Important Bird Areas

of

California

Daniel S. Cooper

Audubon CALIFORNIA

Pasadena, California

Important Bird Areas of California
by Daniel S. Cooper

Published by:
Audubon California
87 North Raymond Ave.
Suite 700
Pasadena, CA 91103
U.S.A

www.ca.audubon.org

Book design, cover design, typography and layout by Beatriz Mojarro

Library of Congress Control Number: 2003115291

Printed by Typecraft Wood & Jones, Pasadena California.

Cover photo: Black Rail (Brian Small)

Back photo: Mendota Wildlife Area, Fresno Co. (Daniel S. Cooper)

About the Author

Daniel S. Cooper graduated from Harvard University in 1995, and received his M.S. in Biogeography from University of California, Riverside 1999, where he investigated bird distribution of the Puente-Chino Hills. From 1995-1996, he worked as a Research Associate at the Kern River Preserve in Weldon, California, and from 1997-1999, worked with Dr. Thomas A. Scott on the Western Riverside County Multi-species Habitat Conservation Plan. Since 1995, he has also conducted research on the distribution of birds of Central and northern South America.

In 1999, Dan was hired by Audubon California to develop a habitat management plan and monitoring program for the Audubon Center in Debs Park, in northeast Los Angeles. In 2001, he became the Director of Bird Conservation for Audubon California, working full-time on statewide conservation issues, including researching and writing the California Important Bird Areas project.

TABLE OF CONTENTS

Important Bird Areas of California

T

The foundation for California's Important Bird Area program was provided by Dr. Meenakshi ("Mini") Nagendran, Bob Barnes and Kathy Gilbert at Audubon California, who introduced the concept to Audubon members and birders around California in the mid 1990s. Their work allowed me to smoothly take over the project when I assumed the role of Director of Bird Conservation in 2001. I am grateful for the support within Audubon California provided by then Executive

Acknowledgments

Director Dan Taylor and Melanie Ingalls, Director of Los Angeles Programs, both of whom allowed me to work on the IBA program during 2000 and 2001 to the exclusion of all else. Jennifer Jacobs at Audubon California assisted in numerous roles at the state office to keep the project rolling, and Lacy Hartford of UC Davis helped with threat analysis and outreach to chapters. National IBA Coordinator Dan Niven and Jeff Wells at National Audubon provided support and encouragement early in the process, and later, California Executive Director Jerry Secundy and the Audubon California Board of Directors kept the book effort a top priority at the state office. I thank President John Flicker and Senior Vice-President Frank Gill for keeping the program a priority at the top levels of the National Audubon Society.

I wish to especially thank Amanda Kochanek of GreenInfo Networks for producing and updating the maps, and Beatriz Mojarro for developing the design and layout for this book.

A large group of birders and field ornithologists generously granted my requests for interviews and data about their areas of expertise. They include:

Robert Allen (San Joaquin Valley – north), Bob Barnes (Tulare Co./So. Sierra Nevada), Alan Barron (Del Norte Co.), Ted Beedy (Sierra Nevada – north), William Bousman

(So. SF Bay), Beverly Brock (Fresno/Madera Co.), Ken Brunges (Central Sierra Nevada), Betty Burridge (Sonoma Co.), Luke Cole (Kings Co.), Dave Compton (Santa Barbara Co.), Bruce Deuel (No. Central Valley), Tom Edell (San Luis Obispo Co.), Sam Fitton (San Benito Co.; San Joaquin Valley – south), David Fix (Humboldt/Del Norte Co.), Kimball Garrett (Los Angeles Co.), Jim Gain (Stanislaus Co.), Steve Glover (Alameda/Contra Costa Co.), Robb Hamilton (Orange Co.), Steve Hampton (Yolo Co.), Tom and Jo Heindel (Inyo Co.), Waldo Holt (San Joaquin Co.), John Hunter (Trinity/Humboldt/Del Norte Co.), Paul Jorgensen (San Diego Co.), Jeri Langham (Sacramento Co.), Joan Lentz (Santa Barbara Co.), Robin Leong (Napa/Solano Co.), Ron LeValley (Humboldt/Del Norte Co.), David Lukas (Sierra Nevada – north), Chet McGaugh (Riverside/San Bernardino Co.), Robert L. McKernan (Lower Colorado River Valley/Imperial Co.), Dan Murphy (San Francisco Co.), Steve Myers (Riverside/San Bernardino Co.), Ed Pandolfino (Sacramento Valley), Don Roberson (Monterey Co.), Michael Rogers (So. SF Bay), Bob Schieferstein (Central Sierra Foothills), Steve Schubert (San Luis Obispo Co.), Alison Sheehey (W. Kern Co.), David Shuford (Marin/Imperial Co.), Robin Smith (San Mateo Co.), John Sterling (Modoc/Lassen/Siskiyou/Trinity Co.), Emilie Strauss (Mono Co.), David Suddjian (Santa Cruz Co.), Dorothy Tobkin (Mendocino Co.), Phil Unitt (San Diego Co.), Ken Weaver (San Diego Co.), Walter Wehtje (Ventura Co.), David Yee (San Joaquin Co.), Bob Yutzy (Shasta Co.)

An informal IBA Advisory Board thoroughly reviewed the final draft and provided excellent advice throughout the process: Bruce Deuel (California Dept. of Fish and Game), Richard Erickson (LSA and Associates), Sam Fitton (Bureau of Land Management), John Luther (Alameda College), Don Roberson (Monterey Peninsula Audubon Society), David Shuford (Point Reyes Bird Observatory), and John Sterling (Jones and Stokes and Associates)

Dozens of other birders and conservationists from around California assisted with specific information on particular sites, providing data, insight and guidance. Rather than listing them all here, I have made every effort to include their names within the accounts of the IBAs.

Daniel S. Cooper
Audubon California
Pasadena

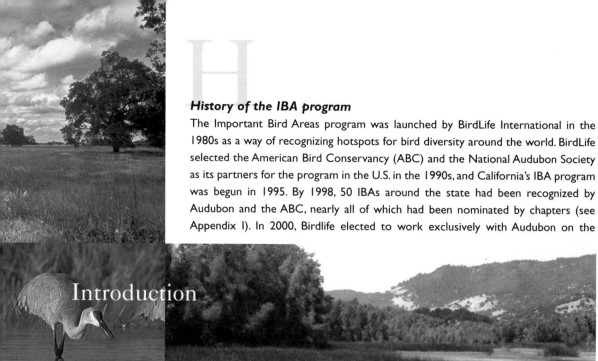

History of the IBA program

The Important Bird Areas program was launched by BirdLife International in the 1980s as a way of recognizing hotspots for bird diversity around the world. BirdLife selected the American Bird Conservancy (ABC) and the National Audubon Society as its partners for the program in the U.S. in the 1990s, and California's IBA program was begun in 1995. By 1998, 50 IBAs around the state had been recognized by Audubon and the ABC, nearly all of which had been nominated by chapters (see Appendix I). In 2000, Birdlife elected to work exclusively with Audubon on the

Introduction

project, and the responsibility of IBA identification and "acceptance" was given to the state offices of Audubon.

California's IBA program was expanded in 2000 to make it more representative of the state's complex diversity. The site criteria for California were standardized to objective numeric goals to ensure that the areas identified were truly stand-out locales in a state with exceptional biological importance. Because California (like other states) had relied on just a handful of local volunteers to nominate sites, vast regions had produced no nominations despite having exceptional bird habitat. A "top-down" system was initiated that began by meeting with and interviewing bird conservation experts for each county to allow them to suggest sites, compiling these suggestions into this report, and supplementing their recommendations with literature research.

Another major change initiated in 2000 was the elimination of the need for landowner approval in identifying IBAs in California, and the shift away from only focusing on public lands. Since the designation of an area as an IBA does not connote any regulatory authority, any bird habitat, regardless of the land ownership, could be identified thus. Though this change may reduce buy-in by local residents in the short run, it is critical to the scientific validity of the project that worthy private lands are not overlooked.

The selection process was originally based on nomination forms submitted by local volunteers, and these forms, many of which included bird lists, pamphlets and survey data, were rolled into the new IBA program. Ultimately, much of the information in this report was based on dozens of conversations with local bird distribution experts around the state representing many different state and federal agencies, conservation groups, and institutions. These advisors are generally also current or past local compilers for North American Birds, a quarterly journal of bird distribution published by the American Birding Association. They were able to quickly and accurately summarize the distributions of sensitive birds within their counties better than most published sources. I was able to personally visit with most advisors, which enabled us to sketch out regions on an atlas that supported the IBA criteria (see below). In cases where data were lacking for a site or a species, local experts were called for information, including refuge and reserve managers, environmental consultants and field biologists whose research intersected the suggested IBA. Audubon's Christmas Bird Count data (refered to as "CBC" in the text) proved extremely useful for documenting winter concentrations of waterbirds and shorebirds. Published data from journal articles, annotated checklists and books (esp. breeding bird atlases) filled out the accounts. This information was compiled into regional summaries that formed the basis for the accounts of each site.

Definition of an IBA

California IBAs are defined as:
1. <100,000 acres in extent
2. Possessing a bird community distinct from the surrounding region
3. Satisfying one of the "IBA Criteria" (see below)

The boundaries of California IBAs were intentionally loosely defined, and were described as precisely as the various advisors felt would be useful in working toward their conservation. Political boundaries were used in cases with specific management regimes, such as around military installations, but in general, every effort was made to identify areas that were definable by natural boundaries, both geologic (e.g. portions of mountain ranges) and biotic (wetlands and associated uplands). It was difficult to find any area within the state where a single owner had complete control over 1000 contiguous acres (particularly so for lowland sites); multiple management regimes are the norm. Future analyses may arrive at different configurations for sites and this report is intended to be a starting place.

Several IBAs were actually a complex of individual sites (e.g. Sierran Meadows, North Mojave Dry Lakes). These "disjunct IBAs" were only identified if one of the constituent sites could qualify as an IBA. For example, "Channel Islands – Northern" includes several islands that could stand alone as IBAs (e.g. Santa Cruz, Santa Rosa), but it seemed to make sense to combine them based on a shared geographic area, a similar (or at least somewhat coordinated) management regime, and, especially, the similarity of their avifauna. These were subjective groupings, and, again, based largely on the suggestions of local advisors.

I tried to avoid geographical bias by selecting advisors from around the state. The IBAs do not exist in a vacuum, and the advisors (including the author) were all aware of current conditions, which inevitably influenced their recommendations for sites. All assumed that the geo-political landscape of the state would not soon change dramatically. National forests would continue to cover most of our mountains; our national parks would be kept intact and protected; that the Desert Protection Act of 1994 would stand, etc. At the same time, they also assumed that any habitat on level, private land near urban and agricultural areas would continue to be lost, in many cases at alarming rates. Because the amount of bird knowledge about each site is highly variable, and since much of the accounts, including the site descriptions and the conservation issues, are so subjective, some sites were described in much greater detail than others. However, this should not imply that these are somehow more important than others.

Many people mistakenly think of IBAs as important birding areas, but this is not an accurate characterization. While some IBAs do indeed offer excellent birding, such as Elkhorn Slough, the Salton Sea, and the Del Norte Coast, to name a few, others do not. They were all identified based on their importance to birds, rather than to birders. Several sites that are exceptional bird-ing sites did not meet any of the criteria for IBA stauts. Small oases and migrant traps for example, like Butterbredt Springs (Kern Co.), Pt. Pinos (Monterey Co.) and Pt. Loma (San Diego Co.) are among the most exciting spots in the state to observe birds, particularly during migration, but don't support enough sensitive species – or those in sufficient numbers – to warrant their inclusion in this report. Readers should refer to Brad Schram's excellent Birder's Guide to Southern California (Lane/ABA Birdfinding Guide), or John Kemper's Birding Northern California (FalconGuide) for a treatment of "important birding areas".

Coordination

Several efforts are ongoing or have been attempted recently to synthesize bird distribution information for conservation purposes statewide. The most similar is a parallel effort to identify the top IBAs in the country, spearheaded by the American Bird Conservancy. Partners-in-Flight, a consortium of agencies and conservation groups, has attempted to summarize research needs at a bioregional scale across North America by identifying broad physiographic units across (e.g. Sonoran Desert) and identifying target species and conservation objectives for each one. It should be noted that this scale is much broader than the site-specific analysis conducted in the IBA report. Partners-in-Flight has also produced, through Pt. Reyes Bird Observatory, a series of Bird Conservation Plans that are easy-to-interpret habitat management plans for the major California bird habitats (e.g. riparian, grassland). The Nature Conservancy has produced several "Ecoregional Reports" for the major floristic subregions of the state, but these have largely been based on rare natural communities rather than specifically focused on birds. Other conservation groups involved in identifying important areas for birds include the non-profit Institute for Bird Populations, which has embarked on a massive monitoring program for Sierra Meadows (described in this report).

The California Department of Fish and Game, under the Resources Agency, has identified hundreds of Significant Natural Areas ("SNAs"), but these are simply circles drawn around areas known to contain one or more sensitive species (plants, mammals, birds) with little accompanying information. Since they depend on voluntary submission of data, certain areas of the state are better covered than others, and bird data are still more uneven. Furthermore, they don't have specific information that puts each area into a statewide context. Pt. Reyes Bird Observatory is involved in updating the California list of Bird Species of Special Concern, used by state agencies to manage populations of rare species not formally listed as threatened or endangered. Detailed, legally-binding recommendations are also issued for threatened or endangered birds by the U.S. Fish and Wildlife Service or the Dept. of Fish and Game in the form of (federal or state) Recovery Plans. All of these efforts are best considered complimentary to Audubon's IBA program, which is more focused on drawing attention to specific places than on species or habitat types.

Numerous local governments around the state are involved in developing habitat conservation plans (HCPs) with the help of regulatory agencies to focus conservation efforts within their jurisdictions while providing for development. Predictably, their recommendations are generally influenced strongly by local political realities, and should not be confused with plans developed by conservation groups or natural resource specialists. Further, they, like the recommendations of state or federal agencies, differ significantly in that they are legally binding, unlike those forwarded by conservation groups (including the California IBA program).

Purpose

A network of IBAs can become a cornerstone of Audubon's conservation activities throughout California. Their identification will help guide conservation activities, both at the chapter and at the national levels of Audubon, and can serve to showcase their resources to other interested groups and agencies. Over the next few years, Audubon will work with local chapters (see Appendix II) to defend these sites and to develop systems to monitor their avifauna.

Several advisors joked that the entire Sierra Nevada, or the entire Bay Area (or, in one case, the entire city of San Francisco) could be identified as an IBA. Indeed, global assessments of biodiversity have long singled out the entire California Floristic Province as globally important, but what could the average conservationist or resource manager possibly do with this information? Throughout the project, I would imagine myself in the position of buying land or suggesting areas for habitat restoration, and thinking about what kind of information would be useful to bring to politicians, funders and the media to highlight the features of each site.

Regarding the conservation power of the IBA program to save birds, it is simply not the tool for saving particular species or for stemming sprawl across beautiful and intact landscapes. We have two Endangered Species Acts (state and federal) and entire branches of resource agencies devoted to species conservation. The National Audubon Society has spearheaded campaigns in California to save species such as the California Condor and the Snowy Plover and places like Mono Lake and the South Fork Kern River. Other conservation groups such as The Nature Conservancy have made tremendous strides in protecting rare and unique vegetation communities and landscapes, and local land trusts have taken up growth issues that lie beyond the scope of national conservation groups. The IBA program is simply a way to identify special places around California known to be important for birds, and to mobilize other like-minded citizens to act in their conservation.

Reading the IBA Accounts

The site name (in bold) is followed the county name (in italics), followed by the name of the city (generallly w/ population >10,000) within or adjacent to the IBA. The remaining criteria are described below.

IBA Criteria

P = >10% of California/1% Global population (breeding and/or wintering) of one or
   more sensitive taxa
L = >9 Sensitive Species
S = >10,000 possible on a 1-day count
W = >5000 waterfowl possible on a 1-day count

P - >1% of Global or >10% of California population of one or more sensitive taxa.

These numbers were difficult to pin down, especially for rapidly-declining species (e.g. Light-footed Clapper Rail) and those difficult to survey (e.g. Marbled Murrelet). Every effort was made to use recently published, peer-reviewed sources to arrive at a good estimate, and even this was possible only for a few taxa. This proportion may include only breeding or wintering populations, or may refer to the entire population in sedentary species. Most IBAs identified support significant populations of non-sensitive taxa (e.g. certain waterfowl or shorebird species), and to identify all of these would be a near-impossible task.

Taxa restricted to just a handful of breeding or wintering sites in California for which a population estimate would not be useful for determining population thresholds were marked "limited range". The regular occurrence of any number of individuals of these taxa were generally enough to hit the threshold numbers for global and state populations.

Table 1. Sensitive Species of California and their population estimates

Species	Global Population Estimate	CA Population Estimate	Source(s)	Status
Fork-tailed Storm-Petrel *Oceanodroma furcata* (breeding)	5 – 6 million "breeders"	Limited Range	Carter *et al.* 1992; Kushlan *et al.* 2002	C,P
Ashy Storm-Petrel *O. homochroa* O. homochroa (breeding)	<10,000 "breeders"	7209 birds	Carter *et al.* 1992; Kushlan *et al.* 2002	C,P,I
Black Storm-Petrel *O. melania* (breeding)	>2 million "breeders"	Limited Range	Carter *et al.* 1992; Kushlan *et al.* 2002	C,P
American White Pelican *Pelecanus erythrorhynchos* (breeding)	>120,000 "breeders"	Limited Range	Kushlan *et al.* 2002	C,P
Brown Pelican *P. occidentalis* (breeding)	c. 190,000 "breeders" (N. America and Caribbean)	Limited Range	Carter *et al.* 1992; Kushlan *et al.* 2002	S,F,FP

Important Bird Areas of California

Species	Global Population Estimate	CA Population Estimate	Source(s)	Status
White-faced Ibis *Plegadis chihi* (breeding)	>100,000 "breeders"	4554 pr.	Ivey *et al.* 2002; Kushlan *et al.* 2002	C
White-faced Ibis *P. chihi* (wintering)	N/A	28,000 birds	Shuford *et al.* 1996 (last published estimate – still increasing)	C
Least Bittern *Ixobrychus exilis*	?	?	N/A	C,P
Wood Stork *Mycteria americana*	32,000 – 42,000 breeders (N. America and Caribbean)	Limited Range	Small 1994; Kushlan *et al.* 2002	C,P
California Condor *Gymnogyps californianus* **EC**	205 birds; roughly half free-flying	N/A	K. Sorenson, *pers. comm.*	S,F,FP,I
Pacific Black Brant *Branta bernicla nigricans* (wintering/staging)	120,000-140,000	< 30,000	Sedinger *et al.* 1994	P
Fulvous Whistling-Duck *Dendrocygna bicolor*	?	Limited Range	Garrett and Dunn 1981	C,P
Tule Greater White-fronted Goose *Anser albifrons elgasi* (wintering/staging)	5,500 birds	N/A	USFWS 2003a	P
Aleutian Canada Goose *Branta canadensis minima* (wintering/staging)	30,600 birds	N/A	USFWS 2003a	(F)
Harlequin Duck *Histrionicus histrionicus* (breeding)	?	Limited Range	Small 1994	C,P
Bald Eagle *Haliaeetus leucocephalus* (breeding)	?	180 territories	California Department of Fish and Game 2000	S,F,FP
Northern Harrier *Circus cyaneus* (breeding)	?	?	N/A	C,P
Northern Goshawk *Accipiter gentilis* (breeding)	?	?	N/A	C,P
Harris' Hawk *Parabuteo unicinctus* (breeding)	?	Limited Range	R. McKernan, *unpubl. data,* 2002	C,P
Swainson's Hawk *Buteo swainsoni* (breeding)	?	800 pr.	California Department of Fish and Game 2000	S
Ferruginous Hawk *B. regalis* (wintering)	?	?	N/A	C,I
Golden Eagle *Aquila chrysaetos* (breeding)	?	?	N/A	C,FP
Peregrine Falcon *Falco peregrinus* (breeding)	?	193 pr.	California Department of Fish and Game 2000	S,FP
Prairie Falcon *F. mexicanus* (breeding)	?	?	N/A	C,P
Greater Sage-Grouse *Centrocercus urophasianus*	4000-8000 birds	N/A	S. Blankenship, *pers. comm.*	C,P
Mt. Pinos Blue Grouse *Dendragapus obscurus howardi* **EC**	?	Limited Range	N/A	P
Catalina California Quail *Callipepla californica catalinensis* **EC**	?	Limited Range	Garrett and Dunn 1981	P
Yellow Rail *Coturnicops noveboracensis*	?	Limited Range	M. San Miguel, *pers. comm.*	C,P
California Black Rail *Laterallus jamaicensis coturniculus*	<9000 birds	N/A	J. Evens, *unpubl. data,* 2002	S,FP,I

Species	Global Population Estimate	CA Population Estimate	Source(s)	Status
California Clapper Rail *Rallus longirostris obsoletus* **EC**	500-1000 birds	N/A	Thelander and Crabtree 1994	S,F,FP
Light-footed Clapper Rail *R. l. levipes*	c. 900 pr. (incl. 750 pr. in Mexico)	325 pr.	E. Palacios, *via email*; Zembal *et al.* 1997	S,F,FP
Yuma Clapper Rail *R. l. yumanensis*	1000-2000 birds	N/A	Shuford *et al.* 2000; Rosenberg *et al.* 1991	S,F,FP
Sandhill Crane *G. canadensis* (wintering/staging)	?	c. 30,000 birds	Small 1994	P
Greater Sandhill Crane *Grus canadensis tabida* (breeding)	?	465 pr.	Ivey and Herzinger 2001	S,FP
Western Snowy Plover *Charadrinus alexandrinus nivosus* (Pacific Coast population)	c. 2000 birds (U.S.), c. 2000 in Mexico (Baja California)	1444 in 2003	K. Clark, USFWS	F
Western Snowy Plover *C. alexandrinus nivosus* (Interior population)	21,000 birds	1745 birds	Brown *et al.* 2001; Page *et al.* 1991	C,P
Mountain Plover *C. montanus*	9000 birds	4000 birds	Brown *et al.* 2001; K. Hunting, *unpubl. data*, 2002	C,I,P
Long-billed Curlew *Numenius americanus*	20,000 birds	N/A	Brown *et al.* 2001	C,I
Van Rossem's Gull-billed Tern *Sterna nilotica vanrossemi* (breeding)	c. 700 pr.	N/A	Molina 2000	C,P
Royal Tern *S. maxima* (breeding)	100,000 – 150,000 "breeders" (N. America and Caribbean)	20-40 pr.	Kushlan *et al.* 2002; K. Molina, *unpubl. data*	P
Elegant Tern *S. elegans* (breeding)	30,000 pr.	N/A	Burness *et al.* 1999	C,P,I
California Least Tern *S. antillarum browni* (breeding)	c. 4500 pr.	4141 pr.	California Department of Fish and Game 2000 (for U.S.); K. Keane, *unpubl. data*; E. Palacios Castro (for Mexico), *via email*	S,F,FP
Black Tern *Chlidonias niger* (breeding)	100,000 – 500,000 "breeders"	4150 pr.	Shuford *et al.* 2001; Kushlan *et al.* 2002	C,P
Black Skimmer *Rhyncops niger* (breeding)	c. 70,000 "breeders"	1200 pr.	Collins and Garrett 1996; Kushlan *et al.* 2002	P
Marbled Murrelet *Brachyramphus marmoratus* (breeding)	300,000 – 800,000 birds	6000 birds	Ralph *et al.* 1995; Kushlan *et al.* 2002	S,F,I
Xantus' Murrelet *Synthliboramphus hypoleucus* (breeding)	5000 – 11,000 birds	2500 – 2800	Carter *et al.* 1992	P
Cassin's Auklet *Ptychoramphus aleuticus* (breeding)	c. 3.5 million "breeders"	53,562 birds	Carter *et al.* 1992; Kushlan *et al.* 2002	P
Tufted Puffin *Fratercula cirrhata* (breeding)	2.75 – 3 million "breeders"	276 birds	Carter *et al.* 1992; Kushlan *et al.* 2002	C,P
Yellow-billed Cuckoo *Coccyzus americanus*	?	30-50 pr.	Thelander and Crabtree 1994	S
Elf Owl *Micrathene whitneyi*	?	Limited Range	Halterman *et al.* 1989; R. McKernan, *unpubl. data*, 2002	S
Burrowing Owl *Athene cunicularia*	?	c. 9000 pr.	CBD *et al.* 2003	C,P
Northern Spotted Owl *Strix occidentalis caurina*	?	1000 pr.	Thelander and Crabtree 1994	F,I

Species	Global Population Estimate	CA Population Estimate	Source(s)	Status
California Spotted Owl *S. o. occidentalis* **EC**	1500 pr.	N/A	G. Gould, *unpubl. data*	C,P,I
Great Gray Owl *S. nebulosa*	?	120-150 birds	Thelander and Crabtree 1994	S
Long-eared Owl *Asio otus*	?	?	N/A	C,P
Short-eared Owl *A. flammeus*	?	?	N/A	C,P
Vaux' Swift *Chaetura vauxi*	?	?	N/A	C,P
Gila Woodpecker *Melanerpes uropygialis*	?	70 pr.	R. McKernan, *unpubl. data*, 2002	S
Gilded Flicker *Colaptes chrysoides*	?	Limited Range	R. McKernan, *unpubl. data*	S
Southwestern Willow Flycatcher *E. t. extimus*	933 territories	305 territories (but possibly no more than 100 breeding pr.)	Sogge *et al.* 2002; M. Whitfield, *pers. comm.*	F
Willow Flycatcher (non-Southwestern) *Empidonax traillii adastus and E. t. brewsterii* (breeding)	?	c. 150 breeding pr.	California Partners in Flight 2001	S
Vermilion Flycatcher *Pyrocephalus rubinus* (breeding)	?	50-100 pr.	Various sources	C,P
Loggerhead Shrike (island forms) *L. l. anthonyi* and *L. l. mearnsi* **EC**	Limited Range	N/A	P. Collins, *unpubl. data*	*
Loggerhead Shrike *Lanius ludovicianus ludovicianus* (breeding)	?	?	N/A	P
Least Bell's Vireo *Vireo bellii pusillus* **EC**	2000 pr. in 2002	c. 1300 pr. (2000 males) in 1998	J. Greaves, *via email*, 2002; B. Kus, *in litt.*	S,F
Arizona Bell's Vireo *V. b. arizonae*	?	Limited Range	R. McKernan, *unpubl. data*, 2002	S
Gray Vireo *V. vicinior*	?	?	N/A	C,P
Catalina Hutton's Vireo *V. huttoni unitti*	Limited Range	N/A	P. Unitt, *unpubl. data*	P
Purple Martin *Progne subis* (breeding)	?	800-1000 pr.	Williams 1998	C,P
Bank Swallow *Riparia riparia* (breeding)	?	8210 pr.	California Department of Fish and Game 2000	S
Cactus Wren *Campylorhynchus brunneicapillus* (coastal-slope populations)	?	?	N/A	**
Clark's Marsh Wren *Cistothorus palustris clarkae*	?	?	Unitt *et al.* 1996	P
California Gnatcatcher *Polioptila alifornica*	5300 pr.	N/A	Thelander and Crabtree 1994	F,C
California Swainson's Thrush *Cathartus ustulatus oedicus*	?	?	N/A	P
Bendire's Thrasher *Toxostoma bendirei*	?	<200 pairs	Remsen 1978	C,P
Crissal Thrasher *T. crissale*	?	?	N/A	C,P
Le Conte's Thrasher *T. lecontei*	?	?	N/A	C
San Joaquin Le Conte's Thrasher *T. lecontei macmillanorum* **EC**	Limited Range	N/A	S. Fitton, *unpubl. data*	P
Lucy's Warbler *Vermivora luciae*	?	?	N/A	P

Species	Global Population Estimate	CA Population Estimate	Source(s)	Status
Yellow Warbler *Dendroica petechia*	?	?	N/A	C,P
Saltmarsh Common Yellowthroat *Geothlypis trichas sinuosa* **EC**	5,705 birds	N/A	H. Spautz, PRBO; *unpubl. data*, 2002	C,P
Yellow-breasted Chat *Icteria virens*	?	?	N/A	C,P
Summer Tanager *Piranga rubra*	?	100 pr.	P. Unitt, *unpubl. data*	C,P
Inyo California Towhee *Pipilo fuscus eremophilus* **EC**	Limited Range	N/A	Various sources	S,F,C
San Clemente Spotted Towhee *P. maculatus clementae* **EC**	Limited Range	N/A	P. Collins, *unpubl. data*	P
Santa Cruz Isl. Rufous-crowned Sparrow *Aimophila ruficeps obscura* **EC**	Limited range	N/A	Various sources	P
Oregon Vesper Sparrow *Pooecetes gramineus affinis*	?	15-20 pr.	R. Erickson, *unpubl. data*	P
Sage Sparrow (coastal-slope populations) *Amphispiza b. belli and A. b. canescens*, in part	?	?	N/A	*
San Clemente Island Sage Sparrow *A. b. clementeae* **EC**	300 birds in 1997	N/A	Institute for Wildlife Studies 2002	F
Bryant's Savannah Sparrow *Passerculus sandwichensis alaudinus* **EC**	?	?	N/A	P
Belding's Savannah Sparrow *P. s. beldingi*	?	2350 pr.	California Department of Fish and Game 2000	S
Large-billed Savannah Sparrow *P. s. rostratus*	?	?	N/A	C,P
Grasshopper Sparrow *Ammodramus savannarum*	?	?	N/A	P
Alameda Song Sparrow *Melospiza melodia pusillula* **EC**	15,204 birds	N/A	H. Spautz, PRBO; *unpubl. data*, 2002	C,P
Suisun Song Sparrow *M. m. maxillaris* **EC**	44,464 birds	N/A	H. Spautz, PRBO; *unpubl. data*, 2002	C,P
San Pablo Song Sparrow *M. m. samuelis* **EC**	77,457 birds	N/A	H. Spautz, PRBO; *unpubl. data*, 2002	C,P
Channel Islands Song Sparrow *M. m. graminea* **EC**	Limited Range	N/A	P. Collins, *unpubl. data*	P
Kern Red-winged Blackbird *Agelaius phoeniceus aciculatus* **EC**	Limited Range	N/A	T. Gallion, *unpubl. data*	P
Tricolored Blackbird *A. tricolor* **EC**	163,000 birds	N/A	Hamilton 2000	C,P

*   Loggerhead Shrike (Island forms): C (*L. l. anthonyi*) F (L. l. mearnsi)

** Cactus Wren: C,P (*C. b. sandiegensis*) (other coastal populations, e.g. Ventura Co., also treated here as "Sensitive")

EC = Taxon endemic to California or nearly so

S = State Threatened/State Endangered
F = Federally Threatened/Fed. Endangered
C = California Bird Species of Special Concern (The Resources Agency 1992)
P = Proposed California Bird Species of Special Concern CDFG and PRBO 2001
FP = "Fully-protected" by State of California
I = Considered "Threatened" or "Near-threatened" by Birdlife International (2000)
() = Recently de-listed
* No formal protection or listing, but widely extirpated from former range in California

BLM   –   Bureau of Land Management
DFG   –   California Dept. of Fish and Game
DoD   –   Department of Defense (U.S.)
NWR   –   National Wildlife Refuge
OHV   –   Off-highway Vehicle
PRBO   –   Point Reyes Bird Observatory, Stinson Beach, California
USFS   –   U.S. Forest Service
USFWS –   U.S. Fish and Wildlife Service
WTP   –   Water Treatment Plant

L - > 9 Sensitive Species

"Sensitive species" were considered to be all those listed as threatened or endangered by state and/or federal agencies (CFDG 2000), as well as most of the species under consideration as California Species of Special Concern (CFDG and PRBO 2001). A handful of taxa treated as Bird Species of Special Concern were not counted as Sensitive Species here, either because of the lack of precision in their ranges (Modesto Song Sparrow, T. Gardali, *pers. comm.*), or because their ranges are so large that their inclusion would probably not contribute appreciably to the analysis (Olive-sided Flycatcher, California Horned Lark).

The conservation consortium Partners-in-Flight has developed a list of "priority" species absent from threatened/endangered species lists that are of conservation concern for a variety of reasons, such as having small global ranges (Pashley *et al.* 2000). National Audubon Society has developed this list into its "WatchList" program, a later incarnation of the "Blue List". Many of these species are treated in the California IBA report as sensitive species. However, those felt by various advisors to be too widespread and common (e.g. Short-billed Dowitcher, California Thrasher) or that occurring marginally in California and for short periods of time (e.g. Least Storm-Petrel) were not included. Finally, the IUCN (International Union for the Conservation of Nature) has produced its own list of vulnerable species, published through BirdLife International (2000). Eleven of the 13 taxa on their "Red List" that occur in California area treated in the IBA report; the other two are either found far out at sea (Black-footed Albatross, Craveri's Murrelet) or are clearly thriving in the U.S. portion of their range (Heerman's Gull).

Unlike IBA programs in other states, sites were not included for simply supporting species of conservation concern – California has too many and they occur too widely. A concerted effort was made to exclude as "present" taxa if they that only occur as transients when relatively plastic in their ecological requirements (e.g. Willow Flycatcher), or those that only occur on foraging runs from distant breeding locales (e.g. gulls, terns). For example, Willow Flycatcher would only be considered "present" if breeding or suspected of breeding within the given IBA. In two special cases, Sage Sparrow and Cactus Wren, all coastal-slope populations were included, since both are widespread in the desert and rare and declining elsewhere in the state.

The current presence of sensitive species at the various IBAs was determined through published sources where possible, but was confirmed principally via interviews with local birders. Various statewide (e.g. Grinnell and Miller 1944, Grenfell and Laudenslayer 1983, Small 1994) and regional references (e.g. Garrett and Dunn 1981, Unitt 1984) were consulted for this information prior to the interviews, though not generally cited specifically within the site accounts.

S - >10,000 shorebirds
An arbitrary number, but one that seems to identify the top sites fairly well (i.e. seemed neither particularly low or high). Data were drawn from several sources, especially surveys done by PRBO (e.g. Page et al. 1999).

W - >5000 waterfowl
(see "S" above). Audubon Christmas Bird Count data were a major source of information for this criterion. One variance from earlier iterations of the IBA program (and ABC's effort) is my exclusion of waterfowl that are only passing by (e.g. coastal promontories).

Alternate Criteria

Migrant Traps
There are many ways to define an area's importance to birds. This report attempted to rely on quantitative data wherever possible. Many criteria were suggested that were simply not defensible based on existing data. For example, other states' IBA programs have included a criteria that reflects high numbers of migrants at a site, especially sites that seem to be important stopover ares for birds that are spending a few days refueling during migration. Despite the presence of numerous bird-banding sites, we still have a very poor understanding of the statewide distribution of migrants, much less how different areas to compare to one another. Though most birders consider desert oases and coastal headlands to be key migrant spots (e.g. Butterbredt Springs, Kern Co.; Pt. Pinos, Monterey Co.), recent work has shown very high numbers of migrants in the Central Valley (e.g. Humple and Geupel 2002) and in tamarisk scrub near the Salton Sea, exceeding recorded counts from "traditional" migrant hotspots along the coast. Clearly, more research is needed, and until it appears we could not use this as a criterion.

Raptors

Others recommended using a criterion that identified a site as important for raptor concentrations. California supports very large numbers of many species of raptors, both as transients (e.g. Turkey Vulture) and as winterers (e.g. Golden Eagle). Several sites may be globally important for these species, but in most cases, the criteria for assessing this have not been developed, and the research is still developing. With the notable exception of long-term raptor migration observational data from southern Marin County and more recent work in the Mojave Desert (see Rowe and Gallion 1996), our current methods of censusing birds over wide areas of the state (e.g. the Christmas Bird Count) are not always precise enough for identifying discrete areas of high wintering raptor density, and for accurately censuing birds within count circles.

Further, many grassland sites are dry in December and early January, and don't "green up" until weeks or months after the Christmas Counts are done. Finally, there are also several sites that are critical for one or two species (e.g. Ferruginous Hawk winter roosts, Burrowing Owl colonies), but not for raptors in general.

Nonetheless, certain areas of the state support large numbers of raptors, and looking at simple numbers on Christmas Bird Counts (15-mile diameter circles), the counts with the highest raptor numbers in California were (table developed by E. Pandolfino):

Table 2. Christmas Bird Counts with the highest raptor numbers

CBC	County	Ave. # raptors 1998 – 2002	Corresponding IBA
Lincoln	Placer	793	None
Rio Cosumnes	Sacramento	751	Cosumnes River Preserve; Stone Lakes NWR Area
Benicia	Solano	740	Suisun Marsh; Benicia SRA
Sacramento	Sacramento, Yolo	725	Yolo Bypass
Point Reyes	Marin	703	Pt. Reyes - Outer
Los Banos	Merced	601	Grasslands Ecol. Area
Stockton	San Joaquin	556	Sacramento – San Joaquin Delta
West Sonoma	Sonoma	470	Bodega Harbor
Moss Landing	Monterey	430	Elkhorn Slough
Orange Co. (NE)	Orange	417	Orange Co. Wilderness Parks; Puente-Chino Hills
E. Contra Costa	Contra Costa	343	Sacramento – San Joaquin Delta; Byron Area
Salton Sea (S)	Imperial	328	Salton Sea; Imperial Valley

Important Bird Areas of California

Research

Another criteria discussed was an area's supporting long-term research. Compared to other states, California's birds are very well-studied, and it is difficult to find areas with absolutely no research on birds. The problem involved defining the type of research – is a report on the food habits of a single species, published in a major science journal, somehow more important than an unpublished breeding bird survey? Though it would have been possible to only consider published research as an IBA criteria, some of the most important monitoring is being done by non-academics birders scouring local patches on a regular basis and keeping personal records of movements, nesting, etc. These are mentioned in the text where possible, but research is not included as a criterion.

Ownership

Though the IBA report makes every effort to ignore political boundaries, several contributors felt that the ownership of a given site should somehow "count" toward it's being identified as an IBA. Specifically, if a site was being managed in a way that put wildlife (and, especially, birds) first, such as an Audubon Sanctuary, this should automatically make it an important bird area. To preserve the integrity of the analysis, however, we had to "let the birds determine the IBAs" – there were simply too many ways to claim an area's importance to birds, and we had to limit ourselves to a defined list of bird-related criteria.

Threat

Critical: Most of habitat at immediate risk of alteration by human activity
High: Most of habitat at some level of risk, or substantial amount of habitat at immediate risk
Medium: Substantial amount of habitat at some level of risk, or small amount at immediate risk
Low: Small amount of habitat at some level of risk, or area well protected and well managed

Local Audubon Chapter

This is the chapter to which Audubon members living within or adjacent to the IBA would be assigned, (per Audubon California's maps) or the nearest chapter to the IBA (see Appendix II). Of course, any number of other chapters may be active at the same IBA without being identified as the local chapter.

Bird Conservation Region

California's ecological regions have been divided up countless ways, but currently, most state agencies and programs are using ten divisions (California Resources Agency 1994) These have also been used by the various authorities on California's flora (e.g. Hickman 1993).

Klamath (northwestern coast and mountains)
Modoc (northeastern corner)
Sierra
Sacramento Valley and San Joaquin Valley
San Francisco Bay
Central West
South Coast
Colorado - Mojave Desert

These may be variously lumped and split, and the maps for this report combine Modoc with Sierra and Mojave with Sonoran Desert.

Important Bird Areas of California

Major bird initiatives (e.g. Partners-in-Flight, North American Bird Conservation Initiative) recognize 37 "Bird Conservation Regions", or BCRs for the U.S. and Canada (NABCI-US 2002) California contains five of these:

Northern Pacific Rainforest (BCR 5)
> (incl. "Klamath" bioregion)

Great Basin (BCR 9)
> (incl. "Modoc" and part of "Sierra" bioregions)

Sierra Nevada (BCR 15)
Coastal California (BCR 32)
> (incl. "Sacramento Valley", "Bay-Delta", "Central Coast", "San Joaquin Valley" and "South Coast" bioregions)

Sonoran and Mojave Desert (BCR 33)

Initials of frequently-cited individuals:

BD – Bruce Deuel
RE – Richard Erickson
SF – Sam Fitton
KG – Kimball Garrett
SH – Steve Hampton
RH – Rob Hansen
RL – Robin Leong
RM – Robert McKernan
DR – Don Roberson
MSM – Mike San Miguel
DS – Dave Shuford
JS – John Sterling

Summary of findings

This report treats over 150 sites representing 58 counties which were evaluated from several hundred suggested sites with the help of dozens of experts statewide. Some of these sites include sprawling refuges that support millions of birds, such as Klamath Basin on the Oregon border or the Salton Sea. Others are less well-known yet contain truly imperiled bird habitats, in some cases the only viable remnants for miles around, such the vernal-pool-rich grasslands of eastern Merced County, or the remnant freshwater wetlands of Bolsa de San Felipe between Gilroy and Hollister. Though many of the sites in this report are secure, managed by agencies aware of their habitat values, others are seeing their resources eroding away. Audubon California's mission not only includes the identification of these sites, it is committed to their long-term protection.

California is an extremely biologically diverse state at all scales for virtually every group of plants and animals. It boasts the richest flora of any state (over 5000 recognized species) and has a rate of floristic endemism (species found nowhere else) exceeding any other state save Hawaii. For birds, its state list is rivaled only by Texas, with which it is neck-and-neck, and many of its counties (e.g. San Diego, Los Angeles, Marin, Monterey) have higher species lists than most states.

California stands out in virtually every category of assessing importance to birds, from numbers to diversity to endemism. The tremendous regional habitat variation, largely due to great elevational and climatic changes within small areas, has allowed for the evolution of a staggering number of distinct races of bird species. California may have more recognized subspecies of birds than any comparably-sized region of North America, which contributes to the high number of rare species (birds with small ranges are generally more vulnerable to disturbance and extinction). Located on the Pacific Flyway (and extending for hundreds of miles along the coast), the state supports huge numbers of migrant shorebirds and waterfowl in spring and fall migration. With its mild climate, the California Floristic Province (land west of the Sierra axis) is the winter home to vast numbers of species, from waterbirds to sparrows. Offshore, rich cold upwellings host concentrations of seabirds from as far away as New Zealand and the Arctic Circle in numbers unprecedented elsewhere in U.S. waters.

North Coast - Klamath

The northwestern corner of the state is dominated by the northern Coast Ranges and by several ancient mountain ranges (e.g. Klamath, Salmon, Marble and Trinity Alps) cloaked with a diverse coniferous forest. Some of the largest and least-impacted rivers in the state drain to the Pacific, connecting the relatively dry oak and juniper woodland of the interior with the temperate rainforest of the coast. Relatively pristine wetlands and coastal dunes remain at the river mouths, and other unique microhabitats that contribute to bird diversity include mountain prairies along ridge tops and remnant old-growth Douglas-Fir and Coast Redwood forests. Taxa restricted in California to the northwest include breeding Fork-tailed Storm-Petrel and Tufted Puffin (nearly so) on offshore rocks, Aleutian Canada Goose (in spring), Ruffed Grouse, Barred Owl, Gray Jay, Black-capped Chickadee and breeding American Redstart. The majority of the state's Purple Martins breed here, as do most of its Peregrine Falcons.

Modoc

A region of vast sagebrush flats, freshwater and alkali lakes, and unbroken tracts of coniferous forest, this lonely corner of the state is actually one of the most important for breeding and migrating waterbirds and raptors. The impoundments of the Klamath Basin and elsewhere support literally millions of birds each year. Many species of waterbirds breed in California only these northeastern wetlands, including American White Pelican, Northern Pintail, Blue-winged Teal, Canvasback, Ring-necked Duck, Lesser Scaup, Common Goldeneye and Bufflehead. Most of the state's breeding Sandhill Crane, Sage Grouse, Willet and Long-billed Curlew occur here, with isolated outposts in Mono and Inyo Co. (e.g. Mono Basin, Owens Valley). In winter, this region hosts impressive concentrations of raptors, especially irruptive northern species such as Rough-legged Hawk. Interesting summer outposts of eastern species (e.g. Least Flycatcher, Eastern Kingbird and Bobolink) have been detected in the extreme northeastern corner of the state.

Sierra

Boasting the highest point in the state (Mt. Whitney), the Sierra Nevada range is one of the major landscape features of the western U.S., and retains one of its most significant, largely intact blocks of coniferous forest. A century and a half of logging, gold-mining and grazing have left a legacy of ecological alteration, with meadows, riparian systems and old-growth especially vulnerable. Though most montane species of the state are found in a crescent around the northern Central Valley, from the Coast Ranges (mainly northern) across the Cascades and Modoc Plateau and south, the Sierra are still home to several bird species found nowhere else in California, including Great Gray Owl, breeding American Pipit, Pine Grosbeak, Gray-crowned Rosy-Finch. One of the great ornithological mysteries of the state, breeding Harlequin Duck, may persist along rugged, undisturbed canyons in the central Sierra east of Sacramento (breeding was recently confirmed in Yosemite Valley!). There are several distinct but little-known subspecies of birds resident in the Great Basin Ranges (esp. the White Mtns.) just east of the Sierra Nevada, but fortunately their habitat is well protected and little-disturbed.

Sacramento and San Joaquin Valleys

Undoubtedly the most impacted portion of the state, these bioregions, collectively known as the "Central Valley" bear little resemblance to the landscape of just fifty years ago, with their meticulously regulated water-delivery systems and miles of laser-leveled agricultural fields. Still the scattered significant patches of un-plowed land, especially along its borders (the eastern base of the Coast Ranges and the lower Sierran foothills) provide a glimpse of historic savannah and vernal pool-rich grassland habitat. Several major refuges and duck clubs have recreated aspects of its wetlands, and are intensively managed for wintering (and, increasingly, breeding) waterbirds. Riparian habitat has been pushed to the brink, though vital remnants remain along every major river, providing corridors of woodland from the Sierra with the valley floor. Even agricultural lands are important for certain species (wintering Mountain Plover and raptors) to the extent they mimic grassland, and when flooded, these fields attract tens of thousands of shorebirds. Species confined to the valley include the Aleutian Canada Goose, and a race of Le Conte's Thrasher in the dry scrub in the southwestern San Joaquin Valley.

San Francisco Bay Area

The San Francisco Bay Area is a major region of endemism, at least for subspecies, hosting three recognized races of Song Sparrow, plus Saltmarsh Common Yellowthroat and California Clapper Rail. The wetlands of San Francisco Bay support a half-million shorebirds during migration and winter, and those of the Sacramento-San Joaquin Delta (often included with San Joaquin Valley bioregion) provide the ecological link between the Pacific coast and the Central Valley. Among its millions of wintering waterfowl, the Delta supports most of the world's wintering population of Tule White-fronted Goose, as well as large numbers of Sandhill Crane and Tundra Swan. One of the major seabird colonies of the eastern Pacific, the Farallon Islands, is just offshore of San Francisco.

Central West

One of the most diverse sections of the state, this bioregion encompasses the entire southern Coast Range from Santa Barbara Co. north to the southern San Francisco Bay Area. Seemingly endless tracts of chaparral dominate the landscape, interspersed with pockets of grassland and oak and evergreen woodland. Though difficult to quantify, it is likely that California's chaparral species occur in their highest concentrations and densities within this bioregion, and most of California's breeding Golden Eagles are resident here. Fairly extensive (though disturbed) riparian habitat is associated with the Napa, Salinas and Santa Ynez rivers. The most extensive coastal marshes and estuaries are associated with Elkhorn Slough and Morro Bay, which are major wintering and staging grounds for waterbirds along the coast. This bioregion's signature species must be the California Condor, of which there are now about 50 released birds in the rugged southern Coast Range between Monterey and Los Angeles, each carefully monitored by the Ventana Wilderness Society.

South Coast

This bioreigon, which includes the Channel Islands, the coastal plain and the high mountains of the Transverse and Peninsular Ranges, is by far the most diverse and biologically rich in the state. Due to the urbanization associated with Los Angeles and San Diego, it rivals the Central Valley in its degree of human transformation, particularly in the lowlands. Though a ring of undeveloped mountains and foothills, protected by several national forests, has been the saving grace of several wide-ranging animals (e.g. Mountain Lion, Golden Eagle), many of the most interesting and unique natural communities lie along the coastal zone. Offshore, several distinct island races (taxonomy of some in dispute) have been recognized for California Quail, Loggerhead Shrike, Hutton's Vireo, Scrub Jay (now considered a full species, "Island Scrub-Jay"), Bewick's Wren, Spotted Towhee, Rufous-crowned Sparrow, Sage Sparrow and Song Sparrow. Several have gone extinct on various islands. Black Storm-Petrel, the "California" race of Brown Pelican and Xantus' Murrelet breed nowhere else in the U.S. except for the northern Channel Islands. Along the mainland coast, remnant saltmarshes support endemic, resident races of Clapper Rail and Savannah Sparrow, and in its freshwater marshes hold a recently-described race of Marsh Wren. Elegant Tern has its only U.S. nesting colonies in its coastal marshes, where it is joined by Royal Tern, another species otherwise unknown in the state as a breeder. Just inland, coastal sage scrub, a unique, summer-deciduous habitat, holds the entire U.S. populations of California Gnatcatcher and Coastal Cactus Wren, which also occur in adjacent Baja California, Mexico. The riparian scrub of southwestern California supports most of the world's breeding Least Bell's Vireo, also found at tiny outposts in the desert and in Baja California.

Colorado – Mojave Desert

Though southwestern California may have more taxa found nowhere else on earth, the varied habitats of the deserts certainly support more that are not found elsewhere in the state. These are generally confined either to desert woodlands (incl. Joshua Tree and mesquite), isolated mountain ranges in the eastern Mojave (with White Fir on highest peaks), wetlands or to riparian corridors (esp. the Amargosa, Mojave and lower Colorado Rivers), many of which have been seriously degraded. Several taxa are strongly associated with the Salton Sea/Imperial Valley, such as Wood Stork, Fulvous Whistling-Duck, Laughing Gull, Yellow-footed Gull and Gull-billed Tern. The Sea has emerged as one of the most important sites in the state for migrant and wintering birds, with over a million individuals representing over 150 species present for most of the year. The desert bioregion supports all of California's populations of Gambel's Quail, Inca Dove, Gilded Flicker, Ladder-backed Woodpecker, Arizona Bell's Vireo, Vermilion Flycatcher, Brown-crested Flycatcher, Verdin, Black-tailed Gnatcatcher, Lucy's Warbler and Inyo California Towhee, plus three thrashers: Bendire's, Crissal and Le Conte's. Several taxa are found only in the Colorado Desert in the southeastern corner of the bioregion, including Yuma Clapper Rail, White-winged Dove, Elf Owl, Gila Woodpecker, Abert's Towhee, Northern Cardinal and Bronzed Cowbird. Most of the state's populations of Least Bittern, Whip-poor-Will, Burrowing Owl, Gray Vireo, Hepatic and Summer tanagers and Scott's Oriole are found in the deserts or along its border with other bioregions.

Ranking

To rank sites by the California IBA Criteria (see IBA Criteria above), I assigned single points for each taxon who cleared the population threshold (10% state/1% global population present at an IBA), and a point each for the other 3 criteria (>9 sensitive species, >10,000 shorebirds, >5000 waterfowl). This allowed sites to be assigned a score and ranked in roughly the order of their importance to birds, although using these criteria alone to determine importance of a site is overly simplistic. One may also rank IBAs by the sheer number of sensitive species known to occur in the area treated, which is more of a measure of diversity not obtained by simply adding the scores of the IBA Criteria.

The table below presents the top ten sites using both measures.

IBA	IBA Score	IBA	# Sensitive species
Lower Colorado River Valley	17	Camp Pendelton	24
Channel Islands - Northern	12	Lower Colorado River Valley	22
Imperial Valley	10	Imperial Valley	21
Salton Sea	10	Southern Orange County	21
San Diego Bay	10	Surprise Valley	20
Suisun Marsh	10	Honey Lake Area	20
Orange Coast Wetlands	9	Klamath Basin/Clear Lake	20
Del Norte Coast	9	Vandenberg Air Force Base	20
San Francisco Bay – south	8	Salton Sea, San Jacinto Valley and Orange Coast Wetlands	19
San Pablo Bay Wetlands	8		

Note that four of the top sites, Lower Colorado River Valley, Imperial Valley, Salton Sea and the Orange Coast Wetlands were listed in the top 10 by both measures. All four are in southern California, and three are largely in a single county: Imperial Co., in extreme southeastern California.

Threats

An analysis of conservation issues across the IBAs revealed that the most commonly-cited threat was urban development and associated habitat transformation, even in remote locations (where mainly due to second-home construction). This factor was mentioned for over half the sites, and was the most-cited threat for IBAs in each region, except for Northeastern California where population pressure is still light. The face of urbanization is different in each area. Many sites in southwestern California, the western Mojave Desert and the central coast (esp. the Hwy. 101 corridor) are seeing direct destruction of large areas of habitat via subdivision construction. Urbanization in the Central Valley certainly includes local hotspots of tract home construction, but more widespread are the development of "ranchettes" – large mansions often placed on hilltops, surrounded by 10 or so acres of land, with roads cutting across grassland and savannah to the next home the next hill over. This ranchette development style has also gained popularity in Central West, Southwestern California, and locally, in the Sierra Nevada.

The next most cited threats were exotic species and direct human disturbance, which includes trampling by humans and unleashed dogs, as well as undirected OHV use. Species invasions are most detrimental when they alter the native biological functions of a site. Exotic plants have most dramatically affected lowland riparian and wetland systems, with infamous examples being giant cane (*Arundo donax*) and tamarisk (*Tamarix spp.*) invasions in Southwestern California and the deserts. Wetland plants, including an invasive cordgrass (*Spartina alternifolia*) were cited as major threats to San Francisco Bay Area systems, and two other noxious exotics Perennial Pepperweed (*Lepidium latifolium*) and Purple Loosestrife (*Lythrum salicaria*), are invading wetland systems throughout the state. "Constructed wetlands", including those on state and federal refuges, continue to be specifically managed to encourage the growth and proliferation of several exotic grasses felt to be beneficial to wintering waterfowl, a practice that could be re-examined locally where this comes at the expense of declining taxa. Exotic and/or invasive animals (e.g. feral cats, Brown-headed Cowbirds) continue to pose a threat locally.

Direct human disturbance is most acute around urban centers and in areas of high recreation use, including many coastal sites. There is still no stigma against encouraging one's dog to run into a flock of roosting shorebirds on the beach, and efforts by coastal parks to fence-off portions of beaches for rare nesting birds meets considerable resistance by the general public. Since so many IBAs are located within public lands designated for "mixed-use", it is up to managers to try to balance human recreation with wildlife protection, often with highly-restrictive budgets and seasonal (and often voluntary and transitory) staff. Threats from OHVs and arson/accidental fire ignition are most prevalent in the deserts and in Southwestern California. This threat, combined with loss of open space due to sprawl, will only intensify in coming decades.

Other threats mentioned often include over-grazing, which is most acute in the Central Valley and the Sierra Nevada. This is most detrimental to riparian corridors, many of which are located in extremely arid regions (e.g. the San Joaquin Valley) where much of the surface water is already tapped for agricultural uses long before it reaches the valley floor. Grazing is also extensively impacting montane and foothill meadow systems, which are often the only non-forest/shrubland habitat for miles around, and extremely important for birds at various stages in their life histories. Agricultural expansion, always an issue for the state's avifauna, has become most dramatic in grape-producing regions (e.g. Hwy. 101 corridor; central Sierra foothills) where large tracts of former ranchland (often excellent grassland wildlife habitat) are being lost to manicured and heavily-sprayed vineyards. Finally, the manipulation of water, often embedded in other "threats" (e.g. urbanization, agricultural expansion), is nearly ubiquitous in California – countless federal, state and local agencies exist solely to move water from one area of the state to another – and it would be impossible to begin to summarize their impact here.

Several sites were felt by local conservationists to be "critically" threatened, with most of their habitat and/or bird communities under immediate risk of major alteration by human activity (detailed in text).

Harris Hawk (Brian Small)

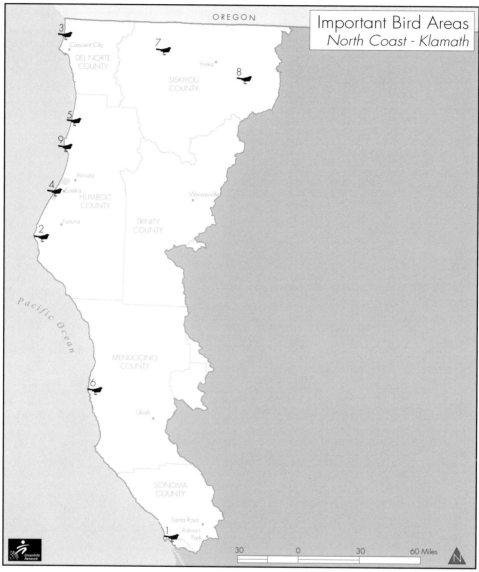

Important Bird Areas
North Coast - Klamath

OREGON

Crescent City
DEL NORTE
COUNTY

SISKIYOU
COUNTY

Yreka

Arcata

Eureka
HUMBOLT
COUNTY

Fortuna

Weaverville

TRINITY
COUNTY

Pacific Ocean

MENDOCINO
COUNTY

Ukiah

SONOMA
COUNTY

Santa Rosa
Rohnert
Park

GreenInfo
Network

30   0   30   60 Miles

1	Bodega Harbor	4	Humboldt Bay	7	Seiad Valley
2	Cape Mendocino Grasslands	5	Humboldt Lagoons	8	Shasta Valley
3	Del Norte Coast	6	Mendocino Coast	9	Trinidad Rocks

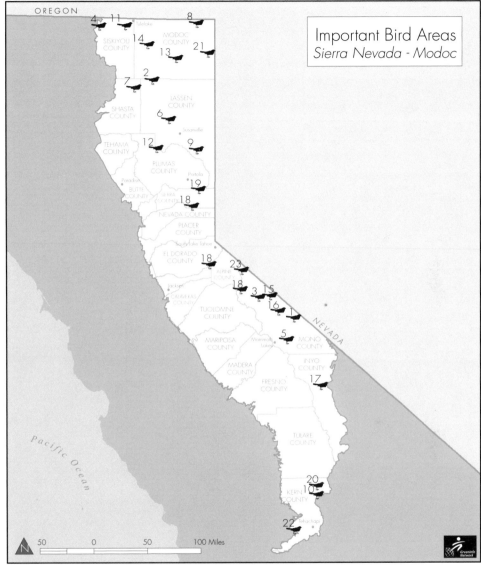

Important Bird Areas
Sierra Nevada - Modoc

1	Adobe Valley	9	Honey Lake Valley	17	Owens River
2	Big Valley/Ash Creek	10	Kelso Creek	18	Sierra Meadows - Northern
3	Bridgeport Valley	11	Klamath Basin/Clear Lake	19	Sierra Valley
4	Butte Valley	12	Lake Almanor Area	20	South Fork Kern River Valley
5	Crowley Lake Area	13	Modoc NWR Area	21	Suprise Valley
6	Eagle Lake	14	Modoc Plateau	22	Tehachapi Oaks
7	Fall River Valley Area	15	Mono Highlands	23	Topaz Lake Area
8	Goose Lake, Modoc County	16	Mono Lake Basin		

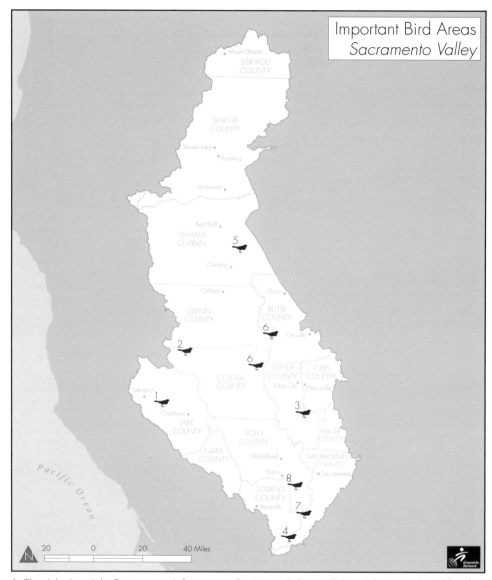

Important Bird Areas
Sacramento Valley

1 Clear Lake Area, Lake County
2 East Park Reservior
3 Feather River - Lower

4 Sacramento - San Joaquin Delta
5 Sacramento River - Upper
6 Sacramento Valley Wetlands

7 Stone Lake National Wildlife Refuge
8 Yolo Bypass

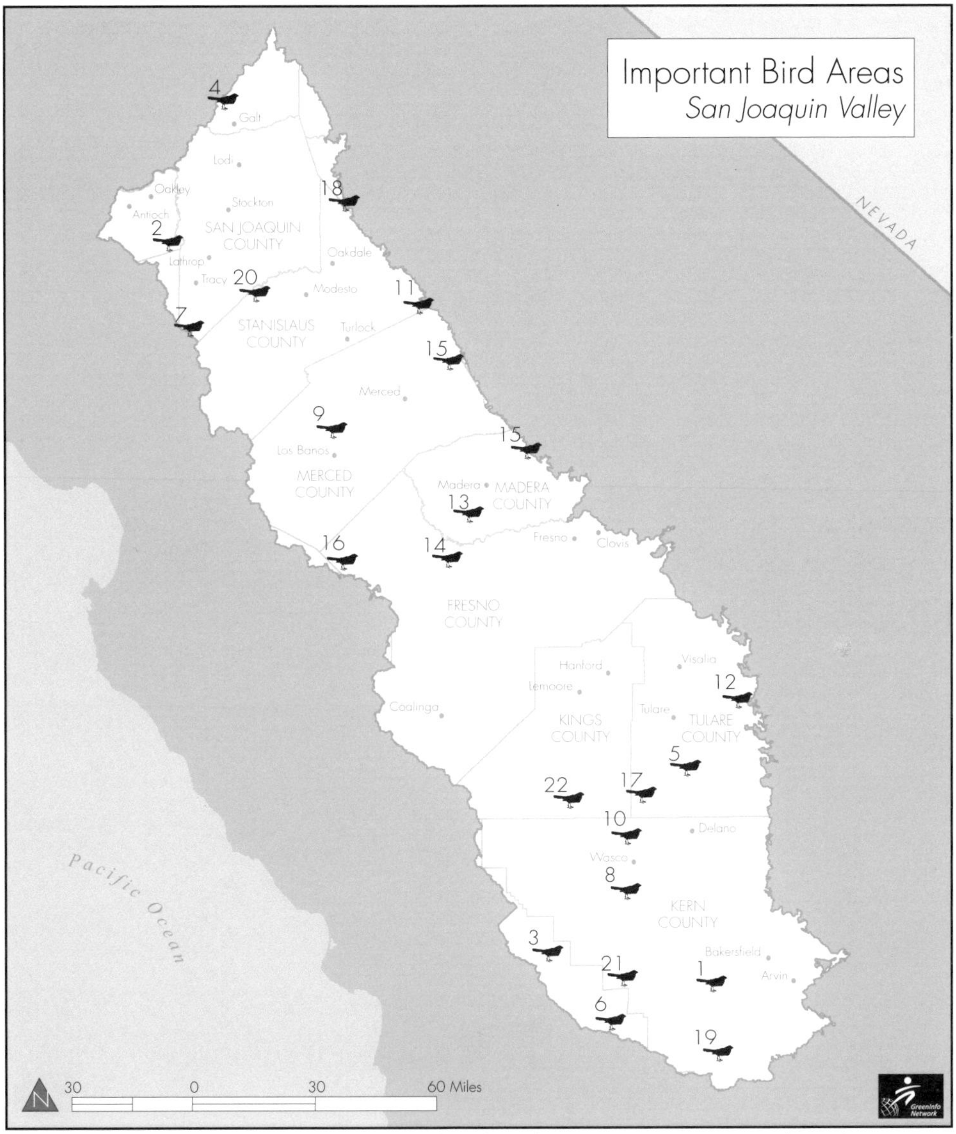

NEVADA

Galt
Lodi
Stockton
Oakley
Antioch
Lathrop
Tracy
Modesto
Turlock
Merced
Los Banos
Madera • MADERA COUNTY
Fresno • Clovis
Hanford
Lemoore
Visalia
Coalinga
Tulare
Delano
Wasco
Bakersfield
Arvin

SAN JOAQUIN COUNTY
STANISLAUS COUNTY
MERCED COUNTY
FRESNO COUNTY
KINGS COUNTY
TULARE COUNTY
KERN COUNTY

Pacific Ocean

30   0   30   60 Miles

GreenInfo Network

1	Buena Vista Lake Bed	9	Grasslands Ecological Area	17	Pixley NWR Area
2	Byron Area	10	Kern NWR Area	18	Salt Spring Valley
3	Carrizo Plain	11	La Grange - Waterford Grasslands	19	San Emigdio Canyon
4	Cosumnes River Preserve	12	Lake Success Area	20	San Joaquin NWR Area
5	Creighton Ranch Area	13	Lone Willow Slough	21	Taft Hills
6	Cuyama Valley	14	Mendota Wildlife Area	22	Tulare Lake Bed
7	East Diablo Range	15	Merced Grasslands		
8	Goose Lake, Kern County	16	Panoche Valley		

Important Bird Areas
San Francisco Bay Area

1   Alameda Naval Air Station
2   Ano Nuevo Area
3   Benicia State Recreation Area
4   Bolinas Lagoon
5   Brooks Island Regional Preserve
6   Concord Marshes

7   Corte Madera Marsh
8   Eastshore Wetlands
9   Farallon Islands
10   Jepson Grasslands
11   Napa Lakes
12   North Richmond Wetlands

13   Point Reyes - Outer
14   Richardson Bay
15   San Francisco Bay - South
16   San Pablo Bay Wetlands
17   Suisun Marsh
18   Tomales Bay

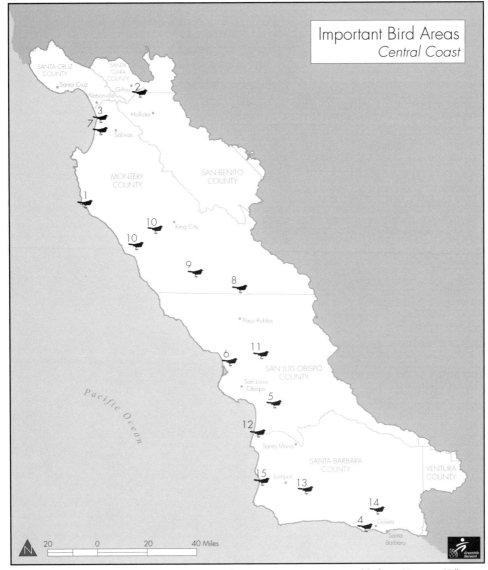

Important Bird Areas
Central Coast

SANTA CRUZ COUNTY
• Santa Cruz

SANTA CLARA COUNTY
• Gilroy
• Watsonville
2

3
7
• Hollister
• Salinas

MONTEREY COUNTY

SAN BENITO COUNTY

1

10
• King City

10

9

8

• Paso Robles

11
6
SAN LUIS OBISPO COUNTY
• San Luis Obispo
5

12
• Santa Maria

SANTA BARBARA COUNTY

VENTURA COUNTY

15 • Lompoc
13

14
4 • Goleta
Santa Barbara

Pacific Ocean

20   0   20   40 Miles

1	Big Sur Area	6	Morro Bay	11	Santa Margarita Valley
2	Bolsa de San Felipe	7	Salinas River - Lower	12	Santa Maria River Valley
3	Elkhorn Slugh	8	Salinas River - Middle	13	Santa Ynez River Valley
4	Goleta Coast	9	San Antonio Valley	14	Santa Ynez River - Upper
5	Lopez Lake Area	10	Santa Lucia Peaks	15	Vandenberg Air Force Base

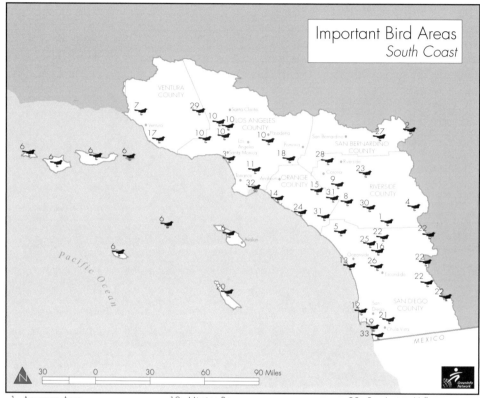

Important Bird Areas
South Coast

30   0   30   60   90 Miles

1 Aguanga Area	12 Mission Bay	23 San Jacinto Valley
2 Baldwin Lake	13 North San Diego Lagoons	24 San Joaquin Hills
3 Ballona Valley	14 Orange Coast Wetlands	25 San Luis Rey River
4 Bautista Creek	15 Orange County Wilderness Parks	26 San Pasqual Valley
5 Camp Pendleton	16 Pamo Valley	27 Santa Ana River - Upper
6 Channel Islands - Northern	17 Pt. Mugu	28 Santa Ana River Valley
7 Lake Casitas Area	18 Puente-Chino Hills	29 Santa Clara River Valley
8 Lake Elsinore	19 San Diego Bay	30 Skinner Reservoir Area
9 Lake Mathews/Estelle Mountain	20 San Clemente Island	31 Southern Orange County
10 Los Angeles Flood Control Basin	21 San Diego NWR - East	32 Terminal Island Tern Colony
11 Lower Los Angeles River	22 San Diego Peaks	33 Tijuana River Reserve

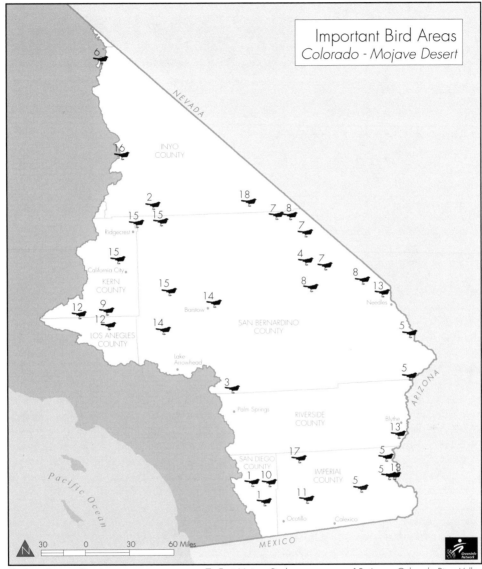

Important Bird Areas
Colorado - Mojave Desert

1 Anza-Borrego Riparian	7 East Mojave Peaks	13 Lower Colorado River Valley
2 Argus Range - Southern	8 East Mojave Springs	14 Mojave River
3 Big Morongo Canyon	9 Edwards Air Force Base	15 North Mojave Dry Lakes
4 Cima Dome	10 Elephant Tree Forest	16 Owens Lake
5 Colorado Desert Microphyll Woodland	11 Imperial Valley	17 Salton Sea
6 Deep Springs Valley	12 Lancaster	18 Shoshone-Tecopa Area

Adobe Valley

Mono

Nearest town(s): Benton
Size: 1000-10,000 acres
Threat: High
Local Audubon Chapter: Eastern Sierra
BCR: 9

IBA Criteria		Source/Notes
L	10 sensitive species: Redhead, Greater Sage-Grouse, Northern Harrier, Ferruginous Hawk, Golden Eagle, Prairie Falcon, Western Snowy Plover, Long-eared Owl, Loggerhead Shrike, Yellow-headed Blackbird	J. Fatooh, *via email*

Description: Adobe Valley, southeast of Mono Lake near the Nevada border, resembles a smaller version of Long Valley (the next major valley to the west, see Crowley Lake Area IBA), and is characterized by spring-fed, ephemeral lakes and ponds rimmed by moist alkali meadows and sagebrush, with open juniper woodland on the surrounding hills. Consistent bodies of water (fullest in spring) include (north to south): Adobe Lake, River Spring Lakes, Antelope Lake and Black Lake. The entire area represents a patchwork of public and private lands, with areas managed by both BLM and DFG.

Birds: Adobe Lake is notable for small numbers of breeding Snowy Plovers, and Black Lake represents an outpost of Great Basin breeding species, including Willet and Wilson's Phalarope. Additional shorebird and marsh species (e.g. Long-billed Curlew) may be expected to begin breeding with improvement of alkali meadow habitat through cattle exclosures. Very isolated within a dry, mountainous area, they appear to be locally important stopover site for migrant waterbirds, with several hundred shorebirds occurring, particularly in spring when water levels peak. A distinct, isolated sub-population of Greater Sage-Grouse occurs in Adobe Valley, with its only strutting ground on private land.

Conservation issues: Cattle grazing occurs throughout the area, and signs of periodic over-grazing have been noted in the past. The BLM and DFG have recently installed fencing around River Springs. Land in this IBA comes up for sale every few years, and several conservation groups and agencies have expressed interest in purchasing and preserving these wetlands for conservation.

Aguanga Area

Riverside/San Diego

Nearest town(s): Temecula
Size: 10,000 - 50,000 acres
Threat: Critical
Local Audubon Chapter: San Bernardino Valley
BCR: 32

	IBA Criteria	Source/Notes
L	17 sensitive species: Northern Harrier, Ferruginous Hawk, Golden Eagle, Prairie Falcon, Burrowing Owl, Loggerhead Shrike, Least Bell's Vireo, Gray Vireo, Cactus Wren, California Gnatcatcher, California Swainson's Thrush, Yellow Warbler, Yellow-breasted Chat, Sage Sparrow, Grasshopper Sparrow, Tricolored Blackbird, Yellow-headed Blackbird	San Diego Natural History Museum 2002; K. Weaver, *via email*

Description: This IBA is dominated by Temecula and Wilson creeks, which drain the north face of Palomar Mountain and the southwestern slope of the San Jacinto Mountains, and include Vail Lake. Floristically, it is one of the most biologically diverse areas of southern California, supporting both coastal and desert elements, as well as several narrow endemics (particularly around Vail Lake). Many biologists find it reminiscent of northwestern Baja California: extensive coastal sage scrub (including Jojoba), alluvial fan scrub, and mesquite bosque mix with Coast Live Oak woodland and, along Temecula Creek, mature Fremont Cottonwood-willow woodland (one of the finest stands south in southern California). Though most of the land is in private hands, it is bounded on the south by the Agua Tibia Wilderness area and the Cleveland National Forest, and on the east by several Indian Reservations.

Birds: The broad floodplain of Temecula Creek east of Vail Lake supports Least Bell's Vireo among the expected riparian breeders (though much of the best habitat remains unexplored). Fascinating "desert-meets-coast" bird assemblages of the scrub habitats occur along Wilson Creek and Tule Creek, where Bell's Sage Sparrow from the coast breeds side-by-side with Black-throated Sparrow from the desert, California and Black-tailed Gnatcatcher maintain adjacent territories (Weaver 1998), along with all three California orioles: Scott's, Hooded and Bullock's. Other interesting sibling species in the area include Nuttall's and Ladder-backed woodpecker and California and Gambel's quail. Localized species found here include breeding Yellow-headed Blackbirds in Lancaster Valley (RE). The canyons running south from Palomar Mountain support a wide variety of foothill and montane birds, as well as several rare non-birds, including Arroyo Southwestern Toad.

Conservation issues: The uniqueness of this region (at a global scale) and its unprotected status would make it a high priority for conservation whatever the threats. The Aguanga Area is one of the few areas of the state where conservation attention is urgently needed to avoid massive habitat alteration. Already, the boom in "ranchettes" has left large lots denuded of native vegetation (cleared by landowners worried about snakes and fire). Current threats include grazing along Temecula Creek that has nearly eliminated the understory. Efforts by the Western Riverside Habitat Management Plan (WRMSHCP) to protect the wide floodplain of Temecula Creek, and to retain its linkages with more extensive habitat to the north and south, should be monitored and supported. Due to the threat of the urban sprawl from Temecula (housing tracts) and the booming casino construction on Indian tribal lands to the east, a "Critical" level of threat is warranted. The land around Vail Lake is slated for massive housing developments, with similar developments planned for the Wilson Valley area. If approved, these will necessitate the widening of Hwy. 79, which cuts through the center of this IBA, which will lead inexorably to the channelization of at least portions of Temecula Creek (a pattern that has been repeated virtually throughout California).

Alameda Naval Air Station

Alameda/San Francisco

Nearest town(s): Borrego Springs
Size: 1000-10,000 acres
Threat: High
Local Audubon Chapter: San Diego
BCR: 33

IBA Criteria		Source/Notes
P	>1% Global population of California Least Tern	287 pr. in 2002; K. Keane, *unpubl. data*

Description: Slated to become a National Wildlife Refuge (one of the few in the U.S. within an urban area), Alameda is one of the most intensely studied IBAs in the state. It is an island composed of fill, featuring about 500 acres of wetlands and grassy, ruderal areas (incl. former airfield) and 400 acres of open water in east-central San Francisco Bay, across from San Francisco.

Birds: The main attribute of this IBA is the sheer number of nesting terns and gulls, which thrive due to the lack of predators (esp. non-native Red Fox) now occurring in wetlands on the "mainland." Alameda NAS has supported one of the largest breeding colonies of Caspian Tern in California within its brackish wetlands (>1000 nests in 1991, although none have bred since 1999, DS). The colony of California Least Tern is one of the world's largest, and the only large group north of Los Angeles. Both California (scarce) and Western Gulls maintain colonies as well, both in the wetland and (Western Gull) on a long breakwater. The site is also emerging as an important reservoir of open-country species in the central Bay Area, as it supports ground-nesters that have been pushed out by urbanization elsewhere, such as Northern Harrier, Burrowing Owl and Horned Lark (M. Shaefer, *in litt.*).

Conservation issues: The crash of Caspian Tern populations has been attributed to the increase in vegetation around the nesting area, as well as to interactions between the terns and nesting gulls (California and Western). Other conservation concerns include helicopters and small aircraft making low flights over the island that disturb the nesting and roosting birds here (M. Elliot, PRBO, via email). Residential and commercial development presently being constructed adjacent to the base may exacerbate the problem of urban-subsidized predators (e.g. feral cats, skunks), which are currently under control. Plans to construct a golf course adjacent to the proposed refuge may present additional threats (e.g. an increase in crows and ravens, etc.). There are also clean-up issues that must be resolved before the transfer is made, which may result in temporary disruption of habitat.

Important Bird Areas of California

Ano Nuevo Area

San Mateo/Santa Cruz

Nearest town(s): Santa Cruz
Size: 10,000 - 50,000 acres
Threat: Low
Local Audubon Chapter: Sequoia
BCR: 32

IBA Criteria		Source/Notes
L	12 sensitive species: Northern Harrier, Golden Eagle, Peregrine Falcon, Marbled Murrelet, Short-eared Owl, Northern/California Spotted Owl, Vaux's Swift, Bank Swallow, California Swainson's Thrush, Yellow Warbler, Bryant's Savannah Sparrow, Grasshopper Sparrow	Sequoia Auduobn Society 2001; D. Suddjian, *pers. comm.*

Description: This complex of protected lands at the base of the San Francisco Peninsula protects some of the richest and most varied bird habitats on the Central Coast. The coastline at Ano Nuevo State Reserve features small offshore islands, rocky headlands, extensive dunes with seep vegetation and bluff-top grassland. East of Hwy. 1, the vegetation switches to a dense, old-growth Coast Redwood and Douglas-Fir forest, with alders lining the numerous streams, where Big Basin Redwood and Butano state parks protect several thousand acres of open space (and the largest block of old-growth forest in the Santa Cruz Mtns.).

Birds: This IBA marks the southernmost regular distribution limit for several species along the coast of California, including Marbled Murrelet, Vaux's Swift, Pileated Woodpecker, Bank Swallow, Varied Thrush and Hermit Warbler. Other "redwood coast" taxa such as Winter Wren and Black Swift (breeds in coastal bluffs) become decidedly less common farther south. Scattered patches of grassland in the area support nesting Northern Harrier and colonies of Grasshopper Sparrow, and American Dipper nests along streams. Ano Nuevo Island, just offshore, provides nesting habitat for seabirds and, remarkably, Heermann's Gull (one of the few California colonies of this primarily Mexican breeder).

Conservation issues: Though this area receives heavy year-round visitation by tourists, particularly to see the breeding Elephant Seals, it is carefully managed by California State Parks. Offshore threats to seabirds include occasional oil spills from the San Francisco area drifting south on currents and affecting species like Marbled Murrelet (SH).

Anza-Borrego Riparian
San Diego

Nearest town(s): Borrego Springs
Size: 1000-10,000 acres
Threat: High
Local Audubon Chapter: San Diego
BCR: 3

IBA Criteria		Source/Notes
P	>1% Global population of Least Bell's Vireo	71 pr. in 2000, Wells and Kus 2001
P	Probably >10% CA population of Vermilion Flycatcher	<5 pr.; P. Jorgensen, *via email*
P	Probably >10% CA population of and Summer Tanager	10 pr.; P. Jorgensen, *via email*
L	12 sensitive species: Northern Harrier, Ferruginous Hawk, Long-eared Owl, Southwestern Willow Flycatcher, Vermilion Flycatcher, Loggerhead Shrike, Least Bell's Vireo, Le Conte's Thrasher, Summer Tanager, Yellow Warbler, Lucy's Warbler, Yellow-breasted Chat	P. Jorgensen, *via email*

Description: Anza-Borrego Desert State Park, located in extreme eastern San Diego County, is one of the jewels of California's state park system, and at over 600,000 acres, is the largest state park in the U.S. Though sensitive species and unique natural communities are scattered throughout its rugged canyons and bajadas, its riparian habitat, which includes natural groves of California Fan Palm, mesquite bosque, and wet meadows, stand out as being among the most important for birds. Unfortunately, much of this habitat is located on private lands adjacent to the park or within in-holdings inside its boundaries. Four main areas are especially critical:

- Lower Willows of Coyote Canyon (Public; 100 acres of willow and fan palm just north of the town of Borrego Springs)
- San Felipe Creek (½ private, ½ California State Parks; 8-mile-long section of perennial creek, including over 200 acres of cottonwood/willow habitat and about 30 acres of marsh/wet meadow; along Hwy. 78 just east of Tamarisk Grove Campground)
- Vallecito Creek at Campbell Grade (Private; 55 acres of riparian habitat 10 miles southeast of Scissors Crossing)
- Vallecito Cienega (Mainly private; 150 acres of mesquite bosque and wet meadow that includes Butterfield Stage Station; five miles downstream of Campbell Grade)

Birds: Many of the sensitive species of birds are confined to the private lands within this IBA, making their management challenging. The extensive mesquite bosque at Vallecito Creek supports the largest number of Least Bell's Vireos (c. 50 pr., *fide* P. Jorgensen), and 12-16 pr. occur at the Lower Willows of Coyote Canyon. Summer Tanager was only recently confirmed breeding within the IBA, with an estimated seven pairs along San Felipe Creek in 2000 (*Ibid*) and scattered pairs elsewhere. In San Diego

County, breeding Long-eared Owl is probably most reliable within this IBA, with San Felipe Creek and Vallecito Cienega traditional nesting sites. Vallecito Cienega features summering Northern Harrier, nesting Vermilion Flycatcher and, in winter, Ferruginous Hawk. Brown-crested Flycatcher has recently established itself as a breeder at a golf course in Borrego Springs and was recorded in 2001 on San Felipe Ck., making it a likely future addition to the list of breeding species in this IBA (San Diego Natural History Museum 2002). Long-term bird monitoring at Vallecitos Ck. (see Massey and Evans 1994) provides excellent baseline data for this dynamic ecosystem.

Conservation issues: Agricultural conversion of extremely fragile desert riparian (including mesquite bosque) habitat remains one of the top concerns on private property here, with 100 acres threatened in the Vallecitos area. Impacts from overgrazing (on private lands) have also been noted, which has included vegetation damage and mesquite cutting to "improve" rangeland for cattle. These cattle support a large population of Brown-headed Cowbirds, which have prompted a region-wide trapping program. Region-wide, depletion of groundwater has been a growing concern, with levels in nearby Borrego Valley having recently been estimated dropping at 1.5 feet/year due to urban development in this arid outpost. As with nearly every desert riparian area, exotic species invasion (esp. tamarisk) remains a major concern, and State Parks has devoted substantial resources controlling it.

Vallecito area, part of "Anza-Borrego Riparian" IBA

Argus Range – Southern

Inyo

Nearest town(s): Trona
Size: 1000-10,000 acres
Sensitive species: 4 (Prairie Falcon, Loggerhead Shrike, Le Conte's Thrasher, Inyo California Towhee) (L. Sutton, *in litt.*)
Threat: Medium
Local Audubon Chapter: Kerncrest
BCR: 33

IBA Criteria		Source/Notes
P	Entire global population of Inyo California Towhee	L. Sutton, *in litt.*

Description: The Argus Mountains lie at the southwestern edge of the Basin and Range geologic province, but are biologically within the Mojave Desert. Several small riparian corridors scattered across a hundred-square-mile region within the southern portion of these mountains west of the town of Trona support the entire global population of the "Inyo" race of the California Towhee. The habitat occurs both on DoD lands (China Lake Naval Weapons Center) and on BLM land, the latter recognized as "Area of Critical Environmental Concern" by the BLM.

Birds: Aside from the towhee, whose numbers average around 150 individuals, this IBA is not particularly distinguished from other desert springs in the north Mojave.

Conservation issues: Grazing by feral horses and burros has been a chronic problem here, as is the case at many desert springs in California. The BLM and the Navy engages in sporadic removal programs.

Baldwin Lake
San Bernardino

Nearest town(s): Big Bear City
Size: <1000 acres
Sensitive species: 1 (Golden Eagle)
Threat: Critical
Local Audubon Chapter: San Bernardino Valley
BCR: 32

IBA Criteria		Source/Notes
W	Probably >5000 Waterfowl	R. McKernan, *via email*

Description: A truly unique natural habitat, Baldwin Lake is a large, ephemeral lake in the northeastern San Bernardino Mountains that forms on alkali soils that were uplifted several thousand feet from the floor of the Mojave Desert. It is surrounded by Great Basin Sage Scrub, probably the most extensive example of this habitat in southern California. The lakeshore can be marshy or dusty depending on the rainfall the previous winter. Extensive pinyon-juniper woodland surrounds the eastern side of the lake, while the southern side features yellow pine woodland contiguous with that of the central San Bernardinos, the most extensive block of such forest in southern California. Unfortunately, increased water diversions for subdivisions in the Bear Basin have resulted in Baldwin Lake being dry for most of the late 1990's.

Birds: Baldwin Lake has supported an exceptionally large breeding population of Eared Grebe (>1000 birds), breeding ducks (at least 4 species) as well as flocks of thousands of shorebirds and waterfowl during migration, especially in fall. As in northeastern California, the shrub-steppe bird community mingles with that of the forest, resulting in a very high diversity of certain groups of birds (up to 15 species of sparrows, including Vesper and Brewer's, breed in the IBA). The vast grassland surrounding the lake is an important raptor foraging area and traditional wintering area for Bald Eagles – up to thirty have wintered.

Conservation issues: Like Mono Lake prior to the lawsuit that saw its feeder stream flow restored, Baldwin Lake is dying of thirst. With the increasing number of diversions, rainfall alone is insufficient to keep open water on the lakebed throughout the spring and summer, much less through fall when waterbird migration peaks. Unless water policy in the area is modified to ensure water collects on the lakebed, Baldwin Lake, like Owens Lake, may cease to exist.

Ballona Valley

Los Angeles

Nearest town(s): Los Angeles (incl. Playa del Rey, Marina del Rey, Venice)
Size: <1000 acres
Sensitive species: 3 (California Least Tern, Loggerhead Shrike, Belding's Savannah Sparrow)
(K. Keane, *unpubl. data; pers. obs.*)
Threat: High
Local Audubon Chapter: Los Angeles, Santa Monica Bay
BCR: 32

IBA Criteria		Source/Notes
P	>1% Global population of California Least Tern	331 pr. in 2001, K. Keane, *unpubl. data*

Description: The Ballona (pronounced "Bah-YO-nuh") Valley features one of the largest remaining expanses of Los Angeles Basin-floor habitat, and the most significant coastal wetland in Los Angeles County, being the only natural saltmarsh between Point Mugu in Ventura County and Los Cerritos Marsh on the Orange/Los Angeles County border (both IBAs). Associated with the mouth of now-channelized Ballona Creek, the valley's habitats have developed in a low-lying portion of the coast behind a nearly-extinct dune system that extended the length of Santa Monica Bay. The area's habitats include coastal (largely-muted) saltmarsh with salt pans (all of which is privately-owned and not open to the public), freshwater marsh (including a new 20-acre constructed freshwater wetland/water treatment lagoon), dune remnants, grassland, riparian thickets, and along the south edge, coastal sage and coastal bluff scrub. Though most of the habitat is located on the south side of Ballona Creek ("Playa del Rey"), significant pieces near Marina del Rey include the 16-acre restored Ballona Lagoon and the fenced and guarded Venice Least Tern colony along the beach.

Birds: This IBA is most notable for the Least Tern colony, which has long supported around 300 pr., with birds foraging at wetlands throughout the valley. Though several wetland and open-country birds have been extirpated from the IBA (e.g. Snowy Plover, Light-footed Clapper Rail, Short-eared and Burrowing owls), vagrants and lingerers (in the case of the plover) still occur. Belding's Savannah Sparrow maintains a small but apparently viable population in the salt marsh, among the most northerly in the world. Hundreds of terns (esp. Elegant) and shorebirds, especially Black-bellied Plover and Willet, congregate at various times of the year along the rocky borders of Ballona Creek, within the wetlands, or along the public beaches at the creek mouth.

Conservation issues: The Ballona Wetlands have been the site of one of the most publicized and long-running conservation battles in the state, and one that is still not over. During the late 1990s, a deal was reached to develop roughly half of some 1000 acres of open land in and around the valley, with the least-developable wetland and hillside habitat left intact. Currently, the State of California is interested in purchasing the rest, and restoring water flows to the saltmarsh, which has been extensively overtaken by exotic weeds. Introduced Red Fox may still be a problem here – public opposition prohibited their trapping several years ago. The Venice Beach Tern Colony requires constant vigilance from volunteers to ward off both animal predators and careless beach-goers alike.

Belding's Savannah Sparrow (Peter LaTourrette)

Bautista Creek

Riverside

Nearest town(s): Hemet
Size: <1000 acres
Threat: Medium
Local Audubon Chapter: San Bernardino Valley
BCR: 32

IBA Criteria		Source/Notes
L	10 sensitive species: Ferruginous Hawk, Golden Eagle, Prairie Falcon, Loggerhead Shrike, Least Bell's Vireo, Cactus Wren, California Gnatcatcher, Yellow Warbler, Yellow-breasted Chat, Sage Sparrow	C. McGaugh, *pers. comm.*

Description: Bautista Creek drains the northwestern San Jacinto Mountains, west of and parallel to the Garner Valley. Notable more for its size and undisturbed qualities than for its bird community, this permanent stream supports strong populations of foothill riparian and woodland species.

Birds: Bautista Creek is apparently important migration corridor for passerines moving up California from the Colorado Desert, specifically connecting the Anza-Borrego Region with the San Jacinto Valley. It supports a full compliment of breeding riparian species, including Least Bell's Vireo, Yellow Warbler, Yellow-breasted Chat and Blue Grosbeak.

Conservation issues: This region is to the east of the main housing boom area of western Riverside County, though plans to site Indian casinos in the area north and south of Bautista Creek are moving forward, with accompanying road-widening plans. The residential sprawl of Hemet-San Jacinto will probably move southeast to affect this IBA, which currently receives no formal protection.

Benicia State Recreation Area

Solan

Nearest town(s): Benicia, Vallejo
Size: <1000 acres
Threat: Low
Local Audubon Chapter: Napa-Solano
BCR: 32

IBA Criteria		Source/Notes
P	>1% Global population Saltmarsh Common Yellowthroat	H. Spautz, *unpubl. data*
P	Probably >1% Global population of California Clapper Rail	6 birds on 1994 Benecia CBC
P	Probably >1% Global population of Suisun Song Sparrow	H. Spautz, *unpubl. data*
L	10 Sensitive species: Northern Harrier, Peregrine Falcon, Black Rail, California Clapper Rail, Long-billed Curlew, Short-eared Owl, Loggerhead Shrike, Saltmarsh Common Yellowthroat, Bryant's Savannah Sparrow, Song Sparrow	R. Leong, *pers. comm.*

Description: Benicia State Recreation Area protects a small area of tidal marsh within Southampton Bay, sandwiched between the cities of Vallejo and Benicia. It is noteworthy both because of its proximity to urbanized areas and because of the concentration of sensitive species it protects.

Birds: This IBA supports a large, apparently stable population of Black Rail (e.g. 25 birds on 1998 Benicia CBC), as well as other wetlands breeders such as Northern Harrier and (winter only) Short-eared Owl. Benicia is situated near the interface of the ranges of several of the San Francisco Bay Area's races of Song Sparrow, whose genetics are currently being investigated. Nonetheless, it is known to support nearly 3% of the global population of what are probably Suisun Song Sparrows, as well as 5-10% of the global population of Saltmarsh Common Yellowthroat (H. Spautz, PRBO, *unpubl. data*). The abundance of migrant and wintering waterbirds in the Carquinez Straits region provide food for Peregrine Falcon, which have maintained one of the Bay Area's few nesting areas on nearby bridges. As with most protected parts of the San Francisco Bay, large numbers of waterfowl winter here, particularly rafting bay species like Canvasback, scaup and both goldeneyes.

Conservation issues: Following the Goals Project (1999), suggested activities for these marshes include the protection and restoration of existing tidal marsh (e.g. elimination of exotic species and barriers to flow) and the removal of trash. Human disturbance, both direct and indirect, continues to threaten this increasingly urban site. Feral cats seem to be increasing, and people walking off-trail through the marsh, often with unleashed dogs, remain a major threat to its bird community (RL).

Big Morongo Canyon
San Bernardino/Riverside

Nearest town(s): Morongo Valley
Size: 1000-10,000 acres
Threat: High
Local Audubon Chapter: San Bernardino Valley
BCR: 33

IBA Criteria		Source/Notes
P	>10% CA population of Summer Tanager	Ave. of 12 nesting pr.; R. Kobaly, *in litt.*
L	10 sensitive species: Golden Eagle, Prairie Falcon, Long-eared Owl, Vermilion Flycatcher, Loggerhead Shrike, Least Bell's Vireo, Lucy's Warbler, Yellow Warbler, Yellow-breasted Chat, Summer Tanager	R. Kobaly, *in litt.*

Description: Big Morongo, located in the Little San Bernardino Mountains about 20 miles north of Palm Springs is one of the largest desert oases in California. It is located adjacent to the town of Morongo Valley, the first of the "gateway towns" to Joshua Tree National Monument along Hwy. 62. The habitat consists of riparian woodland and freshwater marsh habitat along perennial streams within the canyon bottom; a broad large alkali meadow (a portion of which is used as athletic fields) surrounded by riparian thickets and microphyll woodland; and dry, desert scrub-covered hillsides. The BLM manages much of the canyon as the Big Morongo Canyon Preserve (formerly The Nature Conservancy), though a significant amount of habitat (160 acres, incl. most of the alkali meadow) is located on lands owned by San Bernardino Co. and managed with a Memorandum of Understanding with the BLM. The entire area is currently managed for biodiversity, and aside from tiny Covington Park's five acres of county land, human use is limited to foot traffic along a boardwalk and trail system that winds through the preserve. South of here, the area's creeks converge and enter a steep-walled canyon with a narrow band of riparian vegetation decidedly less attractive to birds, finally emerging in the lower Colorado Desert west of Desert Hot Springs.

Birds: Avian use of the IBA is remarkable, and has been well-known to ornithologists for decades. Its breeding bird community is unique and exceptionally rich, with over 70 nesting species documented from just a few hundred acres of habitat. Long-term research into the breeding bird diversity, mainly by Gene Cardiff of the San Bernardino Co. Museum of Natural History, has estimated densities of more than 1400 territories per square kilometer, one of the densest concentrations in North America. It currently boasts one of the largest populations of Brown-crested Flycatchers and Summer Tanagers in the state. The Bell's Vireos breeding here appear the coastal Least Bell's Vireo (breeding in mesquite bosques), one of just a handful of desert outposts for this race. Long-eared Owl maintains a small breeding population within the willow forest, and Yellow-billed Cuckoo has graced the IBA several times in recent summers, suggesting it may be at least prospecting for breeding locations. Other riparian obligates such as Yellow-breasted Chat nest in strong numbers both at the preserve and at Covington Park, with Vermilion Flycatchers nearly restricted to the latter site. This region (western Little San Bernardino Mtns.) appears to be a contact zone between desert and coastal species (e.g. Ladder-backed and Nuttall's Woodpecker). During spring, songbirds migrating north through the state from the Colorado Desert stop here in huge numbers, particularly in late April, when there can be hundreds of flycatchers, warblers, tanagers and orioles at the oasis. Fall migration is more subdued, but can be impressive in September.

Conservation issues: The fact that much of the most important bird habitat within this IBA is not protected by the preserve but is in fact county-owned presents a strong argument for constant vigilance at the site. Recent proposals by San Bernardino Co. include the construction of a campground with concessions at the entrance to the preserve (*fide* R. Kobaly). The growth of the surrounding desert communities within the Morongo Basin represent another concern to the water supply, the lifeblood of the preserve, which is otherwise well managed and carefully maintained (most of the canyon bottom protected by the BLM as an "Area of Critical Environmental Concern"). Cowbird parasitism exists, but its impacts are not quantitatively known. A fire in the early 1990s burned much of the riparian forest (including many mature cottonwoods), but this has regenerated well.

Long-eared Owl (Peter LaTourrette)

Big Sur Area

Monterey

Nearest town(s): Big Sur
Size: 1000-10,000 acres
Threat: Low
Local Audubon Chapter: Monterey Peninsula
BCR: 32

IBA Criteria		Source/Notes
P	Consistent roosting and foraging area for California Condor	C. Hohenberger, *in litt.*
L	10 Sensitive species: Ashy Storm-Petrel, California Condor, Ferruginous Hawk, Western Snowy Plover, Cassin's Auklet, California Spotted Owl, Vaux's Swift, Purple Martin, California Swainson's Thrush, Grasshopper Sparrow	Roberson and Tenney 1993

Description: This IBA is centered on Pt. Sur, a major promontory about 30 miles south of Monterey, and encompasses a collection of unique natural features of the northern "Big Sur Coast." At its north end, near the famous Bixby Creek Bridge (the photograph most associated with Big Sur) lies Castle Rock and the offshore islets and rocky shores of Hurricane Pt. Moving south, Hwy. 1 crosses the Little Sur River, which forms a small estuary at the Pacific; the grassy headlands of Pt. Sur; and finally the floodplain and mouth of the Big Sur River, much of which is protected by Andrew Molera State Park. The Santa Lucia Mtns. (mostly protected as the Ventana Wilderness Sanctuary), rise to 3400' above the coast and form the backdrop to this IBA, whose vegetation represents an intersection of northern-mesic and southern-arid, with Desert Spiny Lizard and yucca thriving a few feet from Coast Redwoods and Banana Slugs. The vegetation along the Big Sur River represents one of the few mature cottonwood-willow forests along the Central Coast. The Ventana Wilderness Society has maintained the Big Sur Ornithology Lab bird-banding station here since the early 1990s, and assists in the federal recovery program for the California Condor.

Birds: The U.S. Fish and Wildlife Service (USFWS) has identified the Ventana Wilderness as a key release site for the California Condor, and, in the late 1990s, decided to release a few birds each year into the nearby mountains, which now forage consistently within this IBA. Several pairs of Peregrine Falcon breed in the area and forage at creek mouths. The Little Sur River mouth is a regionally important non-breeding roost site for Brown Pelican and Snowy Plover in winter, and plovers have bred at Pt. Sur. Purple Martin, essentially extirpated along the coast of California farther south, maintain a small breeding colony (8-12 pr.) in Western Sycamores along the Big Sur River. The Hurricane Point area in the north is the southernmost regular Common Murre colony in the eastern Pacific, and supports large colonies of nesting Pigeon Guillemots and cormorants (Brandt's and Pelagic). Recently, it was discovered to support small numbers of breeding Ashy Storm-Petrels and Cassin's Auklets, making it the only nesting site for these species between the Farallons off San Francisco and the Channel Islands off southern California (McChesney *et al.* 2000). Species diversity within this IBA is among the highest in the state (over 375 species known from the site, *fide* D. Roberson). The Pt. Sur Area, specifically the lower Big Sur River, hosts a large number and diversity of migrant landbirds (e.g. 300-400 Yellow Warblers banded each year during migration), and a significant migration of Turkey Vultures (ave. 5000/season) has been noted in the spring and fall.

Conservation issues: This IBA is being carefully monitored and managed for conservation by California State Parks and the Ventana Wilderness Sanctuary, but some lingering issues include the potential extirpation of Purple Martin as a nester and the proliferation of Brown-headed Cowbirds, whose effect on nesting passerines in the area is imperfectly known. Control programs for European Starling and cowbirds should be investigated.

California Condor (Kelly Sorenson, courtesy Ventana Wilderness Society)

Big Valley/Ash Creek
Modoc/Lassen

Nearest town(s): Adin, Beiber
Size: 10,000 - 50,000 acres
Threat: Low
Local Audubon Chapter: None
BCR: 9

IBA Criteria		Source/Notes
P	>10% of CA population of Greater Sandhill Crane	c. 80 pr. in 2000; Ivey and Herzinger 2001
L	12 sensitive species: Redhead, Northern Harrier, Swainson's Hawk, Ferruginous Hawk, Greater Sage-Grouse, Sandhill Crane, Long-billed Curlew, Black Tern, Burrowing Owl, Short-eared Owl, Yellow Warbler, Yellow-headed Blackbird	S. Collins, in litt.
W	>5000 Waterfowl	c. 300,000 Snow and Ross' Geese in Feb-Mar.; L. Ashford, in litt.

Description: Big Valley is the middle of three large valleys formed by the Pit River in northeastern California, with Fall River Valley and the South Fork Pit River Valley (which contains Modoc NWR) being the other two. All feature a blend of wetland (freshwater marsh, alkali meadow) and "upland" (sagebrush scrub) habitat, with stringers of riparian woodland along waterways, surrounded by juniper-dotted hillsides. Big Valley, like the others, features large wildlife areas managed primarily for waterfowl and sensitive species. Straddling two counties, the 14,000-acre Ash Creek Wildlife Area includes a large portion of the wetland habitat, but significant wildlife habitat is also found on the private ranches of the valley. The entire valley, including the wildlife area, is grazed and "hayed", whereby the alkali meadow grasses are harvested in summer for hay.

Birds: Big Valley supports huge numbers of north-bound waterfowl in early spring, as well as large breeding populations of Great Basin species. Many species of ducks remain to breed, including Bufflehead, a localized nester in the state. Ash Creek Wildlife Area supports thousands of the tiny Cackling race of Canada Goose during early spring staging, as well as hundreds of thousands of Snow and Ross' geese. Up to 5800 Greater Sandhill Cranes arrive in early spring (nearly equal to the entire California breeding population), and those that remain to breed represent the largest California nesting population of this taxon (Ivey and Herziger 2001). The upland habitat in the IBA protects one of the few consistently Greater Sage-Grouse leks left in California (BD).

Conservation issues: Unlike many large wetland areas in the state, this IBA is remote and still relatively pristine, with conservation issues mainly centered around management for Greater Sandhill Crane. Hay-cutting schedules (late June on private lands vs. August on state lands) have been a major point of controversy. The manager at Ash Creek Wildlife Area mentions the need for increased riparian habitat restoration, particularly on the wildlife area, but also cites strong support for conservation projects (coordinated by the local Resource Conservation District) by area landowners (*fide* L. Ashford). About 1200 acres of floodplain wetlands at the west end of Big Valley can be restored by rehabilitating deep incisions in Ash Creek, and additional wetland and riparian restoration opportunities exist along the Pit River (*fide* G. Ivey). Large mammals are predictably abundant here, notably multiple bands of Pronghorn (S. Collins, *in litt.*).

Sandhill Cranes (Peter LaTourrette)

Bodega Harbor

Sonoma

Nearest town(s): Bodega Bay
Size: 1000-10,000 acres
Sensitive species: 8 (Brant, Northern Harrier, Ferruginous Hawk, Black Rail, Western Snowy Plover, Long-billed Curlew, California Swainson's Thrush, Bryant's Savannah Sparrow) (Burridge 1995)
Threat: Medium
Local Audubon Chapter: Madrone
BCR: 32

IBA Criteria		Source/Notes
S	>10,000 Shorebirds	12,000 in winter; PRBO, *unpubl. data*
W	>5000 Waterfowl	K. Wilson and R. Olsen, *in litt.*

Description: The Bodega Harbor area features a natural, protected estuary/harbor fed by several small, freshwater creeks that flow out of the surrounding hills. Tidal action transforms the harbor into a vast mudflat, making it attractive to large numbers of waterbirds year round. A sand-spit juts out across its southern end, protecting extensive Doran Marsh, a brackish, tidal wetland. Another peninsula comes down from the north, and forms grassy Bodega Head, surrounded by sand dunes. The area is a popular destination for tourists exploring the California coast and with fishermen. The U.S. Coast Guard maintains a station on the sand spit, and UC Davis operates the Bodega Marine Lab on Bodega Head. Just south of Bodega Harbor, two major estuaries flow into Bodega Bay, Estero Americano (on the Marin/Sonoma Co. line) and Estero San Antonio (Marin Co.), which are located on private ranches and virtually unstudied and inaccessible.

Birds: The large numbers of migrant and wintering waterbirds are the primary value of this IBA, particularly the hundreds of Brant that stop in migration and winter (Sedinger *et al.* 1994). Located within a few minutes' bird-flight from the wetlands of Tomales Bay (see below), it may be seen as the northernmost outpost of the larger Pt. Reyes wetland ecosystem, with a similar array of species (e.g. nesting Black Rail). Though rare in recent years, Snowy Plover have both bred and wintered here (K. Wilson, *in litt.*).

Conservation issues: Though the site seems reasonably secure from further development, direct disturbance of birds by human use (recreational fishing boats, windsurfers) may impact wintering flocks of water birds. Incursions of exotic plant species (esp. Pampas grass) threaten the native flora, especially the wetland habitats.

Bolinas Lagoon

Marin

Nearest town(s): Stinson Beach, Bolinas
Size: 1000-10,000 acres
Sensitive species: 4 (Black Rail, Long-billed Curlew, California Swainson's Thrush, Bryant's Savannah Sparrow) (Shuford 1993)
Threat: Low
Local Audubon Chapter: Marin
BCR: 32

IBA Criteria		Source/Notes
S	>10,000 Shorebirds	Up to 35,000 in spring; Shuford *et al.* 1989
W	>5000 Waterfowl	Shuford *et al.* 2002

Located at the southern base of Pt. Reyes, this estuary lies between the communities of Bolinas and Stinson Beach. A popular nature center, Audubon Canyon Ranch is situated at the eastern edge of the lagoon. Though Bolinas Lagoon is encircled by a paved road, residential development is largely confined to the large sand spit at the mouth of the lagoon. Bolinas Lagoon is a major stopover and wintering spot for waterbirds along the Pacific Coast, and its tidal marsh supports a small population of Black Rail. Ecological research on shorebirds (PRBO) and waders (Cypress Grove Research Station) here has been ongoing since the mid-1970s. Various ecological enhancements to restore the lagoon to a more natural state are being coordinated by a local non-profit conservation group, the Bolinas Lagoon Foundation.

Bolsa de San Felipe
Santa Clara/San Benito

Nearest town(s): Gilroy, Hollister
Size: 10,000 - 50,000 acres
Threat: Critical
Local Audubon Chapter: Santa Clara Valley, Monterey Peninsula
BCR: 32

	IBA Criteria	Source/Notes
P	>1% Global population of Long-billed Curlew	600 birds in recent (late 1990s) counts; S. Fitton, *pers. comm.*
L	10 sensitive species: Northern Harrier, Ferruginous Hawk, Long-billed Curlew, Burrowing Owl, Loggerhead Shrike, Least Bell's Vireo, California Swainson's Thrush, Yellow Warbler, Yellow-breasted Chat, Tricolored Blackbird	M. Rogers, S. Fitton, *pers. comm.*

Description: The Bolsa de San Felipe area lies just east of the Monterey Bay area, in a triangle formed by Hwy. 101, Hwy. 152, and Hwy. 156. Major features for wildlife include San Felipe Lake, a natural, formerly-seasonal freshwater pond rimmed by a freshwater marsh and willows just south of Hwy. 152 about 10 miles east of Gilroy. The lake is surrounded by pastureland and agricultural fields that extend to the west and south, which are intersected by riparian vegetation, notably along Llagas Creek and the upper Pajaro River. Just northeast of the Bolsa, along Pacheco Creek (visible from Hwy. 152) is one of the most extensive sycamore riparian woodlands on the entire Central Coast. The southwest portion of the IBA is a raised area known as the Flint Hills, which feature extensive grassland and scattered seasonal wetlands. Though it has been virtually unexplored by biologists (SF), it likely contains many surprises, perhaps even vernal pools. Finally, a former gravel pit on the southeast side of the IBA (vic. Hollister), known locally as the Southside Ponds, support good numbers of waterbirds and have excellent restoration potential (SF).

Birds: Public access is virtually impossible throughout this IBA, and any ornithological investigation has been done from public roads. It is known that a large colony of Tricolored Blackbirds (localized in the region) regularly breeds here, along with a handful of American Bittern (also along nearby Llagas Ck.) and several species of waders and ducks. The agricultural lands provide important winter foraging and roosting habitat for Long-billed Curlew and all the expected species of geese, which join the thousands of waterbirds that commute between here, the South San Francisco Bay, the Central Valley and the Monterey Bay lowlands. This IBA is the winter home of such communally roosting raptors as White-tailed Kite and Ferruginous Hawk, and a tiny, remnant population of Burrowing Owl. The riparian thickets support many of the nesting lowland riparian bird species that were once common north to the San Francisco Bay but that have now been widely extirpated, including Yellow Warbler and a large population of Yellow-breasted Chat. Least Bell's Vireo has even nested here recently (M. Rodgers, *pers. comm.*). These riparian birds may also be found along Pacheco Creek, along with taxa more typical of foothill streams (e.g. Western Wood-Pewee).

Conservation issues: Each year, more houses, in particular large "ranchettes", continue to claim more open habitat here, and more surface water in the area is lost to agricultural diversions and is pumped for the area's burgeoning human population. Other direct effects include road-widening and sprawl from the growing communities of Hollister and Gilroy. Unless urgent conservation measures are taken (land easements, acquisitions), the unique resources of this nearly un-studied IBA will be lost.

"San Felipe Lake" along Hwy. 152 east of Gilroy, Bolsa de San Felipe IBA (Daniel S. Cooper)

Bridgeport Valley
Mono

Nearest town(s): Bridgeport
Size: 10,000 - 50,000 acres
Sensitive species: 8 (Northern Harrier, Ferruginous Hawk, Gold Eagle, Prairie Falcon. Loggerhead Shrike, Bank Swallow, Yellow Warbler, Yellow-headed Blackbird) (E. Strauss, *via email*)
Threat: High
Local Audubon Chapter: Eastern Sierra
BCR: 9

IBA Criteria		Source/Notes
W	>5000 Waterfowl	27,050 waterfowl on 17 September 1997, D. House, *unpubl. data*

Description: Bridgeport Valley is formed by the east fork of the Walker River, one valley south of the branch that forms Topaz Lake/Antelope Valley. Bridgeport Reservoir, formed by a small dam about five miles north of the town of Bridgeport, is fed by numerous creeks out of the eastern Sierra Nevada, and in fall features a broad draw-down area of mudflats at its southern end. The valley itself extends for about five miles south of town (south and west of Hwy. 395), and supports extensive grassland and wet meadow vegetation. Grazing pressure is tremendous within this IBA, and riparian habitat is limited to thin strips of willows along Swanger and Virginia creeks, both of which follow Hwy. 395.

Birds: The Bridgeport Valley was one of two locales in California ever known to support breeding Yellow Rail, with the last egg sets collected in the mid-1900s (the other site was Long Valley, see below; Grinnell Miller 1944). This scarce northern breeder has been essentially extirpated from the state. Recent summer records of Short-eared Owl suggest that enough wet grassland habitat may remain to be supporting at least a fragmentary Great Basin wetland bird community. The riparian habitats have been thoroughly altered, although Bank Swallow nests just east of town at a borrow pit. Forster's Tern has bred in recent years at Bridgeport Reservoir (*fide* E. Strauss), although lowered water levels have forced them to abandon nests. On the bright side, the drawdown area of the reservoir can support over a thousand shorebirds during fall (esp. Killdeer and phalaropes, Shuford *et al.* 2002), and, at the peak of movement in late September, thousands of ducks, especially Mallard, Green-winged Teal and Gadwall (D. House, *unpubl. data*).

Conservation issues: The entire IBA, including the shore of Bridgeport Reservoir is heavily grazed by cattle and sheep. This has eliminated most of the marsh habitat of the valley, and may be precluding the establishment of certain sensitive Great Basin breeders. Water levels of the reservoir determine the availability of nesting sites for island-nesting waterbirds such as terns. Like the Antelope Valley to the north, this IBA may be relatively stable, but ecologically, it is a pale shadow of its former state.

Brooks Island Regional Preserve

Contra Costa

Nearest town(s): Richmond, El Cerrito, Albany
Size: <1000 acres
Sensitive species: 0 (J. Hedgecock, *in litt.*)
Threat: Low
Local Audubon Chapter: Golden Gate
BCR: 32

IBA Criteria		Source/Notes
W	>5000 Waterfowl	Highs of 10,000 Greater Scaup, 5000 Surf Scoter; J. Hedgecock, *in litt.*

Description: Brooks Island is a naturally-formed, 373-acre patch of dry land in the east San Francisco Bay, about 10 miles northeast of the city of San Francisco. It is managed by the East Bay Regional Park District, and may be visited only by kayak. The San Francisco Bay Bird Observatory and the Cypress Grove Research Station have been conducting long-term bird research on its breeding water birds.

Birds: Brooks Island, like the Alameda NAS just to the south, supports one of the largest breeding colonies of Caspian Tern in California, with 900 pr. in 1998. Aside from this distinction, there was a sizable heron rookery here, which consisted of primarily of Black-crowned Night-Heron (max. 100 pr.) and Snowy Egret (max. 95 pr.), with a handful each of Great Blue Heron and Great Egret. This was apparently abandoned in the 1996, coinciding with the two-month appearance of a single Red Fox on the island (J. Kelly, via email). In winter, the waters around Brooks Island support exceptional concentrations of certain inshore sea ducks and hundreds of shorebirds roost on the island during migration and winter (esp. Western Sandpiper, Dunlin, Willet and Black-bellied Plover).

Conservation issues: Brooks Island is adjacent to Richmond Harbor where high levels of DDT have been detected. Introduced Red Foxes have been implicated in recent declines in nesting waders, and the occasional recreational kayaker ignoring the signs prohibiting approach by boat has caused major disturbance to the tern colony during the breeding season.

Buena Vista Lake Bed

Kern

Nearest town(s): Bakersfield
Size: 10,000 - 50,000 acres
Threat: Medium
Local Audubon Chapter: Kern
BCR: 32

IBA Criteria		Source/Notes
L	16 sensitive species: White-faced Ibis, Redhead, Northern Harrier, Swainson's Hawk, Ferruginous Hawk, Mountain Plover, Long-billed Curlew, Black Tern, Burrowing Owl, Short-eared Owl, Long-eared Owl, Loggerhead Shrike, Yellow Warbler, Sage Sparrow, Tricolored Blackbird, Yellow-headed Blackbird	A. Sheehey, *pers. comm.*

Description: Until the mid-1800s, the southern San Joaquin Valley boasted the largest freshwater wetland complex in the western U.S., extending a half-million acres across what was to be known as the Tulare Lake Basin. Three main basins were involved, with the massive Tulare Lake Bed in the north and the Buena Vista and Kern Lake Beds southwest of present-day Bakersfield. Agriculture, both row crops and grazing, expanded through the early 1900s, and by the mid-1900s, Isabella Dam largely halted the regular winter floods in the area. During the 1960s and 70s, the region was converted to a highly mechanized landscape of "manicured" corporate farms with heavy pesticide use and highly limited bird habitat. Today, cracks in the levees have allowed water to escape containment, fields to go fallow, and habitat to flourish again, mostly out of sight to the thousands of motorists along I-5, which cuts through the middle of the Buena Vista Lake Bed. Key areas for birds here include large (1000s of acres) water banks both east and west of I-5 within the historic Kern River bed that are flooded by the county when water reserves are above normal; Cole's Levee Ecosystem Preserve, a 6000-acre, privately-owned gem of riparian, grassland and alkali sink scrub just north of the Buena Vista Aquatic Recreation Area west of I-5; and several smaller overflow basins just north of South Lake Rd. east of the town of Taft. Other patches of un-plowed valley floor (e.g. Tule Elk Preserve, southeast of Buttonwillow) have received little attention from field ornithologists but have high potential for grassland and riparian birds

Birds: Though historical records from this IBA include such phenomena as nesting colonies of American White Pelican (e.g. Linton 1908), a surprisingly large subset of the former avifauna persists, albeit in reduced numbers. So, while the region's bird communities have not returned to pre-1950s conditions, they are certainly occupying every shred of available habitat. The Kern Water Bank east of I-5 has recently hosted up to 100 White-faced Ibis summering, along with breeding Northern Harrier, White-tailed Kite (c. 15 pairs summer when flooded), and is one of the few San Joaquin Valley-floor areas where scarce riparian birds such as Yellow Warbler and Yellow-breasted Chat persist in summer. The water bank west of I-5 was found to support Forster's and Black Terns during surveys in 1998 (Shuford *et al.* 1999). Cole's Levee has been little studied by birders, but is expected to support a similar

Important Bird Areas of California

subset of birds. Tricolored Blackbirds have a traditional breeding area at the Tule Elk Preserve (TNC 1998). The overflow ponds east of Taft are notable for large numbers of shorebirds and waterfowl in migration and winter (when at least partially flooded), and for high numbers of Burrowing Owl, which seem associated with the dirt banks of the California Aqueduct through this area. Prairie Falcons summer in this area, and often forage around these ponds, where they are joined by numerous other raptors during migration and winter, many of which roost in trees along the Kern River (SF).

Conservation issues: Due to the high degree of degradation to this IBA, and the fact that any habitat is either in private hands or is managed by county agencies with no clear habitat conservation mandate, a "Critical" threat designation is warranted for the entire IBA. Though Conservation issues affecting the area range from unreliable water levels to toxins in the soil and water, the fact that so little habitat remains means that any amount of conservation activity through easements and management agreements can have marked effects on bird populations in this portion of the San Joaquin Valley. Though an overwhelming majority of the region is in private hands, the Buena Vista Aquatic Recreation Area, basically in the center of the IBA, is a county-run fishing and boating park (incl. Lake Webb/Lake Evans) with tremendous (unrealized) conservation potential, both along its borders and in the area outside the levees of the lake. Patches of riparian thickets here could be expanded and protected, and freshwater marsh vegetation encouraged where appropriate. Recent expansion of urban sprawl west from Bakersfield continues to degrade habitat within this IBA through encroachment and direct habitat loss, particularly along the Kern River.

Butte Valley

Siskiyou

Nearest town(s): Macdoel
Size: 10,000 - 50,000 acres
Threat: Low
Local Audubon Chapter: Mt. Shasta
BCR: 9

IBA Criteria		Source/Notes
P	Nearly 10% of CA breeding population of Swainson's Hawk	70 pr.; K. Novick, *unpubl. data*
L	11 sensitive species: American White Pelican, Redhead, Northern Harrier, Swainson's Hawk, Ferruginous Hawk, Sandhill Crane, Black Tern, Short-eared Owl, Long-eared Owl, Yellow Warbler, Yellow-headed Blackbird	K. Novick, *pers. comm.*
W	>5000 Waterfowl	100,000+ waterfowl during peaks; K. Novick, *pers. comm.*

Description: Butte Valley lies in extreme north-central California, near the town of Macdoel about halfway between I-5 and the Klamath Basin. It includes Butte Valley National Grasslands (c. 20,000 acres, USFS) in the north and Butte Valley Wildlife Area (DFG) in the south, which includes 4000-acre Meiss Lake (ephemeral, drying every 10-15 years), 4,400 acres of managed wetlands, and about 5000 acres of other habitats such as croplands, meadows, grasslands and woodland (oak-juniper, pine-fir and riparian). Additional seasonal wetlands dot the National Grasslands, mainly in spring.

Birds: The Butte Valley Wildlife Area is notable for exceptional concentrations of waterfowl in migration, with 100,000 ducks regularly stopping over. Tens of thousands of geese (Canada, Greater White-fronted, Snow and Ross') occur in spring, as well as up to 5000 Tundra Swans. About 50 species of birds nest in the wildlife area, including 13 species of ducks. Shuford *et al.* (1998) considered this IBA among the top five most important sites for "inland-breeding seabirds" in northeastern California, with Meiss Lake especially important. In recent years, Meiss has supported 2-3000 pr. each of California and Ring-billed gulls, along with colonies of terns and Double-crested Cormorants. Small numbers of American White Pelican have bred here in recent wet years (1999 and 2000, K. Novick, *unpubl. data*). Swainson's Hawk breed in exceptional numbers, and other raptors abound in fall and winter, including up to 75 wintering Bald Eagles.

Conservation issues: During the mid-1900s, the hydrology of Butte Valley was extensively altered, which included draining of wetlands and channelizing of streams. Much of this damage is being repaired by the State of California, at least within Butte Valley Wildlife Area. Riparian areas, heavily-impacted by years of cattle grazing, are being fenced and replanted. Butte Valley is often visited by natural floods after wet winters, and has long piped "excess" water north into the Klamath River. Crop yields, particularly of "cereal grains" that support migrating waterfowl and Sandhill Cranes, vary considerably from year to year, though their acreage has actually decreased considerably due to wetlands restoration.

Byron Area

Contra Costa

Nearest town(s): Byron, Brentwood, Tracy
Size: 10,000 - 50,000 acres
Sensitive species: 9 (Northern Harrier, Swainson's Hawk, Ferruginous Hawk, Golden Eagle, Long-billed Curlew, Burrowing Owl, Short-eared Owl, Loggerhead Shrike, Tricolored Blackbird) (Glover 2001)
Threat: High
Local Audubon Chapter: Mt. Diablo
BCR: 32

IBA Criteria		Source/Notes
P	>1% Global population of Long-billed Culew	276 birds on 2001 East Contra Costa County CBC
W	>5000 Waterfowl	7233 waterfowl on 2002 East Contra Costa County CBC

Description: This IBA encompasses a large patch of grassland and constructed wetlands in one of the fastest-growing regions of California, on the outer ring of bedroom communities for the East San Francisco Bay Area that includes Oakley, Brentwood and Tracy. The "Byron Grasslands" (no formal name) lie in the ecotone between the eastern shoulder of the Diablo Range and the floor of the Central Valley, west of Byron Hwy. and south of Hwy. 160. Some of the best habitat here is centered on the Byron Airport. The non-profit Trust for Public Land has recently entered into a contract to acquire the 4000-acre "Cowell Ranch" property near Brentwood, but much of the grassland here remains in private hands. The Clifton Court Forebay is a 2000-acre water retention basin managed by the California Dept. of Water Resources at the southernmost portion of the current Sacramento Delta wetlands ecosystem.

Birds: This region has become increasingly important for wintering raptors that cannot persist in intensively-farmed and/or developed areas of the southern Delta. Large numbers of waterfowl utilize the open water of the forebay during winter and migration (e.g. c. 3000 Tundra Swan on 2002 East Contra Costa Co. CBC), particularly for nighttime roosts. Short-eared Owl breeds in the wet grassland here (one of the few nesting areas left in the Central Valley), and Burrowing Owls utilize the raised, sandy spots here for nesting, having been eliminated from much of the valley floor. Lesser Nighthawk also breed in sandy, scrubby areas that have been extensively converted to agriculture elsewhere, and Swainson's Hawk nest in scattered clumps of trees (mainly planted eucalyptus), about the closest they breed to the Bay Area.

Conservation issues: Although Clifton Court Forebay is fairly well protected, the grassland habitat within IBA is being whittled away each year by housing tracts and associated road construction. Hopefully, the acquisition of Cowell Ranch can leverage additional conservation acquisitions in the region.

Important Bird Areas of California

Camp Pendleton
San Diego/Riverside

Nearest town(s): Oceanside, Fallbrook
Size: >50,000 acres
Threat: High
Local Audubon Chapter: Buena Vista, South Coast
BCR: 32

IBA Criteria		Source/Notes
P	>1% Global population of California Least Tern	602 nests in 2002; K. Keane, *unpubl. data*
P	>1% Global population of Southwestern Willow Flycatcher	23 territories; Sogge *et al.* 2002
P	>1% Global population of Least Bell's Vireo	300 pr. 1993; B. Foster, *in litt.*
P	>1% Global population of California Gnatcatcher	USFWS 1998
L	24 sensitive species: Least Bittern, Redhead, Northern Harrier, Ferruginous Hawk, Golden Eagle, Light-footed Clapper Rail, Western Snowy Plover, Long-billed Curlew, Least Tern, California Spotted Owl, Long-eared Owl, Southwestern Willow Flycatcher, Loggerhead Shrike, Least Bell's Vireo, Cactus Wren, Clark's Marsh Wren, California Gnatcatcher, California Swainson's Thrush, Yellow Warbler, Yellow-breasted Chat, Summer Tanager, Sage Sparrow, Belding's Savannah Sparrow, Grasshopper Sparrow	San Diego Natural History Museum 2002

Description: The Santa Margarita River watershed stands alone in southern California as having an unbroken, unchannelized corridor of lowland riparian habitat along its floodplain from its headwaters to an intact coastal estuary at its mouth. With most of its 27-mile length skirting the southern border of vast Camp Pendleton (DoD), it has survived the major modification of its banks for agriculture and urbanization that has affected virtually every other lowland river in Central and Southern California. North of the river, within Camp Pendleton, the rugged hills of the southern Santa Ana Mountains provide important habitat for the remaining wide-ranging "megafauna" of coastal southern California, including Mountain Lion. The base is also home to over 95% of the endemic Pacific Pocket Mouse (*Perognathus longimembris pacificus*), restricted to sandy soils on marine terraces. Other important habitat features for birds within this IBA include the tributaries Sandy Creek and De Luz Creek, as well as San Mateo Creek on the northern border of Camp Pendleton and O'Neil Lake, one of the most extensive freshwater marshes along the coast of southern California. The headwaters of the Santa Margarita are the site of intensive ecological research (through California State University, San Diego) and conservation efforts to connect with the Peninsular Ranges of western Riverside and northern San Diego County via the "Tenaja Corridor."

Birds: The most outstanding feature of the avifauna of the Santa Margarita River watershed is the veritable abundance of many species that are otherwise reduced to scattered pairs in the region. Predictably, the diversity of breeding species is remarkable – around 90 bird species have been found nesting within a 10-square-mile block on recent surveys (K. Weaver, *pers. comm.*). For riparian bird species, the population of Least Bell's Vireo is by far the largest in the state (roughly half the global population, *fide* B. Kus, *unpubl. data*). and that of Southwestern Willow Flycatcher is one of the largest in the state away from the Lower Colorado River, the others being on the San Luis Rey River and the South Fork Kern River (Stephenson and Calcarone 1999). Its population of Long-eared Owl, once abundant in willow thickets bordered by grassland throughout southern California, is now apparently the only one left along the coast (west of I-5). The extensive grassland supports multiple territories of Northern Harrier (by comparison, <10 pairs breed in all of Los Angeles and Orange County each year). Three distinct "Core Populations" (up to 150 pr. each) of California Gnatcatcher occur along the River at the southern boundary of Camp Pendelton, and another two core popuations are near San Onofre/San Mateo Ck. at the north end (USFWS 1998). The estuary and salt flats at the mouth of the Santa Margarita River are equally impressive, with possibly the largest breeding colony of California Least Tern in the world and one of state's largest populations of breeding Snowy Plover (89 nests in 2001); as well as over 100 pairs of Belding's Savannah Sparrow. More than 1500 shorebirds per day refuel at the river mouth during the fall (PRBO, *unpubl. data*). The lack of public access has been important for the low level of disturbance to these species, but more critical has been the fact that development has been so limited within the borders of the base, in sharp contrast to everywhere else along the coastal plain of southern California (all bird survey numbers B. Foster, *unpubl. data*).

Conservation issues: The explosion of population growth in western Riverside Co. (headwaters of the Santa Margarita River) have resulted in unprecedented invasions of exotic plants throughout the river system (esp. Arundo and tamarisk). Feral cats are a local but growing problem along the river, and education programs would be warranted around developed areas within the upper watershed (e.g. Fallbrook). Channelization proposals for tributaries of the Santa Margarita (e.g. Murrieta Creek) remain a constant threat to riparian habitat, and powerline construction proposals threaten to encourage exotic species invasions into intact habitat. Though the habitat on Camp Pendleton is secure for now, it receives no formal protection as an ecological reserve or wildlife refuge, and should be considered at risk from future development schemes. Recently, residential development on the base has claimed several hundred acres of coastal sage scrub and grassland habitat.

Cape Mendocino Grasslands

Humboldt

Nearest town(s): Ferndale
Size: 10,000 - 50,000 acres
Threat: Low
Local Audubon Chapter: Redwood Region
BCR: 5

	IBA Criteria	Source/Notes
L	11 sensitive species: Northern Harrier, Ferruginous Hawk, Golden Eagle, Peregrine Falcon, Tufted Puffin, Burrowing Owl, Northern Spotted Owl, Short-eared Owl, Long-eared Owl, Purple Martin, Bryant's Savannah Sparrow, Grasshopper Sparrow	Harris 1996; J. Sterling, *pers. comm.*

This area supports one of the largest expanses of grassland in northwestern California, reached via a long, sinuous road west from Hwy. 101. Bounded by the King Range Wilderness Area (a.k.a. "The Lost Coast", BLM) to the south, the ownership of this IBA is almost entirely private, with most of the land in two large holdings of long-time ranching families. About 10% of the area, including remnant patches of Douglas-Fir forest, is controlled by timber companies. In addition to an exceptionally rich and diverse wintering raptor community, the Cape Mendocino grasslands support colonies of nesting Grasshopper Sparrows and Horned Larks, both regionally rare breeders. This is one of the few reliable places in northwestern California mentioned by Harris (1996) for Long-eared Owl, which occur in fall. Offshore rocks in the area (incl. False Cape Rocks, Sugarloaf Island and Steamboat Rock) support a diverse breeding seabird colony, including over 20,000 Common Murre, which represented nearly 10% of the state's nesting population in the late 1980s (Carter *et al.* 1992).

Carrizo Plain

San Luis Obispo/Kern

Nearest town(s): Taft, Maricopa
Size: >50,000 acres
Threat: Low
Local Audubon Chapter: North Cuesta or Kern
BCR: 32

IBA Criteria		Source/Notes
P	>1% Global population of Mountain Plover	Up to 300 birds during 1980s; S. Fitton, *pers. comm.*
P	>1% Global population of Long-billed Curlew	2505 birds, Carrizo Plains CBC, 1995
P	>1% Global population of San Joaquin Le Conte's Thrasher	S. Fitton, *pers. comm.*
P	>10% CA population of Sandhill Crane	2900 birds, Carrizo Plains CBC, 1992
L	15 sensitive species: Northern Harrier, Ferruginous Hawk, Golden Eagle, Prairie Falcon, Sandhill Crane, Mountain Plover, Long-billed Curlew, Burrowing Owl, Short-eared Owl, Long-eared Owl, Loggerhead Shrike, San Joaquin Le Conte's Thrasher, Sage Sparrow, Grasshopper Sparrow, Tricolored Blackbird	J. Benson, *in litt.*; S. Fitton, *pers. comm.*
S	Probably >10,000 Shorebirds	S. Fitton, *pers. comm.*
W	Probably >5000 Waterfowl	S. Fitton, *pers. comm.*

Description: This IBA encompasses 180,000 acres along the San Andreas Fault between the Central Valley and the coast, and includes two large valleys (Carrizo Plain and Elkhorn Plain), a massive seasonal alkali lake (Soda Lake), and low, rolling hills of grass and arid scrub. Jointly managed by the BLM and a host of other public agencies and non-profits, it represents one of the most significant swaths of protected lands in the state. Taken together with Bitter Creek National Wildlife Refuge just to the southeast, the Wildlands Conservancy's recently-designated Wind Wolves Preserve (see San Emigdio Canyon IBA), and the Sespe Wilderness Area, this is one of the few areas in the state that is large and protected enough where, as it is often said, condors can soar down from the hills to feed on the carcasses of Pronghorn and Tule Elk. This IBA contains the largest remaining example of the San Joaquin Valley ecosystem – most within the valley itself were eliminated over a century ago.

Birds: The flocks of several thousand Sandhill Cranes that form winter roosts on Soda Lake have put Carrizo Plain on the map, ornithologically, and as native, natural habitat for open country birds continues to decline in the state, the importance of this IBA only increases. Breeding Northern Harrier, Golden Eagle, Prairie Falcon, Burrowing Owl, the canescens race of Sage Sparrow – all of which have become localized or have all but disappeared from the San Joaquin Valley – thrive at Carrizo. Swainson's Hawk was known as a breeder from the San Juan Creek drainage just west of Carrizo (Walton 1978), and may persist in the area. In spring after wet winters, Soda Lake becomes a haven for thousands of waterfowl and for northbound shorebirds, but their numbers are imperfectly known due to the difficulty of accessing the habitat at this time (SF). Wintering Ferruginous Hawk and resident Short-eared and Long-eared owls occur in one of their last strongholds toward southern California, and in winter, flocks of several hundred Long-billed Curlews may be found in the grassland on the valley floor. Mountain Plover formerly wintered in flocks totalling about 300 birds, but recent wet years have apparently decreased the amount of suitable habitat for them (SF). Aside from birds, Carrizo Plain is notable for protecting numerous rare species, including several San Joaquin Valley endemic plants virtually eliminated elsewhere.

Conservation issues: This area is one of the most carefully-managed areas of California, and no changes are recommended.

Island Scrub-Jay (Peter LaTourrette)

Channel Islands – Northern

Ventura, Santa Barbara, Los Angeles

Nearest town(s): none
Size: >50,000 acres
Threat: High
Local Audubon Chapter: Ventura, Santa Barbara
BCR: 32

IBA Criteria		Source/Notes
P (5)	Entire Global populations of Catalina California Quail, Catalina Hutton's Vireo, San Clemente Spotted Towhee, Santa Cruz Isl. Rufous-crowned Sparrow and Channel Isl. Song Sparrow	Garrett and Dunn 1981
P (3)	>1% of Global population of breeding California Brown, Pelican, Ashy Storm-Petrel and Xantus' Murrelet	Carter et al. 1992
P (2)	>10% CA population of breeding Black Storm-Petrel and Cassin's Auklet	Carter et al. 1992
P	>10% California population of coastal-breeding Western Snowy Plover	196 birds in summer 1995; USFWS 2001
L	16 sensitive species: Brown Pelican, Ashy Storm-Petrel, Black Storm-Petrel, Peregrine Falcon, Catalina California Quail, Snowy Plover, Cassin's Auklet, Xantus' Murrelet, Tufted Puffin, Burrowing Owl, Short-eared Owl, Loggerhead Shrike, Catalina Hutton's Vireo, San Clemente Spotted Towhee, Santa Cruz Island Rufous-crowned Sparrow, Channel Islands Song Sparrow	Garrett and Dunn 1981

Description: The northern Channel Islands lie south of Santa Barbara and Ventura, off the coast of southern California, and their peaks looming offshore are a familiar sight to millions of residents of the Los Angeles metropolitan area. For a variety of reasons, they have remained virtually undeveloped, and thus represent some of the best examples of aspects of pre-settlement southern California. Four are arranged in an east-west chain: San Miguel (9000 acres), Santa Rosa (50,000 acres), Santa Cruz (60,000 acres) and tiny Anacapa (700 acres). Santa Barbara (640 acres) lies to the southeast, and San Nicolas (13,000 acres), southwest of here, is the most isolated of the islands. Santa Catalina Island (a.k.a. "Catalina", 50,000 acres), to the southeast, is due south of Los Angeles. All except Catalina are managed by the federal government, with San Nicolas operated as a U.S. Navy Base and the remaining five under Channel Islands National Park. The waters off the northern islands, San Miguel, Santa Rosa, Santa Cruz, Anacapa and Santa Barbara have also been recognized as one of three National Marine Sanctuaries (NOAA) in California. Nearly 90% of Catalina is owned by the non-profit Santa Catalina Island Conservancy, a conservation group, and it is the only island with a permanent town, Avalon. Both Santa Rosa and Santa Cruz have in-holdings of private land (large ranches) that pre-date their park designation.

Birds: As with most large islands on earth, several bird taxa have evolved here in isolation and are not found elsewhere, with each island sharing some races and not others. Of the sensitive endemic taxa, their distribution is as follows: Catalina California Quail (native to Catalina and introduced to Santa Cruz and Santa Rosa, *fide* Garrett and Dunn 1981), Island Loggerhead Shrike (all except San Nicolas), Catalina Hutton's Vireo (Santa Catalina), San Clemente Spotted Towhee (Santa Catalina and Santa Rosa), Santa Cruz Island Rufous-crowned Sparrow (Santa Cruz and Anacapa) and Channel Islands Song Sparrow (San Miguel and Santa Rosa). Island Scrub-Jay – a recently-split species not currently considered sensitive – occurs only on Santa Cruz Island. This IBA is the single most important seabird nesting area in southern California, with birds concentrated on coastal bluffs and on large offshore rocks around each island (except San Nicolas and Catalina). Three seabird taxa – California Brown Pelican, Black Storm-Petrel and Xantus' Murrelet – do not nest regularly elsewhere in the U.S. Though Black Storm-Petrels are much more common in the Gulf of California, the population of Brown Pelicans represents about 10% of the global population of the californicus race, our local subspecies. The entire U.S. breeding population of Xantus' Murrelet is confined to the Channel Islands (the endemic scrippsii race), with the largest colony on Santa Barbara Isl. (1400 birds, Carter *et al.* 1992). Tiny Prince Island, off San Miguel Isl., hosts nearly 20% the state's breeding Cassin's Auklets (c. 9,000, Carter *et al.* 1992). Several other seabirds, including Rhinoceros Auklet and Tufted Puffin, formerly bred more widely within this IBA, but were extirpated by rats and other introduced pests except for a remnant population of both on and around San Miguel Isl. (Carter *et al.* 1992). The northern Channel Islands population of Snowy Plovers (breeding on Santa Rosa, San Miguel and San Nicolas Isl.) is comprised of 250-400 birds (J. Greaves, *in litt.*), one of the largest concentration of the coastal-breeding Western Snowy Plover in the world. Most of the breeding Peregrine Falcons in southern California nest here, as well as several endemic races of songbirds whose relatedness to each other (and to mainland birds) is still being debated. Burrowing Owl and both Mountain Plover and Pacific Golden-Plover winter on the windswept grasslands of San Nicolas (W. Wehtje, *pers. comm.*), and each island supports large numbers of migrant songbirds, particularly in fall.

Conservation issues: Overgrazing (by sheep, goats and cattle) has been a historical problem for this IBA, but largely through the efforts of the National Park Service, this threat has been isolated to Santa Rosa Island and a small portion of Santa Cruz Island. Predation of ground nesting seabird nests by exotic rats remains an issue, recently addressed by an eradication effort 2002 on Anacapa Isl. Most recently, avian conservation battles have been waged over high-powered lights from night-fishing squid boats and their potentially deleterious effects on nesting seabirds. Rare oil spills have resulted in impacts to some seabirds here, particularly Brown Pelican (SH). Other threats to pelagic seabirds include "oil and gas development, busy shipping lanes in nearby waters, non-point source pollution, and commercial and recreational fishing" (http://www.sanctuaries.nos.noaa.gov/oms/omschannel/omschannel.html).

Cima Dome
San Bernardino

Nearest town(s): Baker
Size: >50,000 acres
Sensitive species: 9 (Golden Eagle, Prairie Falcon, Burrowing Owl, Long-eared Owl, Loggerhead Shrike, Gilded Flicker, Bendire's Thrasher, Crissal Thrasher, Le Conte's Thrasher) (S. Myers, *pers. comm.*)
Threat: Low
Local Audubon Chapter: San Bernardino Valley
BCR: 33

IBA Criteria		Source/Notes
P	>10% CA population of Gilded Flicker	S. Myers, *pers. comm.*
P	Probably >10% CA population of Bendire's Thrasher	England and Laudenslayer 1989

Visible to drivers along I-15 to and from Las Vegas, Cima Dome is a 70-squre-mile granitic mass that rises almost imperceptibly out of the Mojave Desert to an elevation of 5700'. Located within the Mojave National Preserve (formerly "East Mojave Scenic Area"), it is famous among naturalists for its vast expanse of Joshua Tree woodland – the largest in the world – and its spectacular wildflower displays after wet winters. Cima Dome supports nearly all of California's Gilded Flickers, as well as strong populations of three scarce desert thrashers (see above), all of which appear to be very sensitive to habitat encroachment, requiring large areas of undisturbed scrubland. Characteristic high desert birds (e.g. Scott's Oriole) are abundant here. Grazing, a relict of old BLM leases prior to its designation as a National Preserve, remains an issue in this fragile environment, though many conservation groups (notably Sierra Club) are currently battling to eliminate cattle from the preserve.

Clear Lake Area, Lake Co.

Lake

Nearest town(s): Clearlake, Lakeport
Size: >50,000 acres
Threat: Medium
Local Audubon Chapter: Redbud
BCR: 32

IBA Criteria		Source/Notes
L	14 sensitive species: Least Bittern, Bald Eagle, Northern Harrier, Ferruginous Hawk, Peregrine Falcon, Burrowing Owl, Short-eared Owl, Purple Martin, Yellow Warbler, Yellow-breasted Chat, Sage Sparrow, Grasshopper Sparrow, Tricolored Blackbird, Yellow-headed Blackbird	J. White, *pers. comm.*
W	>5000 Waterfowl	24,425 Western Grebes, Clear Lake CBC, 2001

Description: Clear Lake, at the southern end of the north Coast Range, is the largest natural lake wholly within the borders of California. It lies in a broad, dry valley just north of Napa Valley, and is fed by several small streams, with an outlet at the southeastern end (Cache Creek) that flows into the Sacramento Valley. The habitats represent a cross-section of the Californian Floristic Province, with mixed evergreen and oak woodland (incl. Black, Blue and Valley oaks) dominating the hillsides and remnant freshwater marsh and riparian habitats associated with creek mouths around the border of the lake. Among the various unique microhabitats are Borax Lake, an ephemeral, alkali lake just north of the town of Clearlake, and a large area of chamise chaparral and grassland east of town. The major natural areas scattered across this IBA include:
- Rodman Slough on the northwest side of the lake (200 acres; DFG, Lake County Land Trust)
- Clear Lake State Park east of Lakeport, which includes mudflats at the lakeshore that concentrate birds year round (565 acres)
- Anderson Marsh State Historic Park/McVicar Sanctuary (National Audubon Society) on the southeastern edge of the lake (1000 acres)
- High Valley, extensive grassland on the northeast side of the lake (vic. Clearlake Oaks)

Birds: With its abundance and diversity of natural habitats, including natural wetlands, Clear Lake is a major resource for birds in northwestern California. Rodman Slough, including the adjacent "reclamation area" now in rice cultivation, supports a full compliment of breeding riparian and wetland birds within this IBA, including a rookeries of Great Blue Heron (100+ nests, *fide* R. Lyons) and Double-crested Cormorant, plus American Bittern and Yellow-breasted Chat. The mudflats of Clear Lake State Park supports large concentrations of roosting waterbirds (incl. terns and American White Pelican) during fall migration, and during summer, the bulrush marsh along the lakeshore between the park and

South Lakeport host what is likely the second-highest concentration of breeding Clark's and Western Grebes in the state (2000 pairs, D. Anderson, *unpubl. data*) as well as recently-confirmed breeding Least Bittern (JS). Anderson Marsh protects a remarkable mix of natural wetlands and mature bottomland riparian forest, with breeding Bald Eagles in the area and intriguing recent summer records of Yellow-billed Cuckoo (J. White, via email). The wetlands here are particularly productive for breeding rails and waders, and support Short-eared Owl in winter. Grassland birds are found north of the town of Clearlake (esp. Burrowing Owl, which may breed) in the High Valley area, which supports the most diverse wintering open-country bird community within this IBA (e.g. Prairie Falcon, Lewis' Woodpecker, Loggerhead Shrike), as well as breeding Yellow-billed Magpie (J. White, via email). Borax Lake has had breeding Tricolored Blackbirds (otherwise confined as nesters to Adobe Creek Reservoir, southwest of Kelseyville). Finally, the chamise chaparral north east of Clearlake support resident Greater Roadrunner and Bell's Sage Sparrow.

Conservation issues: Encouraging restoration projects within this IBA include plans to remove levees in the Rodman Slough area to permit a re-establishment of wetland habitat there (J. White, via email). Though several natural areas within the IBA are protected either as state parkland or as conservation lands managed by the Clear Lake Land Trust, other areas are still largely private and are thus vulnerable. Of particular concern are the extensive bulrush beds along the edges of the lake that are easily destroyed by marina construction. Residential and agricultural (mainly vineyard) development represents a major threat to the chaparral and grassland habitat on the east side of the lake.

Rodman Slough; Clear Lake Area, Lake Co. IBA (Suzanne McDonald)

Colorado Desert Microphyll Woodland
Imperial/Riverside/San Bernardino

Nearest town(s): Needles, Parker, Blythe; Lake Havasu City, AZ
Size: 1000-10,000 acres
Sensitive species: 8 (Elf Owl, Long-eared Owl, Loggerhead Shrike, Gila Woodpecker, Bendire's Thrasher, Crissal Thrasher, Le Conte's Thrasher, Lucy's Warbler) (R. McKernan, *pers. comm.*)
Threat: High
Local Audubon Chapter: Yuma
BCR: 33

IBA Criteria		Source/Notes
P	>1% CA population of Elf Owl	R. McKernan, *pers. comm.*
P	Probably >10% CA population of Gila Woodpecker	S. Myers, *pers. comm.*

Description: The lower Colorado Desert has one of the most arid climates in California, but includes several widely-spaced patches of microphyll woodland, much of which is associated with washes that flow east into the Colorado River. The larger ones include Chemehuevi Wash (San Bernardino Co., opposite Lake Havasu City, AZ), Vidal Wash (San Bernardino/Riverside Co., southwest of Parker, AZ) and Milpitas Wash (Imperial Co., west of Cibola NWR). Another major occurrence of this habitat lies along the northeastern base of the Algodones Dunes about 30 miles west of the river, halfway between the river and the south end of the Salton Sea. Dominant trees include Ironwood *(Olneya tesota)*, Paloverde and Honey Mesquite. Essentially the entire IBA falls under the jurisdiction of the BLM.

Birds: Because this area is located along the flight path of migrant songbirds moving up into California from Mexico (toward the Transverse Ranges and into the Sierra Nevada), any patch of green vegetation can attract large numbers of birds in April. In the Algodones Dunes woodland, any rain from the previous winter runs off the Chocolate Mtns. to the east and collects in sumps that can remain boggy for months (occasionally with small ponds forming), which make the habitat even more attractive to migrants. Long-eared Owls breed locally, and can form large winter roosts here. The scrubby woodland here also represents westernmost outposts for several primarily Mexican species more common in Arizona, such as Elf Owl (recently discovered in the Indian Pass Wilderness southeast of the Chocolate Mtns.), Gila Woodpecker (west to the Algodones Dunes), and Northern Cardinal (Vidal Wash). Vidal Wash also reaches the southern portion of the range of Bendire's Thrasher (England and Laudenslayer 1989).

Conservation issues: While portions of these sites are secure due to their remoteness, those closest to roads are heavily used by OHV enthusiasts. The unique woodland at the Algodones Dunes has been the site of recent controversy between the BLM and OHV riders, thousands of which descend upon the "town" of Glamis during winter weekends. Various lawsuits over the management of these riders have forced the closure of several areas, further angering riders and inviting retaliation. Mining is also an issue locally. Resort/marina development associated with the Colorado River has removed large tracts of mesquite woodland within this IBA (e.g. "Big River", part of Vidal Wash), which has led to regional extirpations of scarce taxa such as Elf Owl.

Restoring Mesquite Bosque near Cibola NWR (Marty Jackle)

Concord Marshes
Contra Costa

Nearest town(s): Martinez, Concord, Pittsburg
Size: 10,000 - 50,000 acres
Threat: Medium
Local Audubon Chapter: Mt. Diablo
BCR: 32

IBA Criteria		Source/Notes
P	>1% Global population of California Black Rail	150+ pr. in 1981; J. Hedgecock, *in litt.*
P	>1% Global population of California Clapper Rail	6 birds in 1994; J. Hedgecock, *in litt.*
P	>1% Global population of Suisun Song Sparrow	H. Spautz, *unpubl. data*
L	10 sensitive species: Northern Harrier, Black Rail, California Clapper Rail, Long-billed Curlew, Least Tern, Short-eared Owl, Loggerhead Shrike, Saltmarsh Common Yellowthroat, Bryant's Savannah Sparrow, Suisun Song Sparrow	J. Hedgecock, *in litt..*; Glover 2001
W	>5000 Waterfowl	c. 5000 Greater Scaup on 1994 Napa-Solano CBC, J. Hedgecock, *in litt.*

Description: The Concord Marshes lie along the southern shore of Suisun Bay at the western edge of the Sacramento River Delta. Along with Suisun Marsh to the north (see below), they ecologically connect the wetlands of the Central Valley with those of San Francisco Bay. Extending east from the town of Martinez to near Pittsburg, the best habitat is now mainly on the north side of Waterfront Rd., extending to the edge of the bay. The wetlands may be divided into three main areas: Martinez Regional Shoreline, which includes a large, constructed "duck pond" and tidal saltmarsh; McNabney Marsh/Pt. Edith (DFG), a large area of freshwater and saltmarsh on either side of the Benicia-Martinez bridge; and the Concord Naval Weapons Station, which extends this habitat to the east. The amount of tidal marsh vegetation varies greatly from year to year, which in turn affects the number and types of bird species. Access to the wetlands is limited to a few roads into the marshes, some of which require checking-in at guard posts. The NWS also includes about 8000 acres of grassland interspersed with riparian stringers extending inland, south of Waterfront Rd.

Birds: The Concord marshes support thousands of waterfowl from fall through spring, as well as high numbers of resident waders (esp. American Bittern) and rails. A full suite of baylands birds occurs here (Black Rail, California Clapper Rail, Suisun Song Sparrow), as do thousands of migrant and wintering shorebirds when conditions are favorable (exposed mudflats). Short-eared Owl is known to winter (*fide* S. Glover), and a handful of California Least Tern have begun breeding adjacent to the Pacific Gas and Electric Plant in Pittsburg, foraging within this IBA. A pair of Peregrine Falcon has begun nesting on the Benicia Bridge, and also forages heavily in this IBA.

Conservation issues: Since much of the habitat is either formally protected and managed for conservation, or protected and managed on DoD property, the most pressing conservation threat is that of exotic plants, the target of recent conservation plans.

California Clapper Rail (Peter LaTourrette)

Corte Madera Marsh

Marin

Nearest town(s): Corte Madera, San Rafael
Size: 1000-10,000 acres
Sensitive species: 6 (Peregrine Falcon, Black Rail, California Clapper Rail, Forster's Tern, Loggerhead Shrike, San Pablo Song Sparrow) (Shuford 1993)
Threat: Low
Local Audubon Chapter: Marin
BCR: 32

IBA Criteria		Source/Notes
P	>1% Global population of California Black Rail	Shuford 1993
P	>1% Global population of California Clapper Rail	Shuford 1993
P	>1% Global population of San Pablo Song Sparrow	1,600 birds; H. Spautz, *unpubl. data.*
S	Probably >10,000 Shorebirds	L. Stenzel, *via email*

Corte Madera Marsh is a patch of tidal marsh southwest of the San Pablo Bay Wetlands, and is largely protected by the 1000-acre Corte Madera Marsh Ecological Preserve (DFG). This IBA supports a sizable population of California Clapper Rail (with a few Black Rail), as well as vast mudflats during low tide that are heavily used by migrating shorebirds in the region. The Goals Project (1999) suggests establishing and enhancing upland buffers around the border of the wetlands to allow for the formation of seasonal ponds and to protect the wetlands from disturbance. Because the hydrology of this area has been so impacted, large areas of marsh are now dry, and exotic species are a growing threat.

Cosumnes River Preserve

Sacramento

Nearest town(s): Elk Grove, Rancho Murrieta
Size: 10,000 - 50,000 acres
Threat: Medium
Local Audubon Chapter: Sacramento
BCR: 32

	IBA Criteria	Source/Notes
P	>1% Global population of Long-billed Curlew	795 birds on Rio Cosumnes CBC, 2000; J. Trochet, *via email*
P	>10% CA population of Sandhill Crane (incl. Greater Sandhill Crane)	Ave. 1500; J. Trochet, *via email*
L	13 sensitive species: Least Bittern, Northern Harrier, Swainson's Hawk, Ferruginous Hawk, Golden Eagle, Black Rail, Sandhill Crane, Burrowing Owl, Short-eared Owl, Loggerhead Shrike, Grasshopper Sparrow, Tricolored Blackbird, Yellow-headed Blackbird	J. Trochet, *via email*
W	>5000 Waterfowl	15,508, Rio Cosumnes CBC, 2001; Ave. 20,000+ waterfowl winter on preserve; J. Trochet, *via email*

Description: The Cosumnes River is the only major river draining the western Sierra Nevada that remains entirely un-dammed and with a natural, snowmelt-fed flood regime. Managed by a consortium of non-profits and agencies, the Cosumnes currently protects about 15,000 acres of floodplain riparian woodland (both original and restored); grassland (including vernal pools); and freshwater wetland just south of Sacramento. Protected lands, including cooperative agricultural ventures and easements, extend from the confluence of the Cosumnes and the Mokelumne rivers (just west of I-5) then northeast to beyond I-99 to the town of Wilton east of Elk Grove.

Birds: The Cosumnes is a year-round magnet for birds, including many sensitive species that have long been extirpated from the most of the Central Valley. Numbers of Greater Sandhill Crane (a rare subspecies) wintering on the preserve alone average 1500 birds, a significant proportion of the state's population (J. Trochet, *in litt.*, citing A. Engelis). Breeding raptors include Swainson's Hawk (3-5 pr.), White-tailed Kite (5-10 pr.) and Northern Harrier (at least 5 pr.). The preserve appears to also be important for summer (pre-migrantion) concentrations of raptors, which have included up to 100 Swainson's Hawks and 200 White-tailed Kites. Up to 25 American Bittern per year have been bred in the freshwater marshes, which recently supported calling (and presumably breeding) Least Bittern and even the occasional Black Rail. The grassland toward the eastern portion of the preserve supports presumably-breeding Grasshopper Sparrow and Tricolored Blackbird, as well as a diverse community of wintering raptor such as Ferruginous Hawk and Burrowing, Short-eared and Long-eared owls.

Northbound shorebirds in spring regularly exceed 1000 birds, with a high of 8500 recorded on one day in mid-April, 1998. Songbird migration is also well-documented here (in contrast to many Central Valley sites), with counts of up to 50 Willow Flycatchers utilizing the riparian forest edge. The riparian woodland, currently being augmented by restoration plots on former orchards and pastures, supports mainly the common obligate passerines, though a smattering of summer records for Yellow Warbler and Yellow-breasted Chat offer hope that the original riparian avifauna of the area can be restored. Ornithological monitoring has been ongoing at the Cosumnes since the late 1980s (PRBO, Sacramento Audubon, John Trochet).

Conservation issues: The importance of this IBA increases each year, as the surrounding area becomes dominated by office parks, corporate farms and vineyards. Cowbird parasitism remains a threat to the reproduction of songbirds within this IBA, as it is surrounded by dairies and pastureland, though no agency or group has committed to supporting a long-term trapping program (J. Trochet, *pers. comm.*). Although most of the lands within the preserve itself are secure, threats to the surrounding landscape could seriously impact its resources, including urban encroachment from the burgeoning suburbs of Sacramento on the north and Stockton on the south, which very realistically threaten to constrict the preserve to a narrow corridor from the Sierra foothills to the Sacramento River Delta. Agricultural run-off continues to pose a threat, especially given the proliferation of vineyards in the area (TNC 1998).

Cosumnes River Preserve (The Nature Conservancy, Staff Photo)

Creighton Ranch Area
Tulare

Size: 1000-10,000 acres
Nearest town(s): Corcoran
Threat: High
Local Audubon Chapter: Tulare County
BCR: 32

IBA Criteria		Source/Notes
L	12 sensitive species: Redhead, Northern Harrier, Swainson's Hawk, Ferruginous Hawk, Sandhill Crane, Mountain Plover, Long-billed Curlew, Burrowing Owl, Short-eared Owl, Loggerhead Shrike, Tricolored Blackbird, Yellow-headed Blackbird	R. Hansen, *pers. comm.*

Description: The Nature Conservancy's former Creighton Ranch Preserve lies along the historic path of the lower Tule River, just east of the town of Corcoran. It features over 3000 acres of Valley Oak and cottonwood-willow riparian woodland, freshwater marsh and alkali grassland with vernal pools. TNC gave up the property in the mid-1990s, and it is now managed by the owner (J.G. Boswell Co.) as a de facto preserve (RH). Several other patches of native valley floor habitats in the area similar to Creighton Ranch include the 40-acre Pixley Vernal Pools Preserve east of the community of Pixley, considered one of just 34 National Natural Landmarks in California (J. Bayliss, NPS, *pers. comm.*). Over 700 acres of grassland/vernal pool habitat at "Herbert Ranch" east of Tulare was recently purchased by the Visalia-based Sierra-Los Tulares Land Trust (RH), and the Stone Corral Ecological Reserve (DFG) protects several hundred acres of a 3000-acre wetland/vernal pool/grassland complex about 20 miles to the north along I-99 (called "Cross Creek/Cottonwood Creek by TNC [1998]). All of these sites, though widely-scattered, are key habitat remnants in an area overwhelmingly dominated by industrial agriculture (mainly orchards and vineyards). Furthermore, most are connected to habitat in the Sierra via the Tule and Kaweah rivers and their tributaries.

Birds: Some of the farthest-south nesting Swainson's Hawks in the state breed at Creighton Ranch, as do localized wetland species such as Northern Harrier and Tricolored Blackbird, given appropriate water conditions. Creighton Ranch and similar properties lie along the massive water conduit system of the Central Valley that ensures that water flows along irrigation canals. In wet winters, Creighton is flooded, which attracts thousands of waterfowl and shorebirds. Mountain Plover and flocks of Sandhill Cranes formerly wintered at Cross Creek/Cottonwood Creek site up until the 1980s (*fide* B. Barnes), and still use fields and grassland in the area.

Conservation issues: According to The Nature Conservancy (1998), over 90% of Creighton Ranch is potential seasonal freshwater marsh, yet water management practices often fluctuate water levels during summer, when nesting birds would require consistent levels for nest placement. For conservationists working in the area, saving these unique habitat patches in western Tulare Co. is literally a race against the clock. Valley floor habitat continues to be ploughed-under for agriculture, increasingly for vineyards on the eastern side of the valley. Several acres of alkali scrub and grassland were recently lost at Creighton Ranch for a "soil borrowing" project (RH). The Sierra-Los Tulares Land Trust is working to link this and other sites in the area with open space corridors along the Kaweah and Tule rivers before their isolation irreparably degrades their resources.

Crowley Lake Area

Mono

Nearest town(s): Mammoth Lakes, Tom's Place
Size: 10,000 - 50,000 acres
Threat: Medium
Local Audubon Chapter: Eastern Sierra
BCR: 9

	IBA Criteria	Source/Notes
P	>1% Global population of Greater Sage-Grouse	248 birds in 2003; S. Blankenship, *unpubl. data*
P	>10% CA population of Bank Swallow	2000 pr.; Gaines 1988
L	14 sensitive species: Northern Harrier, Swainson's Hawk, Ferruginous Hawk, Golden Eagle, Peregrine Falcon, Prairie Falcon, Greater Sage-Grouse, Western Snowy Plover, Short-eared Owl, Long-eared Owl, Loggerhead Shrike, Bank Swallow, Yellow Warbler, Yellow-headed Blackbird	T. and J. Heindel, *pers. comm.*
W	>5000 Waterfowl	12,035 waterfowl on 17 Sept. 1997; D. House, *unpubl. data*

Description: Long Valley, one of the most volcanically active areas of California, lies north of the head of the Owens Valley in the eastern Sierra. Fed by several streams rushing down from mountains (incl. Convict Ck. and Upper Owens River), this vast alkali meadow is surrounded by robust Sagebrush scrub which climbs up high, conifer-covered slopes on all sides. Though it originally filled with water seasonally, it now supports both seasonal wetlands as well as Crowley Reservoir. Crowley, at 6,500 acres, is one of the largest bodies of water in California east of the Sierran axis, and its shallow edges remain marshy year round, providing exceptional wildlife habitat. Cattle graze much of Long Valley, though an ambitious project to fence critical stream banks and lakeshore beginning in the late 1990s resulted in a partial recovery of the meadow system, including dense rush and sedge marshes and willow thickets. The entire IBA is owned by the Los Angeles Dept. of Water and Power (LADWP) and is leased to ranchers.

Birds: Long Valley supports what is now one of the largest populations of Greater Sage-Grouse in the state, a species that depends on the area's low level of development for unobstructed seasonal elevational migrations (e.g. upslope in summer following nesting). Bank Swallow maintains its southernmost colony remaining in California on the eroded banks of Crowley, and Snowy Plover nest in small numbers at the north end of the reservoir and on the alkali lakes scattered across the valley floor (e.g. west of Benton Crossing Rd., DS). Prairie Falcons breed in nearby rock outcroppings, and up to 24 Peregrine Falcon chicks have been successfully hacked out of a tower installed by LADWP (G. Coufal, LADWP, *in litt.*). The concentrations of waterfowl year round (but especially in fall and spring) are nearly unduplicated in the region, especially Mallard and Gadwall in early fall (D. House, *unpubl. data*).

Important Bird Areas of California

Several species of ducks and grebes have large breeding populations in the expansive marshy meadows here. Like other interior wetlands, Crowley supports large numbers of post-breeding waterbirds in late summer (e.g. American White Pelican), which concentrate at the Owens River mouth. Shorebirds pour through by the hundreds (occasionally thousands) in spring and fall, with over 100 Spotted Sandpipers recorded on recent single-day surveys (D. Shuford *unpubl. data*). It is conceivable that with continued recovery of the wet meadow ecosystem here, Long Valley could once again support breeding Yellow Rail, known historically from the area (Grinnell and Miller 1944). In winter, the grassland of Long Valley hosts one of the major raptor concentrations east of the Sierra.

Conservation issues: Concern over the Greater Sage-Grouse has led to the LADWP's installing specialized fencing around leks, and working with the DFG to suspend hunting until the species recovered (G. Coufal, LADWP, *in litt.*). LADWP has also fenced large areas of feeder streams on the north side of the reservoir (incl. the Owens River), and has conducted Bald Eagle and Sage Grouse monitoring for several years. On the other hand, the area receives very high (and increasing) recreational use, particularly during the nesting season when birds are the most sensitive. A landfill on the northeast side of the lake is responsible for a surprising amount of trash strewn across the valley, and both this and plans to site a major airport just north of Crowley along Hwy. 395 to serve Mammoth's burgeoning population deserve close monitoring.

Crowley Lake (Daniel S. Cooper)

Cuyama Valley

Santa Barbara/San Luis Obispo

Nearest town(s): New Cuyama
Size: 10,000 - 50,000 acres
Threat: Medium
Local Audubon Chapter: None
BCR: 32

	IBA Criteria	Source/Notes
L	12 sensitive species: Ferruginous Hawk, Golden Eagle, Prairie Falcon, Long-billed Curlew, Burrowing Owl, Short-eared Owl, Long-eared Owl, Loggerhead Shrike, San Joaquin Le Conte's Thrasher, Sage Sparrow, Grasshopper Sparrow, Tricolored Blackbird	Lehman 1994

Description: The Cuyama Valley extends for about 15 miles along the middle Cuyama River, which flows west through the Coast Range about 80 miles inland of Santa Maria. Surrounded by dry hills, its habitat represents a fascinating intersection of Central Valley, Mojave Desert, and coastal influences virtually unique in the world. Where uncultivated, the valley floor alternates between alkali sink scrub and grassland, and the hills support a sparse sage scrub with pinyon-juniper woodland on north-facing slopes. The valley has long been under intensive agricultural cultivation (mainly alfalfa) and cattle grazing, both of which have left the Cuyama River and the underlying water table drastically depleted. The protected Carrizo Plain Natural Area lies just over the Caliente Range to the north, and several wilderness areas of the Los Padres National Forest are to the south, affording the IBA a level of security found in only a handful of areas (notably the South Fork Kern Valley).

Birds: Due to the preponderance of private land in the area, the bird communities of Cuyama Valley are poorly known (see Lehman 1994), but represent a subset of what may be found at Carrizo Plain to the north, with the addition of a handful of desert species. The winter raptor community is large and diverse, though variable based on rainfall. The valley floor sustains breeding colonies of Tricolored Blackbird and Burrowing Owl and the low hills support nesting Prairie Falcon, canescens Sage Sparrow, and San Joaquin Le Conte's Thrasher (just north of Ballinger Canyon, fide S. Fitton). These are joined by a disjunct population of Black-throated and Brewer's sparrows and Scott's Oriole that reach the northwestern limit of their ranges in the southern Caliente Mountains that form the north side of the Cuyama Valley. While only patches of riparian habitat remain along the Cuyama River, the restoration potential, given the amount of open space in the area, should be considered very high.

Conservation issues: The avifauna of the Cuyama Valley should be considered pushed to its limits by the intensive agriculture that dominates this IBA. Because of this, it is likely that even limited restoration projects, such as fencing streams and rotating grazing on pasture, would result in dramatic responses by the birds here.

Deep Springs Valley

Inyo

Nearest town(s): Big Pine
Size: 1000-10,000 acres
Threat: Low
Local Audubon Chapter: Eastern Sierra
BCR: 33

IBA Criteria		Source/Notes
L	12 sensitive species: Northern Harrier, Swainson's Hawk, Ferruginous Hawk, Golden Eagle, Prairie Falcon, Western Snowy Plover, Burrowing Owl, Short-eared Owl, Loggerhead Shrike, Yellow Warbler, Yellow-breasted Chat, Yellow-headed Blackbird	T. and J. Heindel, *pers. comm.*

Description: The Deep Springs Valley is located in eastern California just inside the border of Nevada, in a deep valley separating the White and Inyo Mountains. The town of Big Pine, in the Owens Valley, lies about 20 linear miles to the west (over Westgard Pass). Though federal lands (incl. wilderness areas, national forests and Death Valley National Park) surround the valley, this IBA is largely privately held. The two key habitats are the riparian habitat within the campus of Deep Springs College, and alkali meadow/playa habitat of Deep Springs Lake, a few miles to the south. The college includes ancient Fremont Cottonwoods and several small stock ponds rimmed with willow thickets, and the lakebed, though generally dry, becomes soggy with lush grasses after rainy winters.

Birds: Deep Springs is best known among birders for its spectacular songbird migration that peaks in spring during late April and May and again in September, with June and September bringing vagrant warblers and vireos from the east. Most of the grassland/meadow species that breed here, especially Northern Harrier and Short-eared Owl, are highly dependent upon rainfall to produce an ample growth of grasses. Snowy Plovers place nests near pools of water around seeps on the bleached playa of Deep Springs Lake. Swainson's Hawks breed in the cottonwoods around the campus, and hunt in the adjacent alfalfa fields. Several rare plants and animals occur here, including the endemic Black Toad *(Bufo exul)*, found nowhere else on earth.

Conservation issues: None at this time

Del Norte Coast

Del Norte

Nearest town(s): Crescent City
Size: 1000-10,000 acres
Threat: High
Local Audubon Chapter: Redwood Region
BCR: 5

	IBA Criteria	Source/Notes
P	Entire global population of Aleutian Canada Goose stages here in spring	Harris 1996
P	Entire CA breeding population of Oregon Vesper Sparrow	Harris 1996
P	Majority of CA breeding population of Fork-tailed Storm-Petrel	Carter *et al.* 1992
P	>10% of CA populations of Cassin's Auklet	5600 birds; Carter *et al.* 1992
P	>10% of CA populations of Tufted Puffin	50+ during 1980s; Carter *et al.* 1992
P	>10% of CA populations of Marbled Murrelet	Ralph *et al.* 1995
L	18 sensitive species: Fork-tailed Storm-Petrel, Aleutian Canada Goose, Northern Harrier, Ferruginous Hawk, Peregrine Falcon, Western Snowy Plover, Marbled Murrelet, Cassin's Auklet, Tufted Puffin, Northern Spotted Owl, Short-eared Owl, Vaux's Swift, Bank Swallow, Purple Martin, Yellow Warbler, Martin, Yellow Warbler, Yellow-breasted Chat, Oregon Vesper Sparrow, Grasshopper Sparrow	Harris 1996; A. Barron, R. Erickson *via email*
S	>10,000 Shorebirds	13,000+ at Lake Talawa during fall; PRBO, *unpubl. data*
W	>5000 Waterfowl	7676 American Wigeon, 1992 Del Norte Co. CBC

Description: This IBA refers to a 15-mile long strip of coastline just south of the Oregon border that is one of the most ornithologically significant coastal areas in the state. It is anchored on the south by Point St. George and by the Smith River estuary in the north. Just north of Crescent City the pastures give way to a mixed conifer forest on the coastal plan surrounding two large lagoons rimmed with freshwater marsh vegetation, Lake Earl and the smaller Lake Talawa, together comprising the largest coastal lagoon complex on the Pacific coast south of Alaska. North of the lagoons are the Smith River Bottoms, an area of wet pastures, riparian stringers, and patches of coniferous rainforest. Public lands protect only a portion of the IBA, with state lands (Lake Earl State Park/Lake Earl Wildlife Area) extending from the lagoons south to include some of Point St. George. This headlands of the point, mostly in private ownership, feature extensive pastureland set atop bluffs overlooking the Pacific. A half-mile offshore lies Castle Rock, protected as a National Wildlife Refuge, at seven acres the smallest of its kind in the state. The Smith River Bottoms and estuary are wholly privately-owned. Another interesting feature of the IBA is "Pacific Shores", a massive, partially-built subdivision on the north side of Lake Earl, where 1500 lots were carved out in the mid-1960s but never developed.

Birds: This IBA is one of the most popular birding sites in northwestern California, with many visitors coming in winter to see Harlequin Duck, alcids and Rock Sandpiper. Castle Rock supports the second-largest seabird colony in California (and possibly the Pacific coast of the U.S.), after the Farallon Islands. Though population numbers have fluctuated in recent years, it has consistently supported the state's largest breeding aggregations of Common Murre (100,000+ in the late 1980s); Cassin's Auklet, Rhinoceros Auklet (1000); and Tufted Puffin (only 2 pr. in 2001, *fide* A. Barron). Offshore rocks just north of the Smith River mouth (incl. Hunter Rock, Prince Isl.) also support breeding seabirds (incl. some of California's only breeding Fork-tailed Storm-Petrels and Tufted Puffin at Prince, *fide* Carter et al. 1992) and a large rookery (c. 100 pr.) of Great Blue Heron, Snowy Egret (farthest north in the western U.S., *fide* Harris 1996) and Black-crowned Night-Heron. The coastal pasturelands from of Point St. George north to the Smith River Bottoms are a major staging and wintering area for Aleutian Canada Goose, with nearly the entire global population (40,000+ birds in 2001) pausing here during spring to refuel. The birds commute each day between night roosts on Castle Rock and diurnal foraging areas on the mainland. Inland, old-growth forests, especially within Jedediah Smith Redwoods State Park, support strong populations of redwood breeders such as Marbled Murrelet.

The Lake Earl/Lake Talawa complex is a very important nesting and wintering area for waterfowl and marsh birds (notably breeding American Bittern) and each fall, the lagoons provide an important staging area for thousands of Canvasback (3456 on 1994 Del Norte Co. CBC.). The broad, sandy beach opposite Lake Talawa has been a winter concentration area for Snowy Plover (Harris 1996), though breeding has not occurred in several years. The grasslands support a nesting population of Oregon Vesper Sparrow (Pooecetes gramineus affinis), a race unknown elsewhere as a breeder in California (D. Fix, *pers. comm.*), and a large and diverse winter bird community (incl. Long-billed Curlew). Finally, the riparian bird community along the Smith River is enhanced by the presence of a traditional Bank Swallow breeding colony, the only consistent one extant in northwestern California.

Conservation issues: The Conservation issues affecting this IBA are complex and not as one might predict. Although the entire Smith River Bottoms/estuary and much of Point St. George are private, their resources have not changed appreciably over the last few decades, and, if anything, seem to be increasing in their attractiveness to several sensitive bird species (notably Aleutian Canada Goose, whose recent population increases have resulted in its removal from the Endangered Species list by USFWS in 2001). Goose preservation has long been driving much of the conservation (and ecotourism) in the area; about 230 acres of the wildlife area were recently opened to dairy cattle to provide alternative foraging areas for the bird (Boxall 2000). Unfortunately, other sites within this IBA have fared less well. Castle Rock's breeding seabird colonies may be put at risk both by the surge in goose numbers (their mass night-roosting coincides with the breeding season for seabirds) and by the recent establishment of Double-crested Cormorant as a breeder displacing other nesters. Most troubling of all, however, has been the situation that has developed at Lake Earl/Lake Talawa, where a recent surge in OHV riders and "cat colonies" (fed by people) has been responsible for frequent disturbances to shorebirds (esp. Snowy Plover, which formerly bred) and Burrowing Owl (probably extirpated). Another issue here involves the sandbar across the mouth of Lake Talawa, which for 100 years prior to 1988 (when the state assumed management) had been quietly dug open by locals to drain the lagoon. In the past decade, the DFG has kept the water levels higher and left the entrance naturally blocked, which has encouraged an extensive marsh to develop, greatly increasing its attractiveness to breeding birds and rare fishes (notably Tidewater Goby). This management has been extremely controversial, pitting "environmentalists" against ranchers concerned about flood risk posed by high lake levels.

Castle Rock, part of Del Norte Coast IBA (Steve Hampton)

Eagle Lake

Lassen

Nearest town(s): Susanville
Size: 10,000 - 50,000 acres
Threat: High
Local Audubon Chapter: Eagle Lake
BCR: 9

IBA Criteria		Source/Notes
L	11 sensitive species: Redhead, Bald Eagle, Northern Harrier, Northern Goshawk, Golden Eagle, Black Tern, Long-eared Owl, Vaux's Swift, Willow Flycatcher, Yellow Warbler, Yellow-headed Blackbird	D. Shaw, *pers. comm.*
W	>5000 Waterfowl	c. 8000 breeding Clark's, Western and Eared Grebes; D. Shaw, *pers. comm.*

Description: Eagle Lake is situated east of Lassen Volcanic National Park, just northwest of the town of Susanville. At 28,000 acres, it is the second-largest natural lake wholly in California (after Clear Lake, Lake Co.), and its closed freshwater environment supports an abundance of native fish, notably the Eagle Lake Rainbow Trout, a large subspecies wholly endemic to the lake. Extensive freshwater wetlands remain at the borders of the lake. Most of the land surrounding the lake is managed by the BLM and the USFS, and is surrounded by USFS land (Lassen National Forest). Since the mid-1970s, Eagle Lake has seen a surge in visitation by fisherman during summer, with most activity centered at its southern end. The surrounding landscape represents a transition from the Cascades on the south (pine forests) with the Great Basin desert on the north.

Birds: The waterbirds of Eagle Lake have been studied since the early 1900s, with major investigations in the 1970s (Gould 1974) and the late 1990s (Shaw 1998). It supports California's largest nesting colonies of Western and Clark's grebes (4-5000 pr., *fide* D. Anderson) and possibly Eared Grebe (>3000 pr. in 1997), and was identified by Shuford (1998) as one of 10 key breeding sites for Black Tern in California, supporting over 100 pr. in 1997 (but see Shaw 1998, who found fewer). Large concentrations of nesting Osprey and Bald Eagle (>25 and up to 10 pr., resp.) in the state are found here (D. Shaw, *pers. comm.*). Several sensitive forest species, including Northern Goshawk, Vaux's Swift and Willow Flycatcher, are known to breed in the Lassen National Forest surrounding the lake, but not within the lake basin itself. American White Pelican formerly nested on the lake's "Pelican Point", but have not been seen since more than 1000 birds were bludgeoned to death by fishermen in the early 1900s (see Shaw 1998). This species still over-summers in breeding condition and its re-establishment is conceivable given changes in management of the lake.

Important Bird Areas of California

Conservation issues: Human visitation essentially doubled at Eagle Lake during the 1980s (Shaw 1998), and development pressure along its shoreline continues apace. Eagle Lake is an entirely closed system, with very little surface flow of water into the lake and no outlet to release exhaust inputs from recreational watercraft. Direct disturbance by boaters during the summer remains the most pressing threat to waterbirds, as well as to post-breeding dispersers from other sites around the Great Basin (e.g. pelican, terns). However, the fact that the original suite of inland seabirds (except for pelican) continues to breed at the lake, some in high numbers, suggests that its ecosystem remains somewhat intact.

Black Tern (Brian Small)

East Diablo Range

Alameda/San Joaquin/Santa Clara/Stanislaus

Nearest town(s): Livermore, Tracy
Size: >50,000 acres
Threat: Medium
Local Audubon Chapters: Ohlone, San Joaquin, Santa Clara Valley, Stanislaus
BCR: 32

IBA Criteria		Source/Notes
L	13 Sensitive species: Bald Eagle, Northern Harrier, Ferruginous Hawk, Golden Eagle, Prairie Falcon, Burrowing Owl, Long-eared Owl, Loggerhead Shrike, Purple Martin, Yellow-breasted Chat, Sage Sparrow, Grasshopper Sparrow, Tricolored Blackbird	Glover 2001; S. Glover, *pers. comm.*

Description: This area encompasses the eastern slopes of the Coast Range separating the east San Francisco Bay Area and the Central Valley. A natural intersection of habitats – the hot, arid valley and the cool, mesic coast – support a number of interesting plants and animals that do not co-occur elsewhere. Practically all ornithological investigation has been conducted along the few public roads through the area, focusing on four areas: Corral Hollow, Mines Rd., San Antonio Valley and Del Puerto Cyn. Corral Hollow Rd. connects the towns of Tracy in the Central Valley with Livermore, and is located in a prominent low pass through the Coast Range. Though the area is dominated by private ranchland, there are several public holdings, including Del Valle Regional Park (west of Mines Rd.), Frank Raines Regional Park (Del Puerto Cyn. Rd.) and tiny Corral Hollow Ecological Area. Mines Rd. runs north-south through the entire area for about 40 miles, and Del Puerto Cyn. intersects the south end of Mines Rd. within the San Antonio Valley, and then heads east, dropping into the Central Valley southwest of Modesto.

Birds: The savannah-covered hills near Livermore have been found to support one of the highest densities of breeding Golden Eagles in the state, with at least 44 territories (http://www2.ucsc.edu/scpbrg/eagles.htm). The chaparral in this area supports breeding populations of sage scrub and arid country species reminiscent of southern California, such as Greater Roadrunner, Costa's Hummingbird, Cassin's Kingbird, Bell's Sage Sparrow, Black-chinned Sparrow and Lawrence's Goldfinch (Edwards 2000). Riparian obligates such as Yellow-breasted Chat breed in small, willow-filled drainages, and even Least Bell's Vireo apparently occurred in the riparian draws in Corral Hollow (Grinnell and Miller 1944), and may yet return given recent successes in southern California. Long-eared Owl and Lewis' Woodpecker, both local in the region, have bred in the oak savannah here. At higher elevations, Coulter Pine forest dominates, which supports breeding montane birds such as Olive-sided Flycatcher and Yellow-rumped Warbler (*fide* S. Glover), contributing to the exceptional breeding diversity of the area. The patches of grassland within the IBA, especially near Livermore and along the eastern base of the IBA, still support breeding populations of Northern Harrier, White-tailed Kite (incl.

communal winter roosts, Small 1994), Burrowing Owl (one of the few remaining Bay Area locales), Loggerhead Shrike, Grasshopper Sparrow, Tricolored Blackbird and in winter, good numbers of Ferruginous Hawk. The area boasts an exceptional diversity of reptiles and amphibians, and the Livermore grasslands, long isolated from the Central Valley, support several sensitive species such as the federally threatened Red-legged Frog. About 20 pr. of Prairie Falcons are believed to breed in the Diablo Range, mainly in the east (*fide* S. Glover), and a pair of Bald Eagles breeds at Del Valle Reservoir (Alameda Co.) just west of Mines Rd.

Conservation issues: While the habitat in the center of this IBA is probably secure simply because of the ruggedness of the terrain, that on its borders, especially the grassland expanses around Livermore and at the edge of the Central Valley, remain particularly threatened by development. Corral Hollow, renowned for its rich and unique reptile and amphibian community, is threatened by a nearby OHV park (The Nature Conservancy 1998).

Golden Eagle (Peter LaTourrette)

East Mojave Peaks
San Bernardino

Nearest town(s): Baker
Size: >50,000 acres
Sensitive species: 7 (Golden Eagle, Prairie Falcon, Long-eared Owl, Gilded Flicker, Gray Vireo, Bendire's Thrasher, Crissal Thrasher) (S. Myers, *pers. comm.*)
Threat: Low
Local Audubon Chapter: San Bernardino Valley
BCR: 33

IBA Criteria		Source/Notes
P	Probably >10% CA population of Gilded Flicker, Gray Vireo and Bendire's Thrasher	S. Myers, *pers. comm.*

Description: The extreme eastern Mojave Desert features three large mountain ranges whose unique natural habitats warrant their recognition as an IBA: the Kingston, Clark and New York ranges. Visible from I-15 just inside the border of Nevada, each supports large tracts of Joshua Tree woodland on lower slopes, grading into Pinyon-Juniper woodland and a floristically diverse desert chaparral, and finally into tiny groves of White Fir above 7000' on their peaks. Unique in California, these "sky islands" of forest separated by vast deserts are miniature versions of their larger counterparts in southern Nevada (e.g. Spring Mtns.) and Arizona, with which they share several species. The habitat within the Kingstons is entirely protected as a BLM wilderness area, and the New Yorks are located within the Mojave National Preserve. About ¾ of Clark Mountain is protected by the Mojave National Preserve, with the exception of the southeast corner just north of Mountain Pass, which was left outside the preserve boundary for a mining operation. These mountains have been the subject of long-term studies in biogeography since the early 1900s, and continue to captivate ornithologists (see Cardiff and Remsen 1981).

Birds: The relatively lush Joshua Tree woodland on the lower slopes of these peaks support strong populations of desert birds, notably Bendire's Thrasher, Juniper Titmouse, Scott's Oriole, and, in the New Yorks, Gilded Flicker. Broad-tailed Hummingbird, Plumbeous Vireo and Virginia's Warbler are common in pinyon-rich chaparral on Clark Mountain, and wherever this habitat occurs on steep-sloped canyons, Gray Vireo breed in what is likely their largest population away from eastern San Diego County. The most unusual bird communities, however, are restricted to the tops of these peaks, occurring most consistently in the fir grove on Clark Mountain. Hepatic Tanager and Whip-poor-will (arizonae race) virtually unknown elsewhere in California, are regular nesters on Clark (and at least the former in the New Yorks as well), and joined by occasional strays from Arizona, including Painted Redstart, Red-faced Warbler, and Grace's Warbler.

Conservation issues: Owing to its remoteness, much of the habitat within this IBA is secure. However, massive new mining operations at Clark Mountain should be closely watched.

Important Bird Areas of California

East Mojave Springs

San Bernardino

Nearest town(s): Baker
Size: <1000 acres
Threat: Medium
Local Audubon Chapter: San Bernardino Valley
BCR: 33

IBA Criteria		Source/Notes
L	11 sensitive species: Long-eared Owl, Vermilion Flycatcher, Loggerhead Shrike, Least Bell's Vireo, Bendire's Thrasher, Crissal Thrasher, Le Conte's Thrasher, Summer Tanager, Lucy's Warbler, Yellow Warbler, Yellow-breasted Chat	R. McKernan, *pers. comm.*

Description: This IBA draws attention to three major springs in the east Mojave Desert with similar avifauna. All are oases of riparian habitat associated with desert ranges surrounded by arid scrub. Horsetheif Spring, in the north, lies at the eastern edge of the Kingston Range (see East Mojave Peaks IBA above), and is reached by taking Excelsior Mine Rd. north 30 miles from I-15. It features a small grove of Fremont Cottonwoods. Piute Spring, adjacent to Ft. Piute about 20 miles due west of Bullhead City, AZ, flows above ground for several hundred meters through volcanic rock, supporting a thin strip of willow forest. Cornfield Spring emerges from the western flank of the Providence Mountains just east of Kelso. Horsetheif is located on BLM land, and the latter two sites are within the Mojave National Preserve. There are several other springs with vital riparian scattered across the east Mojave, mostly associated with desert ranges (e.g. Sunflower and Panamint Springs, Old Woman Mtns.; Cove Spring, Granite Mtns.). All should be considered important for birds in this harsh environment.

Birds: These springs are most heavily-used by birds during spring migration (April-May), when songbirds are moving up into the state from the Colorado River. The nesting avifauna, including Least Bell's Vireo and Yellow-breasted Chat, is highly dependent on the condition of the riparian vegetation at each, which is at times overgrazed (by cattle and by feral horses and burros) or burned (due to arson).

Conservation issues: Efforts to fence cattle and vandals from these springs have met with limited success. As long as the desert is seen by a subset of its users as a place to "raise hell", these fragile habitats will need to be protected and closely monitored. Recent (court-ordered) actions by BLM to close particularly sensitive areas have caused a serious backlash among the OHV community, exacerbating an already tenuous truce between desert preservationists and others (R. Kobaly, *pers. comm.*).

East Park Reservoir

Colusa

Nearest town(s): Williams
Size: 1000-10,000 acres
Threat: Low
Local Audubon Chapter: Redbud
BCR: 32

IBA Criteria		Source/Notes
P	>1% Global population of Tricolored Blackbird	10,000 birds during 1900s; B. Bird, *in litt.*
L	11 sensitive species: Ferruginous Hawk, Golden Eagle, Prairie Falcon, Burrowing Owl, Short-eared Owl, Long-eared Owl, Loggerhead Shrike, San Joaquin Le Conte's Thrasher, Sage Sparrow, Grasshopper Sparrow, Tricolored Blackbird	B. Bird, *in litt.*

Description: East Park Reservoir is located at the ecotone between the Northern Coast Range and the Central Valley, about 60 miles northwest of Sacramento. A mid-sized reservoir surrounded by Blue Oak savannah and chaparral, its woodland and riparian habitats have been the site of migrant and resident songbird research since 1997 (Point Reyes Bird Observatory). Though significant wetlands have developed here, dramatic water fluctuations tend to leave them either dry or flooded, and thus unattractive to nesting birds.

Birds: This site is notable for having three large breeding colonies of Tricolored Blackbird. The riparian habitat is locally significant in that it has retained elements of the lowland riparian avifauna of the northern Central Valley (e.g. Yellow-breasted Chat nests in small numbers). The site is well-used by Neotropical migrants, but probably not with any greater frequency than other sites in the Northern Coast Ranges (e.g. upper Cache Creek).

Conservation issues: For the past six years, the staff has worked hard to minimize the effects of grazing in riparian and wetlands areas. They have also proposed a boardwalk through the wetland areas, specifically for viewing Tricolored Blackbirds.

Eastshore Wetlands
Alameda

Nearest town: Berkeley
Size: <1000 acres
Sensitive species: 6 (Peregrine Falcon, Black Rail, California Clapper Rail, Long-billed Curlew, Burrowing Owl, Alameda Song Sparrow) (S. Granholm, *unpubl. data*)
Threat: High
Local Audubon Chapter: Golden Gate
BCR: 32

IBA Criteria		Source/Notes
P	>1% Global population of Alameda Song Sparrow	2% of Global population; H. Spautz, *unpubl. data*
P	Possibly >1% Global population of California Clapper	S. Granholm, *pers. comm.*
S	>10,000 Shorebirds	LSA Associates 2001
W	>5000 Waterfowl	LSA Associates 2001; 20,000+ waterfowl on the 2002 Oakland CBC

Description: This narrow band of wetland habitat (tidal mudflats, salt marsh) and limited upland (grassland-covered fill) extends across several hundred acres in the highly-urbanized central San Francisco Bay near Berkeley, between the Richmond-San Rafael Bridge (I-580) and the Bay Bridge (I-80). It may be divided into two sections, the "Albany mudflats" and adjacent "Berkeley Meadows" (former landfill) in the north, and the "Emeryville Crescent" to the south, hard up against I-580 and the Bay Bridge. Most of the tidal marsh is associated with the Emeryville Crescent, including several small "high marsh ponds" that fill with water intermittently.

Birds: Lying between two larger wetland areas (North Richmond Wetlands in the north and South San Francisco Bay in the south), this IBA provides refuge for a wide variety of waterbirds in an otherwise inhospitable section of the bay where nearly all of the historical wetlands have been filled for marina developments and other urban uses. Shorebird numbers regularly exceed 10,000 birds at both sites, making them, along with Corte Madera Marsh across the bay (see above) the most productive shorebird areas of the central bay. Waterfowl numbers are also impressive, with thousands of ducks, mainly "diving" species (e.g. Lesser Scaup, Ruddy Duck). This IBA (esp. Berkeley Meadows) has been found to be an important area for open-country species in the central bay, including the occasional Burrowing Owl in winter. The Emeryville Crescent supports the most intact tidal marsh bird community within the IBA (S. Granholm, *pers. comm.*), which includes Black and California Clapper rails (both winter, and may breed) and at least one of the two endemic songbird races of the Bay Area, the Alameda Song Sparrow (c. 2% of the global population, *fide* H. Spautz, PRBO). Saltmarsh Common Yellowthroat has not been detected on recent surveys (H. Spautz, PRBO, via email). A pair of Peregrine Falcons nest on the Bay Bridge, foraging heavily within the IBA. With proper management, three species may become regular breeders within this IBA, Northern Harrier (1 pr. nested at Berkeley Meadows in 2001), Least Tern (12 pr. nesting on an artificial island within Albany mudflats in 2000 only) and potentially Saltmarsh Common Yellowthroat (all bird survey numbers LSA Associates 2001).

Conservation issues: With most of the open space earmarked for preservation as parkland ("Eastshore State Park"), development is less of a threat than human disturbance. The Albany mudflats are located adjacent to the major off-leash dog area in the East Bay (Pt. Isabel), and, as such, receive heavy use by dogs (estimated 1 million visits by dogs per year, *fide* A. Feinstein). Exotic wetland species remain a threat, including Spartina alterniflora in the marsh, and both black rats and feral cats in upland areas. Potential future threats include proposed increases in public recreational use (including a "kayak camp" at the Albany mudflats).

Yellow-headed Blackbird (Peter LaTourrette)

Edwards Air Force Base

Los Angeles, Kern

Nearest town(s): Lancaster
Size: >50,000 acres
Threat: Critical
Local Audubon Chapter: San Fernando Valley
BCR: 33

	IBA Criteria	Source/Notes
L	13 sensitive species: White-faced Ibis, Redhead, Northern Harrier, Ferruginous Hawk, Prairie Falcon, Western Snowy Plover, Long-billed Curlew, Burrowing Owl, Short-eared Owl, Long-eared Owl, Loggerhead Shrike, Le Conte's Thrasher, Tricolored Blackbird, Yellow-headed Blackbird	Allen and Garrett 1995; K. Garrett, *pers. comm.*
S	>10,000 Shorebirds	High of 12,000 Western Sandpipers in spring surveys, late 1990s; Shuford *et al.* 2002
W	>5000 Waterfowl	7265 Northern Shoveler, 1998 Lancaster CBC

Description: Edwards Air Force Base, about 1.5 hrs. north of Los Angeles along the Kern County border, encompasses 300,000 acres of largely pristine west Mojave Desert habitats. These include some of the most extensive mesquite woodland in the region, as well as several massive dry lakes, (Buckhorn, Rosamond and Rogers) that fill with water during wet winters and support variably-sized, marshy alkali grassland and alkali flat habitats. These wetlands are augmented by water from treatment facilities that is spread into two main sets of large ponds on the southern edge of the base, including "Piute Ponds" in Los Angeles Co. Both sets of ponds feature extensive cattail and bulrush marsh (best developed at Piute Ponds), as well as exposed mudflats when water levels are optimal. Because these wetlands are not used directly by the military, a select number of birders have been granted access privileges. A long-term data set of observations of the wetlands been maintained by Kimball Garrett, and the base has conducted bird monitoring programs (e.g. base-wide point counts) for years.

Birds: The Piute Ponds support some of the only large breeding colonies of White-faced Ibis and Tricolored Blackbird in the Mojave Desert, all of which have been widely extirpated from coastal southern California. They also support a sizable proportion of southern California populations of several breeding marsh birds, such as Redhead, Gadwall and Yellow-headed Blackbird. The shorebird migration through here can be phenomenal from July to September, with somewhat lower numbers in spring (KG, MSM). These wetlands are an important post-breeding congregation area for many waterbirds, notably American White Pelican, Black Tern and numerous herons and egrets. Small numbers of Snowy Plover breed on alkali playas here (e.g. Rosamond Dry Lake), which can support large numbers of north-bound shorebirds after winter rains. Spring, fall and winter bring tens of thousands of ducks, which are also present at the Lancaster Water Treatment Plant, square, unvegetated ponds of the just southwest of the base, near the intersection of Hwy. 14 and Avenue D. The mesquite woodlands on Edwards, as those in other parts of the desert, can be alive with migrating passerines in March and April, and numerous isolated (and undisturbed) rock outcrops still support nesting raptors in a region where they are constantly disturbed by vandals, OHV riders, etc.

Conservation issues: These wetlands receive no formal protection whatsoever, and are increasingly being seen as a liability to the DoD, which fears that the incidence of bird strikes with aircraft outweigh the value of providing or retaining wildlife habitat. Changes in water treatment practices could have devastating effects on the waterbird community that has developed associated with the constructed wetlands and with Rosamond Dry Lake, which collects leakage from the impoundments. As the Antelope Valley urbanizes (Lancaster-Palmdale's population is already nearly 350,000 people and increasing), the lands surrounding these wetlands will be increasingly urban, which will bring the associated ills (e.g. feral cats).

Gray Vireo (Brian Small)

Elephant Tree Forest
San Diego

Nearest town(s): Borrego Springs
Size: <1000 acres
Sensitive species: 3 (Loggerhead Shrike, Gray Vireo, Le Conte's Thrasher) (Unitt 2000)
Threat: Low
Local Audubon Chapter: San Diego
BCR: 33

IBA Criteria		Source/Notes
P	Entire CA wintering population of Gray Vireo	Unitt 2000a

This tiny natural community of microphyll woodland dominated by Elephant Tree (Bursera microphylla) on the western edge of the Colorado Desert is located entirely within massive Anza-Borrego Desert State Park. Specifically, the habitat is best developed along Alma Wash, which crosses Split Mtn. Rd. south of Hwy. 78. Known to ornithologists only since 1999, it is apparently unique in the state, being the northernmost extension of a plant community otherwise restricted to northwest Mexico. This IBA is notable as the sole wintering ground for Gray Vireo in California. This declining species that nests in desert-slope foothills in southern California was thought to winter exclusively outside the state when biologists from the San Diego Museum of Natural History discovered the population here. This site is secure and rarely-visited.

Elkhorn Slough
Monterey

Nearest town(s): Watsonville
Size: 10,000 - 50,000 acres
Threat: High
Local Audubon Chapter: Monterey Peninsula
BCR: 32

	IBA Criteria	Source/Notes
P	>1% Global population of Long-billed Curlew	211 birds, 1999 Moss Landing CBC
P	Possibly >10% CA population of coastal-breeding Western Snowy Plover	146 birds in "Monterey Bay" region in summer 1989; USFWS 2001
L	11 Sensitive species: Northern Harrier, Ferruginous Hawk, Golden Eagle, Short-eared Owl, Western Snowy Plover, Long-billed Curlew, Burrowing Owl, Loggerhead Shrike, California Swainson's Thrush, Bryant's Savannah Sparrow, Tricolored Blackbird	Roberon and Tenney 1993; D. Roberson, *pers. comm.*
S	>10,000 Shorebirds	30,000 birds; PRBO, *unpubl. data*
W	>5000 Waterfowl	c. 7000 birds, 1999 Moss Landing CBC

Description: Encompassing a large region of coastal bottomlands midway between Santa Cruz and Monterey, the Elkhorn Slough ecosystem is one of the richest estuaries in the state. Designated a National Estuarine Research Reserve (one of three in the state). It includes the main slough channel through tidal marshes, the abandoned salt evaporation ponds near the mouth of the channel, as well as myriad side channels, potholes, feeder streams, and regularly-flooded pastures. These wetlands are surrounded by low hills with dense oak woodland and chaparral, with scattered riparian thickets and grassland. The bulk of the wetlands of Elkhorn Slough (c. 1000 acres) are well protected as federal and state conservation reserves (Elkhorn Slough Preserve/Elkhorn Slough Ecological Reserve, *resp.*).

Birds: The Elkhorn Slough region, which includes associated agricultural fields and pastureland, is a critical wintering and stopover site for shorebirds along the Pacific Flyway – any damp spot in the area can be filled with shorebirds during fall migration. Though breeding populations of California Clapper Rail and Short-eared Owl have been extirpated, other sensitive marsh birds persist in strong numbers, including resident Savannah Sparrow (the coastal *alaudinus* race), nesting ducks (incl. Gadwall, Northern Pintail, Northern Shoveler), Northern Harrier and American Bittern (scarce). The large salt flats at Moss Landing are unique in the Monterey Bay area, and support large numbers of breeding Snowy Plover. Both Caspian and Forster's terns have bred recently. Re-colonization by Least Tern and colonization by Black Skimmer as nesters is also possible (DR). Around 300 species of birds have been recorded here, and unlike migrant traps with similar totals, one can see over 100 on nearly any day of the year, making it among the most species-rich sites for birds in the state.

Conservation issues: Red Fox continues to pose a grave threat to Snowy Plover and other ground-nesting birds. Though the protected portions of Elkhorn Slough will probably remain free from development, the upland areas, including oak woodland, are currently under major threat from suburban sprawl associated with the Hwy. 101 corridor. During the 1990s, Audubon California was involved in a major planning effort for the Elkhorn Slough watershed to develop solutions for these concerns. If urbanization is not contained, conservationists anticipate increased problems with exotic species, including invasive plants and feral dogs and cats that prey upon ground-dwelling birds, and pollution from urban runoff.

Elkhorn Slough (Robert Stephens, Audubon California Board of Directors)

Fall River Valley Area
Shasta

Nearest town(s): Fall River Mills
Size: 10,000 - 50,000 acres
Threat: Low
Local Audubon Chapter: None
BCR: 9

IBA Criteria		Source/Notes
L	17 sensitive species: Redhead, Bald Eagle, Northern Harrier, Ferruginous Hawk, Golden Eagle, Sandhill Crane, Long-billed Curlew, Black Tern, Short-eared Owl, Vaux's Swift Loggerhead Shrike, Bank Swallow, Purple Martin, Yellow Warbler, Yellow-breasted Chat, Tricolored Blackbird, Yellow-headed Blackbird	B. Yutzy, *via email*
W	>5000 Waterfowl	c. 4000 of each Mallard, American Wigeon, Ruddy Duck on 1999 Fall River Mills CBC

Description: About halfway between Redding and Alturas, this large valley lies in the triangle formed by Hwy. 89 and Hwy. 299, and is formed by the Fall River which runs along the floor of the valley, and by the much larger Pit River, which drains west from the Warner Mtns. into Shasta Lake and forms the southern edge of this IBA. Habitat diversity is high in this transition area between the Cascades and the Modoc Plateau, with mixed oak-coniferous forest, oak-dominated chaparral, and large, shallow lakes with extensive, marshy borders. Private lands, nearly all of it grazed, dominate here, and the floor of the Fall River Valley is covered by irrigated agricultural land. Public lands are limited to Ahjumawi Lava Springs State Park in the northeast Fall River Valley, and McArthur Burney Falls Memorial State Park in the far west, which includes Lake Britton along the Pit River. Though public lands protect excellent examples of upland habitat, much of the wetland habitat is privately held, including large wetlands associated with Eastman Lake (a.k.a. Big Lake) adjacent to Ahjumawi S.P., which is owned by Pacific Gas and Electric.

Birds: The Fall River Valley supports a high diversity of breeding ducks and shorebirds (incl. Long-billed Curlew, Willet and Wilson's Phalarope) and a handful of breeding Sandhill Cranes. Thousands of ducks and geese over-winter here, and large numbers of the tiny Cackling Canada Geese (a rare subspecies) stage during spring migration. Both the Pit and Fall rivers support large populations of breeding and wintering Bald Eagle and Osprey, and the agricultural areas and grasslands are an important foraging area for wintering raptors. Bank Swallows nest locally along the Pit River, and more than 20 pairs of Black Swift, by far the largest colony in the state (C. Collins, *pers. comm.*), breed at McArthur-Burney State Park. The oak woodland here supports one of the few regular Purple Martin colonies in northeastern California (Williams 1998). As an interesting biogeographical note, California's characteristic oak woodland avifauna approaches its northeastern limit here, with Band-tailed Pigeon,

Important Bird Areas of California

Acorn and Nuttall's woodpecker, Oak Titmouse, Wrentit and Lawrence's Goldfinch all breeding north to vic. Day, Modoc Co. (JS).

Conservation issues: Fairly remote and still very undeveloped, this IBA seems to have remained a well-kept secret. Though recent shifts in agriculture from cattle pasture to wild rice cultivation have made the habitat more appealing to certain waterbirds (esp. shorebirds) and less suitable for raptors, the overall landscape is still attractive to a thriving bird community (B. Yutzy, via email). Potential conflicts involve the allocation of water from Big Lake, which is owned by Pacific Gas and Electric. The ranchers don't want wetlands expanded to impact grazing opportunities, and PG&E wants the water reserved for hydropower, which may leave relatively little for wildlife (B. Yutzy, via email).

Tufted Puffins (Peter LaTourrette)

Farallon Islands

San Francisco

Nearest town(s): none
Size: <1000 acres
Sensitive species: 3 (Ashy Storm-Petrel, Cassin's Auklet, Tufted Puffin) (C. Abraham, *in litt.*)
Threat: Medium
Local Audubon Chapter: Golden Gate
BCR: 32

IBA Criteria		Source/Notes
P	Majority of Global breeding population of Ashy Storm-Petrel	2500+ pr. in 2000; Abraham *et al.* 2000
P	>10% of CA breeding populations of Cassin's Auklet	15,000+ pr. in 2000; Abraham *et al.* 2000
P	>10% of CA breeding populations of Tufted Puffin	50 – 130 birds during 1990s, Abraham *et al.* 2000

Description: The Farallon Islands are a barren cluster of rocks about 30 miles west of San Francisco. The largest of the islands, Southeast Farallon Island and West End Island, cover just 110 acres, and have been the focus of important research on breeding seabirds and migratory songbirds for decades. The waters around the islands are managed as the Gulf of the Farallons National Marine Sanctuary (National Oceanic and Atmospheric Administration), and the USFWS owns the islands and manages it as part of the San Francisco Bay NWR Complex. Ecological research on birds is coordinating jointly by USFWS and PRBO.

Birds: These islands support an astounding number and diversity of breeding California seabirds, and in 2000, hosted the world's largest breeding colonies of Ashy Storm-Petrel, and some of largest aggregations of breeding Brandt's Cormorant (5500+ pr.), Western Gull (nearly 20,000 pr.), Pigeon Guillemot (800+ pr.) and Cassin's Auklet (Abraham *et al.* 2000).

Conservation issues: The islands are accessible only to researchers, and in this regard are well protected. However, oil spills at sea remain a threat. Half of the ten known oil spills in California since 1985 have occurred around the Farallons (located along a major shipping lane), which have resulted in population-wide impacts at least to Common Murre (S. Hampton, *pers. comm.*). Gill-net fisheries may also pose a threat to breeding seabirds, both by direct impacts to birds (incidental catch) and by reduction of their food source.

Feather River - Lower
Yuba/Sutter

Nearest town(s): Yuba City, Marysville
Size: <1000 acres
Sensitive species: 8 (Northern Harrier, Swainson's Hawk, Ferruginous Hawk, Golden Eagle, Yellow-billed Cuckoo, Loggerhead Shrike, Bank Swallow, Yellow-breasted Chat) (T. Manolis, via email)
Threat: High
Local Audubon Chapter: Altacal
BCR: 32

IBA Criteria		Source/Notes
P	>10% CA breeding population of Yellow-billed Cuckoo	Laymon and Halterman 1987

Description: This IBA includes particularly rich lowland riparian woodland along the lower Feather River between Yuba City/Marysville and Sacramento. Specifically, it includes the area from Abbott Lake south to the Highway 99 bridge at Nicolaus. Private land dominates here, though a portion has been nominated as "Oso Plumas National Natural Landmark" (National Park Service) for being an exceptional example of Great Valley Riparian Forest (R. Holland, *in litt.*). This IBA, along with the Sacramento River – Upper IBA, represents some of the finest examples of lowland riparian woodland remaining in the entire Sacramento Valley (BD), of which a meager 2% remain. Several areas of a few hundred acres in extent are managed by the state as units of Feather River Wildlife Area, and a ¹/₂-mile-wide strip totaling 400 acres is protected as the Bobelaine Audubon Sanctuary (J. Persson, *in litt.*). Point Reyes Bird Observatory has monitored riparian breeding birds here since the mid-1990s.

Birds: The lower Feather supports one of a handful of breeding populations of Western Yellow-billed Cuckoo in the state, a taxon that has been reduced to fewer than 50 pairs in California (Thelander and Crabtree 1994). Bank Swallow, also widely extirpated in the Sacramento Valley, is also known to breed within the IBA (*fide* T. Manolis), along with several other sensitive riparian species such as Swainson's Hawk and Yellow-breasted Chat. The restoration potential within the IBA is arguably more impressive than the actual resources present today.

Conservation issues: Large areas in the area remain in private hands, and even on certain public holdings, over-grazing by cattle gravely threatens the riparian bird community both by its direct damage to vegetation and by encouraging the proliferation of cowbirds and exotic vegetation. Fires, including those set by levee district personnel to remove vegetation and to discourage ground squirrel tunneling, periodically burn out of control and into the riparian vegetation, devastating bird habitat for several years. This occurred in 1985 (R. Holland, *in litt.*), 1992 (J. Persson, *in litt.*), and 1998 (B. Clark, via email). However, TNC (1995) identified this area as having high restoration potential, owing largely to the presence of set back levees (TNC 1995).

Goleta Coast

Santa Barbara

Nearest town(s): Goleta, Santa Barbara
Size: <1000 acres
Sensitive species: 9 (Least Bittern, Western Snowy Plover, Long-billed Curlew, Burrowing Owl, Short-eared Owl, Loggerhead Shrike, Yellow Warbler, Yellow-breasted Chat, Belding's Savannah Sparrow, Grasshopper Sparrow) (Lehman 1994)
Threat: High
Local Audubon Chapter: Santa Barbara
BCR: 32

IBA Criteria		Source/Notes
P	>10% CA wintering population of Western Snowy Plover	c. 200 birds; D. Kisner, *in litt.*

Description: This area, one of the first nominated during the early years of the IBA program, encompasses a narrow, partially-developed strip along the coast west of Santa Barbara. It may be divided into the following major areas:

- Devereux Slough (UC Santa Barbara)
- Goleta Slough (Santa Barbara Co. Parks, City of Santa Barbara, UC Santa Barbara)
- Campus Lagoon (UC Santa Barbara)
- More Mesa/Ellwood Mesa (Private)
- Atascadero and Maria Ygnacio Creek (Santa Barbara Co.; So. Calif. Gas Co.)
- Lake Los Carneros (Private; Santa Barbara Co. Parks)
- Goleta Point/Coal Oil Point (UC Santa Barbara)

More and Ellwood mesas are two sizable patches of remnant coastal grassland, with patches of Coast Live Oak woodland and riparian vegetation west of the community of Isla Vista. Atascadero and Maria Ygnacio creeks are channelized streams with mud bottoms, which support a narrow strip of riparian vegetation (mostly willow). Lake Los Carneros is a small, cattail-rimmed pond with some riparian vegetation on the west side of Goleta, north of Hwy. 101. Goleta Slough is a true tidal wetland essentially separating UC Santa Barbara from Santa Barbara Municipal Airport and Hwy. 101. Moving west from Goleta Slough is Campus Lagoon, a salt-water-filled pond on the UCSB campus, and to its east is Devereux Slough, another tidal wetland

Birds: Devereux Slough is a major southern California wintering area for Snowy Plover (up to 200 birds in winter) and host to locally significant numbers of migrant and wintering waterfowl, shorebirds, gulls and terns. In 2001, a pair of Snowy Plover successfully produced a chick at the mouth of the slough for the first time in over 30 years, due largely to a volunteer "chick watch" organized by the Coal Oil Point Reserve (D. Chirman, via email). Devereux is also the northernmost outpost of Belding's Savannah

Sparrow in the world. Nearby Goleta Slough supports a much larger population of this taxon (at least 69 pr. in 1992, *fide* D. Compton) and similar usage by migrant and wintering waterbirds. Numerous species of raptors utilize the grassland surrounding the slough. More Mesa supports a communal roost of White-tailed Kite (a few stay to breed), and a handful of Burrowing and Short-eared owls and Northern Harrier continue to winter here (and, less frequently, at nearby Ellwood Mesa). Atascadero and Maria Ygnacio creeks are notable for the high number of migrants they support, particularly during September and October, which are monitored by a long-term banding program. Lake Los Carneros is also one of a handful of breeding locales on the coast of California for Least Bittern. Finally, Coal Oil and Goleta Points appear to be very important resting points for northbound rocky-shore shorebirds (notably Surfbird), and tens of thousands of migrant inshore seabirds (loons, scoters, phalaropes, etc.) stream north just offshore during March and April. Though not as important for birds, several vernal pool complexes have recently been discovered in the flat grassland between Hwy. 101 and Isla Vista.

Conservation issues: This area is still experiencing high pressure for more development, as well as increasing use from current residents. Public education about the threats posed by feeding feral cats and introduced Red Fox, running dogs off-leash and casual disturbance by people would help the birds of More Mesa, Campus Lagoon and Coal Oil Point. Exotic flora and fauna (esp. Arundo, Castor Bean and Pampas Grass) pose an increasingly grave threat to the bird communities of this IBA, and their management should be encouraged.

Western Snowy Plover (Brian Small)

Goose Lake, Kern Co.

Kern

Nearest town(s): Wasco
Size: 1000-10,000 acres
Threat: Medium
Local Audubon Chapter: Kern
BCR: 32

	IBA Criteria	Source/Notes
L	14 sensitive species: White-faced Ibis, Redhead, Northern Harrier, Swainson's Hawk, Ferruginous Hawk, Sandhill Crane, Western Snowy Plover, Long-billed Curlew, Burrowing Owl, Short-eared Owl, Loggerhead Shrike, Sage Sparrow, Tricolored Blackbird, Yellow-headed Blackbird	A. Sheehey, *via email*
W	Probably >5000 Waterfowl	A. Sheehey, *via email*

Description: Goose Lake covers roughly 5000 acres in the southwestern San Joaquin Valley, straddling I-5 about 20 miles south of Kern National Wildlife Refuge. Primary used as a water recharge area during wet winters by Semitropic Irrigation District, it includes alkali sink scrub, grassland, and freshwater marsh, typically holding water until May or June. Aside from a small (40-acre) BLM holding (SF), it is legally unprotected.

Birds: Goose Lake is known among area biologists for supporting thousands of waterfowl and shorebirds during winter and spring, and for its large breeding colony of Yellow-headed Blackbirds. This IBA is the farthest-south wintering area for Sandhill Crane in the Central Valley, and like many habitat patches on the floor of the San Joaquin Valley, its alkali sink scrub is highly isolated by the agricultural (mostly cotton) landscape. As such, it supports a unique natural community (incl. nesting Sage Sparrows) essentially gone from the floor of the southern San Joaquin Valley.

Conservation issues: Though the area's wildlife receives no formal protection, currently management practices seem to be ideal for marsh species (*fide* D. Germano), at least in winter and spring. The atriplex scrub habitat in the area, however, is highly fragmented and isolated, and is being seriously degraded (November 2001, *pers. obs.*) by OHV use and dumping.

Important Bird Areas of California

Goose Lake, Modoc Co.

Modoc

Nearest town(s): Alturas
Size: >50,000 acres
Threat: Medium
Local Audubon Chapter: Eagle Lake
BCR: 9

IBA Criteria		Source/Notes
L	13 sensitive species: Redhead, Bald Eagle, Northern Harrier, Swainson's Hawk, Ferruginous Hawk, Golden Eagle, Sandhill Crane, Western Snowy Plover, Long-billed Curlew, Short-eared Owl, Loggerhead Shrike, Yellow Warbler, Yellow-headed Blackbird	D. Shuford, J. Sterling, *pers. comm.*
S	>10,000 Shorebirds	15,000+ Western Sandpipers in spring and fall; 10,000+ American Avocet in fall during late 1990s; Shuford *et al.* 2002
W	>5000 Waterfowl	D. Shuford, J. Sterling, *pers. comm.*

Description: One of the largest natural lakes in California, Goose Lake straddles the Oregon border just west of the Nevada line. An enclosed system fed only by rainfall, the lake is still fresh water (somewhat alkaline), and supports an important native fish community. Its levels fluctuate depending on the previous year's rainfall, which supports vast alkali mudflats along its southern end. This section of the IBA also features impressive natural sand dunes and constructed impoundments with freshwater wetlands. Along its east end, irrigated alfalfa fields along Hwy. 395 give way to extensive wet alkali meadow habitat leading down to the shore of the lake. The more remote west side is rocky with lava deposits, but supports extensive bulrush marshes. Several low-lying islands along the east end are alternately exposed and submerged depending on rainfall the winter before.

Birds: Remote and rarely visited by birders, Goose Lake is known to be a critical late-summer staging area for waterfowl where tens of thousands of Canada Geese and ducks, including large numbers of Canvasbacks, molt (and are therefore flightless) during August. A sizable breeding colony of Snowy Plover occurs on alkali flats, and upwards of 30,000 migrant shorebirds per day utilize the impoundments and the southeastern lake shore in spring and fall (DS). Over 10,000 American Avocets were recorded here during a single aerial survey in August 1995 (Warnock *et al.* 1998), a period when lowered water levels results in little shorebird habitat on the state's refuges. These shorebirds have been shown to commute between this site, Honey Lake to the south, and Summer/Abert lakes in Oregon (*Ibid*). The wetlands surrounding Goose Lake support very large numbers of breeding terns (Forster's and Caspian) and in 1997 held almost 10% of the state's nesting Ring-billed Gull population (Shuford and Ryan 2000). Regionally, this IBA was found to hold some of the largest colonies of Caspian and Forster's terns in northeastern California, and historically supported breeding American White Pelican (Shuford 1998). The area also contains one of the largest Pronghorn Antelope breeding areas left in California.

Conservation issues: As with most wetlands in the Great Basin, water levels are critical to avian use and productivity at Goose Lake. Low lake levels cause a decline in marsh and island habitat, and poor nesting success for breeding birds. Fortunately, the area is still very remote, and increased development is probably at least several decades away.

Tricolored Blackbird (Peter LaTourrette)

Grasslands Ecological Area
Merced/Stanislaus

Nearest town(s): Los Banos, Merced, Gustine
Size: >50,000 acres
Threat: Low
Local Audubon Chapter: Stanislaus
BCR: 32

	IBA Criteria	Source/Notes
P	>1% Global population of Long-billed Curlew	767 birds on 1996 Los Banos CBC; Ave. 2000+ in winter throughout GEA; R. Allen, *unpubl. data*
P	>1% Global population of Tricolored Blackbird	Ave. 5 – 10,000 breeding birds; 22,406 on 1995 Los Banos CBC (60,000+ in winter); R. Allen, *unpubl. data*
P	>10% California population of Sandhill Crane	Up to 12,000 in winter; R. Allen, *unpubl. data*
P	>10% California population of White-faced Ibis	c. 10,000 birds in winter; Shuford *et al.* 1996
L	17 sensitive species: White-faced Ibis, Aleutian Canada Goose, Redhead, Northern Harrier, Swainson's Hawk, Ferruginous Hawk, Sandhill Crane, Mountain Plover, Long-billed Curlew, Black Tern, Burrowing Owl, Short-eared Owl, Loggerhead Shrike, Yellow-breasted Chat, Grasshopper Sparrow, Tricolored Blackbird, Yellow-headed Blackbird	R. Allen, J. Fulton; *pers. comm.*
S	>10,000 Shorebirds	200,000+ during peaks in spring, fall and winter; Shuford *et al.* 1998
W	>5000 Waterfowl	165,265 waterfowl on San Luis NWR alone on 15 Jan. 2003; USFWS 2003b

Description: The Grasslands Ecological Area is a 160,000-acre mosaic of Central Valley floor habitats located between I-5 and I-99 in the northern San Joaquin Valley, west of a line between Modesto and Fresno. It lies in the historic plain of the San Joaquin River, in an area historically prone to devastating floods and poor farming soils. This vast network of freshwater marshes (permanent and seasonal), alkali grassland and riparian thickets is the result of decades of collaborative conservation agreements between private duck clubs, California State Parks, DFG (Volta and Los Banos wildlife areas), and the National Wildlife Refuge System (San Luis, Merced NWRs). It is among the largest remaining areas of unplowed land on the floor of the Central Valley, and The Nature Conservancy (1998) has identified its Valley Sacaton Grassland (see Holland 1986) as the finest example of such habitat in the state.

Birds: This IBA is most notable for its abundance of native valley grassland and for its staggering concentrations of wintering waterfowl. It hosts a half-million individual ducks, geese, and swans each year between November and February, with Northern Pintail, Green-winged Teal, Northern Shoveler and Gadwall all having registered 100,000+ counts (J. Fulton, *in litt.*). It is also a major post-breeding dispersal area for American White Pelican (1000 counted on 20 August 1995; J. Fulton, *in litt.*). This IBA consistently hosts large numbers of breeding Tricolored Blackbirds and may support over a third of the global population of this species in winter. A comparable percentage of Sandhill Cranes may occur here in winter (including c. 25 Greater Sandhill Crane) and Long-billed Curlew forage in its open pastures and fields, which host breeding colonies of Grasshopper Sparrow in the spring (*Ibid*). Winter roosts of White-faced Ibis were estimated at over 10,000 birds, making it the second-largest concentration of the species in winter in California after the Imperial Valley, supporting roughly a third of the state's population. It is a major stopover site for shorebirds moving through the Central Valley, with an average of 10,000 each fall, winter and spring, and over 200,000 counted during peaks (see Shuford *et al.* 1998), earning it a distinction as a Western Hemisphere Shorebird Reserve Site in addition to its recognition as a RAMSAR site. Several heron rookeries have developed here, with an average of 300 nests of Double-crested Cormorant, Great Blue Heron and Great Egret. Dozens of pairs of Swainson's Hawk breed, a significant percentage of the entire San Joaquin Valley population. The riparian bird community is best developed along the San Joaquin River in the northwest section of the IBA, which supports breeding Yellow-breasted Chat, large numbers of Blue Grosbeak as well as what is likely the southernmost large population of the California-endemic Yellow-billed Magpie on the floor of the Central Valley (*Ibid*). Waterbird monitoring has been ongoing here for decades, and riparian songbird monitoring was initiated in the late 1990s, run in partnership with Point Reyes Bird Observatory.

Conservation issues: Under the terms of the Central Valley Project Improvement Act (1992), a minimum flow of water must be maintained to the refuge and to private lands with easements for wildlife habitat. The GEA oversees 76 stream miles of existing or potential riparian habitat, and recent management plans have included the fencing of streambeds from cattle, the re-watering of ancient oxbows, and, remarkably, the de-authorization of portions of San Joaquin River flood control levees to restore the natural riparian ecology. Despite a vast network of easements and reserves within the GEA, the progression of land conversion, including urban sprawl along the Hwy. 152 corridor (e.g. Los Banos) and agricultural and industrial development region-wide, threatens the wildlife of this IBA. Non-native plants (incl. Yellow Star Thistle *Centaurea solstitalis*) remain a constant obstacle to conservation, but are being managed for by refuge staff. The conversion of native scrub habitats to grain crops (to attract game birds) has been an issue in the past, but current management seems sympathetic to the concerns of native wildlife. Interestingly, lack of grazing in portions of the IBA may become a possible threat to certain open-country species that thrive on the sparse, scrubby grassland maintained by cattle (TNC 1998). As an historical note, this IBA contains the infamous former Kesterson Reservoir, where thousands of water birds experienced acute selenium poisoning (including horrific birth defects and deformities) in the early 1980s due to improper storage of agricultural runoff. The site has since been cleaned up, filled in with soil, and absorbed into the GEA, and refuge managers are now keenly aware of the need to carefully manage runoff in and around the IBA.

Honey Lake Valley

Lassen

Nearest town(s): Susanville
Size: >50,000 acres
Threat: Medium
Local Audubon Chapter: Eagle Lake
BCR: 9

	IBA Criteria	Source/Notes
P	>10% CA breeding population of White-faced Ibis	1000 pr. at Leavitt Lake in late 1990s; D. Shuford, *pers. comm.*
P	>10% CA breeding population of interior-breeding Western Snowy Plover	208 birds 1978; Page and Stenzel 1981
P	Probably >1% Global population of Greater Sage-Grouse	W. Broadhead, *via email*
L	20 sensitive species: White-faced Ibis, Redhead, Bald Eagle, Northern Harrier, Swainson's Hawk, Ferruginous Hawk, Golden Eagle, Prairie Falcon, Greater Sage-Grouse, Western Snowy Plover, Long-billed Curlew, Sandhill Crane, Black Tern, Burrowing Owl, Short-eared Owl, Long-eared Owl, Loggerhead Shrike, Bank Swallow, Tricolored Blackbird, Yellow-headed Blackbird	D. Shuford, T. Manolis, *pers. comm.*
S	>10,000 Shorebirds	17,884 birds in late 1990s; Shuford *et al.* 2002
W	>5000 Waterfowl	13,191 Snow Geese, 2000 Honey Lake CBC

Description: Honey Lake is one of the largest of several large natural alkali lakes of the Great Basin (remnants of ancient Lahontan Lake), lying just inside the California-Nevada border about 70 miles north of Reno, Nevada. The ownership of the lake and surrounding valley is complex, with the Sierra Army Depot (DoD) dominating the eastern end of the lake, and the 8000-acre Honey Lake Wildlife Area (State of California) at the northwestern end. On the south, the Jay Dow, Sr. Wetlands (private) protect about 1500 acres of wetlands in large impoundments. Several private holdings, mainly dedicated to alfalfa production, are found along Hwy. 395, beyond which lie the heavily-forested Diamond Mountains, essentially a spur of the Sierra Nevada. The broad "sagebrush ocean" of the western Great Basin extends to the north and east. Major bird habitats of the Honey Lake Valley include the vast alkali mudflats around the margins of the lake; grassland and sagebrush flats; and extensive constructed wetlands (impoundments) on the wildlife area and within the Jay Dow, Sr. Wetlands. Lake Leavitt, just to the northwest, is a 2500-acre natural depression that supports wetland and riparian (willow thicket) habitat, managed by the local irrigation district with assistance from DFG (F. Hall, *pers. comm.*). Other riparian habitats are limited to scrub associated with the Susan River in the north, and large rock outcrops are found in the Diamond Mtns. to the west.

Important Bird Areas of California

Birds: The Honey Lake Valley is situated along a major transition area between the Sierra Nevada and the Great Basin, and supports a very high diversity of breeding species. Huge numbers of waterfowl and shorebirds utilize the wetlands from spring through fall, including breeding Snowy Plover, which maintained one of its largest nesting aggregations in California here during the 1970s (Page and Stenzel 1981). Together with Goose Lake in Modoc Co. and Oregon's Summer and Abert Lakes, Honey Lake comprises one of major natural wetland complexes of the western Great Basin, sharing 300,000 shorebirds (that commute among the four sites), based on recent surveys in spring and fall (Warnock *et al.* 1998). Interior species such as American Avocet and Wilson's Phalarope are particularly numerous, and are joined in summer by large numbers (1000+ pr.) of breeding California and Ring-billed gulls (Shuford and Ryan 2000), as well as one of three large Caspian Tern colonies in northeastern California (Shuford 1998). Hartson Reservoir was identified by Shuford (1998) as a key site for the reestablishment of a breeding population of the widely-extirpated American White Pelican in California, which last bred in the 1970s. Leavitt Lake has supported one of the largest White-faced Ibis colonies in northern California (D. Shuford, *pers. comm.*) and Greater Sage-Grouse have maintained a traditional lek just northeast of Honey Lake in the Amadee Hills/Skedaddle Mountains. This area is tremendously important for raptors year round. A breeding population of Long-eared Owls occurs here, nesting under sagebrush (BD), and a colony of Burrowing Owl persists on the Sierra Army Depot (W. Broadhead, via email).

Conservation issues: Honey Lake itself is dependent on rain and snowmelt flowing into the Susan River, and during dry years, it shrinks considerably. Many of the productive wetlands rimming the lake are dependent on increasingly expensive water piped out of the Susan River, and compete with agricultural uses (e.g. alfalfa) in the region. During droughts, the amount of wetland habitat is reduced considerably, and land that would be islands become connected to land, allowing predators access. Although Honey Lake is still remote, increasing numbers of second homes are being constructed along Hwy. 395 as Susanville's popularity as a vacation destination increases.

Important Bird Areas of California

Humboldt Bay
Humboldt

Nearest town(s): Arcata, Eureka
Size: 10,000 - 50,000 acres
Threat: Medium
Local Audubon Chapter: Redwood Region
BCR: 5

IBA Criteria		Source/Notes
P	>1% Global population of Pacific Black Brant (spring)	30,000 birds; Sedinger *et al.* 1994
P	>1% Global population of Long-billed Curlew	C. Ogan, *pers. comm.*
P	>10% CA population of Marbled Murrelet	Ralph *et al.* 1995
L	16 sensitive species: Bald Eagle, Northern Harrier, Ferruginous Hawk, Peregrine Falcon, Western Snowy Plover, Long-billed Curlew, Marbled Murrelet, Burrowing Owl, Short-eared Owl, Long-eared Owl, Vaux's Swift, Purple Martin, Yellow Warbler, Yellow-breasted Chat, Bryant's Savannah Sparrow, Grasshopper Sparrow, Tricolored Blackbird	D. Fix, R. Hewitt, C. Ogan, J. Sterling, *pers. comm.*
S	>10,000 Shorebirds	80,000 birds during peaks; Colwell 1994
W	>5000 Waterfowl	57,868 birds on 15 Jan. 2003; USFWS 2003b

Description: This mosaic of wet pastures, tidal wetlands, and two major estuaries (Mad River, Eel River) extends from McKinleyville north of Arcata south to the confluence of the Eel and Van Duzen rivers along Hwy. 101. One of the premiere natural estuaries in the state, Humboldt Bay transforms from a placid lagoon to an extensive mudflat rimmed with saltmarsh during low tide, with much of its habitat managed as Humboldt Bay National Wildlife Refuge. Just south of the bay, a vast system of tidal channels cuts through wet pastures and dairy farms along the Eel River. Historically prone to major flooding events in early spring, it has remained undeveloped, and is partially protected as the Eel River Wildlife Area (DFG). The Nature Conservancy's Lanphere-Christensen Dune Preserve, one of the finest examples of coastal dunes in the state, lies within this IBA, separating the bottomlands from the ocean. A significant amount of freshwater marsh habitat has been restored/recreated at Arcata Marsh, a progressive, city-owned wetland/water treatment facility on the northeast side of Humboldt Bay that has become a model for such efforts worldwide. Other key habitats in this area include the boggy willow thickets near the town of Fairhaven on the Samoa Peninsula, which are within BLM's Samoa Dunes Recreation Area, a popular off-road vehicle playground, and Indian Island off Eureka, which supports a large heron rookery. Long-term bird banding stations were established two decades ago adjacent to the Mad River Slough and the dunes preserve (Humboldt Bay Banding Lab) and, more recently, at the confluence of the Eel and the Van Duzen rivers.

Birds: Up to 80,000 shorebirds have been estimated on Humboldt Bay and associated habitats during peak days in spring and fall. The state's largest concentration of Brant (c. 25% of Pacific Flyway population) occurs here in spring, when large flocks feed on eelgrass in the bay. Both the tidal wetlands and agricultural fields provide important roosting habitat for wintering shorebirds. A remarkable breeding population of Snowy Plover occurs on gravel bars along the Eel River, on the adjacent beach, and along the south spit of Humboldt Bay. The broad, sandy beach at the mouth of the Mad River in the north also supports a small nesting population of plovers (R. Hewitt, *pers. comm.*). A large heron rookery on Indian Island adjacent to the town of Eureka is among the largest in the state, with another located at Teal Island on the southeast corrner of the bay. Near-shore waters off the coast appear to be vital for non-breeding concentrations of Marbled Murrelet, which maintain one of the largest populations in the state within the Eel River drainage southeast of the bay (J. Hunter, *pers. comm.*). Riparian habitat, somewhat limited on the immediate coast in this bioregion, is particularly well developed along the Mad River in the Blue Lake area and along the Eel River, which supports Black-capped Chickadee and an unusual west coast outpost of American Redstart. These rivers are also important foraging areas for Bald Eagle, which breeds just inland of the bay (Harris 1996). Several species highly localized in northwestern California occur in this IBA and at very few other locales, particularly open-country species such as Ferruginous Hawk and breeding Northern Harrier, Short-eared Owl and Grasshopper Sparrow. A breeding outpost of Tricolored Blackbirds has long been active in the Fortuna area, with birds foraging on nearby dairy farms. For migrant passerines coming in off the Pacific, the willows near Fairhaven offer the first suitable foraging habitat in the area, and are probably the best place to observe fall songbird migration on the northwest coast.

Conservation issues: This IBA is a patchwork of public and private lands, with much of the latter in agricultural production (with clear benefits to certain bird species, such as wintering raptors and roosting shorebirds). Much of the Eel River Bottoms are still in private ownership and are therefore vulnerable to development and/or alteration. However, since this area is so flood-prone and is under active agricultural production, development seems unlikely at this point. Though the edges of the bay are reasonably well protected as a national wildlife refuge, the bay itself must contend with the effects of a major oyster-culture operation, which periodically dredges the eelgrass beds, and covers them with used shells (Harris 1996). Many sensitive species depend on the non-wetland vegetation (grassland, riparian stringers), and maintenance of these habitats even on public lands has been a challenge to local conservationists. One recent decision to convert a large area of the Mad River Wildlife Area to cattle pasture (at the urging of local dairymen) led to the elimination of a major communal raptor roost (47 White-tailed Kites, 12 Short-eared Owls, *fide* D. Fix). Similar management conflicts have occurred at the "Ocean Ranch" section of the wildlife area, one of the premiere shorebird sites (extensive mudflats) that DFG has proposed converting to diked impoundments (D. Fix, *pers. comm.*). The fact that the "Fairhaven Willows" are located within a major off-road vehicle area, Samoa Dunes Recreation Area, leaves them open to degradation, and they should be considered vulnerable to alteration unless given formal recognition for their habitat value. Finally, this IBA was hit by two major oil spills, in September of 1997 and 1999, resulting in major mortality of Marbled Murrelets (SH).

Humboldt Lagoons
Humboldt

Nearest town(s): Orick
Size: 10,000 - 50,000 acres
Sensitive species: 8 (Peregrine Falcon, Western Snowy Plover, Marbled Murrelet, Burrowing Owl, Northern Spotted Owl, Vaux's Swift, Purple Martin, Yellow Warbler) (*fide* D. Fix)
Threat: Medium
Local Audubon Chapter: Redwood Region
BCR: 5

IBA Criteria		Source/Notes
P	>10% CA population of Marbled Murrelet	Ralph *et al.* 1995
W	>5000 Waterfowl	D. Fix, *pers. comm.*

Encompassing the coastal lowlands from the southern portion of Prairie Creek Redwoods State Park south to Patrick's Point, this is an area of large coastal lagoons surrounded by redwood forest. Most of the land is protected as state and federal parks (incl. Humboldt Lagoons State Park, Redwood National Park) with scattered parcels of private lands. Like Lake Earl to the north, this is a major coastal wintering area for non-marine waterfowl. The mature redwood forest in the hills east of the lagoons supports a significant proportion of California's nesting Marbled Murrelets, many of which winter just offshore, as well as breeding Vaux's Swift and Peregrine Falcon (in an ancient redwood snag). Most of the northwestern "specialty" birds such as Ruffed Grouse, Barred Owl and Gray Jay are found here. Though this site is fairly secure from development, chronic management concerns include trampling of sensitive nesting and roosting habitat by dogs and beach-goers.

Imperial Valley

Imperial

Nearest town(s): Brawley, El Centro, Calexico
Size: >50,000 acres
Threat: High
Local Audubon Chapter: San Diego, San Bernardino Valley
BCR: 33

	IBA Criteria	Source/Notes
P	>1% Global population of Mountain Plover	3758 birds in December 1999; Shuford *et al.* 2000
P	>1% Global population of Long-billed Curlew	5000+ birds in December, 1999; Shuford *et al.* 2000
P	>10% CA population of Wood Stork	"Small and declining post-breeding population"; Shuford *et al.* 2000
P	>10% CA population of White-faced Ibis	40,000 birds in October 1999; Shuford *et al.* 2000
P	>10% CA population of Burrowing Owl	DeSante and Ruhlen 1995
P	>10% CA population of Gila Woodpecker	5 – 10 pr. in Brawley, *pers. obs.*
P	>10% CA population of Vermilion Flycatcher	Up to 20 pr. vic. Holtville; RM
L	21 sensitive species: Least Bittern, White-faced Ibis, Wood Stork, Fulvous Whistling-Duck, Redhead, Ferruginous Hawk, Black Rail, Yuma Clapper Rail, Sandhill Crane, Mountain Plover, Long-billed Curlew, Gull-billed Tern, Burrowing Owl, Short-eared Owl, Gila Woodpecker, Vermilion Flycatcher, Loggerhead Shrike, Crissal Thrasher, Lucy's Warbler, Yellow-breasted Chat, Yellow-headed Blackbird	Shuford *et al.* 2000; RM, *pers. comm.*
S	>10,000 Shorebirds	G. McCaskie, *pers. comm.*
W	>5000 Waterfowl	G. McCaskie, *pers. comm.*

Description: The Imperial Valley, located in extreme southeastern California between the Salton Sea and the U.S.-Mexico border, is one of the premiere winter birding spots in the country. Most of the wetland habitat is contained within units of the Sonny Bono Salton Sea National Wildlife Refuge and the Imperial State Wildlife Area (including Finney-Ramer Lakes), as well as a handful of private duck clubs. The refuges also contain large fields of grains adjacent to marshes, similar to those hundreds of miles northwest in California's Central Valley. Limited wetland and riparian (mainly tamarisk) vegetation is also associated with the two main rivers, the New and the Alamo, that flow north across the valley into to Sea. Both rivers are fed nearly exclusively by agricultural runoff, a situation that has been implicated in massive die-offs of birds at the Salton Sea. A mosaic of irregularly-flooded row crops, irrigation canals, and occasional remnants of native alkali sink scrub also contribute to the area's staggering number and diversity of bird species nearly year round. The Imperial Valley is also one of the most important agricultural areas of the state, and its farmland extends south from the international border nearly to the head of the Gulf of California, with the Mexico side at least doubling the size of the habitat. Thus, the economy of the region, like that of the Central Valley, lives and dies with agriculture. Other players include the DoD (Naval Air Facility El Centro), and recently, geothermal energy exploration, which has added a new dimension to the increasingly industrial landscape here. In many ways, the Imperial Valley resembles Mexico more than the U.S., with the workforce and population overwhelmingly Hispanic, and Spanish heard far more often than English in its towns and on radio stations.

Birds: The habitats of the Imperial Valley, like other agricultural areas of the state, are heavily dependent upon water levels and water delivery infrastructure. First, it should be noted that the largest California populations of several species occur here. Between 30-40% of the global population of Mountain Plover winters within the Imperial Valley, almost exclusively in agricultural fields. Gila Woodpecker maintains its only California population away from the Colorado River in the Brawley area, and over 70% of the state's Burrowing Owls are found here (DeSante and Ruhlen 1995). Late summer sees an influx of birds dispersing north from the Gulf of California which utilize the marshes and flooded fields of the Valley, including variable numbers of Yellow-footed and Laughing gulls and Gull-billed Tern, all of which are nearly restricted to this IBA and the adjacent Salton Sea in California (Yellow-footed Gull found nowhere else in the U.S.). Fulvous Whistling-Duck is an increasingly rare visitor to marshy fields and impoundments, and may be extirpated as a nester.

The impoundments within Finney-Ramer Lakes represent a critical year-round nocturnal roosting site for herons that forage during the day throughout the valley and at the Salton Sea, whose numbers build up during the summer and early fall with post-breeding dispersants. Fall roost surveys during 1999 (Shuford et al. 2000) recorded counts of 40,000 Cattle Egrets (August) and nearly 40,000 White-faced Ibis (October). About half California's wintering population of White-faced Ibis may occur here (e.g. 16,000 birds in mid-1990s, Shuford et al. 1996). These roosts are also critical for southern California's remaining wintering Sandhill Cranes (widely extirpated elsewhere), about 300 of which forage during the day in grain fields south of Brawley. Major nesting colonies of egrets are found at Ramer Lake (Great Egret) and in eucalyptus groves near Westmoreland (Cattle Egret) (Shuford et al. 2000). Agricultural fields, particularly when partially flooded, support thousands of wintering White-faced Ibis, Long-billed Curlew (At least 10% of global population), both Snow and Ross' geese, along with tens of thousands of gulls (mainly Ring-billed). Shorebird use of these fields is exceptionally high during migration, both in spring and fall. Nearly 10,000 Whimbrel were recorded here on one count in April 1989 (Shuford et al. 2000), and fall migrants are joined by hundreds of Black Terns, particularly on fields close to the Salton Sea itself in the northern portion of the valley. Raptors have never been systematically censused here, but the wintering raptor community seems particularly dense, especially during "invasion" years of northern buteos.

Unlined irrigation canals where grown to marsh vegetation support Least Bittern and scarce rails, including small numbers of California Black and Yuma Clapper rails (esp. Lower Finney Lake and Holtville Main Drain, RM). These are often concentrated around wet spots where water seeps out of bases of the levees, a situation that also supports lush mesquite and riparian vegetation. These micro-wetlands surrounded by arid desert also support desert riparian species such as Lucy's Warbler and California's largest population of Vermilion Flycatchers (up to 20 pairs associated with the Highland Canal east of Holtville, RM). The riparian vegetation associated with unlined irrigation canals throughout the valley

Important Bird Areas of California

and with marshy impoundments appears to be very important for migrant songbirds, and a recent banding study by PRBO documented spring capture rates of Wilson's Warblers alone to be an order of magnitude higher than at Coyote Creek Riparian Station, a long-term banding station in the San Francisco Bay Area. This vegetation is also critical for the persistence of Colorado Desert species in the area, including Crissal Thrasher, Black-tailed Gnatcatcher, and Abert's Towhee.

Conservation issues: Shuford *et al.* (2000) summarize major conservation concerns for the Salton Sea and Imperial Valley. Those that pertain to this IBA include:

- Protecting and enhancing habitats for species of conservation concern, and those used by large numbers of roosting, nesting and foraging birds (incl. reducing disturbance by humans and predators).
- Continuing research on the impacts to birds of concentrations of heavy metals within the Imperial Valley/Salton Sea ecosystem.
- Evaluating the impacts of reduced water supplies and crop conversion (e.g. alfalfa to vineyards) agricultural fields in the IBA.
- Restoration of native riparian areas, including control of non-native species (e.g. tamarisk).

Mountain Plover (Peter LaTourrette)

Jepson Grasslands

Solano

Nearest town(s): Rio Vista, Fairfield
Size: 1000-10,000 acres
Threat: Critical
Local Audubon Chapter: Napa-Solano
BCR: 32

IBA Criteria		Source/Notes
P	Possibly >1% Global population of Mountain Plover	65 birds on 2 February 2002; K. Hunting, *unpubl. data*
P	Possibly >1% Global population of Long-billed Curlew	R. Leong, *via email*
L	10 sensitive species: Northern Harrier, Swainson's Hawk, Ferruginous Hawk, Golden Eagle, Mountain Plover, Long-billed Curlew, Burrowing Owl, Short-eared Owl, Loggerhead Shrike, Tricolored Blackbird	R. Leong, *via email*

Description: This IBA, adjacent to the Jepson Prairie Preserve, lies about 15 miles east of Fairfield, centered on the intersection of Highways 12 and 113. It features a cluster of dry agricultural fields and pastureland at the edge of the Delta ecosystem.

Birds: These grasslands have emerged as a key site within the Bay Area and Delta for several declining grassland species, notably an exceptional diversity of wintering raptors and for breeding Swainson's and Northern Harrier. Burrowing Owl and Loggerhead Shrike, both widely extirpated in the region, are resident, and one of two wintering flocks of Mountain Plover in northern California favors the fields along Robinson Rd., and is not found in the vernal pool habitat on nearby Jepson Prairie Preserve.

Conservation issues: The habitat in this area has received no protection from wildlife agencies and conservation groups, and it is likely that it will be eliminated soon unless conservation easements can be put in place to maintain current agricultural uses (RL, via email). The area is steadily seeing more vineyards and is quickly urbanizing; a golf/retiree community has just been constructed at nearby Rio Vista, and a large windfarm was recently installed at Bird's Landing.

Kelso Creek

Kern

Nearest town(s): Weldon, Lake Isabella
Size: <1000 acres
Threat: High
Local Audubon Chapter: Kerncrest
BCR: 33

IBA Criteria		Source/Notes
P	>1% Global population of Kern Red-winged Blackbird	T. Gallion, *in litt.*
L	10 sensitive species: Ferruginous Hawk, Burrowing Owl, Long-eared Owl, Loggerhead Shrike, Bendire's Thrasher, Le Conte's Thrasher, Yellow Warbler, Yellow-breasted Chat, Summer Tanager, Kern Red-winged Blackbird	K. Axelson, *pers. comm.*

Description: Kelso Creek is one of the major streams of the southernmost Sierra Nevada, dividing the Piute and the Scodie ranges on the south side of the Kern River drainage. It runs north for about twenty miles toward the South Fork Kern River, but now only reaches the Kern during flood events. Normally, it flows above ground year-round to a point about five miles south of the Kern, supporting several hundred acres of exceptionally lush woodland of Fremont Cottonwood and willows, with stinging nettle thickets so attractive to birds and other wildlife. Above the streambed, dense stands of Joshua Tree woodland are found on terraces, interspersed with tracts of lush desert scrub and desert chaparral. Wildflower displays in this area can be spectacular in April and May. About 150 acres of creek bed has recently been purchased by Audubon California, in hopes of augmenting holdings of the most critical bird habitat throughout the South Fork Kern River watershed. The ownership in this IBA is very complex, being a mosaic of private ranchland (the majority) and BLM holdings. Most of the mountainous lands surrounding the stream were designated as Wilderness Areas by the BLM following the Passage of the Desert Protection Act in 1994, but this did little to protect the riparian areas.

Birds: Following a long history of grazing and OHV abuse within the streambed of Kelso Creek, its bird community is recovering each year with the help of conservation easements and acquisitions. Although Yellow-billed Cuckoo and Willow Flycatcher have yet to appear as nesters (as they do along the South Fork Kern River to the north), most of the other riparian obligate species of the Mojave are present, with the addition of the narrowly-endemic Kern race of Red-winged Blackbird. Toward the north, the creek opens up to form a broad, sparsely-vegetated floodplain that supports breeding Burrowing Owl (along sandy river cuts) and Le Conte's Thrasher. Migrant songbirds can pass through in exceptionally large numbers during spring and early fall, although access to the habitat has been difficult due to fencing and ranchers that have barred public access. During fall, thousands of Turkey Vultures migrate south along Kelso Creek from the Kern Valley, en route to the Colorado River and Mexico.

Important Bird Areas of California

Conservation issues: Since most of the lands surrounding this IBA are secure from development, conservation is focused on managing the riparian habitat for birds and reducing threats such as overgrazing and destructive recreation activities. This area of vast federal wilderness areas is contiguous (and occasionally interspersed) with one of the most heavily-used OHV areas in the country, which has led to inevitable challenges managing human use in an area that has long tolerated lawlessness. The occasional motorcyclist that sneaks into the habitat along Kelso Creek often leads to a "rediscovery" of the site by other OHV enthusiasts, which restarts the degradation (K. Axelson, *pers. comm.*).

Kelso Creek (Alison Sheehey © NatureAli)

Kern NWR Area

Kern

Nearest town(s): Wasco, Delano
Size: 1000-10,000 acres
Threat: High
Local Audubon Chapter: Kern
BCR: 32

IBA Criteria		Source/Notes
P	>1% Global population of Tricolored Blackbird	J. Allen, *pers. comm.*
P	>10% CA population of White-faced Ibis	Ivey *et al.* 2002
L	15 sensitive species: Least Bittern, White-faced Ibis, Redhead, Northern Harrier, Ferruginous Hawk, Sandhill Crane, Mountain Plover, Long-billed Curlew, Burrowing Owl, Long-eared Owl, Short-eared Owl, Loggerhead Shrike, Sage Sparrow, Tricolored Blackbird, Yellow-headed Blackbird	J. Allen, A. Sheehey, *unpubl. data*
S	>10,000 Shorebirds	Recent (late 1990s) high of 18,000 birds in spring; J. Allen, *pers. comm*
W	>5000 Waterfowl	71,485 ducks between Kern and Pixley NWR and 3000 acres of private duck clubs in January 2003; USFWS 2003b

Description: The Kern National Wildlife Refuge protects just over 10,000 acres of alkali grassland, constructed freshwater marsh (impoundments and channels) and scrubby riparian stringers in the southern San Joaquin Valley, about 40 miles northwest of Bakersfield. Geologically, this area lies just south of the massive historic Tulare Lake Bed (see below). What little alkali scrub habitat remains here is greatly augmented by the 3000-acre Semitropic Ridge Preserve at its southern border (maintained by the non-profit Center for Natural Lands Management), which, according to The Nature Conservancy (1998), supports the "largest and best example of Valley Saltbush Scrub and Valley Sink Scrub community" on the floor of the Central Valley, as well as the "largest and highest quality natural area remaining in the southern San Joaquin Valley bottom." Several private duck clubs in the area contribute additional important wetland and native scrub/grassland habitat.

Birds: This IBA may be most notable for the recovering valley grassland and alkali scrub bird community that has developed following the recent removal of grazing from large areas of the refuge. Short-eared Owl has re-colonized the area as a breeder (SF), one of the only places it nests on the San Joaquin Valley floor. The constructed marshes have proven attractive to large colonies (several hundred pairs) of breeding White-faced Ibis (fourth-largest colony in the state, Ivey *et al.* 2002) and Tricolored Blackbird, now localized breeders in the industrialized agricultural landscape of the modern-day San Joaquin Valley. Swainson's Hawk has bred in the past 10 years (SF), and may do so again. Burrowing Owl, declining drastically statewide, remains a common resident in the area. The canescens race of Sage Sparrow, resident in low numbers on the refuge, is common at Semitropic Ridge, as do Greater Roadrunner, a scrubland species otherwise very rare on the agricultural San Joaquin Valley floor (DS). Tens of thousands of wintering waterfowl utilize the refuge's flooded fields and constructed wetlands, mainly Northern Shoveler (c. 25,000 in 2003), Ruddy Duck and Green-winged Teal; geese are much scarcer here than in refuges to the north (USFWS 2003b). Spring migration has brought thousands of shorebirds into the impoundments as they are being drained for the summer. In winter, small flocks of Sandhill Crane and Mountain Plover occur in drier agricultural fields in the area, both with much-reduced populations in the southern San Joaquin Valley. Though the original riparian bird community has not recovered, the refuge receives very little visitation from birders in the summer, and as the habitat continues to improve, it is likely that colonization by riparian obligates will occur. Interestingly, several native amphibians persist here in vernal pools on the valley floor, including Spadefoot Toad and possibly California Tiger Salamander (TNC 1998).

Conservation issues: Although the management plan at the NWR specifies a goal of 7000 acres of wetland habitat, difficulties in obtaining water have resulted in about half that amount on average (TNC 1998). Most of this water is present in winter only, which diminishes its value to breeding species. A more pressing threat involves ever-increasing and intensifying agriculture just outside its boundaries, which continue to alter the hydrology of the region by lowering the water table and pumping toxins into the air and water, which ends up in the refuge. Several thousand acres of evaporation ponds (for agricultural runoff) on the Tulare Lake Bed just to the north may pose a serious risk to birds in the area (these types of structures were implicated in the disaster at Kesterson NWR in the 1980s). Finally, exotic plants (e.g. tamarisk, Russian Thistle) pose a serious threat to recovery of riparian species at Kern NWR. In 2001, $1 million was awarded to Audubon California and Ducks Unlimited for wetland habitat enhancement projects in the area, which will contribute toward the recreation of the historic Tulare Lake Bed.

Klamath Basin/Clear Lake

Siskiyou/Modoc

Nearest town(s): Tulelake
Size: >50,000 acres
Threat: High
Local Audubon Chapter: Klamath Basin, Eagle Lake
BCR: 9

	IBA Criteria	Source/Notes
P	Entire CA breeding population of American White Pelican	2559 pr. in 1997; Shuford 1998
P	>10% CA breeding population of White-faced Ibis	1000+ pr.; Ivey et al. 2002
L	20 sensitive species: American White Pelican, Least Bittern, White-faced Ibis, Redhead, Bald Eagle, Northern Harrier, Swainson's Hawk, Ferruginous Hawk, Golden Eagle, Peregrine Falcon, Prairie Falcon, Greater Sage-Grouse, Sandhill Crane, Long-billed Curlew, Short-eared Owl, Loggerhead Shrike, Bank Swallow, Yellow Warbler, Tricolored Blackbird, Yellow-headed Blackbird	D. Shuford, J. Sterling, pers. comm.
S	>10,000 Shorebirds	c. 20,000 on 27 April 2001 at Tule Lake; Shuford et al. 2002
W	>5000 Waterfowl	c. 1 million waterfowl during spring; K. Novick, in litt.

Description: This enormous complex of seasonal wetlands, impoundments, agricultural lands, expansive grassland and sagebrush steppe habitat is considered by many to be the most important bird area in the state in terms of sheer numbers that utilize the habitats year round. This IBA straddles the Oregon border east of I-5, and includes three major national wildlife refuges, Tule Lake NWR and Lower Klamath NWR, on the floor of the Klamath Basin, and Clear Lake NWR, on the edge of the Modoc Plateau just to the east (which drains into the basin). During summer, when most refuges throughout the West have drawn down their water, the Klamath Basin can retain about 23,000 acres of wetlands, possibly the largest aggregation of any site in California in the breeding season (D. Mauser, pers. comm.).

Birds: Nearly 1 million waterfowl, an estimated 10% of the total number of individuals using the Pacific Flyway, pass through this IBA during migration. Up to 200,000 Greater White-fronted Goose of the "Pacific" race stage here in early spring (D. Mauser, in litt.). The number of northbound shorebirds in spring is also exceptional. This IBA supports both of California's last remaining colonies of American White Pelican, with birds nesting on undisturbed islets on Clear Lake and at Sheepy Lake (Lower Klamath NWR), where most of northeastern California's nesting Double-crested Cormorant breed (>1000 pr., ibid.). Breeding White-faced Ibis numbers have surged here, and the IBA was found to support over 1000 nesting pairs (c. ¹/₄ of the state's population) in the late 1990s (Ivey et al. 2002). In winter, the IBA is particularly critical for Bald Eagle – 60-80% of the 1000 eagles that winter in the Klamath Basin use Tule Lake and Lower Klamath NWRs, by far the largest concentration in the state. Two active Greater Sage-Grouse leks are known from the southern shore of Clear Lake (S. Blankenship, via email). The islets of Clear Lake also support large numbers of breeding Great Basin gulls and terns, including one of three large colonies of Caspian Tern in northeastern California (Shuford 1998). Surveys in the 1990s ranked Clear Lake in the top five sites in the state for numbers of breeding California and Ring-billed gulls (Shuford and Ryan 2000). The shallow marshes on the basin refuges support large numbers of breeding waterbirds, as well as major post-breeding aggregations of species such as Black Tern (several thousands of birds, Shuford *et al.* 2001).

Conservation issues: Despite the area's importance to birds in western North America, it remains highly threatened by agricultural practices, because of water diversions and habitat clearing (including farming on the refuges). Much of the wetland habitat of this IBA is the result of the Klamath Project, a massive water re-routing network that moves water to and from the region's major rivers (Klamath River, Lost River), reservoirs and fields. The region's agricultural operations are currently (2001) being reviewed at the federal level in light of increased restrictions on water diversions to provide adequate flows for salmon and several threatened and endangered fishes (e.g. Lost River and Shortnose suckers) in the Klamath drainage. A recent drought (2001) has affected breeding bird habitat at Clear Lake by creating land bridges to nesting islands. Recent refuge activities have addressed this problem by constructing fenced exclosures to protect nesting American White Pelicans from coyotes (DS). Increasingly, exotic plant species are invading these artificial wetlands, the most noxious being Perennial Pepperweed *(Lepidium latifolium)* and Purple Loosestrife *(Lythrum salicaria)* (K. Novick, *pers. comm.*).

Important Bird Areas of California

La Grange-Waterford Grasslands

Stanislaus/Tuolumne

Nearest town(s): Knights Ferry, La Grange
Size: 10,000 - 50,000 acres
Threat: Critical
Local Audubon Chapter: Stanislaus, Central Sierra
BCR: 32

	IBA Criteria	Source/Notes
P	>1% Global population Long-billed Curlew	200 birds on 1996 La Grange-Waterford CBC
L	10 sensitive species: Northern Harrier, Ferruginous Hawk, Golden Eagle, Burrowing Owl, Short-eared Owl, Loggerhead Shrike, Yellow-breasted Chat, Sage Sparrow, Grasshopper Sparrow, Tricolored Blackbird	J. Gain, K. Brunges, R Schieferstein, *pers. comm.*

Description: Extending between the Stanislaus and the Tuolumne rivers, the eastern borders of their eponymous counties features flat, extensive grassland dotted with vernal pools (of "excellent" quality, per TNC 1998) grading into a broad band of oak savannah to the east, at the toe of the Sierra foothills. Though rarely visited by ornithologists, hundreds of thousands of people drive past this northern edge of this area each year along Highway 120, the main thoroughfare between the Bay Area, Yosemite National Park and, farther east, Mono Lake. Much of the best grassland habitat is now limited to the center of this IBA, along Rock River and Cooperstown roads. Numerous and largely unexplored riparian areas are scattered throughout, with the best examples toward the east along Red Hills Road (Dry Creek).

Birds: The grasslands surrounding Cooperstown support a high diversity of wintering raptors, especially Ferruginous and Rough-legged hawks, and both Bald and Golden eagles. Burrowing (esp. along Tim Bell Rd.) and wintering Short-eared Owls (esp. along Rock River Rd.) are still familiar sights here, and Lewis' Woodpeckers winter in good numbers in the oaks along Cooperstown Rd. The riparian areas along the major rivers and the moist spots within grasslands near Chinese Camp in the north have Yellow-breasted Chat and breeding colonies of Tricolored Blackbird. Bell's Sage and Black-chinned sparrows, somewhat local in the Sierra, are common in the Chamise chaparral associated with the Red Hills on the eastern portion of the IBA.

Conservation issues: Planned communities are sprouting up each year along the Highway 120 corridor, and agricultural expansion (mainly orchards and vineyards) continues to claim more land here. Virtually no protected land occurs within this rapidly-developing IBA, which justifies its being assigned a "Critical" threat level.

Important Bird Areas of California

Lake Almanor Area

Plumas/Lassen

Nearest town(s): Chester, Westwood
Size: >50,000 acres
Sensitive species: 8 (Bald Eagle, Northern Goshawk, Golden Eagle, Sandhill Crane, Black Tern, California Spotted Owl, Willow Flycatcher, Yellow Warbler) (S. McDonald, *in litt.*)
Threat: High
Local Audubon Chapter: Eagle Lake, Plumas
BCR: 15

IBA Criteria		Source/Notes
P	>10% CA population of Willow Flycatcher	72 birds in 1997; California PIF 2001
W	>5000 Waterfowl	46,370 American Wigeon on 1989 Lake Almanor CBC

Description: Lake Almanor and Mountain Meadows Reservoir lie at the boundary between the Sierra Nevada and the Cascades, between Red Bluff and Susanville. These two large reservoirs (13 and 6 miles long, *resp.*) were constructed on the North Fork of the Feather River by Pacific Gas and Electric to provide hydropower and are separated by a short stream known as "Hamilton Branch". Between the reservoirs and the surrounding meadows and forest, this IBA features a wide diversity of northern Californian habitats, including several distinct coniferous forest associations, sagebrush flats, riparian thickets, wet meadows, and freshwater marshes. The spectacular scenery (Mt. Lassen looms to the northwest) and abundance of private land has led to a recent building boom, most severe at Lake Almanor. An exceptionally diverse community of mammals occurs in this IBA, including Mountain Lion, Pronghorn, Sierra Nevada Red Fox, Snowshoe Hare, Pine Marten and Northern Flying-Squirrel.

Birds: This IBA is notable for supporting one of the largest populations of Willow Flycatchers in the state, which breed in meadows with willow thickets in and around Westwood. Several Great Basin waterbirds, including small numbers of Greater Sandhill Crane (up to 6 nesting pr., *fide* S. McDonald), breed in wet meadows and the marshy margins of the two lakes, and 300 pr. of Eared Grebe were estimated nesting at Mtn. Meadows Reservoir in 1999. The Feather River "delta" at the northwestern end of Lake Almanor is especially attractive for breeding Clark's and Western grebes, congregating waterbirds during migration, and the number of ducks wintering on the lake can be staggering (esp. American Wigeon and Ruddy Duck). The vast tracts of unbroken coniferous forest around this IBA support strong numbers of northerly breeding species such as Northern Goshawk, Black-backed Woodpecker and Gray Jay, and have been popular with California birders for decades (see Green and Airola 1997).

Conservation issues: The principal conservation battle of this IBA involves the "Westwood and Dyer Mountain Resort Community", a 6800-acre mega-development within Lassen Co. on the southwestern side of Mountain Meadows Reservoir. A recently-formed land trust, the Mountain Meadows Conservancy, is attempting to ensure land and cultural artifact conservation in the face of the project, which is slated for some of the most biologically diverse portions of the IBA.

Mouth of Goodrich Ck., Lake Almanor Area IBA (Suzanne McDonald)

Lake Casitas Area

Ventura

Nearest town(s): Ojai, Ventura
Size: 1000-10,000 acres
Threat: Medium
Local Audubon Chapter: Ventura
BCR: 32

IBA Criteria		Source/Notes
L	11 sensitive species: Least Bittern, Northern Harrier, Ferruginous Hawk, Golden Eagle, Long-eared Owl, Loggerhead Shrike, Yellow Warbler, Yellow-breasted Chat, Sage Sparrow, Grasshopper Sparrow, Tricolored Blackbird	R. Smith, *in litt.*; J. Greaves, *via email*

Description: Lake Casitas is a large reservoir north of the City of Ventura formed by the damming of several tributaries of the Ventura River. It is situated in a valley at the southern end of the Coast Range, which extends south and east into an area referred to as Canada Larga. The important bird habitats here include the extensive grassland along Canada Larga Rd. and the freshwater marsh and adjoining grassland associated with Lake Casitas.

Birds: Several marsh species scarce in the region occur within this IBA, including breeding Osprey and Northern Harrier, as well as a colony of several hundred Tricolored Blackbirds. A consistent breeding population of Grasshopper Sparrow may be found along Canada Larga Rd., along with the expected grassland species such as White-tailed Kite and (in winter) Ferruginous Hawk. The riparian habitat in the area, especially along the Ventura River, supports breeding Yellow-breasted Chat and perhaps Yellow Warbler (*fide* J. Greaves).

Conservation issues: The land around Lake Casitas is owned by a regional Water District, which may eventually consider it "excess", given the recent upgrade of the reservoir's filtration system (*fide* W. Wehtje). The Canada Larga area, being all private ranchland, could be sold at any time.

Lake Elsinore

Riverside

Nearest town(s): Lake Elsinore
Size: <1000 acres
Sensitive species: 9 (Ferruginous Hawk, Loggerhead Shrike, Least Bell's Vireo, Cactus Wren, California Gnatcatcher, Yellow Warbler, Yellow-breasted Chat, Sage Sparrow, Tricolored Blackbird) (D. Cooper, *unpubl. data*)
Threat: High
Local Audubon Chapter: San Bernardino Valley
BCR: 32

IBA Criteria		Source/Notes
W	>5000 Waterfowl	D. Cooper, *unpubl. data*

Description: Lake Elsinore is one of the largest natural lakes in southern California. It is surrounded on the east by arid, coastal sage scrub-covered hills, and on the west by the steep eastern escarpment of the Santa Ana Mountains, which are cloaked in chaparral and oak woodland. The lake is fed by Temescal Creek and the San Jacinto River, which enter from the Lake Mathews/Estelle Mtn. IBA from the north. Though largely surrounded by trailer parks, campgrounds and marinas, the southern end features an extensive constructed wetland ("Wetland Habitat Area", City of Lake Elsinore) with small islets, mudflats, and freshwater marsh vegetation bounded by a large dike. More freshwater marsh and riparian habitat is found just north of the lake, associated with Temescal Creek, and accessible from Hwy. 74. South of the lake (though also separated from the lake by the large dike) is the historic drawdown area of the lake, now a broad plain covered with alkali grassland (mainly exotic) and scattered clumps of mulefat-dominated riparian scrub. More intact grassland (mixed with coastal sage scrub) is found just west of Temescal Creek north of Hwy. 74, but is slated for development. Pockets of willow-cottonwood riparian woodland are also found along the lakeshore, particularly at the southwestern corner (vic. Rome Hill).

Birds: The grassy drawdown area and adjacent impoundments at the south end of Lake Elsinore support a diverse raptor community, and several species of locally scarce waterbirds (incl. Caspian Tern) breed in the constructed wetlands. Currently, access limits thorough exploration of the wetlands (it's a 2-mile walk out to the habitat). Several heron rookeries are found in the riparian growth around the lake, especially in willow clumps. The Coastal Sage Scrub is especially lush on the east side of the lake, and though seriously fragmented by roads and houses, supports high densities of California Gnatcatcher (USFWS 1998), Cactus Wren and Bell's Sage Sparrow (*pers. obs.*).

Conservation issues: Human disturbance (OHV use, dumping) and arson threatens the remaining patches of coastal sage scrub, particularly those on the eastern side of the lake. The entire IBA is widely popular with OHV enthusiasts, and fences and signage are nearly impossible to maintain given current activities. Riparian thickets are especially at risk, both from vehicles and from serious infestation by exotic plants, especially tamarisk, which was found to be completely lining the constructed wetlands and much of the drawdown area in 2001 (*pers. obs.*).

Lake Mathews/Estelle Mtn.
Riverside

Nearest town(s): Riverside, Corona, Perris, Lake Elsinore
Size: 1000-10,000 acres
Threat: High
Local Audubon Chapter: San Bernardino Valley
BCR: 32

IBA Criteria		Source/Notes
P	>1% Global population of California Gnatcatcher	USFWS 1998
L	12 sensitive species: Northern Harrier, Ferruginous Hawk, Golden Eagle, Burrowing Owl, Loggerhead Shrike, Least Bell's Vireo, Cactus Wren, California Gnatcatcher, Yellow-breasted Chat, Sage Sparrow, Grasshopper Sparrow, Tricolored Blackbird	C. McGaugh, *pers. comm.*

Description: This largest undeveloped expanse of habitat in western Riverside Co. features a large reservoir (Lake Mathews) surrounded by annual grassland and arid, Riversidean Coastal Sage Scrub that extends over hilly terrain about 10 miles south to Interstate 15. Much of the land has been designated the Estelle Mountain – Lake Mathews Reserve with parcels owned by the Metropolitan Water District (MWD), the Riverside County Habitat Conservation Authority, DFG and BLM. Day-to-day management is coordinated by the non-profit Center for Natural Lands Management. At 13,000 acres, this reserve encompasses most of the open space immediately surrounding Lake Mathews and the hills to the south. While the reserve south of the lake is fenced and tightly monitored, an annex of the reserve west and northwest of the lake is afforded minimal protection. Arlington Mountain and Estelle Mountain are floristically similar with the addition of large tracts of chamise chaparral and even Western Juniper-dotted scrub on the latter, a unique habitat type here restricted to the foothills of Peninsula Ranges. Temescal Wash drains the southern flank of Estelle Mountain, and supports lush riparian woodland with oaks, willows and sycamores.

Birds: This avifauna of this IBA is notable for supporting one of the largest populations of California Gnatcatchers in Riverside Co. (50-80 pr. in the Lake Mathews-Dawson Cyn. "Core Population", USFWS 1998), as well as for its high number and diversity of wintering raptors. Lake Mathews has become an important wintering area for Bald Eagle in southern California. Temescal Wash, on the southern end of the IBA, supports an intact riparian bird community with both foothill and lowland elements.

Conservation issues: Originally designated to provide Critical Habitat (per USFWS) for the Stephen's Kangaroo-Rat, this area has emerged as one of the key areas for conservation attention under the Western Riverside County Multi-species Habitat Conservation Plan. As such, its protection under this plan should be carefully monitored. The ongoing conversion of high-quality coastal sage scrub to exotic, annual grassland (largely through arson) represents the foremost threat (R. Baxter, Center for

Natural Lands Management, *pers. comm.*). Away from patrolled areas within the Estelle Mountain – Lake Mathews Reserve, major human disturbance (including OHV use, arson, illegal hunting, dumping) threatens the remaining patches of Riversidean Coastal Sage Scrub (especially vic. Arlington Mountain). Urban sprawl continues to claim open space in the region – the development on the northwest slope of Arlington Mtn. (mid-1990s) is now infamous for knowingly causing the extirpation of one of the last pairs of Golden Eagle in western Riverside Co. Educational outreach to the Metropolitan Water District could greatly enhance riparian habitat there – the willow forest surrounding Lake Mathews has long been cleared for the specific purpose of eliminating habitat for sensitive bird species (L. LaPre, *pers. comm.*). Although a large area of habitat is protected as open space, habitat on the southwestern flank of Estelle Mtn. and adjacent Temescal Wash is seeing the construction of scattered "dream homes", housing tracts and most recently, a massive mining operation.

Sage Sparrow (Brian Small)

Lake Success Area

Tulare

Nearest town(s): Porterville
Size: 1000-10,000 acres
Sensitive species: 8 (Ferruginous Hawk, Golden Eagle, Prairie Falcon, Burrowing Owl, Loggerhead Shrike, Yellow-breasted Chat, Grasshopper Sparrow, Tricolored Blackbird) (A. Frolich, *pers. comm.*)
Threat: High
Local Audubon Chapter: Tulare County
BCR: 32

IBA Criteria		Source/Notes
P	>1% Global population of Tricolored Blackbird	W. Principe, *via email*

Description: This IBA is centered on Lake Success, a mid-sized Sierra foothill reservoir on the Tule River. It includes the extensive grassland surrounding the lake (particularly well-developed on the north side), as well as the riparian habitat along each arm of the Tule River as it enters the lake from the east, and below the spillway of the dam.

Birds: The open, valley-floor grassland north and west of Lake Success often stays wet into early summer, when it supports large numbers of breeding Grasshopper Sparrow and, in a nearby quarry pond, thousands of breeding Tricolored Blackbirds (W. Principe, *via email*). Burrowing Owl, widely extirpated along the base of the Sierras, is still resident here, and is joined by a diverse raptor community in winter that historically included California Condor. Bald and Golden eagles and Prairie Falcon still winter in numbers, and the latter two breed in the area. The riparian habitat here has received virtually no coverage by birders during summer, but has recently been found to support Yellow-breasted Chat (A. Frolich, *pers. comm.*) and likely holds several other riparian-obligate breeders. Winter brings thousands of waterfowl to the reservoir, especially American Wigeon and Common Merganser, and fall finds hundreds of shorebirds along the muddy border along the north side, many of which over-winter.

Conservation issues: As Porterville expands east toward the foothills, the flat and rolling grassland in the area will continue to come under development pressure, as much of it is still in private ownership. An active conservation constituency in the area, spearheaded by the Sierra-Los Tulares Land Trust, has generated interest in large-scale open space preservation in the region, linking the remaining valley floor grassland with the Sierras via the Tule River corridor.

Lancaster

Los Angeles/Kern

Nearest town(s): Lancaster, Palmdale
Size: 10,000 - 50,000 acres
Threat: Critical
Local Audubon Chapter: San Fernando Valley
BCR: 33

IBA Criteria		Source/Notes
P	>1% Global population of Mountain Plover	95 birds on 1996 Lancaster CBC
P	>1% Global population Long-billed Curlew	K. Garrett, M. San Miguel, *pers. comm.*
L	10 sensitive species: Northern Harrier, Swainson's Hawk, Ferruginous Hawk, Mountain Plover, Long-billed Curlew, Burrowing Owl, Short-eared Owl, Long-eared Owl, Loggerhead Shrike, Le Conte's Thrasher	Allen and Garrett 1995; K. Garrett, M. San Miguel, *pers. comm.*

Description: This area of the western Mojave Desert is within the "Antelope Valley" of northern Los Angeles Co., one of the rapidly-developing regions of the country. As tract homes replace thousands of acres of open space each year, birds are being forced into increasingly smaller areas. Three major bird habitats are present in a mosaic of agriculture and wildland: Joshua Tree woodland and desert scrub, arid grassland/"wildflower fields" and alfalfa fields with tall windbreaks. The land here slopes gradually to drain into the vast alkali playas of Rosamond and Rogers Dry Lakes on Edwards Air Force Base (see Edwards Air Force Base Wetlands IBA above). The land here is overwhelmingly privately-owned, though several hundred acres are protected as the Antelope Valley California Poppy State Reserve along Lancaster Rd. about 10 miles west of Hwy. 14.

Birds: The remnant Joshua Tree Woodland in this area supports one of the farthest-west populations of Le Conte's Thrasher in the state (only the San Joaquin Valley group lies beyond). Now existing as a metapopulation fragmented by subdivisions, its future is uncertain. The largest groups are currently northeast of the intersection of Sierra Hwy. and Ave. P East, and about twenty miles northwest of here, west of Rosamond (mainly Kern Co.). The grassland bird community is most impressive in winter, when large numbers of raptors concentrate in three main areas: along Lancaster Blvd. north of Lake Hughes; along Ave. A west of Rosamond; and along Ave. J east of Lancaster. Large flocks of Vesper Sparrows, Horned Lark and Mountain Bluebirds also occur here, widely extirpated elsewhere in the Los Angeles area. The agricultural fields, especially alfalfa, are productive year round. Winter brings Mountain Plover, whose flocks are among the last in southern California. After wet winters, nesting grassland species like Northern Harrier and Short-eared Owl linger well into spring, and occasionally even breed. Swainson's Hawk maintains its southernmost breeding outpost in the state here, nesting in windbreaks east of Lancaster (1-2 pr.). As this IBA lies in the path of a major spring migrant route for songbirds, these windbreaks can host hundreds of vireos, thrushes and warblers during April and May. Fields that receive

Important Bird Areas of California

effluent from local water treatment facilities can support hundreds of White-faced Ibis and shorebirds, and these fields support a group of around 200 Long-billed Curlews in fall and winter (MSM).

Conservation issues: This IBA is seeing rapid transformation from an agricultural/wildland landscape to an urban zone of tract homes and planted trees. Much of the conservation efforts in the western Mojave (e.g. BLM's West Mojave Habitat Conservation Plan) have focused on protected the Desert Tortoise, and would not be expected to give much attention to bird habitats, such as alfalfa fields in Palmdale. Conservation action could focus on protecting and linking undeveloped lands of east Palmdale with the San Gabriel Mountains, and those west of Rosamond with the Tehachapi Mountains.

Le Conte's Thrasher (Brian Small)

Lone Willow Slough

Madera

Nearest town(s): Madera
Size: 10,000 - 50,000 acres
Threat: Critical
Local Audubon Chapter: Fresno
BCR: 32

	IBA Criteria	Source/Notes
L	12 sensitive species: Redhead, Northern Harrier, Swainson's Hawk, Ferruginous Hawk, Sandhill Crane, Mountain Plover, Long-billed Curlew, Burrowing Owl, Short-eared Owl, Loggerhead Shrike, Tricolored Blackbird, Yellow-headed Blackbird	R. Hansen, *pers. comm.*

Description: East of Firebaugh, in the agricultural "no man's land" between two key Central Valley IBAs (Grasslands Ecological Area and Mendota Wildlife Area), is a 30,000-acre patch of vernal pool-rich grassland, alkali scrub and freshwater marsh (i.e. the slough) with narrow bands of riparian woodland and that has somehow survived the agricultural transformation of western Fresno/Madera Co. Located northeast of Firebaugh, this habitat may represent the largest intact swath of unplowed valley floor in the San Joaquin Valley (R. Hansen, *pers. comm.*). Originally, this site would have supported a rich riparian woodland associated with the San Joaquin River, from which it is now separated by levees, but today only scattered patches remain. Currently, the entire area is totally privately-owned, heavily grazed and virtually unstudied.

Birds: From a handful of visits by ornithologists, this IBA is known to support a sizable population of breeding Swainson's Hawks, of which 50-100 birds have been observed at summer roosts in cottonwoods along the slough. These trees also hold rookeries of Great Blue Heron and probably other waders (*pers. obs.*). The bulrush marsh, which covers several hundred acres, probably supports nesting White-faced Ibis, which summer (*pers. obs.*). The extensive grasslands may be one of the only places on the San Joaquin Valley floor that could potentially support Grasshopper Sparrow, though more fieldwork is needed.

Conservation issues: The slough itself is apparently a water bank for the local irrigation district, and receives no formal protection. The grasslands are managed exclusively for cattle and sheep grazing. This is a site that urgently deserves study and conservation attention, possibly involving its inclusion into the Grasslands Ecological Area.

Important Bird Areas of California

Lopez Lake Area

San Luis Obispo

Nearest town(s): Arroyo Grande, Pismo Beach
Size: 10,000 - 50,000 acres
Threat: Low
Local Audubon Chapter: Morro Coast
BCR: 32

	IBA Criteria	Source/Notes
L	10 sensitive species: Ferruginous Hawk, Golden Eagle, Peregrine Falcon, Prairie Falcon, California Spotted Owl, Loggerhead Shrike, Yellow Warbler, Yellow-breasted Chat, Sage Sparrow, Grasshopper Sparrow	S. Schubert, T. Edell, *in litt.*

Description: Lopez Lake is a large reservoir located in the hills northeast of the Arroyo Grande/Pismo Beach area of the Central Coast. It is fed by several creeks, including Arroyo Grande Creek, which enters from the east and continues its flow southwest from Lopez Canyon Dam. The mountains just east of the lake feature rock outcrops and rugged canyons of mixed evergreen woodland and dense chaparral. The ownership is complex, with the county of San Luis Obispo managing the lake and immediate vicinity, and the US Forest Service (USFS) dominating the woodland and chaparral habitats to the east. The mature riparian habitat along Arroyo Grande Creek to the west lies mainly on private property, though some of this habitat may be found on public land on the southeast side of the lake within Biddle Park (San Luis Obispo Co. Parks).

Birds: This area supports an exceptional diversity of breeding birds, including one of the largest known populations of Yellow-breasted Chat in the county, as well as good numbers of other riparian-obligate species such as Swainson's Thrush and Yellow Warbler. The canyon-lands to the north and east support American Dipper, rare in the Coast Range, as well as Spotted and Long-eared owls, and summering montane birds such as Olive-sided Flycatcher and Western Tanager. A massive cliff face known as "Huff's Hole" north of the lake (now within the Santa Lucia Wilderness Area) was a traditional nesting site for California Condor, which disappeared shortly after the filling of the lake. Prairie and, irregularly, Peregrine falcons continue to breed in the area.

Conservation issues: None at this time.

Important Bird Areas of California

Los Angeles Flood Control Basins

Los Angeles

Nearest town(s): Azusa, Irwindale, Baldwin Park, El Monte, South El Monte, Pico Rivera, Montebello
Size: 1000-10,000 acres
Threat: High
Local Audubon Chapter: Whittier, Pasadena
BCR: 32

IBA Criteria		Source/Notes
L	10 sensitive species: Least Bittern, Loggerhead Shrike, Least Bell's Vireo, Cactus Wren, Clark's Marsh Wren, California Gnatcatcher, California Swainson's Thrush, Yellow Warbler, Yellow-breasted Chat, Tricolored Blackbird	Allen and Garrett 1995; Long 1993; K. Garrett, *pers. comm.*

Description: The Los Angeles Basin is drained by two major rivers, the Los Angeles and the San Gabriel. During the mid-1900s, both were systematically channelized, and large dams were constructed at regular intervals along their lengths. The open land preserved behind (upstream of) these dams, which include Van Norman, Hansen, Whittier Narrows, Rio Hondo (on the adjacent Rio Hondo), and Santa Fe, has been devoted to various purposes that could sustain rare flood events (incl. picnic areas, athletic fields and golf courses) with large areas left undeveloped to contain the sediment that flowed down the river after each large winter storm. Though these debris basins were originally intended to be cleared out annually, this was done so infrequently that several have reverted back to their original habitat, providing a glimpse of how the non-channelized rivers would have appeared.

Birds: Significant habitat for birds adjacent to these flood control structures include the coastal sage scrub in the Montebello Hills (vic. Whittier Narrows Dam) and the Big Tujunga Wash area near Hansen Dam. Hansen and Santa Fe dams support sizeable areas of alluvial fan scrub, a very rare habitat limited to southwestern California with bird community similar to that of coastal sage scrub. The area (including adjacent gravel pits) supports Lesser Nighthawk, Greater Roadrunner, Costa's Hummingbird, Cactus Wren, Loggerhead Shrike, as well as several other sensitive vertebrates nearly gone from the Los Angeles Area, including San Diego Black-tailed Jackrabbit and probably also San Diego Horned Lizard. Long (1993) summarized current knowledge about the birds of Whittier Narrows. The Montebello Hills preserve a major population of California Gnatcatcher (41 pr., K. Clark, USFWS, *pers. comm.*) near the northern edge of their global range, as well as a subset of other coastal sage scrub species such as Cactus Wren and (at least formerly) Greater Roadrunner. Moving east, the riparian habitat of the Rio Hondo and the San Gabriel River areas support all of the riparian-obligate species of the IBA, and Legg Lake supports breeding Least Bittern, Marsh Wren of the endemic clarkae race and Tricolored Blackbird in its bulrush-rimmed islets, as well as locally-large numbers (100s) of wintering waterfowl. A wide diversity of wintering passerines occurs here as well, with Christmas Bird Counts typically finding over 100 species.

Conservation issues: Very little of this area is even nominally managed for biodiversity, with the exceptions of tiny Bosque del Rio Hondo Park and the nearby Whittier Narrows Wildlife Area. The other areas are extremely vulnerable to a variety of habitat loss, including ongoing development for recreation uses (e.g. soccer fields, golf courses). Exotic vegetation (e.g. Arundo and Castor Bean) and Brown-headed Cowbird parasitism currently represent the greatest threats to the riparian resources of the recreation area. Two introduced passerines, Nutmeg Manakin and Orange Bishop, are especially common in the Whittier Narrows area, and may pose a serious threat to native nesting birds. The primary reason for the "High" threat designation is due to the fact that the majority of the habitat in this IBA is managed by the Army Corps of Engineers. This has led to large swaths of riparian woodland being bulldozed in a matter of hours, with only cursory environmental review (e.g. vic. Santa Fe Dam, Rio Hondo Dam). Such destructive maintenance activities as bulldozing only encourages exotic plants and animals. Sparsely-vegetated, un-irrigated areas are now at a premium (and are still being lost), home to once-common Loggerhead Shrike, Western Meadowlark, wintering sparrows, and raptors.

Least Bittern (Brian Small)

Lower Colorado River Valley

San Bernardino/Riverside/Imperial

Nearest town(s): Needles, Blythe; Yuma, AZ
Size: 10,000 - 50,000 acres
Threat: High
Local Audubon Chapter: San Bernardino Valley; Yuma
BCR: 33

IBA Criteria		Source/Notes
P	>1% Global population of Long-billed Curlew	Flocks of 100s in winter, R. Higson, *pers. comm.*
P	>1% Global population of Yuma Clapper Rail	R. McKernan, *pers. comm.*
P	>1% Global population of Southwestern Willow Flycatcher	18 pr.; Sogge *et al.* 2002
P	Possibly >1% Global population of Mountain Plover	47 birds vic. Blythe on 2 February 2002; K. Hunting, *unpubl. data*
P	Nearly entire CA population of Elf Owl	Thelander and Crabtree 1994
P	Nearly entire CA population of Arizona Bell's Vireo	McKernan and Braden 2001
P	>10% CA population of Yellow-billed Cuckoo	McKernan and Braden 2001
P	>10% CA population of Gila Woodpecker	Thelander and Crabtree 1994
P	>10% CA population of Gilded Flicker	Thelander and Crabtree 1994
P	>10% CA population of Vermilion Flycatcher	R. McKernan, *pers. comm.*
P	>10% CA population of Summer Tanager	McKernan and Braden 2001
P	Probably >10% CA population of Least Bittern, Crissal Thrasher, Lucy's Warbler	Garrett and Dunn 1981; Small 1994
L	23 sensitive species: Least Bittern, White-faced Ibis, Ferruginous Hawk, Black Rail, Yuma Clapper Rail, Mountain Plover, Long-billed Curlew, Yellow-billed Cuckoo, Elf Owl, Burrowing Owl, Long-eared Owl, Gila Woodpecker, Gilded Flicker, Southwestern Willow Flycatcher, Vermilion Flycatcher, Crissal Thrasher, Loggerhead Shrike, Arizona Bell's Vireo, Lucy's Warbler, Yellow Warbler, Yellow-breasted Chat, Summer Tanager, Yellow-headed Blackbird	McKernan and Braden 2001; R. Higson, *pers. comm*
S	>10,000 Shorebirds	R. Mckernan, R. Higson; *pers. comm.*
W	>5000 Waterfowl	12,473 waterfowl on 14 January, 2003; USFWS 2003b

Important Bird Areas of California

Description: This IBA draws attention to what is arguably the most important area for California's most imperiled avifauna – that of the wetlands and riparian thickets of the lower Colorado River Valley. The original riparian and wetland habitat of the Colorado River has been extensively altered, but particularly the downstream portions, including all of that within California. Most of the best habitat is (fortunately) located off the beaten path, even for this remote corner of California, with "nodes" of habitat at the Nevada/Arizona/California border at Fort Mohave and then to the south between Blythe, CA and Yuma, AZ. However, scattered patches of habitat elsewhere (e.g. near Headgate Dam just north of Parker, AZ) are probably critically important for birds in this arid landscape. The riparian thicket and woodland here is now generally dominated by tamarisk, but some areas have developed a very significant component of native willows and Arrowweed.

Starting in the north, the Fort Mohave area refers to the portion of the lower Colorado River Valley just south of the Nevada border south to the town of Needles. It is dominated by the Fort Mohave Indian Reservation, but also includes a large private holding to the north "Soto Ranch." The Havasu NWR (part of the lower Colorado River refuge complex) is just south of Fort Mohave, though mostly located in Arizona (incl. Topock Marsh). Although most of the habitat here, mainly Honey Mesquite bosque, was cleared during the 1990s, it is included because it still supports populations (albeit seriously reduced) of sensitive species. These are largely confined to a band of mesquite on the eastern side of the "Needles Hwy." northwest of River Rd., and to a strip of marsh and riparian vegetation (including dense willow thicket) along the main stem of the Colorado River.

Moving south, some of the finest remnants include the Hall Island area on the southern end of Arizona's Parker Valley, and Big Hole Slough (DFG), which protects about 100 acres of riparian and freshwater marsh habitat along an old oxbow of the lower Colorado River on the north side of Blythe. The agricultural fields in the area, though established over former riparian habitat, are considered part of this IBA due to their current importance for birds. On the southern end of Blythe's Palo Verde Valley, Cibola NWR straddles the Arizona/California border about 20 miles south of town, where Hwy. 78 swings west away from the river. Key habitats on the California side of Cibola include Three Finger Slough (40 acres) and Walker Lake (c. 350 acres of riparian), both impoundments built in former oxbows of the river channel with freshwater marsh and willow-tamarisk thickets (including several old habitat restoration sites). Moving south, nearby Draper Lake within Imperial NWR (c. 200 acres of riparian) is another former oxbow with similar marsh-tamarisk-willow habitat along the river. Imperial NWR is notable for its lack of levees along the river channel, which permits the river to form natural meanders and oxbows.

South of here, Picacho State Recreation Area supports about 350 acres of habitat along the river from near Taylor Lake to Ferguson Lake. Significant native plant components are found near the Picacho Camp Store (mainly willows) and at Ferguson Lake (70% native) (McKernan and Braden 2001). Most of the habitat near Imperial Dam is located within Arizona, but within about five miles south of here, several small patches of willow riparian vegetation provide important bird habitat, notably at West Pond, just west of the dam. The levees at West Pond have recently allowed water to seep through, which has resulted in the development of lush, even-aged riparian woodland, now a rare feature along the river.

Birds: The birds of this IBA have been monitored by Robert L. McKernan and Gerald Braden of the San Bernardino Co. Museum since 1996. The species along the river seem to vary somewhat predictably

Important Bird Areas of California

in their occurrence, with some (e.g. Lucy's Warbler, Yellow-breasted Chat) being fairly widespread and others (Elf Owl, Yellow-billed Cuckoo) being very rare, and often occurring only with large aggregations of the commoner taxa. Big Hole Slough supports one of the few California occurrences of Northern Cardinal (RM), and the Fort Mohave area is known as one of the last holdouts for Elf Owl in California (Halterman *et al.* 1989; Rosenberg *et al.* 1991), which, unfortunately, may already be extirpated (5 pr. in 1987, 1 bird as recently as 1997, *fide* R. McKernan). Because the river is emerging as one of the most important corridors in the state for northbound migrants in spring, the agricultural fields to the west of Blythe (esp. along Lovekin Blvd.) support exceptionally high numbers of migrant shorebirds when flooded (e.g. up to 10,000 Whimbrel in recent springs, RM). Long-billed Curlew is also found in migration and winter in large flocks. The fields in this area host one of just two large aggregations of Mountain Plover left in southern California (several hundred birds), the other being in similar habitat in the Imperial Valley. Finally, Mayflower County Park, just north of Big Hole, has emerged as one of the premier spots along the river to observe songbird migration, with large numbers moving through both spring and fall (R. Higson, *pers. comm.*). The Cibola area seems to support the most complete suite of riparian breeders, as well as impressive numbers of migrant and wintering waterfowl (including occasional flocks of wintering Sandhill Crane). Most of the other riparian habitat areas mentioned above have supported all of the sensitive riparian species within the last 10 years, though not all occur at every site each year. One other species of note, Harris' Hawk, maintains a small breeding population just across the river from Ferguson Lake, and could be expected to eventually colonize the habitat toward the southern end of this IBA (RM).

Conservation issues: To say that this area is "critically" threatened almost misrepresents the conservation urgency here. In general, the populations of sensitive species seems to fluctuate from year to year, with taxa like Yellow-billed Cuckoo and Willow Flycatchers breeding for a few years and then vanishing. This underscores the need to thoroughly survey all patches of riparian habitat in the region and speaks to the importance of even small patches for birds that may be displaced by such events as water level manipulation, fires and local habitat clearing. Current threats include ongoing direct habitat destruction (e.g. Senator Wash just north of Imperial Dam is regularly scraped clean of vegetation) and the general problems associated with fragmented riparian habitats (exotic plant invasions, cowbird parasitism). Encouragingly, some of the most sensitive species (incl. Yellow-billed Cuckoo) have partially adapted to nesting in tamarisk, given appropriate "old-growth" structure (RM). The habitat in this portion of the lower Colorado River Valley, though productive, is very limited compared to historic extent, and could be greatly enhanced with additional restoration of public lands along the main stem of the river (e.g. Goose Flats Wildlife Area, just south of I-10). As with other agricultural areas of the state attractive to birds, changing cultivation/irrigation practices (e.g. conversion of alfalfa fields to row crops) could have dramatic effects on the birds using the habitat (e.g. Mountain Plover).

Lower Los Angeles River
Los Angeles

Nearest town(s): Long Beach, Compton, Paramount
Size: <1000 acres
Sensitive species: 1 (Loggerhead Shrike) (D. Cooper, *unpubl. data*)
Threat: Medium
Local Audubon Chapter: El Dorado
BCR: 32

IBA Criteria		Source/Notes
S	>10,000 Shorebirds	D. Cooper, *unpubl. data*

Description: A truly unique (yet nearly entirely un-natural) site, this 7-mile stretch of concrete channel along the Los Angeles River through north Long Beach, Compton and Paramount is one of the most important shorebird stopover sites in southern California. During the summer, a thin sheet of treated wastewater forms in the river channel, and becomes rich with algae and micro-invertebrates that attract shorebirds. An asphalt bicycle path runs along the top of the eastern levee providing excellent viewing conditions that apparently do not disturb the shorebirds, which refuel and rest in the shallower bare spots in the concrete. Although this is a totally human-made environment, it has replaced formerly extensive shorebird habitat once present in the vast marshes along the coast of the Los Angeles Basin (e.g. Long Beach/Wilmington). Plans for freshwater marsh and riparian restoration of the settling ponds just outside the banks of the levees (Dept. of Public Works; California Coastal Conservancy) could substantially improve the area's value for native lowland birds species, particularly in winter, when passerines are crowded into any patch of open habitat in the Los Angeles Basin.

Birds: The heat of midsummer coincides with the height of shorebird migration through southern California, and more than two dozen species of sandpipers and plovers have been recorded along this section of the river. Surveys conducted during 1999 and 2000 documented numbers of birds between 8000-15,000 per day between July and October, peaking in August and early September (D. Cooper, *unpubl. data*). A substantial number of shorebirds also winter along the channel (e.g. 2000+ Western Sandpipers in January, 2001, *pers. obs.*) during dry spells (water level rises following even light rains, which temporarily eliminates shorebird habitat). A strong push of waterfowl occurs in fall, with hundreds of ducks, particularly Cinnamon Teal and Northern Pintail, feeding near the Willow St. over-crossing. Peregrine Falcon and White-tailed Kite forage here year round, and a remnant population of Common Ground-Dove persists in the older sections of Long Beach alongside the river.

Conservation issues: Recent deaths (2001) of Black-necked Stilts and Mallards (*pers. obs.*) suggest that avian botulism could be a problem at this site, and more research is needed. Ironically, periodic vegetation clearing (scraping the concrete bottom of the channel) is apparently necessary to maintain the attractiveness of this particular stretch of the river to migrant shorebirds. Of course, this is a unique situation limited to this section, and the rest of the river, particularly the soft-bottomed sections to the south, see their riparian resources seriously degraded by vegetation removal.

Important Bird Areas of California

McCloud River - Upper

Siskiyou

Nearest town(s): McCloud
Size: 1000-10,000 acres
Sensitive species: 7 (Northern Goshawk, California Spotted Owl, Vaux's Swift, Willow Flycatcher, California Swainson's Thrush, Yellow Warbler, Yellow-breasted Chat) (*fide* J. Mariani)
Threat: Low
Local Audubon Chapter: Mt. Shasta
BCR: 5

	IBA Criteria	Source/Notes
P	>10% CA breeding population of Willow Flycatcher	72 birds in 1997; California PIF 2001

This recently "discovered" birding area is just southeast of Mt. Shasta, only about 20 minutes off I-5. Situated at just 3,200 feet elevation, it nonetheless supports a representative Cascade bird community that is extremely rich in breeding species diversity. The extensive boggy riparian habitat of 800-acre Bigelow Meadow across the river from the Fowlers campground supports large thickets of willows. This area is largely public land (USFS) with some private in-holdings. This IBA is notable for a large population of breeding Willow Flycatchers that may represent about ¼ of the state's nesting population of the brewsteri (Sierra-Cascades breeding) race. Strong populations of other riparian and wet meadow species include Calliope Hummingbird, Swainson's Thrush and American Dipper are also found here (J. Mariani, *via email*). This site is well-protected within Shasta-Trinity National Forest. Grazing was eliminated in the late 1980s, and the riparian habitat is recovering very well (D. Derby, *pers. comm.*).

Mendocino Coast
Mendocino

Nearest town(s): Fort Bragg
Size: 10,000 - 50,000 acres
Threat: Medium
Local Audubon Chapter: Mendocino Coast
BCR: 5

IBA Criteria		Source/Notes
L	12 sensitive species: Ashy Storm-Petrel, Northern Harrier, Ferruginous Hawk, Western Snowy Plover, Tufted Puffin, Burrowing Owl, Northern Spotted Owl, Vaux's Swift, Purple Martin, California Swainson's Thrush, Bryant's Savannah Sparrow, Grasshopper Sparrow	D. Tobkin, *in litt.*

Description: This IBA refers to several distinct habitats along a 20-mile stretch of coast from the mouth of Ten Mile River south through Ft. Bragg to the "Mendocino Headlands." Its diverse natural communities include extensive grassland, pockets of coniferous forest, riparian corridors, freshwater wetlands and small brackish lagoons at creek mouths. A patchwork of state lands and private ranches, major protected areas within this IBA include (north to south) MacKerricher State Park, Caspar Headlands State Reserve/Caspar State Beach, Russian Gulch State Park, Mendocino Headlands State Park and Van Damme State Park. Key bird habitats include the broad, sandy beach of MacKerricher State Park (very rare on the north coast); the grasslands between here and Bald Hill (just inland of Hwy. 1); Lake Cleone, a coastal freshwater lake; Glass Beach in Fort Bragg; the estuary at the mouth of Big Creek; and grasslands in the Mendocino Headlands area. Significant seabird breeding areas include Goat Island, just offshore of the town of Mendocino, and rocks within Van Damme Cove, just to the south.

Birds: Snowy Plover maintains a tiny breeding population (up to 5 pr.) at MacKerricher State Park, one of just a handful of sites in northwestern California, with about 40 birds typically found in winter here. The grasslands within this IBA, particularly those between MacKerricher and Bald Hill, support wintering Tricolored Blackbirds, a diverse raptor community including wintering Ferruginous Hawk and (at least formerly) Burrowing Owl, as well as breeding harrier. Grasshopper Sparrow is known to nest in the hills on the north side of Ten Mile River, and may be more widespread, particularly after wet winters. Other localized nesters include a handful of Purple Martins nesting in drain-holes under Hwy. 1 bridges over Ten Mile River, Big River, and in snags along Caspar Creek. Goat Island is known to support 1000+ breeding Brandt's Cormorant, as well as small numbers of Rhinoceros Auklet and Tufted Puffin, and Van Damme Cove may have the farthest-north known nesting Ashy Storm-Petrels in the world (Carter *et al.* 1992).

Conservation issues: Though the lands within this IBA are reasonably secure from development, human disturbance remains a concern, particularly for breeding Snowy Plovers and nesting seabirds (especially Van Damme Cove Rocks, *fide* Carter *et al.* 1992). Although the plover nesting area at MacKerricher has been fenced, it is not regularly patrolled, and in 2000, the single nest on the site was apparently abandoned due to human disturbance (K. Carter, *in litt.*). Proposals to construct a "hiking/biking/tram" trail through the foredunes the length of Ten Mile Beach (*fide* K. Carter) are also troubling. Glass Beach and the Big Creek drainage are being investigated by the Coastal Conservancy and California State Parks, respectively, for acquisition as conservation areas, an encouraging development (*fide* D. Tobkin).

Mendocino Coast IBA

Mendota Wildlife Area

Fresno

Nearest town(s): Mendota, Firebaugh
Size: 10,000 - 50,000 acres
Threat: High
Local Audubon Chapter: Fresno
BCR: 32

IBA Criteria		Source/Notes
P	>1% Global population of Tricolored Blackbird	7000 birds in late May, 2001; S. Breuggemann, *pers. comm.*
P	>10% CA population of White-faced Ibis	25,000 birds estimated in 2001, S. Breuggemann, *pers. comm.*
L	12 sensitive species: White-faced Ibis, Redhead, Northern Harrier, Swainson's Hawk, Ferruginous Hawk, Sandhill Crane, Long-billed Curlew, Burrowing Owl, Short-eared Owl, Loggerhead Shrike, Tricolored Blackbird, Yellow-headed Blackbird	R. Allen, *via email*
S	Probably >10,000 Shorebirds	S. Breuggemann, *pers. comm.*
W	>5000 Waterfowl	18,325 waterfowl on 15 January, 2003; USFWS 2003b

Description: Located at the historical confluence of the San Joaquin and the Kings rivers, this IBA includes the 12,425-acre Wildlife Area as well as the Producer's Dairy, which covers almost as large an area immediately north of the refuge. Primarily managed for winter waterfowl, Mendota is characterized by large, marshy impoundments with 3000 acres of agricultural lands planted in silage for cattle (esp. Trefoil). Small riparian restoration projects have been attempted that involve setting back levees, but the aridity of the environment and the high cost of water has hampered these efforts (B. Huddleston, *pers. comm.*). Due to diversions of the San Joaquin before it reaches Mendota, all of the water on the refuge is piped down from the Sacramento Valley. Still, a modest amount of riparian vegetation has developed along Fresno Slough in what is referred to as the Mendota Pools, and a narrow band of riparian woodland persists within levees along the San Joaquin River to the north (now pumped dry except during wet winters). Unfortunately, the riparian habitat along the San Joaquin has been routinely cleared for flood control and only scattered large trees remain (TNC 1998).

Birds: Though the avifauna at Mendota is poorly-known within California birding circles, it is one of the key sites for birds in the San Joaquin Valley, and the only significant natural habitat within a vast industrial-agricultural landscape (mainly cotton) between the Grasslands Ecological Area and the Tulare Lake Bed, over 50 miles to the south. Mendota has emerged as hosting the largest nesting aggregation of White-faced Ibis in the state (over 2000 pr. in the late 1990s, Ivey *et al.* 2002), with an estimated 7000

Important Bird Areas of California

birds observed in late May 2001. These birds leave the refuge in the morning to feed in pastures of the adjacent Producer's Dairy, returning at dusk. Tricolored Blackbirds have bred in extremely large numbers at the dairy (25,000 birds estimated in 2001), as previous colonies within the wildlife area were predated upon by another colonial breeder, Black-crowned Night-Heron. Unfortunately, fledging typically coincides with the harvesting of the silage at the dairy with disastrous results to the grassland bird community outside the refuge. Winter and spring shorebird use is high, with over 10,000 birds present on peak spring days (DS). Because some water is available during the summer, the wetlands on the refuge are also utilized by breeding Northern Harrier, and both Black and Forster's terns have summered and may eventually breed (S. Brueggeman, *pers. comm.*). During the late fall, water spread on the refuge attracts up to 200,000 ducks and geese, as well as hundreds of Sandhill Crane that later move north to spend the rest of the winter after the water levels are lowered. In spring, thousands of shorebirds utilize the mudflats left behind in the draining impoundments. Riparian species such as White-tailed Kite and Blue Grosbeak, essentially eliminated from most of the farmed San Joaquin Valley floor, maintain sizable populations here, particularly at the Mendota Pools.

Conservation issues: Because the refuge devotes its scarce water allotments to providing wintering habitat for waterfowl (duck-hunting essentially supports this refuge), other groups of birds, particularly riparian obligates, make do with only limited habitat and attention. Efforts to allow some riparian vegetation along the San Joaquin River could be explored, as could cooperative agreements with neighboring landowners (especially Producer's Dairy), as has been done at Grasslands Ecological Area to the north. According to The Nature Conservancy (1998), "excessive grazing" and "widespread use of rodenticides" remain a threat to the habitat here.

Merced Grasslands

Merced/Mariposa/Madera

Nearest town(s): Merced, Madera
Size: 10,000 - 50,000 acres
Threat: Critical
Local Audubon Chapter: Stanislaus, Fresno
BCR: 32

IBA Criteria		Source/Notes
L	12 sensitive species: Northern Harrier, Swainson's Hawk, Ferruginous Hawk, Golden Eagle, Long-billed Curlew, Burrowing Owl, Short-eared Owl, Long-eared Owl, Loggerhead Shrike, Yellow-breasted Chat, Grasshopper Sparrow, Tricolored Blackbird	J. Vollmar, *pers. comm.*

Description: The uncultivated Central Valley floor of eastern Merced Co. protects the largest and most varied complex of vernal pool-rich grassland in California. Following the area's surprisingly recent "discovery" by botanists, several new species of plants and invertebrates have been found here, a few of which occur nowhere else on earth (Holland 2000). This vast, undulating prairie (characterized by mima mounds) then sweeps south along the base of the Sierra foothills, nearly to the San Joaquin River north of Fresno, though its widest portion is currently centered along La Paloma Rd. in eastern Merced Co.

Birds: This region has traditionally been a major wintering area for large concentrations of raptors, most of which do not occur in the wooded areas of the Sierra foothills or in the agricultural lands of the Central Valley Floor. Though quantitative investigations have only begun, species like Short-eared Owl, Rough-legged Hawk, and Golden Eagle occur in as high concentrations as anywhere in the San Joaquin Valley. Also in winter, the grassland is alive with hundreds of Long-billed Curlew and thousands of grassland sparrows, particularly Vesper and Savannah, which occur in large flocks with clouds of Horned Lark (*pers. obs.*). The riparian birds of this IBA, like other San Joaquin Valley sites, are less well known than the raptors, but the areas with the greatest potential include the Merced River bottomland habitat east of Snelling (Merced Co.), Mariposa Ck. along White Rock Rd. (Mariposa Co.), and below the dam spillways of several reservoirs (e.g. Hensley Lake, Madera Co.).

Conservation issues: This IBA includes some of the most intense conservation battlegrounds in the state. Issues include the construction of a new University of California campus northeast of Merced (originally slated directly atop the heart of the vernal pool area but since realigned); ongoing urban sprawl north and east from Madera and Merced that continues to whittle away at the western edge of this IBA (especially along Road 400, Madera Co.); the expansion of orchards eastward from the I-99, proceeding particularly rapidly within Madera Co.; and numerous proposals to channelize and dam streams in the area for "flood control" (and eventually for agricultural and urban development). Grazing practices throughout this IBA are highly variable and doubtless greatly affect bird diversity of abundance. For example, in mid-February, 2001, when the area should be its greenest, the hills of southwest Mariposa Co. were brownish and seriously overgrazed, in sharp contrast to the verdant mima mounds of nearby Merced Co. (*pers. obs.*). This area has become a high priority for The Nature Conservancy in California, which has been quietly obtaining easements on ranches and riverfront property throughout the IBA (S. Johnson, *pers. comm.*).

Vernal pool northeast of Merced, Merced Grasslands IBA. Note rippled "Mima Mound" topography in background.
(Daniel S. Cooper)

Mission Bay

San Diego

Nearest town(s): San Diego
Size: 1000-10,000 acres
Sensitive species: 9 (Brant, Western Snowy Plover, Light-footed Clapper Rail, Long-billed Curlew, Least Tern, Loggerhead Shrike, Clark's Marsh Wren, Belding's Savannah Sparrow, Large-billed Savannah Sparrow) (San Diego Natural History Museum 2000)
Threat: Low
Local Audubon Chapter: San Diego
BCR: 32

IBA Criteria		Source/Notes
P	>1% Global population of California Least Tern	506 nests in 2002; K. Keane, *unpubl. data*
W	Probably >5000 Waterfowl	J. Martin, *via email*

Description: Mission Bay is a highly-altered estuarine complex within the City of San Diego that is currently developed primarily for aquatic vehicle recreation, with large hotels and vacation homes built atop former saltmarsh. Aside from the open water (which covers 1220 acres of eelgrass), the exposed shoreline of the bay and several scattered sandy and alkali flats (c. 10 acres), the most ecologically valuable habitat, saltmarsh, is restricted to two areas: the 40-acre "Northern Wildlife Reserve" (City of San Diego; University of California Reserve) and the 200-acre wetland that has developed along the soft-bottomed stretch of the San Diego River channel on the south side of Mission Bay.

Birds: Both the Northern Wildlife Reserve and the San Diego River channel support thousands of waterfowl, shorebirds (over 5000 in winter; PRBO, *unpubl. data*), and waders during migration and winter, along with small populations of Belding's Savannah Sparrow and (river channel only) Light-footed Clapper Rail. California Least Tern has begun nesting on specially-constructed sandbars and alkali flats around the Bay, and now represent one of the largest colonies in the world (506 nests in 2002, K. Keane, *unpubl. data*) and Brant appear in small numbers in winter and spring, feeding on eelgrass beds as on nearby San Diego Bay.

Conservation issues: Virtually all of the available open space in and around Mission Bay is addressed in the 1994 Mission Bay Park Master Plan (*fide* J. Martin), which lays out guidelines for restoration and enhancement of remaining and potential saltmarsh and wetland habitat. Though the tiny reserves of Mission Bay and the flood control channel are secure from development, direct human disturbance remains a constant threat, particularly near the mouth of the channel, which has been designated an official off-leash dog area by San Diego Dept. of Parks and Recreation. This often results in harassment to roosting birds (often encouraged by dog owners), especially to several dozen Snowy Plover that roost principally on dry sand during fall and winter. Nightly fireworks displays during the summer from neighboring Sea World (a large amusement park) represent another potential source of disturbance (J. Martin, USFWS, *via email*).

Modoc NWR

Modo

Nearest town(s): Alturas
Size: 1000-10,000 acres
Threat: Medium
Local Audubon Chapter: Eagle Lake
BCR: 9

IBA Criteria		Source/Notes
P	>10% CA breeding population of Greater Sandhill Crane	Ivey and Herzinger 2001
L	12 sensitive species: Least Bittern, Redhead, Northern Harrier, Ferruginous Hawk, Sandhill Crane, Long-billed Curlew, Short-eared Owl, Long-eared Owl, Bank Swallow, Yellow Warbler, Tricolored Blackbird, Yellow-headed Blackbird	P. Walcott, *in litt.*
W	>5000 Waterfowl	16,416 waterfowl on 11 March 2003; Modoc NWR 2003

Modoc NWR, located just south of the town of Alturas, protects 7000 acres of marsh, wet meadow and grassland/sagebrush habitat along the upper Pit River. This IBA has consistently supported some of the highest numbers of breeding Sandhill Cranes in California, along with Big Valley/Ash Creek and Surprise Valley (Littlefield 1995, Ivey and Herzinger 2001). Recently, small numbers of Least Bittern have been found summering here, a species otherwise virtually unknown in northeastern California (JS). White-faced Ibis bred in 1989 and not since (*fide* G. Ivey), although recolonization is conceivable. A large area of rice cultivation just to the south of the refuge along Hwy. 395 (the "Lyneta Ranch") has held several thousand migrating shorebirds per day, particularly in spring (Shuford *et al.* 2002). Like many refuges, obtaining sufficient water for the wetlands is cited most frequently among threats to birds, particularly during spring and summer when demands from agriculture are highest.

Modoc Plateau
Modoc

Nearest town(s): Alturas
Size: >50,000 acres
Threat: Low
Local Audubon Chapter: Eagle Lake
BCR: 9

IBA Criteria		Source/Notes
P	>10% of CA population of Greater Sandhill Crane	Ivey and Herzinger 2001
P	>10% of CA population of Black Tern	Shuford 1998
L	14 sensitive species: Redhead, Bald Eagle, Northern Harrier, Northern Goshawk, Golden Eagle, Peregrine Falcon, Prairie Falcon, Greater Sage-Grouse, Sandhill Crane, Long-billed Curlew, Black Tern, Loggerhead Shrike, Purple Martin, Yellow-headed Blackbird	J. Sterling and D. Shuford, *pers. comm.*
W	Probably >5000 Waterfowl	J. Sterling and D. Shuford, *pers. comm.*

Description: This IBA encompasses the dozens of marshy reservoirs that dot the Modoc Plateau, a high, forested steppe in extreme northeastern California. Its rough boundaries would extend from Clear Lake east to Goose Lake, south to Alturas, and thence west to vic. White Horse on the Siskiyou/Modoc Co. line. Though many of the wetlands are somewhat artificial, being dammed streams constructed in the early 1900s to provide additional water for cattle and to improve waterfowl hunting, they have offset aspects of the destruction of natural wetlands for agriculture elsewhere in northeastern California (especially the Klamath Basin). These wetlands freeze up in mid-winter and burst into life in summer, and occur in a mosaic with extensive grassland, sagebrush flats and large tracts of coniferous forest in this wild and virtually unpopulated corner of the state. Public lands dominate, with most of the Modoc Plateau managed as Modoc National Forest. Some of the more important breeding areas for wetland birds on the plateau include Big Sage Reservoir, Taylor Creek wetlands and Egg Lake.

Birds: The wetlands of the Modoc Plateau boast the highest diversity of breeding waterfowl in the state, and if Common Loon were to be rediscovered breeding in California, the Modoc Plateau might be the most likely area. The network of small, marsh-edged ponds are productive for some of the largest concentrations of breeding Black Tern in the state (e.g. Boles Meadow, Widow Valley; Shuford *et al.* 2001), and support major state populations of Bufflehead, Sandhill Crane and Forster's Tern. Big Sage Reservoir was identified as having California's largest breeding colony of Ring-billed Gull in recent surveys (Shuford and Ryan 2000). The sagebrush scrub between Clear Lake and Big Sage Lake has been one of the last Greater Sage-Grouse strongholds (hundreds of birds) in the state, but even this population is apparently down to just a single lek (DS). The coniferous woods are distinctly northern, with Black-backed Woodpecker and Gray Jay nesting, but also contain Great Basin elements such as Juniper Titmouse.

Conservation issues: Nearly all the land within this IBA falls under management of the Devil's Garden Ranger District of Modoc National Forest. Owing to its remoteness, it is very lightly-used and considered secure at this time.

Prairie Falcon (Peter LaTourrette)

Mojave River
San Bernardino

Nearest town(s): Victorville
Size: 1000-10,000 acres
Threat: Critical
Local Audubon Chapter: San Bernardino Valley
BCR: 33

	IBA Criteria	Source/Notes
P	>10% CA population of Summer Tanager	12 pr.; S. Myers, *pers. comm.*
L	14 sensitive species: Ferruginous Hawk, Burrowing Owl, Long-eared Owl, Vermilion Flycatcher, Loggerhead Shrike, Least Bell's Vireo, Bendire's Thrasher, Le Conte's Thrasher, Lucy's Warbler, Yellow Warbler, Yellow-breasted Chat, Summer Tanager, Tricolored Blackbird, Yellow-headed Blackbird	S. Myers, *pers. comm.*

Description: The Mojave is one of the major rivers in southern California, though very few people are even aware of its existence. Prior to the uplift of the Transverse Ranges (i.e. San Bernardino Mtns.), it flowed south into the Los Angeles Basin to the Pacific, but over the past few million years it has instead watered one of the most arid portions of the Mojave Desert. Today, its origins are the rushing brooks of the northern San Bernardino Mtns., which converge and are alternately above or below ground north past Barstow and east to Baker, where the river disappears permanently beneath the sand. Along its middle length, from Victorville north to Helendale, the riparian vegetation along the river reaches its apex, supporting a wide band of bottomland Fremont Cottonwood-willow woodland for about 15 miles. It is surrounded on the west by bluffs and arid desert, and on the east by agricultural land (alfalfa, cattle). Aside from an exceptionally rich few hundred acres within Mojave Narrows Regional Park in Victorville, the river and its habitat is in private ownership, subject to the whims of ranchers and the San Bernardino County Flood Control District, both of which regularly bulldoze and alter large stretches of the floodplain. Still, the lowland riparian habitat here is some of the finest in southern California. Another important area of the highway lies well downstream, about 20 miles east of Barstow. Here, Camp Cady Wildlife Area (DFG) protects about 1500 acres of riparian woodland, accessible off Harvard Rd.

Birds: Located about halfway between the lower Colorado River and the southern Sierras, the middle stretch of the Mojave has probably always provided a vital link for migratory birds moving north out of Mexico. Today, it is notable for hosting one of the largest populations of Brown-crested Flycatchers in the state (at least 10 pairs along the Victorville – Helendale stretch alone), as well as at least a dozen pairs of Summer Tanagers, second only to the Kern River Preserve. From long-term banding and mid-summer surveys (S. Meyers, *unpubl. data*), several pairs of Bell's Vireo, probably of the "Least" race, has recently been found summering near Victorville, and the river remains one of the westernmost nesting sites for Vermilion Flycatcher in the U.S. The habitat north of Victorville, if managed properly, could support several pairs of Yellow-billed Cuckoo, for which there are only scattered records. Tricolored Blackbird maintains one of its rare desert breeding areas near Camp Cady.

Conservation issues: The unprotected section of the Mojave, from Victorville to Helendale, is a river that has been pushed to the brink – but it's not too late. Once flowing across a broad floodplain, the water has recently been channelized using earthen levees that artificially speed its flow and may be contributing to the slow death of the riparian woodland outside the levee walls. Large areas are apparently being logged by current managers, possibly for misguided flood control purposes (*pers. obs.*). Unauthorized OHV use is common here, and probably contributes to frequent fires in the riparian woodland. Still, enough side channels and old oxbows remain mesic enough to support tall, shady riparian forest with almost entirely native understory that even includes abundant native wildflowers such as Indian Paintbrush. A concerted effort to acquire and manage river-bottom land (e.g. with levee setbacks and possibly riparian plantings) and offer conservation easements/incentives to local landowners, similar to that undertaken along the South Fork Kern River, is necessary for saving this fascinating and intact system.

The Mojave River at Mojave Narrows (Steven Myers)

Mono Highlands
Mono

Nearest town(s): Lee Vining, Bridgeport
Size: >50,000 acres
Sensitive species: 8 (Greater Sage-Grouse, Northern Harrier, Northern Goshawk, Golden Eagle, Prairie Falcon, Long-eared Owl, Loggerhead Shrike, Yellow Warbler) (F. Fatooh, *via email*)
Threat: Medium
Local Audubon Chapter: Eastern Sierra
BCR: 9

IBA Criteria		Source/Notes
P	>1% Global population of Greater Sage-Grouse	c. 150 birds, *fide* S. Blankenship

Description: This IBA encompasses two ranges near the Nevada border in Mono County, the Bodie Hills in the north and Glass Mountain in the south. The Bodie Hills form a vast area of rolling, high-elevation (>8000') sagebrush tracts and stringers of riparian woodland extending from the Mono Lake Basin north to the Bridgeport Valley. The famous ghost town of Bodie, now a State Historic Park, lies near the center of hills that are otherwise undeveloped, with few roads. Glass Mountain separates Adobe Valley from the Crowley Lake area to the south, and also features extensive tracts of sagebrush, along with mixed conifer forest (Jeffrey Pine with Lodgepole Pine at highest elevations) isolated from that of the Sierra Nevada. The Glass Mountain area was the subject of an intensive breeding bird atlas effort (Shuford *et al.* 2002).

Birds: This IBA is notable for its large population of Greater Sage-Grouse, part of the Mono County metapopulations that appear to be genetically distinct from other groups in the Great Basin (J. Fatooh, *pers. comm.*). The sagebrush habitat within the Bodie Hills seems especially lush and intact in contrast to other tracts in the region that have been burned, over-grazed, or otherwise impacted by human activity (e.g. Long Valley). Vesper Sparrows breed in abundance, as do White-crowned Sparrows, occurring in isolated population islands (*fide* E. Strauss). Glass Mountain supports some of the highest densities of nesting Long-eared Owl in the state, as well as an unusual, high-elevation nesting population of Northern Harrier (DS). Songbirds are concentrated in riparian thickets, which are filled with fruiting currants (Ribes spp.) in fall that attract large numbers of migrant songbirds.

Conservation issues: The BLM has managed to reduce grazing pressure in key areas within the Bodie Hills, and fended off a proposal from gold mining (J. Fatooh, *pers. comm.*). The Glass Mountain area is fairly remote and lightly used, and reasonably well managed by the USFS.

Important Bird Areas of California

Mono Lake Basin

Mono

Nearest town(s): Lee Vining
Size: >50,000 acres
Threat: Medium
Local Audubon Chapter: Eastern Sierra
BCR: 9

IBA Criteria		Source/Notes
P	>10% CA population of interior-breeding Western Snowy Plover	119 in May 2001; Abbott and Ruhlen, *in litt.*
L	11 sensitive species: Redhead, Northern Harrier, Northern Goshawk, Golden Eagle, Prairie Falcon, Greater Sage-Grouse, Western Snowy Plover, Willow Flycatcher, Loggerhead Shrike, Yellow Warbler, Yellow-headed Blackbird	Gaines 1988
S	>10,000 Shorebirds	Max. c. 50,000 in spring, 25,000 in fall; Shuford *et al.* 2002
W	>5000 Waterfowl	Up to 1 million Eared Grebes; Gaines 1988; 11,000 – 15,000 ducks each fall; California State Water Resources Control Board 1994

Description: Internationally famous Mono Lake lies on the boundary between the Great Basin and the Sierra Nevada, which rises 6,000 feet above the lake's surface to the west. Hundreds of thousands of years of evaporation have concentrated salts and other minerals within the lake, making it 2 to 3 times as salty as the ocean. Algae in its water supports brine shrimp in the trillions as well as alkali flies that carpet the shore. This simple ecosystem feeds millions of migratory birds each year, which also utilize the marsh and alkali meadows that ring the lake. Upslope, the basin is dominated by sagebrush steppe, with pinyon-juniper forests on the higher elevations. To the south lies a vast Jeffrey pine forest, with mountain mahogany *(Cercocarpus)* on the sun-baked ridges. The lake's tributary streams, in the process of being restored, will support cottonwood-willow riparian forests with dense understory and wet meadows. Also dotting the Mono Basin are irrigated pasture and a few freshwater ponds created to provide waterfowl habitat.

The Mono Basin is one of the most intensively studied natural areas in California, beginning with the pioneering birding and conservation work of David Gaines and David Winkler in the 1970s, and continuing to the present with biologists from PRBO. Litigation by Audubon resulted in the California Supreme Court's 1983 "Public Trust decision", which reaffirmed the state's duty to balance the public trust with water allocations and thereby protect the common natural heritage of Californians. In 1994, the State Water Resources Control Board amended the licenses for water diversions of the Los Angeles Dept. of Water and Power, setting a minimum level for the lake high above the then-current level, thereby "saving" Mono Lake. Most of the land in the Mono Basin is managed by the USFS, the State

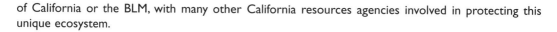

of California or the BLM, with many other California resources agencies involved in protecting this unique ecosystem.

Birds: Islands within Mono Lake support 70-80% of California's nesting population of California Gull (20,000+ pr.), the second-largest rookery in the world after Utah's Great Salt Lake (Shuford and Ryan 2000). These gulls are joined by Caspian Tern and Snowy Plover, the latter historically maintaining one of its largest California breeding areas (Page *et al.* 1991). In summer, over a hundred thousand phalaropes (Wilson's and Red-necked) descend upon Mono Lake, where they complete their molt before continuing on to wintering grounds in South America. Mono Lake is one of the key interior shorebird sites in the state. Over 20,000 Least and Western sandpipers have been recorded on single-day surveys in spring and fall counts of American Avocet have exceeded 10,000 (Shuford *et al.* 2002). After the fall passage of shorebirds, the migration of Eared Grebe through eastern California surges, with up to a million birds recorded on the lake in recent years (the primary fall staging site in the world). Many of these grebes winter at the Salton Sea and in the Gulf of California. Willow Flycatchers, extremely local in the Sierra Nevada and eastern California, have been discovered breeding in the streams on the west side of the basin along Rush Ck. (S. Heath, PRBO, *pers. comm.*), and Virginia's Warbler, even more localized in California, maintains small breeding groups on ridges (M. Green, *pers. comm.*). From research conducted by PRBO, the creeks within the basin (e.g. Lee Vining Creek) support the highest indices of breeding songbird diversity and species richness of 33 creeks surveyed in the eastern Sierra Nevada (*Ibid*). The basin lies between two major populations of Greater Sage-Grouse (Bodie Hills and Long Valley), and small numbers have been observed in lush stands of sagebrush (most recently discovered breeding along Walker Creek, *fide* T. Floyd). Yellow Rail historically bred in the wet meadows of Mono County (Grinnell and Miller 1944), and the only recent summer record for California (1985) is from the marsh at Mono Lake Co. Park (Gaines 1988).

Conservation issues: The 1994 decision by the State Water Board set a target elevation for the water level of Mono Lake by establishing required minimum and peak stream flows into the lake, and called for specific restoration activities. Still, water continues to be diverted (with associated alteration of flows), which inhibits the full development of riparian and wetland habitat. Though banned from most riparian areas, grazing continues to degrade meadows and riparian systems in the basin (*fide* S. Heath, PRBO. Increased recreation at the lake has the potential to impact birds that are resting and feeding, particularly during migration, and development proposals, if implemented, would impact sagebrush and meadow habitat within the basin (L. Cutting, *in litt.*).

Morro Bay

San Luis Obispo

Nearest town(s): Morro Bay, Baywood Park, Los Osos
Size: 10,000 - 50,000 acres
Threat: Medium
Local Audubon Chapter: Morro Coast
BCR: 32

IBA Criteria		Source/Notes
P	>1% Global population of Pacific Black Brant	3391 on 2001 Morro Bay CBC
P	>1% Global population of Long-billed Curlew	681 on 1997 Morro Bay CBC
L	13 Sensitive species: Brant, Ferruginous Hawk, Golden Eagle, Peregrine Falcon, Black Rail, Short-eared Owl, Western Snowy Plover, Long-billed Curlew, California Swainson's Thrush, Sage Sparrow, Bryant's Savannah Sparrow, Large-billed Savannah Sparrow, Grasshopper Sparrow	T. Edell, S. Schubert, *pers. comm.*
S	>10,000 Shorebirds	Up to 20,000 in winter; PRBO, *unpubl. data*
W	>5000 Waterfowl	8000+ waterfowl on 2001 Morro Bay CBC

Description: Aside from some shoreline modification associated with marinas and fill in the communities of Morro Bay and Baywood Park, much of this IBA has remained strikingly unaltered from original conditions, especially compared with other wetlands south of the San Francisco Bay Area. The habitat of may be divided into four main units. Dominating the landscape is the vast, shallow open water of the bay, which is tidally drained. The highly productive saltmarsh of this IBA is restricted to the east and southeast sides of the bay, most extensive along South Bay Blvd. near the community of Baywood Park. Small patches of woodland (both oak and riparian) may be found associated with creeks on the eastern edge of the bay, notably within Morro Bay State Park and the remarkable dwarf Coast Live Oak woodland of Elfin Forest (San Luis Obispo Co. Parks). The western and southwestern edge of the bay, inaccessible by land, is dominated by dune habitats, with their own distinct avifauna, protected as Morro Dunes Natural Preserve (DFG).

Birds: Morro Bay is one of the most important waterbird stopover and wintering locations in California south of San Francisco Bay with up to 20,000 shorebirds spending the winter on its tidally-exposed mudflats. The concentration of migrant and wintering Brant is one of the highest in the state, exceeding 4000 birds during the winter of 2000-01 (J. Roser, via email). Many of the thousands of waterfowl and shorebirds that forage on the waters of the bay (e.g. over 2000 Marbled Godwit and c. 500 Long-billed Curlew regularly winter) roost in the upland habitat at the bay's edge, including the long sand spit on the west side. This IBA also supports a large aggregation of nesting Snowy Plover on the ocean side of the sand spit (126 birds in summer 1989, USFWS 2001). Though California Clapper Rail was last seen in 1973, a small population of Black Rail persisting in the tidal marsh here is one of only three south of the San Francisco Bay Area (desert populations in the Imperial Valley and the Colorado River Valley being the other two). Many species of raptors, including Short-eared Owl and Northern Harrier, winter on the dry portions of the marsh and adjacent grassland. Two areas seem particularly critical for migrant passerines: the willow thickets along Pecho Rd. in Los Osos and the Elfin Forest at Baywood Park. The only major heron rookery on the bay is located in a eucalyptus grove at Fairbanks Point within Morro Bay State Park. Morro Rock, located at the north end of the bay, continues to support a nesting pair (exceptionally two, as in 2001) of Peregrine Falcon. Bell's Sage Sparrow has been resident, at least formerly, in dune scrub on aeolian sand deposits near "Shark's Inlet" at the extreme southern end of the bay in Los Osos, further south on the dunes into Montana De Oro State Park (S. Schubert, via email), and in shrub vegetation on a hillside known as Bayview Heights above the town of Los Osos.

Conservation issues: The natural resources of Morro Bay have long been recognized by government agencies and non-profit organizations, and this IBA enjoys some of the most intensive conservation attention of any site in the state. The fact that residential and commercial development is continuing throughout the relatively small Morro Bay watershed necessitates the assignment of a "Medium" conservation threat – large areas are protected, but the entire area will continue to be subject to encroachment and its associated threats (exotic species, human disturbance) for the foreseeable future.

Pacific Black Brant (Peter LaTourrette)

Napa Lakes

Napa

Nearest town(s): "Napa Valley"
Size: >50,000 acres
Threat: Low
Local Audubon Chapter: Napa-Solano
BCR: 32

	IBA Criteria	Source/Notes
L	11 sensitive species: Bald Eagle, Northern Harrier, Golden Eagle, Peregrine Falcon, Prairie Falcon, Burrowing Owl, Long-eared Owl, Loggerhead Shrike, Yellow Warbler, Sage Sparrow, Tricolored Blackbird	M. Barson, S. Dearn-Tarpley, *in litt.*; R. Leong, *pers. comm.*

Description: This IBA refers to a biologically diverse area of ridges and valleys at the southern end of the northern Coast Range, mid-way between Napa Valley and the Sacramento Valley. Typically "Californian", this rugged country of oak and mixed-conifer woodland, broken by grassland, chaparral, and rocky outcrops, is dominated by giant Lake Berryessa (13,000 acres), a reservoir formed by a dam on Putah Creek. Smaller Lake Hennessey (850 acres) to the west, managed by the City of Napa for water supply, has similar habitat, though on a smaller scale. Berryessa is managed by the federal government (Bureau of Reclamation, BLM) within an area designated the Berryessa Blue Ridge Natural Area, though the surrounding hills are actually mosaic of state, federal and private lands, including several jointly-managed conservation reserves (e.g. Quail Ridge Reserve on the south shore of the lake).

Birds: Owing partially to the inaccessibility of much of this IBA, its avifauna is notable for the abundance and diversity of nesting raptors, which includes c. 10 pr. Osprey and 3 pr. Bald Eagle between Berryessa and Hennessey. Golden Eagle and both Peregrine and Prairie falcons breed in the rock outcrops of Blue Ridge, just east of Lake Berryessa, and forage widely. Grazing was recently eliminated from the draw-down area on the eastern shore of the lake, which has allowed a lush grassland to develop, ideal for breeding Northern Harrier. Napa-Solano Audubon is currently monitoring its progress. Other scarce open country birds increasingly rare in the region include Burrowing Owl (winter only) and Loggerhead Shrike. Both lakes support small Great Blue Heron rookeries (<15 nests, RL). Berryessa supported Purple Martin until their nest trees, snags in a flooded riparian area of the lake, eventually rotted and fell (RL).

Conservation issues: Long the focus of conservation attention and extremely unsuitable for residential development, much of this IBA is considered well protected. However, persistent issues include localized human disturbance of nesting raptors, particularly around areas with high visitation (e.g. Lake Berryessa).

North Mojave Dry Lakes

Kern/San Bernardino

Nearest town(s): Ridgecrest, Barstow
Size: 10,000 - 50,000 acres
Threat: High
Local Audubon Chapter: Kerncrest, San Bernardino Valley
BCR: 33

IBA Criteria		Source/Notes
L	10 sensitive species: Northern Harrier, Ferruginous Hawk, Redhead, Western Snowy Plover, Burrowing Owl, Short-eared Owl, Long-eared Owl, Loggerhead Shrike, Tricolored Blackbird, Yellow-headed Blackbird	S. Myers, *pers. comm.*
W	>5000 Waterfowl	5047 waterfowl on 2000 China Lake CBC

Description: This IBA refers to four large dry lakes and associated seasonal wetlands between Ridgecrest and Barstow in the northern Mojave Desert: China Lake, Searles Dry Lake, Koehn Dry Lake, and Harper Dry Lake. At China Lake, located within the sprawling China Lake Naval Weapons Center just north of Ridgecrest, most of the birds are associated with several large ponds fed by a wastewater treatment plant. Searles Dry Lake, about 20 miles east near Trona, and Koehn Dry Lake, between here and the town of Mojave, feature several spring-fed wetlands that expand after wet winters, producing lush alkali meadows and vast mudflats. Harper Dry Lake, northwest of Barstow, used to be among the most productive wetlands in the Mojave, but recent (1990s) lowering of the water table for agriculture has all but ruined habitat value there. Other dry lakes in the north Mojave, including Superior (north of Barstow) and Cronese (southwest of Baker) could also be included in this IBA, but their current resources are poorly known at this time.

Birds: Avian use of these wetlands is complex and highly variable depending on rainfall. Due to the inaccessibility of large areas of habitat (e.g. marshy borders of lakes prohibit travel), much remains to be learned. This IBA is most quiet in winter, when bird activity is confined to the constructed wetlands at China Lake, which support several hundred waterfowl (e.g. 2500 Snow Geese on 2000 China Lake CBC). Beginning in late March, a build-up of migrant waterfowl and shorebirds begins, which can bring thousands of waterbirds into the lakes, notably Eared Grebe, American White Pelican, White-faced Ibis, Cinnamon Teal, along with hundreds of Wilson's and Red-necked Phalaropes. Several species of waterfowl, including Green-winged Teal and Northern Pintail, remain to breed in the wetlands, as do marsh raptors such as Northern Harrier and Short-eared Owl, both probably regular nesters at least at Koehn Dry Lake. Koehn also supports one of the few desert-breeding colonies of Tricolored Blackbird, which, along with the raptors, also utilize the alfalfa fields in the area. Snowy Plover has been documented breeding at Harper Dry Lake (61 adults) and Searles Dry Lake (16 adults) in 1978 (Page and Stenzel 1981), and likely still breed, at least at Harper (S. Abbott and T. Ruhlen, *unpubl. data*).

Conservation issues: Naturally-occurring desert wetland habitat is very rare in California, and receives virtually no protection. It is threatened both by lowering of the regional water table in association with agricultural practices, as well as by non-directed recreation such as OHV use. Locally (e.g. Searles Dry Lake), runoff from chemical production supports much of the wetland and wet alkali playa habitat, and the effects of this toxic runoff on the region's avifauna have not been adequately documented. The constructed wetlands at China Lake, while secure for now, could eventually be regarded as a threat to "military preparedness", as has been the case with other wetlands at DoD properties in California (e.g. Edwards AFB; Pt. Mugu NWS).

Giant Marsh as seen from Pt. Pinole, part of "North Richmond Wetlands" IBA
(Alan Harper, Audubon California Board of Directors)

North Richmond Wetlands

Contra Costa

Nearest town(s): Richmond, San Pablo, Pinole
Size: 1000-10,000 acres
Sensitive species: 7 (Northern Harrier, Black Rail, California Clapper Rail, Short-eared Owl, Loggerhead Shrike, Bryant's Savannah Sparrow, San Pablo Song Sparrow) (Glover 2001)
Threat: Critical
Local Audubon Chapter: Golden Gate or Mt. Diablo
BCR: 32

IBA Criteria		Source/Notes
P	>1% Global population of California Clapper Rail	S. Glover, *pers. comm.*
S	>10,000 Shorebirds	L. Stenzel, *via email*
W	Probably >5000 Waterfowl	S. Glover, *pers. comm.*

Description: Located at the north end of the heavily-urbanized East Bay region of the San Francisco Bay Area, this little-known area contains two main protected parcels, both managed by the East Bay Regional Park District: Pt. Pinole Regional Park, which protects over 2000 acres of bluff-top and bay front habitats (including mudflats and tidal marsh), and, just to the south, Wildcat Creek Marsh, where one of the Bay Area's last contiguous stretches of riparian thicket empties into the tidal wetlands of San Pablo Bay. Both sites have been the focus of aggressive habitat restoration work, and are a tremendous natural resource for the surrounding urban neighborhoods.

Birds: The mudflats of San Francisco Bay in this region attract thousands of shorebirds and other waterbirds during migration and winter, and serve as a link between the vast wetlands of the San Pablo Bay to the north and those in south San Francisco Bay. Interestingly, Pt. Pinole seems to attract species otherwise uncommon within San Francisco Bay, including Red Knot (over 1000 counted in a recent spring, L. Stenzel, PRBO, *unpubl. data*). San Francisco Bay, and this IBA in particular, is one of just three areas along the Pacific coast of North America that supports large numbers of Red Knot in winter (Goals Report 1999). This area also supports one of the few nesting pairs of Osprey on San Francisco Bay, and the tidal marshes here still have an intact tidal marsh bird community widely extirpated from the Central San Francisco Bay.

Conservation issues: Though a portion of this area is well protected as regional parkland, large swaths of saltmarsh and grassland habitat are still privately owned and threatened by rapidly-developing Richmond (esp. office parks). There are numerous restoration opportunities for former tidal marsh in the area that could add appreciably to the habitat value of the area (e.g. vic. Richmond Landfill to the south).

North San Diego Lagoons

San Diego

Nearest town(s): Oceanside, Carlsbad, Encinitas, Solana Beach, Del Mar
Size: 1000-10,000 acres
Threat: High
Local Audubon Chapter: Buena Vista
BCR: 32

IBA Criteria		Source/Notes
P	>1% Global population of Light-footed Clapper Rail	12 pr. in 1996; Zembal et al. 1997
P	>1% Global population of California Least Tern	226 nests in 2002; K. Keane, unpubl. data
L	15 sensitive species: Least Bittern, Redhead, Light-footed Clapper Rail, Western Snowy Plover, Long-billed Curlew, Least Tern, Black Skimmer, Loggerhead Shrike, Least Bell's Vireo, Cactus Wren, Clark's Marsh Wren, California Gnatcatcher, Yellow-breasted Chat, Belding's Savannah Sparrow, Large-billed Savannah Sparrow	F. Hall, in litt.; K. Weaver, pers. comm.; San Diego Natural History Museum 2000

Description: Driving between San Diego and Los Angeles along I-5, one passes over a series of small, east-west-trending valleys with natural lagoons where creeks flowing from the east meet the Pacific Ocean. Each lagoon has a slightly different geological setting, and while each originally supported varying amounts of freshwater marsh, saltmarsh, coastal sage scrub, and riparian woodland, a century of use has altered their hydrology and habitats. Like the wetlands along the Orange County coast, this chain of estuaries is linked by foraging and dispersing waterbirds that utilize the IBA for breeding, migration refueling, and wintering. The largest of these lagoons, that at the Santa Margarita River mouth, is treated in the Camp Pendleton/ Santa Margarita River IBA. South of here, the others include:

- San Luis Rey River Estuary (Private)
- Buena Vista Lagoon (DFG)
- Agua Hedionda Lagoon (San Diego Gas and Electric, DFG)
- Batiquitos Lagoon (City of Carlsbad)
- San Elijo Lagoon (DFG; San Diego Co. Parks; Non-profit)
- San Dieguito Lagoon (DFG; San Dieguito River Park JPA; San Diego Co.; City of San Diego; Private)
- Los Penasquitos Lagoon (California State Parks; Private; Non-profit)

The San Luis Rey River Estuary consists of about 200 acres of riparian woodland and wetland (freshwater and saltmarsh) habitat west of I-5, within the City of Oceanside. South of here, the next three lagoons are located within the City of Carlsbad. Buena Vista Lagoon, covering just over 200 acres, lacks an outlet to the sea and is rimmed with freshwater marsh vegetation which, due to the lack of tidal flushing or flooding, has invaded much of the surface area. There is an Audubon Center on the west end of the lagoon, near the Pacific Coast Hwy. over-crossing, and another public access point on the northeast side, along Jefferson. Agua Hedionda Lagoon, heavily used by boaters, is sub-divided into several areas for various types of watercraft recreation, with access from the northern edge of the main lagoon east of I-5. A power plant is located on the southwestern side of the lagoon, and the southeastern edge is still agricultural. Residential development dominates the northern end. About 330 acres of wetland habitat persist here (186 acres of which in a recently-designated Ecological Reserve), mainly at its far eastern end, is off-limits to motorized craft.

On the border between Carlsbad and Encinitas, Batiquitos Lagoon, at 600 acres, is hemmed-in by urbanization on all but a portion of the southern border, which features some coastal sage scrub on steep slopes. The mouth of Batiquitos was not open to the sea throughout most of the 20th Century until the mid-1990s, when the silt dam at its mouth was removed as part of a large restoration project as mitigation for Port of Los Angeles activities in the Long Beach area of Los Angeles Co. This project also involved the construction of islands for breeding terns. There is a small interpretive center here along with a hiking trail along the north side of the lagoon.

San Elijo Lagoon lies between the cities of Encinitas and Solana Beach, and covers approximately 1000 acres, mainly salt marsh and mudflat, with smaller areas of freshwater marsh, riparian scrub, and, on the south side, a few hundred acres of coastal sage scrub and maritime chaparral. The mouth is flushed by heavy storms, and is dredged several times a year to allow seawater to enter. San Dieguito Lagoon supports 260 acres of wetlands and several hundred acres of open agricultural lands within the City of Del Mar. Aside from the northwest side, which is dominated by Del Mar fairgrounds and racetrack, the majority of the valley, particularly that east of I-5, is still largely natural. South of Del Mar, Los Penasquitos Lagoon, within the City of San Diego, supports 385 acres of wetlands, including over 100 acres of alkali flat habitat. A small amount of freshwater marsh and riparian scrub is also present. The slopes surrounding the lagoon support lush coastal sage scrub, maritime chaparral and Torrey Pine Woodland, which is rapidly disappearing outside the boundaries of Torrey Pines State Park, which oversees about half the wetlands.

Birds: All of the lagoons support large numbers of wintering waterfowl (tens of thousands) and waders during migration and winter. Those with exposed mudflat habitat (Batiquitos, San Elijo, San Dieguito, and Los Penasquitos lagoons) provide important shorebird foraging habitat during migration and winter, exceeding 5000 individuals on single-day counts (PRBO, *unpubl. data*). These three also feature the most extensive open land, and predictably support most of the sensitive species within this IBA. The saltmarsh habitat at Los Penasquitos Lagoon supports about 150 pairs of Belding's Savannah Sparrow (the second-largest in San Diego Co., after Tijuana Slough) and 2 pairs of Light-footed Clapper Rail (1997), while that at San Elijo Lagoon supports 40 pairs of Belding's Savannah Sparrow and 4 pairs of Light-footed Clapper Rail (1998) (California DFG 2000). The northernmost lagoons, Buena Vista, Agua Hedionda and Batiquitos, have more limited saltmarsh habitat, with small resident populations of Belding's Savannah Sparrows (e.g. 30 pr. at Batiquitos), and a somewhat reduced freshwater marsh avifauna that includes nesting Least Bittern, Clark's Marsh Wren and several species of breeding waterfowl (including Gadwall and Redhead)

Species dependent upon the sandy or alkali flats of the wetlands continue to be a notable feature of this IBA, especially at Batiquitos Lagoon, which supports a major colony of nesting Least Tern (226 nests in 2002, K. Keane, *unpubl. data*). Forster's Tern, Black Skimmer (30 pr. in 1997) and Snowy Plover (16 pr. in 1997) (F. Hall *in litt.*) also breed here. San Elijo Lagoon also supports breeding Least Tern and Snowy Plovers, and Least Tern has bred at San Dieguito Lagoon. Both Least Tern and Snowy Plover bred at Los Penasquitos until c. 1980, and may do so again given specific habitat management (all survey unless noted otherwise).

Coastal scrub habitat is most extensive at San Elijo Lagoon, which holds 20 pr. of California Gnatcatcher. Batiquitos and Los Penasquitos Lagoon have remnant populations (< 10 pr.) of California Gnatcatcher, but Cactus Wren and other scrub species have been widely extirpated from this IBA, as have sensitive riparian bird species. Currently, the San Luis Rey River mouth and San Elijo Lagoon support the bulk of riparian species within this IBA, with Least Bell's Vireo and Yellow-breasted Chat breeding at the former and Yellow-breasted Chat (2-5 pr.) at the latter (F. Hall, *in litt.*).

Conservation issues: The primary threats to the avifauna of these lagoons has been the sealing-off of the tidal outlets and the concurrent encroachment of urbanization. Exotic plant and animal species continue to pose a serious threat, including Red Fox. The restoration at Batiquitos Lagoon, which involved opening the tidal outlet and re-vegetating the native plant communities, should serve as an example of the possibilities for restoration within this IBA.

Black Skimmer (Peter LaTourrette)

Orange Coast Wetlands

Orange/Los Angeles

Nearest town(s): Long Beach, Seal Beach, Sunset Beach, Huntington Beach, Newport Beach
Size: 1000-10,000 acres
Threat: High
Local Audubon Chapter: Sea and Sage, El Dorado
BCR: 32

	IBA Criteria	Source/Notes
P	>1% of Global population of California Least Tern	Up to 500 pr.; K. Keane, *unpubl. data*
P	>1% of Global population Elegant Tern	4000 pr. at Bolsa Chica in 1997 at Bolsa Chica, C. Boardman, *in litt.*
P	>1% of Global population of Light-footed Clapper Rail	158+ pr. at Upper Newport Bay in 1996, Zembal *et al.* 1997
P	>10% CA breeding population of Royal Tern	15-20 pr. at Bolsa Chica in 1997 Gallagher 1997
P	>10% CA breeding population of Black Skimmer	200+ pr. at Bolsa Chica by mid-1990s; Collins and Garrett 1996
P	>10% CA breeding population of Belding's Savannah Sparrow	498 in IBA in 1991, Gallagher 1997
L	19 sensitive species: Brant, Redhead, Light-footed Clapper Rail, Western Snowy Plover, Mountain Plover, Royal Tern, Elegant Tern, Least Tern, Black Skimmer, Long-billed Curlew, Burrowing Owl, Short-eared Owl, Loggerhead Shrike, Cactus Wren, Clark's Marsh Wren, California Gnatcatcher, Yellow-breasted Chat, Belding's Savannah Sparrow, Large-billed Savannah Sparrow	Hamilton and Willick 1996; Gallagher 1997
S	>10,000 Shorebirds	14,800 birds in winter at Upper Newport Bay alone; PRBO, *unpubl. data*
W	>5000 Waterfowl	c. 10,000 waterfowl (excluding scoters) on 2001 Orange County – Coastal CBC

Description: The north coast of Orange County supports some of the most important remnant wetlands in southern California (each one could be a separate IBA), and has been the site of bird research for several decades. Up until the early 1900s, this area was a vast network of coastal marshes, even supporting a commercial waterfowl hunting industry. Today, this IBA still protects some of southern California's most extensive wetlands. From north to south, they include:

- Los Cerritos Wetlands and adj. oil fields (Private)
- Hellman Property (Private)
- Seal Beach NWR/NWS (U.S. Navy; USFWS)
- Bolsa Chica (Private; State of CA)
- Huntington Beach Wetlands (Private; City of Huntington Beach)

- Santa Ana River mouth (Private, Army Corps. of Engineers)
- Upper Newport Bay (State of CA)

Los Cerritos Wetlands includes a small saltmarsh with natural tidal influence within an active oil field, bounded on the south by Westminster Blvd. South of Westminster, also on active oil fields, is a small freshwater marsh and scattered patches of riparian vegetation. The Hellman Property immediately to the east is another active oil field, this in an extensive area of rolling grassland and scattered water-deprived saltmarsh, with small area of mudflat habitat where a tidal channel invades. Moving east, Seal Beach National Wildlife Refuge (across Seal Beach Blvd.) protects one of the largest intact saltmarshes in southern California (1000 acres) and also features significant areas of grassland and agricultural lands, particularly north of Westminster Blvd. within Seal Beach Naval Weapons Station.

South of here is the Bolsa Chica Ecological Area and the adjacent bluff, mesa, and oil fields, separated by the marina development of Sunset Beach. Several smaller saltmarsh remnants of varying degrees of degradation may be found on the east (inland) side of Pacific Coast Highway (collectively called "Huntington Beach Wetlands"). Just south of these, one of the largest patches of native coastal sage scrub habitat in this IBA persists in open space at the Santa Ana River mouth, also east of PCH, where additional water-deprived saltmarsh persists. Finally, at the southern end is the relatively extensive mudflats and saltmarsh of Upper Newport Bay and adjacent uplands that include pockets of coastal sage scrub and riparian thicket. Most of the grassland and coastal sage scrub habitat once found surrounding the bay has been lost to cliff-top development of Newport Beach since the 1980s.

Birds: This IBA supports some of the largest tern nesting colonies on the Pacific Coast, with Bolsa Chica typically supporting the largest. The wide, sandy beach at adjacent Huntington State Beach supported a majority (316 pr.) of Least Tern in 2002 (K. Keane, *unpubl. data*). Seal Beach NWR also supports breeding Least Tern (ave. 150 pr. from 1986-98, *Ibid*), as does the Bolsa Chica and the Santa Ana River mouth. This IBA also supports around one-eighth of the state's population of Belding's Savannah Sparrow scattered throughout the saltmarshes.

Huge flocks of migrating shorebirds (15-20,000 in fall, winter and spring; PRBO, *unpubl. data*) and waterfowl, wintering geese, and foraging raptors travel freely up and down the coast here, obviating the need to treat these sites as a single unit. Predictably, sensitive wetland species are concentrated in the largest patches of healthy habitat. In 1996, the vast saltmarsh of Upper Newport Bay supported c. 158 pr. of Light-footed Clapper Rail – nearly three-quarters of the U.S. population (Zembal *et al.* 1997). Only about 7 pairs may remain at Seal Beach NWR, down from several dozen in the mid-1990s (J. Bradley, USFWS, *pers. comm.*). Los Cerritos Wetlands in Long Beach is currently a foraging area for locally-breeding the terns, and supports a modest number of Belding's Savannah Sparrow (abundant throughout the IBA in saltmarsh). Its freshwater marshes, if restored, could prove regionally important for breeding waterfowl, Least Bittern, and the endemic Clark's race of Marsh Wren. Snowy Plover maintains tiny breeding colonies in alkali flats at Bolsa Chica and at the Santa Ana River mouth. The remnant coastal sage scrub of Upper Newport Bay and (formerly?) the mouth of the Santa Ana River support the only Cactus Wren and California Gnatcatchers in the IBA.

The extensive grassland and open country of Hellman/Seal Beach, Bolsa Chica, the Santa Ana River mouth and Upper Newport Bay represent a majority of the raptor habitat along the immediate coast of the Los Angeles Basin, with the hawk and owl community of Seal Beach NWS/NWR perhaps the largest and most diverse. Ferruginous Hawk, Prairie Falcon and Short-eared Owl are scarce but regular winter residents, and Burrowing Owl nests in weep holes in weapons storage units (one of two breeding colonies in coastal southern California). The sparse, flat grassland at Seal Beach NWS/NWR is one of just 4 sites in the U.S. that supports wintering Pacific Golden-Plover, and a handful of Mountain Plover has recently rediscovered the site as a wintering area. Hundreds of geese, representing all four regularly-occurring species, winter at Hellman/Seal Beach NWR, the largest concentration in coastal southern California.

Conservation issues: The two main bird conservation battles involve saving precious open space from residential home construction and reducing the threat of exotic or pest species that threaten nesting marsh birds. This includes the fight for purchase and/or protection of the Los Cerritos Wetlands and oil fields and adjacent Hellman Property, one of two natural estuaries remaining in Los Angeles County (Ballona Wetlands being the other). At Bolsa Chica, the grassy, open space of the mesa, overlooking the only naturally-functioning estuary on the site, is threatened by a massive housing development that promises to eliminate some of the most important raptor foraging habitat left on the coasts of Los Angeles and Orange Co. An education program against feeding non-native predators, especially Red Fox and feral cats, would benefit ground-nesting birds within the IBA, particularly terns and rails.

Orange County Wilderness Parks
Orange

Nearest town(s): Orange, Tustin, El Toro, Mission Viejo
Size: 1000-10,000 acres
Threat: Medium
Local Audubon Chapter: Sea and Sage
BCR: 32

IBA Criteria		Source/Notes
P	>1% Global population of California Gnatcatcher	120 – 150 birds within El Toro Marine Base Core Population, USFWS 1998
L	10 sensitive species: Long-eared Owl, Loggerhead Shrike, Least Bell's Vireo, Cactus Wren, California Gnatcatcher, California Swainson's Thrush, Yellow Warbler, Yellow-breasted, Grasshopper Sparrow, Tricolored Blackbird	Hamilton and Willick 1996; Gallagher 1997

This IBA encompasses the 20,177-acre Central Subregional Reserve of the Nature Reserve of Orange County, located south and west of the Cleveland National Forest in the foothills and southwestern slopes of the Santa Ana Mountains. From its western boundary at Santiago Oaks Regional Park in the City of Orange, the central subregional reserve extends east about 14 miles to El Toro Road. From its northernmost point in the Coal Canyon Preserve, it continues about 7.5 miles southwest to the southern edge of the Lomas de Santiago. This IBA also takes in O'Neill Regional Park/Oso Reservoir (c. 3500 acres north of Mission Viejo) and Thomas F. Riley Wilderness Park (523 acres east of Mission Viejo). El Toro Marine Base, not yet a park, would be considered part of this IBA, which protects some of largest and least disturbed expanses of grassland, coastal sage scrub, chaparral, oak woodland and riparian habitat near the Orange County metropolis.

Birds: These parks and open spaces support healthy populations of scarce coastal sage scrub and grassland bird species, including California Gnatcatcher and Grasshopper Sparrow. Extensive oak and sycamore woodlands provide breeding areas for such raptors as White-tailed Kite, Cooper's Hawk, and a small number of Long-eared Owls, which are now nearly extirpated on southern California's coastal slope. Lowland riparian thickets are best-developed in Santiago Creek (especially in the Villa Park Flood Control Basin) and in Peters Canyon Regional Park, sites that support nesting Least Bell's Vireos and that may be recolonized by Southwestern Willow Flycatchers.

Conservation issues: Established under the state/federal Natural Communities Conservation Plan for coastal sage scrub, the Nature Reserve of Orange County operates under an endowment and conservation grants that fund long-term monitoring of plant communities and wildlife populations, plus ongoing exotic species control, habitat restoration, and other management actions. The parks outside this system are not subject to this management and monitoring at this time, and are managed by the Orange County Harbors, Beaches and Parks Department. The main Conservation issues in this IBA involve potential conflicts between humans and wildlife. The central subregional reserve is still largely off-limits to people, except in docent-led groups, but with large human populations on three sides of the reserve, pressure to open up more reserve lands to unsupervised hikers, equestrians, and mountain bikers can be expected to grow. Other conservation issues include relatively frequent wildfires, possibly leading to secondary effects such as increased invasion by exotic plants and increased establishment of unauthorized trails.

Grasshopper Sparrow (Peter LaTourrette)

Owens Lake

Inyo

Nearest town(s): Lone Pine, Olancha
Size: >50,000 acres
Threat: Medium
Local Audubon Chapter: Eastern Sierra
BCR: 33

IBA Criteria		Source/Notes
P	>10% CA population of interior-breeding population of Western Snowy Plover	272 birds in 2002; Page and Ruhlen 2002
L	12 sensitive species: Least Bittern, Northern Harrier, Swainson's Hawk, Ferruginous Hawk, Prairie Falcon, Western Snowy Plover, Burrowing Owl, Short-eared Owl, Loggerhead Shrike, Le Conte's Thrasher, Yellow Warbler, Yellow-headed Blackbird	M. Prather, *unpubl. data*
S	>10,000 Shorebirds	18,500 Western/Least sandpipers 18 April 2002; Page and Ruhlen 2002
W	Probably >5000 Waterfowl	M. Prather, *via email*

Description: Owens Lake is a 100-square-mile terminal alkali playa at 3600' elevation at the southern end of the Owens Valley, surrounded by the 14,000' southern Sierra Nevada on the west and the 9000' Inyo Mtns. on the east. Historically, the lake would fill in winter and spring depending on rainfall, and support an unbelievable concentration of waterbirds and native fishes. After 1924, it was turned nearly dry year-round due to a massive network of water diversions associated with the Los Angeles Aqueduct. About a dozen wetlands supported by natural seeps or artesian wells surround the margin of the lakebed, generally on private property. Many of these are visible as large patches of green from Highway 395, the major thoroughfare through eastern California that skirts the western border of the lake. Except for a strip of land at the Owens River delta on the northern end, the entire lake bed is owned by the California State Lands Commission. Beginning in the 1990s, a series of lawsuits over the adverse health effects of dust created by the dry lake bed resulted in the initiation of experimental irrigation projects that continue to be expanded. This has led to a substantial increase in the acreage of wetland habitat on Owens Lake. The Los Angeles Dept. of Water and Power has recently announced plans to irrigate a 14-square-mile area at the Owens River delta beginning in fall 2001.

Birds: Owens Lake appears to be a major stop-over site for shorebirds and waterfowl in the southern California interior. Each spring and fall, brine flies on the lake support thousands of shorebirds, mainly Western and Least sandpipers, and thousands of ducks utilize the wetlands (especially the impoundments along the edges). An estimated 63,000 American Avocets stop at the lake during fall (Page and Ruhlen 2002). A wintering group of 300-400 Snow Geese winters here. Snowy Plover, alkali playa obligates in the interior of California, breed here in very high numbers. Many of the alkali marsh birds associated with northeastern California breed here, including massive colonies of Yellow-headed Blackbird and, recently, Long-billed Curlew (1998 and 1999 only, *fide* T. and J. Heindel) and Wilson's Phalarope. It is likely that with continued increase of surface water on Owens Lake and the recovery of the wetland and meadow habitat, the avifauna will rebound dramatically.

Conservation issues: Owens Lake may be thought of as a globally-important wetland in the making. Though the lakebed itself is probably reasonably secure from disturbance because of its public ownership and relative inaccessibility (surrounding private lands essentially block all public access), most of the conservation issues involve the private holdings along the margin of the lake. Recently, a massive water-bottling plant appeared on the southeast near Olancha, directly atop sensitive alkali wetland and riparian habitat. The ancient cottonwoods associated with the feeder streams on the western side of the lake, critical to breeding Swainson's Hawk and other riparian species, are almost entirely located on private cattle ranches that have with the added conservation challenges involving grazing within riparian zones. Over 300 acres of enhanced wetlands are planned for the Owens River delta as part of the "Lower Owens River Project", to begin in 2003. As Owens Lake recovers, a main conservation challenge will involve treating the entire basin – feeder streams, meadows, marshes, and lake bed – as an integrated, inter-dependent ecosystem, similar to the now-famous situation at Mono Lake to the north.

Owens Lake bed with Inyo Mountains in background, Owens Lake IBA (Daniel S. Cooper)

Owens River

Inyo/Mono

Nearest town(s): Bishop, Big Pine, Independence, Lone Pine
Size: 10,000 - 50,000 acres
Threat: Medium
Local Audubon Chapter: Eastern Sierra
BCR: 9 and 33

	IBA Criteria	Source/Notes
P	>10% CA population of Yellow-billed Cuckoo	T. and J. Heindel, *pers. comm.*
P	>1% Global population of Southwestern Willow Flycatcher	28 territories; Sogge *et al.* 2002
L	17 sensitive species: Least Bittern, Northern Harrier, Swainson's Hawk, Ferruginous Hawk, Prairie Falcon, Yellow-billed Cuckoo, Burrowing Owl, Short-eared Owl, Long-eared Owl, Southwestern Willow Flycatcher, Loggerhead Shrike, Bank Swallow, Le Conte's Thrasher, Yellow Warbler, Yellow-breasted Chat, Summer Tanager, Yellow-headed Blackbird	T. and J. Heindel, *pers. comm.*
W	>5000 Waterfowl	T. and J. Heindel, *pers. comm.*

Description: Draining the eastern Sierras from near Bishop south to Owens Lake, the Owens River is the northernmost of the four desert rivers of California – the Amargosa, Mojave and lower Colorado being the others. It supports an extensive network of riparian woodland, freshwater marsh and alkali meadow habitats at the eastern base of the Sierra Nevada. The saga of the Owens River is well known to Californians, and involves water schemes of the early 1900s to route the stream flow of the eastern Sierra Nevada into the Los Angeles Aqueduct to support the agricultural expansion of the Los Angeles area. While the lowering of Mono Lake is the outcome most associated with this arrangement, the Owens River was arguably even more transformed and degraded. The flow of the lower Owens (from Owens Lake to about 60 miles north) was reduced to nearly nothing and its water tied up in a chain of large reservoirs along Highway 395, controlled by the Los Angeles Dept. of Water and Power (LADWP). The entire floor of the Owens Valley, once a lush valley with swamps and orchards, was soon transformed into comparatively arid ranchland with pitiful stringers of grazed riparian vegetation and trampled marshes along irrigation canals. A few notable exceptions remained, and like Owens Lake, this system is in a state of recovery. Still, nearly all the habitat is still in private ownership or controlled by the DWP (and leased to ranchers) along the main stem of the Owens River and associated tributaries. Key areas include (north to south):

- Fish Slough Area (6,400 acres of freshwater marsh, alkali meadow and limited riparian habitat, jointly-owned by BLM, DFG, DWP/Private; just north of Bishop; includes the slough and associated tributaries at the headwaters of the Owens River)
- Warren and Klondike Lakes (DWP with public access for fishing and boating; large impoundments just north of Big Pine)

- Baker Meadow (DWP/Private; excellent riparian and meadow habitat just west of Big Pine)
- Tinemaha Reservoir Area (DWP with public access for fishing; c. 10 miles south of Big Pine; includes Fish Springs, a large area of marshes and meadows, and mature riparian woodland along the Owens River above and below the reservoir)
- Billy Lake (DWP with public access for fishing; large freshwater marsh just east of Independence)
- Hogback Creek (DWP/Private; excellent riparian habitat west of Highway 395 c. 5 miles north of Lone Pine)
- Edward's Field (DWP/Private; Mature riparian woodland and meadow in town of Lone Pine)

Anchoring the northern end of this IBA, Fish Slough has been identified as a "National Natural Landmark" by the U.S. Park Service (J. Bayliss, *in litt.*) and an "Area of Critical Environmental Concern" by the BLM.

Birds: The riparian habitats associated with the Owens River are already among the most extensive in the state, and with continued commitment by the LADWP to improve their habitat value for birds, this IBA is poised to be one of the most important in the southwestern U.S. in the coming decades. The northern end of the valley has been found to support two riparian breeders widely extirpated as nesters from central and southern California: Bank Swallow and Willow Flycatcher, which persist locally southwest of Fish Slough. Baker Meadow has emerged as one of the consistent spots for Yellow-billed Cuckoo in the state, with up to 9 birds summering recently at Baker Meadow and scattered pairs and singles elsewhere (e.g. Hogback Ck; along the Owens River north and south of Tinemaha Reservoir). Virtually all of the riparian birds of this IBA may be found commonly at Baker Meadow (e.g. Yellow-breasted Chat, Summer Tanager). Summer Tanager nears the northern limit of its California range at Baker Meadow, breeding commonly in remnant patches of mature riparian woodland throughout the IBA. Swainson's Hawk breed throughout the IBA in massive Fremont Cottonwoods on the valley floor, in what is probably the stronghold of their population in Central and southern California. The freshwater marsh habitat supports large numbers of rails, as well as local pockets of summering Least Bittern (e.g. Fish Slough, Billy Lake). At Tinemaha Reservoir, Osprey bred on platforms until recently when they blew down, and winter waterfowl concentrations here are by far the largest in the IBA (and among the highest in the deserts away from the Salton Sea). Klondike and Warren Lakes also see heavy use by waterfowl. Local water conditions (e.g. draw-downs that expose mudflats) can make wet areas attractive to shorebirds in migration, with 1000+ shorebirds during a recent spring survey at Tinemaha Reservoir (D. Shuford *unpubl. data*). This IBA also supports several species typical of Great Basin meadows, including summering Short-eared Owl particularly along the Owens River near Warm Springs Rd. southeast of Bishop. Burrowing Owl, nearing extirpation from the entire Owens Valley, may persist just north of Independence.

Conservation issues: The principle challenge to conserving birds within this IBA involves their management on private lands. Fortunately, recent (c. 2000) changes within the LADWP have resulted in a major shift in management philosophy of their holdings, which hold the lion's share of sensitive bird species in the Owens Valley. The "Lower Owens River Project" (LADWP), scheduled to begin in 2003, should restore flow to the lowermost 60 miles of river (and fence large areas from cattle), including 300 acres of wetlands at the delta of Owens Lake (G. Coufal, LADWP, *in litt.*). Their recent efforts to increase surface water flows along the Owens River and to protect riparian resources from cattle grazing (the main economic force here aside from tourism) should be supported. Millions of people drive along Highway 395 each year to world-famous skiing and fishing areas, and any conservation effort here has great potential to meet a large, diverse audience.

Owens River near Bishop (Daniel S. Cooper)

Pamo Valley
San Diego

Nearest town(s): Escondido
Size: 1000-10,000 acres
Threat: Medium
Local Audubon Chapter: Palomar
BCR: 32

IBA Criteria		Source/Notes
L	11 sensitive species: Ferruginous Hawk, Golden Eagle, Peregrine Falcon, Prairie Falcon, Loggerhead Shrike, Cactus Wren, California Gnatcatcher, Yellow Warbler, Sage Sparrow, Grasshopper Sparrow, Tricolored Blackbird	San Diego Natural History Museum 2000

Description: The Pamo Valley, formed by the confluence of Temescal and Santa Ysabel creeks, supports one of the least-disturbed examples of the southern California native landscape – a mosaic of grassland, oak woodland (incl. Engelmann Oak), riparian woodland, chaparral and coastal sage scrub. Much of the valley floor is covered by ancient oak woodland underlain by White Sage scrub, believed by many to represent a dominant southern California vegetation community prior to the invasion of annual grassland. This habitat rises up nearly unbroken to Coulter/Jeffrey Pine woodland on higher ridges. Though surrounded by the Cleveland National Forest, it is largely owned by the City of San Diego, with much of the open space dedicated to grazing. Just north and west of the Pamo Valley lies the Guejito Ranch/Rodriguez Mtn. area, a large, contiguous block of privately-owned land that has received virtually no coverage by ornithologists.

Birds: Most of the sensitive species of lowland southern California are found here, such as Grasshopper Sparrow and Tricolored Blackbird. This is about as far inland as the Diegan Coastal Sage Scrub bird community (Cactus Wren, California Gnatcatcher) occurs, and the extensive grasslands support good numbers of wintering raptors (though in lower numbers than Ramona Grasslands or Lake Henshaw). Along with Golden Eagle and Prairie Falcon, Peregrine Falcon is believed to breed in the Rodriguez Mtn. area, one of the few natural nesting sites for the species in southern California.

Conservation issues: Although there have been sporadic proposals through the years to dam Temescal and Santa Ysabel creeks and to site a county dump in Pamo Valley, none has succeeded (*fide* K. Weaver). However, this area contains very little public land, and therefore should be considered at some risk.

Panoche Valley

Fresno/San Benito

Nearest town(s): Fresno
Size: 10,000 - 50,000 acres
Threat: Medium
Local Audubon Chapter: Fresno, Monterey Peninsula
BCR: 32

IBA Criteria		Source/Notes
P	>1% Global population of Mountain Plover	630 birds on 1992 Panoche Valley CBC
P	>1% Global population of Long-billed Curlew	373 birds on 1995 Panoche Valley CBC
L	12 sensitive species: Northern Harrier, Ferruginous Hawk, Golden Eagle, Prairie Falcon, Mountain Plover, Long-billed Curlew, Burrowing Owl, Short-eared Owl, Loggerhead Shrike, Sage Sparrow, Grasshopper Sparrow, Tricolored Blackbird	S. Fitton, *pers. comm.*

Description: The Panoche Valley is located just west of I-5, due west of Fresno. One of the few areas of the western San Joaquin Valley with both good access and intact habitat, it has long been a favorite destination of Bay Area birders seeking inland species. This sparsely-populated and remote region of California consists of vast, grassy ranches that extend up over chaparral and oak-covered ridges, interspersed with dry washes with intermittent water. Riparian habitat is limited, but Little Panoche Creek supports a corridor of cottonwood-willow-sycamore woodland. The dry scrub springs to life in April with spectacular wildflower displays after wet winters. A mix of BLM and private lands dominate, with the exception of 828-acre Little Panoche Reservoir Wildlife Area (DFG). Pinnacles National Monument, one of California's least-visited National Park Service properties, lies about 20 miles to the west.

Birds: The broad Panoche Valley proper (San Benito Co.) is notable for its high concentrations of wintering raptors and enormous sparrow flocks, which join a resident population of Burrowing Owl and other grassland species. Grasshopper Sparrow and Short-eared Owl breed, both of which have been virtually eliminated as nesters elsewhere in the San Joaquin Valley. Winter brings Mountain Plover to the short-grass prairie on the valley floor, one of the few areas of the state where this species still winters in semi-natural habitat. Hundreds of Tricolored Blackbirds breed each year at Little Panoche Reservoir near I-5. The interior canescens race of Sage Sparrow breeds here, near the northern limit of its isolated San Joaquin Valley range. Several rare Central Valley endemics, including Blunt-nosed Leopard-Lizard and Giant Kangaroo-Rat, thrive here, as do several lowland riparian species nearly gone from the valley floor like Western Pond-Turtle and Red-legged Frog.

Conservation issues: Agricultural expansion within this IBA is becoming a serious threat, as improved water delivery systems are setting the stage for a shift from dryland farming and grazing to orchards and vineyards. The BLM has made this area a high priority for acquisitions and conservation easements and though exotic species such as tamarisk remain a threat, particularly along riparian areas (TNC 1998).

Pixley NWR Area

Tulare

Nearest town(s): Earlimart, Pixley
Size: 1000-10,000 acres
Threat: Medium
Local Audubon Chapter: Tulare County
BCR: 32

	IBA Criteria	Source/Notes
P	>10% CA population of Sandhill Crane	Up to 5000 birds; J. Allen, *pers. comm.*
L	13 sensitive species: Redhead, Northern Harrier, Swainson's Hawk, Ferruginous Hawk, Sandhill Crane, Mountain Plover, Long-billed Curlew, Burrowing Owl, Short-eared Owl, Long-eared Owl, Loggerhead Shrike, Tricolored Blackbird, Yellow-headed Blackbird	B. Barnes, *pers. comm.*
W	>5000 Waterfowl	71,485 ducks between Kern and Pixley NWR and 3000 acres of private duck clubs in January 2003; USFWS 2003b

Description: Pixley National Wildlife Refuge protects nearly 6000 acres of native alkali grassland, alkali sink scrub, and riparian habitat in the southeastern San Joaquin Valley, about 25 miles west of Porterville. Its alkali grassland grows atop a unique interior dune system associated with the shore of ancient Lake Tulare, the only large remnant of this habitat left (TNC 1998). This ecosystem is extended to the south and east by the 1,500+ acre Allensworth Ecological Reserve (DFG) and the largely undeveloped Colonel Allensworth State Historic Park, as well as by several county-owned parcels of remnant valley-floor habitats. Open to the public only in 2001, Pixley is managed by the Kern NWR to the north, and has remained largely un-studied by ornithologists. The surrounding landscape is dominated by intensive agriculture (mainly cotton), but features several small, scattered patches of native valley floor habitat.

Birds: Pixley NWR is known for its wintering flock of Sandhill Crane, which average about 3000 birds. The IBA also supports variable numbers of Mountain Plover that winter in a band west onto to the Tulare Lake Bed (Kings Co.) and south to the Kern NWR. Pixley is considered to be the most likely spot for breeding Long-eared Owl on the floor of the San Joaquin Valley (RH), and Short-eared Owl summers and probably breeds after wet winters. It is likely that with continued recovery of formerly-grazed grassland and riparian habitat, other species will rediscover this IBA, such as Yellow-breasted Chat and Grasshopper Sparrow.

Conservation issues: Since Pixley is still principally managed for waterfowl and rare alkali scrub taxa, acquiring water for the wetland-breeders or migrants has not been a high priority, and riparian habitat has only recently been given management attention. Though water levels determine much of the avian use of the refuge, the greatest threat to the resources within the IBA may involve its isolation from other natural areas.

Pt. Mugu Area

Ventura

Nearest town(s): Oxnard, Port Hueneme, Camarillo
Size: 1000-10,000 acres
Threat: Critical
Local Audubon Chapter: Ventura, Conejo Valley
BCR: 32

	IBA Criteria	Source/Notes
P	>1% Global population of Long-billed Curlew	331 birds on 1995 Thousand Oaks CBC
P	>1% Global population of California Least Tern	c. 300 pr. in 2002; K. Keane, *unpubl. data*
P	Probably >10% CA population of coastal-breeding Western Snowy Plover	175 birds in summer 1989; USFWS 2001
P	>10% CA population of Belding's Savannah Sparrow	400 pr., California Dept. Fish and Game 2000
L	13 sensitive species: Least Bittern, Northern Harrier, Light-footed Clapper Rail, Western Snowy Plover, Long-billed Curlew, Least Tern, Burrowing Owl, Short-eared Owl, Loggerhead Shrike, Cactus Wren, Belding's Savannah Sparrow, Large-billed Savannah Sparrow, Tricolored Blackbird	W. Wehtje, *pers. comm.*
S	>10,000 Shorebirds	Up to 66,000 birds during spring peaks; PRBO, *unpubl. data*
W	>5000 Waterfowl	8462 Northern Shoveler on 2000 Thousand Oaks CBC

Description: The Point Mugu area, located along the coast halfway between Santa Barbara and Los Angeles, is dominated by the western end of the Santa Monica Mountains terminating in Mugu Rock, a large block of sandstone on the western side of Pacific Coast Highway. The important bird habitats include two estuaries, Mugu Lagoon (c. 2000 acres) at the mouth of Calleguas Creek, and remnant saltmarsh habitat at Ormond Beach (c. 200 acres) farther up the coast. The former is the largest coastal estuary between Morro Bay (San Luis Obispo Co.) and Bolsa Chica Lagoon (Orange Co.). A long, sandy barrier island connecting the two wetlands, runs the length of the Pacific Weapons Station Point Mugu (DoD). Just inland is the broad coastal plain known as the Oxnard Plain, which is bounded by Port Hueneme, Oxnard and Camarillo. These rich agricultural fields are planted with sod, strawberries, and other low-growing crops that are regularly flooded. Scattered windbreaks of eucalyptus and tamarisk dot the landscape, which is quickly losing ground to urbanization (mainly "big box" warehouses) from the north and west. The interface of the plain and the estuaries features several freshwater ponds, the largest ones managed for waterfowl as a private duck-hunting club, one of the last in southern California. Finally, a small portion of the western Santa Monica Mtns. falls within the boundary of the weapons station, including some excellent, cactus-rich coastal sage scrub.

Birds: Mugu Lagoon is one of the key coastal wetlands in the state, supporting tens of thousands of shorebirds each day during spring and up to 10,000 in winter (PRBO, *unpubl. data*), and thousands of ducks during migration and winter. One of the world's largest populations of Belding's Savannah Sparrow is found here, among all the expected southern California saltmarsh and coastal breeders, including the farthest-north remaining population of Light-footed Clapper Rail (declining sharply), and several hundred pairs of California Least Tern (K. Keane, *unpubl. data*). Peregrine Falcon has recently become regular into early summer, causing speculation that a pair may be nesting in the nearby Santa Monica Mtns. (T. Keeney, via email). The lagoon supports the largest remaining natural Brown Pelican roosting area (non-breeders) in southwestern California (Jaques *et al.* 1996). The Oxnard Plain is also important for migrating shorebirds, particularly in fall, when hundreds may be seen foraging in the fields when tidal fluctuations push them out of the mudflats along the coast. The agricultural fields (esp. the sod farms) are one of just four regular wintering areas for Pacific Golden-Plover in the state, and the scattered windbreaks are often filled with migrant songbirds in September and October. Like Goleta Point in Santa Barbara Co. (see Goleta Coast IBA), tens of thousands of seabirds stream north past Mugu Rock just south of Mugu Lagoon each spring.

Conservation issues: This IBA is being seriously encroached upon by "big box" warehouses and residential developments from the north and west. A recent shift in philosophy within the DoD has resulted in the Navy's investigating major changes to Mugu Lagoon and the surrounding wetlands in hopes of minimizing the chances of collisions between birds and aircraft (KG). While some key bird habitats along the immediate coast are receiving much-needed attention from conservation groups like the Coastal Conservancy (e.g. Ormond Beach), others just inland are receiving virtually none (e.g. agricultural fields). Agricultural easements should be explored to halt the conversion of open space to urban use, and the existing open-space connections between coastal wetlands, the Oxnard Plain and the vast Santa Monica Mountains should be maintained. Now essentially an urban area, human disturbance to species, particularly at the remaining wetlands (e.g. at McGrath State Beach) remains high.

Pt. Reyes - Outer

Marin

Nearest town(s): Olema, Inverness
Size: >50,000 acres
Sensitive species: 9 (Ashy Storm-Petrel, Northern Harrier, Black Rail, Western Snowy Plover, Long-billed Curlew, Tufted Puffin, California Swainson's Thrush, Bryant's Savannah Sparrow, Tricolored Blackbird) (Shuford 1993)
Threat: Low
Local Audubon Chapter: Marin
BCR: 32

IBA Criteria		Source/Notes
W	>5000 Waterfowl	D. Shuford, *pers. comm.*
S	>10,000 Shorebirds	Up to 20,000 on Drakes and Limantour esteros; PRBO, *unpubl. data*

Description: Pt. Reyes is a triangular-shaped piece of land jutting out into the Pacific Ocean north of the San Francisco Bay Area. This IBA centers on its western edge, a region of rugged headlands, broad, sandy beaches, windswept pastureland, dune lakes and one of the largest coastal estuaries in California, Drake's Estero. Managed as Pt. Reyes National Seashore, this area has numerous private in-holdings (mainly dairy farms and oyster operations) that pre-date the park. Like other IBAs in the region (Tomales Bay, Bolinas Lagoon), this area has received close scrutiny by Point Reyes Bird Observatory and is exceptionally well covered year-round by birders from California and around the world.

Birds: The areas of this IBA most important for bird conservation include the vast saltmarsh and mudflats of Drake's Estero, which support very large numbers of waterbirds in migration and winter. The headlands and offshore rocks within this IBA are critically important to a diverse nesting seabird population that includes Ashy Storm-Petrel (74 at Bird Rock, off Tomales Pt.), Rhinocerous Auklet and Tufted Puffin (handful on Pt. Reyes proper), all localized in the state (Carter *et al.* 1992). These are concentrated in three areas: Bird Rock, in the north near Tomales Point; the headlands at Pt. Reyes proper (southwest of Drake's Estero); and offshore rocks within Drake's Bay southeast of Drake's Estero. The sandy beaches in the area host nesting Snowy Plover (declining, *fide* D. Shuford), particularly along North Beach and Limantour Spit. The open fields in the area are also important for open-country migrants and winterers, including shorebirds such as the localized Pacific Golden-Plover, which winters at just a handful of sites in California. Finally, the scattered clumps of trees associated with ranch yards within this IBA have long been known as important migration hotspots, with hundreds of songbirds crowding into planted groves of cypress, particularly in fall.

Conservation issues: Common Ravens, increasing in the region have been implicated in recent declines of nesting Snowy Plover, and oil spills (many originating near the Farallon Islands, see above) continue to affect seabirds in this region of the coast. Remarkably, in 2001, the S.S. Jacob Luckenbach, which sank off San Francisco in 1953, was found to have been leaking oil during winter storms, possibly since the 1970s. This oil has now been implicated in major winter mortality of Common Murres in and around this IBA (SH).

North Beach as seen from Pt. Reyes Lighthouse (Alison Sheehey © Nature Ali)

Puente-Chino Hills
Los Angeles/Orange/San Bernardino/Riverside

Nearest town(s): Whittier, La Puente, Rowland Heights, La Habra Heights, Brea, Diamond Bar, Pomona, Chino, Chino Hills, Yorba Linda
Size: 10,000 - 50,000 acres
Threat: High
Local Audubon Chapter: Whittier, Pomona Valley
BCR: 32

	IBA Criteria	Source/Notes
L	14 sensitive species: Northern Harrier, Ferruginous Hawk, Golden Eagle, Prairie Falcon, Loggerhead Shrike, Least Bell's Vireo, Cactus Wren, Clark's Marsh Wren, California Gnatcatcher, Yellow Warbler, Yellow-breasted Chat, Sage Sparrow, Grasshopper Sparrow, Tricolored Blackbird	Cooper 2000

Description: This low (<1500') range of hills on the eastern side of the Los Angeles Basin supports an intact mosaic of lowland terrestrial habitats, notably extensive areas of grassland and, along its southern boundary in Orange Co., coastal sage scrub. The woodland is dominated by California Black Walnut, and small patches of riparian thickets are scattered throughout the hills, particularly along Tonner and Telegraph canyons, permanent stream in the eastern portion of the hills. In the far northeast, a marshy stock-pond within the grassland of upper Tonner Canyon adds habitat diversity to this IBA.

Birds: Several breeding species extremely rare and local in the Los Angeles area maintain small, remnant populations here, including Northern Harrier, Golden Eagle, California Gnatcatcher, Least Bell's Vireo and Sage Sparrow (Cooper 2000). Cactus Wren and Grasshopper Sparrow are more widespread in appropriate habitat throughout the hills. Locally-scarce grassland birds include Prairie Falcon (one pair breeds vic. Gypsum Canyon just to the south) and, in the far east, Vesper Sparrow and Ferruginous Hawk. What is likely Clark's Marsh Wren appears to have persisted along San Jose Creek in Diamond Bar (P. Unitt, *unpubl. data*)., and probably also occurs in Upper Tonner Canyon at Grand Ave. (*pers. obs.*). The avifauna of the adjacent San Jose and Coyote Hills (Los Angeles and Orange counties, *resp.*), is similar, and may be considered part of this IBA.

Conservation issues: A southward extension of Chino Hills State Park to include the coastal sage scrub within and north of the city of Brea would substantially protect this major population area of sensitive species, particularly California Gnatcatcher and Cactus Wren. Similarly, the largest expanse of grassland in the IBA and its only large freshwater marsh, that of Upper Tonner Canyon just northeast of the Firestone Boy Scout Reserve, could either be folded into Chino Hills State Park or purchased by a conservation agency such as the Santa Monica Mountains Conservancy, which has already purchased and established several small reserves along the hills. The extensive grassland south of Rowland Heights may not be defensible from the encroachment of tract homes from all directions, though every effort should be made to establish easements here that maintain the relatively unfragmented configuration of the habitat.

Richardson Bay
Marin

Nearest town(s): Tiburon, Mill Valley
Size: <1000 acres
Sensitive species: 3 (Black Rail, Long-billed Curlew, San Pablo Song Sparrow) (Shuford 1993)
Threat: Low
Local Audubon Chapter: Marin
BCR: 32

IBA Criteria		Source/Notes
W	>5000 Waterfowl	5888 waterfowl within Richardson Bay Audubon Sanctuary on 5 January 1999; K. Howard, *unpubl. data.*

Description: Richardson Bay is located just north of San Francisco in southeastern Marin Co. in the urbanized middle section of San Francisco Bay, across from Berkeley. Though much of the shoreline has been filled and rip-rapped, a small area in the northwest is managed by Marin Co. Open Space District ("Bothin Marsh"). This patch, along with the wetlands of Corte Madera, represents the majority of the tidal marsh habitat of west-central San Francisco Bay. Nearly 1000 acres of open water is protected as the Tiburon Audubon Center (formerly called "Richardson Bay Wildlife Sanctuary"), which has maintained a small center for several decades on 11 acres of coastal scrub, riparian thicket and oak woodland.

Birds: The large numbers of waterfowl (high tide) and shorebirds (low tide) that find refuge in the sanctuary make it an important link of habitat in an otherwise urbanized portion of San Francisco Bay between the extensive refuges to the north and south. Over 8000 scaup (Greater and Lesser) have been recorded within the Audubon sanctuary alone (M. Sundove, *pers. comm.*), though the area normally holds a couple thousand ducks, mainly scaup, Ruddy Duck, and Bufflehead (M. Sundove, *pers. comm.*). Hundreds of shorebirds, especially Western Sandpiper, utilize the exposed mudflats of Bothin Marsh daily during migration.

Conservation issues: The upland portions of this IBA are extensively invaded with exotic vegetation (e.g. Broom, Prunus sp.).

Sacramento-San Joaquin Delta

Solano/Sacramento/Contra Costa/San Joaquin

Nearest town(s): Oakley, Brentwood, Stockton
Size: 10,000 - 50,000 acres
Sensitive species: 9 (Northern Harrier, Swainson's Hawk, Peregrine Falcon, Black Rail, Sandhill Crane, Short-eared Owl, Loggerhead Shrike, Yellow-breasted Chat, Yellow-headed Blackbird) (Glover 2001; W. Holt, *pers. comm.*)
Threat: High
Local Audubon Chapter: Napa-Solano, Sacramento, Mt. Diablo, San Joaquin
BCR: 32

IBA Criteria		Source/Notes
P	>1% Global population of Long-billed Curlew	470 birds on 2000 Stockton CBC
P	>1% Global population of Greater Sandhill Crane/ >10% CA population of Sandhill Crane	15,227 Sandhill Cranes on 2001 Stockton CBC; W. Holt, *pers. comm.*
S	>10,000 Shorebirds	10,101 shorebirds on 1995 Stockton CBC
W	>5000 Waterfowl	152,194 waterfowl in "Delta", 6-8 January, 2003; USFWS 2003b

Description: This IBA is centered on the southwest arm of Sacramento County, roughly halfway between Sacramento and the East Bay cities of Antioch and Concord. This portion of the Sacramento Delta, from Walnut Grove downstream to Oakley, was formerly a vast region of bulrush ("tule") marsh with brackish water. The conversion of this area to agriculture in the late 1800s involved "reclamation" of these wetlands – the construction of levees along channels and draining the resulting islands of land for farming. These large blocks of farmland, many of which have sunk up to 25' below sea level, are alternately known as "islands" or "tracts." Not to be confused with these islands of agricultural are numerous small islets (up to several acres in size) within large river channels that are either natural remnants or mounds of dredge spoils left over from levee construction. These have since converted to or retained native riparian and tidal marsh vegetation, often the only such habitat for miles around. The best examples of in-stream islets are in San Joaquin Co., northwest of Stockton. Major tracts and islands with bird habitat include:

- Liberty/Ryer Islands, Solano Co. (Private)
- Sherman Island, Sacramento Co. (DFG – "Lower Sherman Island W.A.")
- Tyler Island, Sacramento Co. (Private)
- Webb Tract, Contra Costa Co. (Private)
- Holland/Palm Tracts, Contra Costa Co. (Private)
- Big Break/Iron House WTP, Contra Costa Co. (incl. Big Break Regional Shoreline, East Bay Regional Park District)
- Piper Slough, Contra Costa Co. (Private, with public boat access)

- Bouldin/Venice/Mandeville/Medford Islands and Empire/Ringe Tracts, San Joaquin and Contra Costa Co. (Private)
- Brack Tract/White Slough, San Joaquin Co. (DFG – "White Slough W.A.")
- Staten Island, San Joaquin Co. (The Nature Conservancy)

Birds: The vast expanse of regularly-flooded agricultural lands throughout this IBA enable the Delta to support a rich wintering bird community that includes Swainson's Hawk (breeds as well as winters), Short-eared Owl, and very large numbers of Tundra Swan and Sandhill Crane. Several hundred thousand waterfowl occur here in late fall and winter. In San Joaquin Co., Brack Tract and Staten Island are now protected as the Phil and Marilyn Isenberg Ecological Reserve (formerly Woodbridge Ecological Reserve). The reserve includes Blossom Slough, a series of ponds with a former peripheral canal now managed for wildlife. The Christmas Bird Count for this area regularly exceeds 150 species, ranking among the top inland sites in the nation. According to local birder Waldo Holt (*pers. comm.*), the fields in this area are farmed in corn that is harvested "sloppily", and support between 55% and 75% of the state's Greater Sandhill Crane population (the remainder winter at the Cosumnes River Preserve and on the refuges of the Sacramento Valley, *fide* Thelander and Crabtree 1994). In Contra Costa Co., the rice fields of Webb Tract support tens of thousands of wintering geese (particularly Greater White-fronted), and hundreds of Sandhill Crane and White-faced Ibis at this time of year (*fide* S. Glover). Holland and Palm tracts, just northeast of Brentwood, also host large numbers of geese and cranes, as well as wintering flocks of Tundra Swans and both Tricolored and Yellow-headed blackbirds. Thousands of shorebirds move through here during migration, and significant concentrations of Killdeer, Long-billed Curlew and Dunlin overwinter (Shuford *et al.* 1998; Stockton CBC).

Breeding specialties include Short-eared Owl, now very scarce in the state as a nester, and Swainson's Hawk. North of here, the tips of Venice and Mandeville islands (formerly farmed, diked former marshes that were stranded as islands when the channel was straightened in the 1930s) support shallow brackish marsh vegetation with high numbers of waterfowl, as well as breeding waders and the only Double-crested Cormorant colony in San Joaquin Co. Significant concentrations of riparian species occur at Liberty Isl., Sherman Isl., and at Piper Slough, which all support several pairs of Yellow-breasted Chat and Blue Grosbeak each among the more common riparian obligates. Long-eared Owl probably winters in low numbers throughout the IBA, and was recently discovered roosting communally at the tip of Ryer Isl. (RL). Big Break, including the Iron House Sanctuary (part of a water treatment facility) supports tidal marsh along the southern shoreline of the Stockton Deep Water Channel with a significant population of Black Rail, a species that probably also occurs in Salicornia habitat at Sherman Isl. (T. Manolis, *pers. comm.*). Elsewhere in the Delta, Black Rail occurs on most in-stream islands greater than 15 acres that support marsh vegetation elevated above the high tide and wave line (*fide* W. Holt). Piper Slough, up the channel to the northeast at the tip of Bethel Isl., is notable as one of the few known migrant traps in the Delta, (e.g. 20 Willow Flycatchers counted one recent fall morning, *fide* S. Glover). A pair of Peregrine Falcons has nested for years on the Antioch Bridge near the southwestern end of this IBA.

Conservation issues: Many of the corn and rice harvest patterns within this IBA are currently ideal for supporting large numbers of sensitive bird species in winter, as is the presence of numerous private duck clubs that manage for waterfowl and open-country species. Though plans have been floated to create a "North Delta National Wildlife Refuge", only a fraction of this IBA is currently in public hands, which has led to widespread and ongoing destruction of its terrestrial and wetland habitats. The in-stream islands are being eroded away as channelization projects increase water speed through the Delta. Conversion of row crops (including grains) to vineyards continues apace with other parts of the Central Valley, with 1000 acres lost each year during the late 1990s within a three-mile radius of the Phil and Marilyn Isenberg Reserve (*fide* W. Holt). Since the tracts and islands are often lower than the surrounding landscape, breaks in levees leave deep reservoirs that are too deep to support wetland vegetation or, for that matter, rare anadramous fish habitat. Reservoir construction (to provide water to the expanding residential subdivisions from cities surrounding the Delta) remains popular and threatens open space locally, as does urbanization. For example, the 5000-acre Steward Tract was recently annexed to the City of Lathrop, and thousands of acres were added to Stockton during the 1990s.

Yellow-billed Cuckoo (Brian Small)

Sacramento River - Upper
Tehama/Butte

Nearest town(s): Chico, Red Bluff, Corning
Size: 10,000 - 50,000 acres
Sensitive species: 8 (Bald Eagle, Northern Harrier, Swainson's Hawk, Ferruginous Hawk, Golden Eagle, Yellow-billed Cuckoo, Loggerhead Shrike, Bank Swallow) (B. Deuel, *pers. comm.*)
Threat: High
Local Audubon Chapter: Altacal
BCR: 32

IBA Criteria		Source/Notes
P	>10% California population of Yellow-billed Cuckoo	Laymon and Halterman 1987
P	>10% California population of Bank Swallow	Garrison *et al.* 1987

Description: The Upper Sacramento River between Red Bluff and Chico protects some of the finest remaining valley riparian woodland left in the Sacramento Valley, which holds a majority of the contiguous riparian habitat in the state. It is currently a patchwork of protected and private holdings, with federal and state agencies and conservation organizations planning to acquire thousands of acres of riparian woodland, farmland and orchards along the river. These have been earmarked for habitat restoration, including about 18,000 acres proposed for the recently created Sacramento River NWR between Red Bluff and Colusa.

Birds: This stretch of the Sacramento is one of a handful of remaining riparian areas in California large and complex enough to support multiple pairs of Yellow-billed Cuckoo (Laymon and Halterman 1987). The majority of the state's Bank Swallows, widely extirpated throughout the state breed in eroding riverbanks along the upper Sacramento (see Garrison *et al.* 1987). Bald Eagle is resident, and at least one pair is believed to breed within this IBA (BD).

Conservation issues: The most pressing concern to the avifauna of this IBA involves a continuing "bank-stabilization" effort by the US Army Corps of Engineers, which involves the rip-rapping of natural riverbank (stripping off the vegetation and replacing the banks with rock-covered levees). This has had disastrous effects on riparian bird populations, particularly Bank Swallow, which requires freshly-eroded, sandy banks for nesting. Efforts to stop this activity have been unsuccessful, so wildlife agencies have resorted to buying parcels outright and defending them from Corps activities.

Important Bird Areas of California

Sacramento Valley Wetlands

Glenn/Butte/Sutter/Colusa

Nearest town(s): Chico, Gridley, Colusa
Size: >50,000 acres
Threat: Medium
Local Audubon Chapter: Altacal
BCR: 32

IBA Criteria		Source/Notes
P	>1% Global population of Tule Greater White-fronted Goose	Small 1994
P	>1% Global population of Greater Sandhill Crane	B. Deuel, *pers. comm.*
P	>1% Global population of Tricolored Blackbird	B. Deuel, *pers. comm.*
P	>10% CA breeding population of Black Tern	Shuford *et al.* 2001
L	16 sensitive species: Least Bittern, White-faced Ibis, Tule White-fronted Goose, Aleutian Canada Goose, Redhead, Northern Harrier, Swainson's Hawk, Ferruginous Hawk, Sandhill Crane, Long-billed Curlew, Black Tern, Burrowing Owl, Short-eared Owl, Loggerhead Shrike, Yellow-breasted Chat, Tricolored Blackbird	J. Kemper, *in litt.*; B. Deuel, *pers. comm*
S	>10,000 Shorebirds	D. Shuford, *pers. comm.*
W	>5000 Waterfowl	233,545 waterfowl on Butte Sink NWR alone, 13 January 2003; USFWS 2003b

Description: Extending across the central and eastern floor of the Central Valley between 50 and 100 miles north of Sacramento, several National Wildlife Refuges, State Wildlife (Management) Areas and private sanctuaries anchor one of the most significant areas of wetlands habitat in the nation. Ownership of this area is divided into 24,000 acres of federal lands managed as the Sacramento NWR Complex (incl. Sacramento, Delevan, Colusa, Sutter, and Butte Sink NWRs and Llano Seco Ranch), 9000 acres of the state-managed Gray Lodge and Upper Butte Basin Wildlife Management Areas, and 850 acres at National Audubon Society's Paul L. Wattis Sanctuary. Hundreds of thousands of rice fields and private duck clubs in the area contribute substantially to the habitat within this large IBA. The Sacramento River NWR, also managed as the Sacramento NWR complex, is treated under the Sacramento River – Upper IBA.

Birds: This IBA is a principle wintering area for Greater Sandhill Crane in the state, and nearly the entire global population of "Tule" Greater White-fronted Goose winters within the Sacramento Valley, among the 300,000 + White-fronts that regularly occur (BD). Between 5 and 25% of the state's population of Ross' Goose winters at Gray Lodge WMA alone. Tens of thousands of Tricolored Blackbirds breed here, making it one of the most critical areas in the state for this species. Flooded fields and drained impoundments make this IBA "among the most important areas in the interior of the state for wintering and migrant shorebirds" (DS). Many of the significant birds of this IBA are not evenly distributed, and are strongly dependent on local management practices at the individual units of the refuges. Flooded rice fields are found virtually throughout, which can host over a million waterfowl between November and March, with the number increasing through the winter as habitat in northeastern California freezes up. Each winter, the NWRs average 300,000 Northern Pintail, as well as 50,000+ Mallard, American Wigeon and Green-winged Teal (J. Kemper, *in litt.*). In summer, rice fields (on private lands surrounding the refuges) become attractive to wetlands breeders such as Black Tern, which are otherwise largely confined to the Modoc Plateau of northeastern California. Around half the state's nesting population of Black Tern was on wetlands of the Sacramento Valley (Shuford *et al.* 2001). Where watered throughout the summer, the freshwater marsh habitat throughout the IBA hosts nesting White-faced Ibis (especially at Colusa, Delevan and Sacramento NWRs), and represents some of the best remaining breeding habitat in the Central Valley for both American and Least bitterns (BD). Sutter NWR (see Gilmer *et al.* 1998) and Gray Lodge boast the best developed riparian habitat, but recent events have decreased the value of Gray Lodge for several riparian-obligate breeders (see below).

Conservation issues: Major concerns to the avifauna of this IBA include the proliferation of non-native plants and animal species, and the periodic outbreaks of communicable diseases (avian cholera, avian botulism), associated with high concentrations of species coming into contact with each other. Similar outbreaks have been documented at other large wetlands in the state with regular aggregations of several hundred thousand waterfowl (e.g. the Salton Sea). Grassland and riparian birds currently receive much less management attention relative to waterfowl within this IBA, and flooded fields (particularly rice fields) on private lands should be considered important wetland bird habitat (Shuford *et al.* 1998). Fires set for purposes of thinning stands of bulrushes and riparian scrub (to improve waterfowl habitat) remain an impediment locally to the development of riparian habitat, though several managers are making efforts to maintain riparian habitat in various levels of succession, particularly along watercourses. Finally, feral cats are now present throughout this IBA, and may represent a major threat to ground-dwelling birds (Gilmer *et al.* 1998).

Salinas River - Lower

Monterey

Nearest town(s): Salinas, Marina, Castroville
Size: 1000-10,000 acres
Threat: Medium
Local Audubon Chapter: Monterey Peninsula
BCR: 32

IBA Criteria		Source/Notes
L	10 sensitive species: Ferruginous Hawk, Western Snowy Plover, Long-billed Curlew, Short-eared Owl, Loggerhead Shrike, California Swainson's Thrush, Yellow Warbler, Yellow-breasted Chat, Bryant's Savannah Sparrow, Tricolored Blackbird	Roberson and Tenney 1993; D. Roberson, *pers. comm.*

Description: The Salinas River flows north through the southern Coast Range to Monterey Bay. The lower Salinas River is considered the stretch that runs from near Hwy. 101 just south of Salinas and flows northwest through agricultural lands, reaching the coast between Marina and Castroville. Strips of riparian vegetation still remain, best-developed away from the coast, and the estuary at the river mouth passes through the northern end of one of the state's most extensive coastal dune systems. One inland area, the Salinas Wastewater Ponds, features excellent bird habitat (incl. willow thickets and mudflats) within the City of Salinas. About 500 acres at the river mouth is protected as state and federal conservation areas (Salinas River State Beach, Salinas River NWR, *resp.*), but much of the inland stretch runs through private lands, and is managed exclusively for flood control.

Birds: The river mouth represents a largely undisturbed roost site for waterbirds in winter and migration. Four terns, Caspian, Forster's, Least and Black Skimmer, have all attempted to breed in recent years, but none has become established (*fide* D. Roberson). Short-eared Owl, otherwise virtually unknown in Monterey Co., winters here, and nested in the 1980s. The river east through Spreckels supports large numbers of migrant and wintering shorebirds and waders, as well as a diverse wintering raptor community. The wastewater treatment ponds attract an exceptionally diverse array of migrants, host several scarce riparian nesters, and, with proper management could emerge as one of the most important riparian birds sites in the Monterey Bay region.

Conservation issues: Though the mouth of the Salinas River is afforded good protection from development and agriculture, the inland portion is regularly bulldozed and modified for various flood control purposes. Like the Pajaro River, it would greatly benefit from a management plan that takes into account wildlife use. Even with the Red Fox population largely controlled, predation of nesting birds (esp. by skunks and raccoons, DR) remains a chronic problem. The Salinas wastewater ponds, simply because they are not designed or operated for wildlife habitat, should be considered at risk of being converted into a more sterile environment, though the current managers have been doing an admirable job at balancing the needs of wildlife with those of water treatment.

Salinas River – Middle

Monterey

Nearest town(s): King City
Size: 10,000 - 50,000 acres
Threat: High
Local Audubon Chapter: Monterey Peninsula
BCR: 32

	IBA Criteria	Source/Notes
L	12 sensitive species: Northern Harrier, Golden Eagle, Prairie Falcon, Ferruginous Hawk, Burrowing Owl, Loggerhead Shrike, Bank Swallow, California Swainson's Thrush, Yellow Warbler, Yellow-breasted Chat, Grasshopper Sparrow, Tricolored Blackbird	Don Roberson, *pers. comm.*; Roberson and Tenney 1993

Description: The Salinas River is one of the major waterways in Central California, draining north over 100 miles from the San Luis Obispo area toward Salinas and out to sea. The riparian habitat is best developed in the southern portion of Monterey County, where U.S. 101 runs alongside and occasionally crosses over a wide band of willow-cottonwood woodland. Along much of its length, is surrounded by sparse, dry grassland particularly on the east side of the middle Salinas River Valley. This grassland represents an important extension of San Joaquin Valley bird habitats that have been intensively modified for agriculture elsewhere, and that support a mix of birds otherwise rare in this region.

Birds: Though the Inner Coast Range has extensive tracts of grazed grassland, the concentrations of grassland birds that occur east of King City are unusually rich. A nesting colony of Bank Swallow along a tributary of the Salinas River southeast of Bitterwater Rd. is the largest one left in California south of San Francisco. Several resident colonies of Burrowing Owls are known from here in what is apparently their stronghold in the Central Coast (DR). Ferruginous Hawk and Mountain Bluebird are regular in winter, and Golden Eagle, Northern Harrier, Prairie Falcon and Greater Roadrunner – all local breeders in Monterey Co. – are resident. It should be noted that the entire eastern side of the Salinas River Valley south to vic. Cholame has been very lightly-covered by field ornithologists, and more surprises await discovery.

Conservation issues: While urban development of this area is probably several decades away, agricultural conversion of pasture to vineyards, as well as grazing pressure itself, remains intense. This valley is quickly becoming a patchwork of sprawling vineyards that separate the riparian zones from the upland scrub and grassland, and strategic conservation acquisitions are needed to protect the large remaining blocks of habitat and the linkages that remain.

Salt Spring Valley

Calaveras

Nearest town(s): Angels Camp, Jenny Lind
Size: 10,000 - 50,000 acres
Threat: High
Local Audubon Chapter: Central Sierra
BCR: 32

IBA Criteria		Source/Notes
L	10 sensitive species: Northern Harrier, Ferruginous Hawk, Golden Eagle, Prairie Falcon, Burrowing Owl, Long-eared Owl, Loggerhead Shrike, Yellow-breasted Chat, Grasshopper Sparrow, Tricolored Blackbird	P. Bowen, K. Brunges, B. Sheiferstein, *pers. comm.*
W	Probably >5000 Waterfowl	P. Bowen, K. Brunges, B. Sheiferstein, *pers. comm.*

Description: The Salt Spring Valley is located due east of Stockton at the base of the Sierra foothills, separated from the rest of the Central Valley by a low, northwest-southeast-trending range covered with oak woodland (Gopher Ridge). It features extensive, level grassland dotted with large oaks, as well as several small drainages with riparian thickets and about 500 acres of vernal pools (TNC 1998). In the center of the valley, the Salt Spring Valley Reservoir is a typical Sierra foothill reservoir, managed for water storage and active recreation (not to be confused with the Salt Springs Reservoir along the Mokelumne River).

Birds: The Copperopolis area may be a center of abundance for the remaining resident Burrowing Owl in the central Sierra Foothills (*fide* K. Brunges), and supports nesting Loggerhead Shrike, which has also declined sharply recently in the foothills. As with many remnant valley grasslands, the wintering raptor community is diverse. Salt Spring Reservoir receives little coverage by birders, but was recently found to support extremely high numbers of Pied-billed Grebe in late fall (e.g. >400 birds in Nov. 1999, JL).

Conservation issues: Currently, this area sits in the middle of a wide swath of wild open habitat up into the Sierras from the valley floor (via San Andreas and Angels Camp), which is likely to emerge as an important habitat corridor as the foothills develop further. This portion of the foothills (including the Copperopolis area) is experiencing a surge in development of sprawling "active retirement communities", with associated mansions and golf courses. Though the entire area is grazed, much of the Salt Spring Valley is still owned by a single ranching family who have shown concern for keeping the area attractive to wildlife (JL).

Salton Sea
Riverside/Imperial

Nearest town(s): Mecca, Calipatria
Size: >50,000 acres
Threat: High
Local Audubon Chapter: San Bernardino Valley, San Diego
BCR: 33

	IBA Criteria	Source/Notes
P	>1% Global population of Yuma Clapper Rail	c. 40% of the U.S. population; Shuford *et al.* 2000
P	>1% Global population of Long-billed Curlew	1967 birds on 2001; Salton Sea – south CBC
P	>1% Global population of Van Rossem's Gull-billed Tern	101 pr.; K. Molina, *unpubl. data*
P	>10% CA population of Wood Stork	"Small and declining post-breeding population"; Shuford *et al* 2000
P	>10% CA population of Fulvous Whistling-Duck	"Small and declining breeding and wintering population"; Shuford *et al* 2000
P	>10% CA population of interior-breeding Western Snowy Plover	221 birds in 1999; Shuford *et al* 2000
P	>10% CA population of Black Skimmer	377 pr.; Shuford *et al.* 2000
L	19 sensitive species: Brown Pelican, Least Bittern, White-faced Ibis, Wood Stork, Fulvous Whistling-Duck, Redhead, Black Rail, Yuma Clapper Rail, Snowy Plover, Long-billed Curlew, Gull-billed Tern, Black Skimmer, Burrowing Owl, Short-eared Owl, Loggerhead Shrike, Crissal Thrasher, Lucy's Warbler, Large-billed Savannah Sparrow, Yellow-headed Blackbird	Shuford *et al* 2000
S	>10,000 Shorebirds	100,000 in migration; Shuford *et al* 2000
W	>5000 Waterfowl	50,000+ winter, migration; Shuford *et al* 2000

Description: The Salton Sea defies description. Formed in 1905 when a break in a canal from the Colorado River filled the Salton Trough, it is arguably the most important body of water for birds in the interior of California. Those who claim the sea is totally un-natural fail to realize that it is a latter-day echo of ancient Lake Cahuilla, an even larger lake in the same spot that was the life-blood of the local Indian tribes (whose fish traps may be seen today high above the current level of the Salton Sea!). Ecologically, it may be thought of as the northern terminus of the Gulf of California, or an alternate flood plain/delta for the lower Colorado River, itself once among the most ecologically vital biomes in the Southwest. As scientists and conservationists discuss ways to "save the sea" by reducing salinity and preventing mass die-offs of birds, the Sea quietly waits, and rises.

Three main rivers flow into the sea, one in the north and two from the south. The Whitewater River emerges from steep, rocky slopes high in the San Bernardino Mtns. to the northwest and runs year-round nearly to the floor of the Colorado Desert north of Palm Springs. By the time it flows through the Coachella Valley, run-off from over a hundred golf courses and thousands of acres of melon and grapefruit orchards quench its thirst before it meets the warm, brownish brine of the sea, just south of the village of Mecca. In the south, the New and the Alamo Rivers flow from the Imperial Valley (see above) to form vast deltas at the southeastern end of the sea, where there are also several large islands just offshore. The shore of the sea is generally un-vegetated (the water is too salty to support much vegetation), although thickets of tamarisk grow at creek mouths and around impoundments, particularly along its southeastern shore. Politically, the sea is a mosaic of ownership that includes Indian tribal lands (northwest), an inactive DoD training range (southwest), the Sony Bono Salton Sea National Wildlife Refuge (south and southeast), Salton Sea State Park (northeast), and various private holdings.

Birds: The avifauna of the Salton Sea has been studied for decades, and is defined by superlatives. Several bird species occur regularly here and nowhere else in western North America, contributing to the exceptionally high year-round diversity of birds here. These include one breeding species, Laughing Gull; two regular, post-breeding visitors (numbers vary): Wood Stork and Yellow-footed Gull; and a migrant and winter-resident shorebird, Stilt Sandpiper. The rare vanrossemii race of Gull-billed Tern breeds in the U.S. only here and at San Diego Bay. The wintering population of Eared Grebes on the Sea is the largest concentration in the world (estimates range from 0.3 to 3.5 million birds), and they are joined by thousands of Western and Clark's grebes, likely the largest aggregation of these two species in California (Small 1994). Each summer, tens of thousands of American White Pelicans descend on the Sea, in all about 30% of the North American breeding population. Mullet Island, near the mouth of the Alamo River, hosts one of the largest breeding colonies of Double-crested Cormorants in western North America. About 40% of the U.S. population of Yuma Clapper Rail, essentially a lower Colorado River endemic, occurs in marshes at the edge of the sea (Shuford et al. 2000). The 2-300 resident Snowy Plover represent one of the largest aggregations in the interior of the U.S. (Page et al. 1991), with most of the birds concentrated along the shoreline and adjacent alkali flats in the southwest and southeast corners of the sea. The thousands of Black Terns summering (but not breeding) on the Sea may be the largest concentration in North America.

As one might predict, birds are not evenly distributed around the Sea, and patterns have been analyzed by Shuford et al. (2000). Waterfowl and shorebirds tend to concentrate primarily along the southeast shoreline (esp. the Wister Unit of the Salton Sea NWR) and secondarily in the north. Waders and their rookeries (thousands of pairs) have also been found to concentrate in the far north and in the southeast. The delta sand spits along the southeastern shore support thousands of roosting cormorants and pelicans (Brown Pelican has bred recently, and in very low numbers). Several hundred pairs of nesting gulls and terns, including Black Skimmer, are found either at the Whitewater River mouth or at Rock Hill on the southern shore. Land bird populations are strongest in remaining areas of native desert scrub or riparian habitat, including along the main rivers and creeks leading into the sea, and within the Torres Martinez Indian Reservation on the north side of the Sea.

Conservation issues: Along with increasing salinity, "perhaps the greatest imminent, and perhaps preventable, threat" to the avifauna of the Sea (D. Shuford, *in litt.*), Shuford *et al.* (2000) also mentions disease, contaminants and human encroachment as primary conservation concerns. Spectacular die-offs caused by botulism and avian cholera have now become commonplace, with major kills being 150,000 Eared Grebes in 1992 (unknown causes), 9000 American White Pelicans in 1996 (botulism) and over 11,000 waterbirds in 1998 (cholera). These kills affect scores of other species and hundreds of individual waders, shorebirds, waterfowl, gulls and terns. Contaminants include selenium, boron and DDE, leached out of the Imperial Valley (where many of the area's birds feed) and into the Sea. Even sporadic human intrusions (e.g. fishing boats passing to close to nesting colonies) can devastate colonies in a matter of minutes as the intense summer heat cooks eggs and nestlings. For land birds, habitat clearing remains a serious threat. The few remaining populations of Crissal Thrasher, Lucy's Warbler and other native scrub-dwelling species are seeing tract after tract cleared for agriculture, particularly at the north and northwest ends of the sea. Tamarisk invasion of riparian draws (e.g. Salt Creek on the northeast side) remains a chronic threat to healthy populations of desert nesters and to freshwater marsh birds (e.g. rails).

American White Pelican (Peter LaTourrette)

San Antonio Valley
Monterey

Nearest town(s): Jolon, Bradley
Size: >50,000 acres
Threat: Medium
Local Audubon Chapter: Monterey Peninsula
BCR: 32

IBA Criteria		Source/Notes
L	13 sensitive species: California Condor, Bald Eagle, Northern Harrier, Ferruginous Hawk, Golden Eagle, Prairie Falcon, Loggerhead Shrike, Purple Martin, Yellow Warbler, Yellow-breasted Chat, Sage Sparrow, Grasshopper Sparrow, Tricolored Blackbird	Roberson and Tenney 1993

Description: The San Antonio Valley, a large valley within the Outer Coast Range of southern Monterey Co., lies entirely within Ft. Hunter-Liggett (DoD). Encompassing most of the San Antonio River and its tributaries, this IBA is characterized by a vast, unbroken oak savannah and scattered riparian corridors, surrounded by rocky canyon lands. Massive San Antonio Reservoir ("Lake San Antonio"), the dammed eastern portion of the San Antonio River, lies just to the southeast.

Birds: This area supports exceptionally high abundances of oak woodland species (D. Roberson, *in litt.*), as well as strong numbers of riparian and interior chaparral birds (e.g. Bell's Sage Sparrow). San Antonio Reservoir supports nesting Northern Harrier, and several pairs of nesting Bald Eagles (following a reintroduction project by Ventana Wilderness Society in the 1980s), augmented in winter by 50-80 non-breeders (Roberson 1993). California Condor maintained a historic nesting area south of this IBA, and released birds have recently been tracked to this IBA, presumably following Turkey Vultures to cow carcasses (Ventana Wilderness Society 2001).

Conservation issues: The San Antonio Valley is reasonably well protected within Ft. Hunter-Liggett but the oak savanna suffers some degradation as a result of heavy use for military training. Although sensitive species are managed carefully, the oak savannah avifauna as a whole receives comparatively little attention. Conservationists have voiced concerns about the regeneration of large oaks and the long-term survival of this uniquely Californian habitat. In addition, significant numbers of European Starlings breed, negatively impacting native cavity-nesters (e.g. Western Bluebird), and cowbird parasitism may be accelerating in riparian areas (DR).

San Clemente Island
Los Angeles

Nearest town(s): none
Size: >50,000 acres
Sensitive species: 5 (Xantus' Murrelet, Burrowing Owl, Short-eared Owl, Loggerhead Shrike, Sage Sparrow) (N. Warnock, *pers. comm.*)
Threat: Medium
Local Audubon Chapter: None
BCR: 32

IBA Criteria		Source/Notes
P	Entire global population of San Clemente Isl. Sage Sparrow	P. Collins, *unpubl. data*
P	Possibly entire global population of San Clemente Isl. Loggerhead Shrike (taxonomy in dispute)	P. Collins, *unpubl. data*

Description: San Clemente Island, the southernmost of the Channel Islands, is unique in that it was never connected to the mainland via a landbridge like its northerly sisters. Thus, its plant and animal communities evolved in near total isolation, supplemented by whatever drifted west in the sea or air. Its 50,000 acres are currently a mix of arid, cactus-rich scrub interspersed with a mix of exotic annual and native perennial (bunchgrass) grassland. The island is scored by numerous deep canyons (wet only briefly, in mid-winter) that extend from a long, central ridge to the sea, and support clumps of native trees and shrubs at seeps, including Toyon, Lemonadeberry and Island Cherry. Scattered oak groves (of endemic species) cling to the highest ridges. Until the 1980s, San Clemente was nearly destroyed by feral goats, which had been brought decades earlier and had reproduced to overrun the island, converting what was probably native maritime scrub into a dusty moonscape. An ambitious goat eradication program gained success through the late 1980s and by 2000, the vegetation still shows signs of recovery each year. At the time of this writing, all but a handful of goats have been eliminated.

Birds: San Clemente Island is best known for supporting a rare race (taxonomy of current population in dispute) of Loggerhead Shrike, notable for its minute population (c. 60 birds in 2001, *fide* N. Warnock, PRBO), wily temperament and affinity for rocky, inaccessible canyon edges. The conservation of this bird, which includes a captive breeding program, has become a small industry involving dozens of biologists. Other SCI endemics include races of Sage Sparrow, nearly as rare, and Channel Island races of Spotted Towhee and Song Sparrow that are now apparently extinct (P. Collins, *unpubl. data*). Xantus' Murrelet apparently maintains a tiny population here, with nests known from Seal Cove and Bird Rock (Carter *et al.* 1992). The grassland habitat on San Clemente supports large numbers (dozens?) of Burrowing Owls in fall and winter – likely the largest concentration in southern California away from the Imperial Valley. Snowy Plover has bred irregularly in very small numbers (single nests found), but an estimated 30-40 birds winter on the island (B. Foster, *unpubl. data*).

Conservation issues: San Clemente Island has one of the most well-funded wildlife management programs in California, but one surprisingly dependent on Navy-biologist relations, often tested at this remote outpost. Examples of vexing problems include Navy personnel's feeding of a large feral cat population, which in turn prey on rare nesting birds. Thus, the island, home to the "rarest of the rare" of California's flora and fauna remains a major testing ground for bombs as well for endangered species recovery efforts.

China Beach, San Clemente Island (Daniel S. Cooper)

San Diego Bay

San Diego

Nearest town(s): National City, Chula Vista, Imperial Beach, Coronado
Size: 1000-10,000 acres
Threat: Medium
Local Audubon Chapter: San Diego
BCR: 32

	IBA Criteria	Source/Notes
P	>1% Global population of Pacific Black Brant	1118 birds on 2001 San Diego CBC
P	>1% Global population of California Least Tern	Nearly 1000 nests in 2002; K. Keane, *unpubl. data*
P	>1% Global population of Van Rossem's Gull-billed Tern	8 – 30 pr.; K. Molina, *unpubl. data*
P	>1% Global population of Elegant Tern	3100 nests on 27 May 1999; Unitt 2000b
P	>1% Global population of Light-footed Clapper Rail	19 pr. at 5 sites in 1996; Zembal *et al.* 1997
P	>10% CA breeding population of Black Skimmer	"Hundreds of pairs"; K. Molina, *unpubl. data*
P	>10% CA breeding population of Royal Tern	35 nests on 27 May 1999; Unitt 2000b
L	18 sensitive species: Brant, Northern Harrier, Light-footed Clapper Rail, Western Snowy Plover, Long-billed Curlew, Gull-billed Tern, Royal Tern, Elegant Tern, Least Tern, Black Skimmer, Burrowing Owl, Short-eared Owl, Loggerhead Shrike, Cactus Wren, Yellow Warbler, Yellow-breasted Chat, Belding's Savannah Sparrow, Large-billed Savannah Sparrow	San Diego Natural History Museum 2000
S	>10,000 Shorebirds	11,000 – 18,000 during fall, winter and spring; PRBO, *unpubl. data*
W	>5000 Waterfowl	15,740 waterfowl on 2001 San Diego CBC

Description: San Diego Bay is the largest tidal estuary in California south of Morro Bay. While most of its northern shoreline has been converted to marinas, recreation beaches, and other urban uses, much of the southern portion has largely been acquired by the USFWS as the South Bay and Sweetwater units of San Diego National Wildlife Refuge. Other important beach habitat may be found on the "Silver Strand" portion on the west side of the bay up to Coronado Island, much of which is managed by the U.S. (incl. the Naval Amphibious Base, Coronado; Naval Air Station, North Isl.). Historic use (Western Salt Works) has resulted in the construction of large, shallow evaporation ponds that were alternately flooded and dried, which are now being restored for wetlands. An extensive, tidally exposed mudflat, rich in eelgrass, extends north of the ponds, and sizable patches of saltmarsh are also present, best developed at Sweetwater Marsh on the northeast portion of the IBA. Small areas of upland habitat, including grassland, riparian and coastal sage scrub, dot the eastern edge of the bay.

Birds: The salt ponds within this IBA support large numbers of breeding terns, including a recently-formed colony of Gull-billed Tern, one of just a handful of colonies in the world of the rare Van Rossem's race. Several dozen pairs of California Least Tern also nest at the salt ponds, as well as hundreds of pairs each of Black Skimmer, Caspian Tern and Forster's Tern. The Naval lands are even more important for breeding Least Tern, and recently supported nearly 1000 nests in 2002 (K. Keane, *unpubl. data*). Thousands of shorebirds utilize the salt ponds and adjacent mudflats during migration, especially Red-necked Phalarope and Western Sandpiper, with numbers approaching 20,000 in fall, and breaking 10,000 during winter and spring (PRBO, *unpubl. data*). The patches of saltmarsh support a small but signifant population of Light-footed Clapper Rail and about 100 pairs of Belding's Savannah Sparrow. Like other shallow coastal bays in California (e.g. Humboldt, San Francisco, Morro), the open water of central and south San Diego Bay appears to be very important to wintering coastal waterfowl, the vast majority being Surf Scoter, Brant and Lesser Scaup. About 10% of the entire Pacific Coast population of Surf Scoters is thought to winter here, along with up to 30% of California's wintering Brant (C. Sankpill, *in litt.*). San Diego County's only known breeding pairs of Peregrine Falcons nest adjacent to the bay, and forage year-round within the IBA. On the southeast side of the bay, the riparian habitat along the Otay River, though narrowly-channelized by earthen levees, supports a rich riparian avifauna.

Conservation issues: South San Diego Bay has been the site of numerous habitat acquisition and restoration efforts, but threats are similar to any urban site (exotic speices, human disturbance, encroachment, runoff, etc.). Current concerns involve recent efforts by a developer to construct a major residential center, including a 24-story hotel, on 100 acres (privately-held) at the entrance to Sweetwater Marsh (B. Collins, *pers. comm.*).

San Diego NWR – Eastern
San Diego

Nearest town(s): Spring Valley, Bonita, Chula Vista
Size: 10,000 - 50,000 acres
Threat: Medium
Local Audubon Chapter: San Diego
BCR: 32

	IBA Criteria	Source/Notes
P	>1% Global population of Least Bell's Vireo	Several dozen pr.; G. Hazard, *via email*
P	>1% Global population of California Gnatcatcher	500+ pr., USFWS 1998
L	16 sensitive species: Least Bittern, Ferruginous Hawk, Golden Eagle, Prairie Falcon, Burrowing Owl, Long-eared Owl, Southwestern Willow Flycatcher, Loggerhead Shrike, Least Bell's Vireo, Cactus Wren, California Gnatcatcher, Yellow Warbler, Yellow-breasted Chat, Sage Sparrow, Grasshopper Sparrow, Tricolored Blackbird	G. Hazard, *via email*; San Diego Natural History Museum 2000

Description: This large swath of open space extends from the U.S. – Mexico border north to the southern border of San Diego's "East County" residential sprawl. Major geologic features of this IBA include the San Ysidro Mtns, (eastern) Otay Mesa, Jamul Mtns, San Miguel Mtns and the Sweetwater River drainage. It protects the largest contiguous block of coastal sage scrub in the U.S., and also includes extensive grassland habitat (esp. east of Lower Otay Reservoir), as well as large areas of oak woodland and riparian vegetation (esp. Sweetwater River) and pockets of freshwater marsh (esp. Sweetwater Reservoir).

Birds: From intensive recent biological surveys in this area, we know it supports some of the largest populations of coastal sage scrub-breeding birds in the world, including Cactus Wren, California Gnatcatcher and Bell's Sage Sparrow. Five distinct Core Populations (50+ pr.) of California Gnatcatcher have been identified here (USFWS 1998), including 350+ pr. at Otay Ranch, one of the two largest aggregations in the U.S. Riparian species such as Least Bell's Vireo breed in riparian habitat throughout (mostly along Sweetwater River), and Southwestern Willow Flycatcher has attempted nesting at the upper end of Sweetwater Reservoir (*fide* G. Hazard) and has summered at Lower Otay Reservoir. The freshwater marshes here (e.g. Sweetwater and Lower Otay reservoirs) may be a stronghold for breeding Least Bittern in southwestern California, and also host breeding colonies of Tricolored Blackbird. The grassland supports many pairs of breeding Grasshopper Sparrows, and is a major wintering area for raptors in San Diego County, including Ferruginous Hawk and small colonies of Burrowing Owl, some of the last in southern California away from the Imperial Valley. The large size of this area contributes to its being an important regional breeding and foraging area for such wide-ranging species as Golden Eagle.

Conservation issues: As this area becomes more urbanized, already-high development pressure will increase. Efforts by the USFWS to pursue conservation easements and acquisitions to increase the aggregate size of the protected area should be encouraged. Key areas are the rapidly-developing western border of the open space (east of Chula Vista), and lands that link particularly valuable habitats with existing protected lands (e.g. to the BLM-mangaged Otay National Cooperative Land and Management Area south of Dulzura). Cowbird parasitism remains a threat, particularly to riparian breeders.

Lake Cuyamaca area, part of "San Diego Peaks" IBA

San Diego Peaks
San Diego

Nearest town(s): Pauma Valley, Warner Springs, Julian, Pine Valley

Size: >50,000 acres

Sensitive species: 9 (Ferruginous Hawk, Golden Eagle, Prairie Falcon, California Spotted Owl, Gray Vireo, Purple Martin, California Swainson's Thrush, Yellow Warbler, Sage Sparrow) (San Diego Natural History Museum 2000)

Threat: Low

Local Audubon Chapter: San Diego, Palomar

BCR: 32

IBA Criteria		Source/Notes
P	Probably >10% CA population of Gray Vireo	K. Weaver, *pers. comm.*

Description: San Diego's backcountry is dominated by the Peninsular Ranges, high mountains extending northward from the peninsula of Baja California. This IBA is dominated by five main ranges – Palomar, Volcan, Hot Springs, Cuyamaca and Laguna. The montane habitat occurs above 5500', and includes yellow pine woodland alternating with high-elevation chaparral (e.g. Redshanks, Chamise, Manzanita), with pinyon-juniper woodland on eastern slopes facing the desert. Surface water is scarce, though Lake Cuyamaca, a large lake surrounded by meadow and riparian thicket, serves as a notable exception. Scattered grassy meadows serve as magnets for birds, particularly after wet winters.

Birds: The montane bird community of this IBA is basically a reduced Sierran avifauna, closely resembling that of the Transverse Ranges north of the Los Angeles Basin, with several taxa reaching the southern edges of their global ranges, including Red-breasted Sapsucker, White-headed Woodpecker and Mountain Chickadee (the latter of the endemic southern California race P. g. baileyae). The avifauna of these ranges has been monitored over the past few decades (e.g. Unitt 1981), and they appear to have recently been gaining rather than losing avian colonists, with the more interesting summer additions being Zone-tailed Hawk, which bred on Hot Springs Mountain at least through the early 1990s, and high-elevation species such as Red-breasted Nuthatch, Golden-crowned Kinglet and Hermit Thrush (San Diego Natural History Museum 2002). Purple Martin continues to maintain small breeding groups, most recently in the Laguna Mtns., and Swainson's Thrush maintains an interesting montane breeding outpost at Palomar Mountain (San Diego Natural History Museum 2002). Many of the meadow systems are located on private lands and have not been adequately surveyed, though Southwestern Willow Flycatcher and other riparian breeders are known to summer in the willow thicket on the south end of Lake Cuyamaca and may breed. Finally, the desert slopes of these peaks appear to be a stronghold in the state for Gray Vireo, an enigmatic, localized breeder that favors dense, arid chaparral with scattered trees at around 4-6000' elevation.

Conservation issues: While much of the habitat in this IBA is protected by National Forest or State Park designation, numerous in-holdings are scattered throughout, often coinciding with the most

Important Bird Areas of California

sensitive habitats (e.g. meadows, streams). Particularly at risk are montane meadows (e.g. Mendenhall Valley on Palomar Mtn.; Laguna Meadow) that are heavily grazed by cattle, particularly on privately-owned sections. The impact of grazing, along with recreational activities (summer visitation is very high), should be assessed.

Mountain Quail (Brian Small)

San Emigdio Canyon

Kern

Nearest town(s): Frazier Park, Pine Mountain
Size: >50,000 acres
Threat: Low
Additional Source: David Clendenen
Local Audubon Chapter: Kern
BCR: 32

	IBA Criteria	Source/Notes
P	Probably >1% Global population of California Spotted Owl	D. Clendenen, *pers. comm.*
L	15 sensitive species: Ferruginous Hawk, Golden Eagle, Prairie Falcon, Mountain Plover, Burrowing Owl, California Spotted Owl, Long-eared Owl, Southwestern Willow Flycatcher, Loggerhead Shrike, Summer Tanager, Yellow Warbler, Yellow-breasted Chat, Sage Sparrow, Grasshopper Sparrow, Tricolored Blackbird	D. Clendenen, *pers. comm.*

Description: The Wind Wolves Preserve, managed by the non-profit Wildlands Conservancy, covers 91,000 acres (2001) of the northern slope of the Coast Range in the extreme southwestern Central Valley, and protects the watersheds of several major streams, including San Emigdio Canyon, that flow into the San Joaquin Valley. Together with the Carrizo Plain/Bitterwater NWR to the north, Wind Wolves contributes to one of the most extensive wholly-protected areas in California. As such, it is the site of several re-establishment programs for rare or extirpated megafauna, including Pronghorn, Tule Elk and California Condor. Its diverse habitats range from atriplex scrub and grassland on the valley floor at the base of the hills, through chaparral, pinyon-juniper woodland, oak woodland and finally yellow pine woodland on the highest peaks. Substantial areas of riparian woodland and freshwater marsh add diversity to this phenomenal area.

Birds: One of the largest colonies of Tricolored Blackbirds in southern California breeds in its marshes, and the surrounding riparian growth supports breeding Southwestern Willow Flycatcher, Yellow Warbler and Yellow-breasted Chat, along with strong numbers of other riparian obligates. Yellow-billed Cuckoo is expected to colonize at least San Emigdio Canyon, particularly with recent riparian restoration efforts (D. Clendenen, *pers. comm.*). The upper portions of these canyons support a rich foothill breeding bird community, which includes California Spotted Owl, and likely harbors several undescribed species of endemic salamanders (TNC 1998). The atriplex scrub at lower elevations supports breeding populations of Sage Sparrow (canescens race) and Brewer's Sparrow. The grasslands on the lower slopes, some of the most extensive in southern California, support colonies of Grasshopper Sparrow and a large and diverse raptor population, including Burrowing Owl and Golden Eagle, the latter also breeding in the surrounding hills. These grasslands were an important foraging area for California Condor until their removal for captive breeding, and may become so again

Conservation issues: While Wind Wolves itself is secure, proposed development of large areas of the northern Tehachapi foothills just east of I-5 (within the sprawling Tejon Ranch) may have regional effects on the area's avifauna, e.g. by increasing the abundance of urban-adapted species, decreasing the amount of raptor foraging habitat, etc.

Tidal wetlands of Don Edwards NWR on south San Francisco Bay, view east (David Cardinal / Cardinal Photo)

San Francisco Bay - South

Contra Costa/Alameda/Santa Clara/San Mateo

Nearest town(s): San Leandro, San Lorenzo, Hayward, Union City, Newark, Fremont, Milpitas, Santa Clara, Sunnyvale, Mountain View, Palo Alto, Redwood City, Foster City
Size: 10,000 - 50,000 acres
Threat: High
Local Audubon Chapter: Sequoia, Santa Clara Valley, Ohlone
BCR: 32

IBA Criteria		Source/Notes
P	Essentially the entire global population Alameda Song Sparrow	H. Spautz, *unpubl. data*
P	>1% Global population of California Clapper Rail	600+ birds; M. Kolar, *in litt.*
P	>1% Global population of Long-billed Curlew	624 birds on 1999 Hayward-Fremont CBC
P	>1% Global population of Saltmarsh Common Yellowthroat	H. Spautz, *unpubl. data*
P	>10% CA population of coastal-breeding Western Snowy Plover	519 birds on 1999 Hayward-Fremont CBC; 203 birds on "South San Francisco Bay" summer 1991; USFWS 2001
L	15 sensitive species: Northern Harrier, Peregrine Falcon, Black Rail, California Clapper Rail, Western Snowy Plover, Long-billed Curlew, Least Tern, Black Skimmer, Burrowing Owl, Short-eared Owl, Loggerhead Shrike, Saltmarsh Common Yellowthroat, Bryant's Savannah Sparrow, Alameda Song Sparrow, Tricolored Blackbird	Sequoia Audubon Soceity 2001; M. Rogers, B. Bousman, *pers. comm.*
S	>10,000 Shorebirds	M. Kolar, *in litt.*
W	>5000 Waterfowl	144,572 waterfowl on "San Francisco Bay", 6-7 January 2003; USFWS 2003b

Description: The wetlands of south San Francisco Bay extend in a U-shaped band from near Milbrae (vic. San Francisco International Airport) southeast through the "Silicon Valley" cities of San Mateo Co. (Redwood City, Palo Alto) to Milpitas/Alviso (Santa Clara Co.), then north up the East Bay into Alameda Co. (Newark, Hayward) to Alameda (vic. Oakland International Airport). Over 20,000 acres of habitat here is protected as the Don Edwards San Francisco Bay National Wildlife Refuge, where many of the bird habitats of this IBA are represented, including tidal marshes at creek deltas, tidal flats, salt pans (barren areas, either naturally formed within salt marshes, or left after salt evaporation ponds have dried), diked wetlands (incl. both brackish and freshwater marshes) and open water. Smaller areas of protected habitat (e.g. Martin Luther King, Jr. and Coyote Hills regional parks; Hayward Regional Shoreline) are scattered throughout. Vast, shallow salt evaporation ponds, located mainly on private lands, are the focus of much conservation and restoration attention. Massive salt pans with interwoven fingers of tidal marsh dominate the area near the western end of the Dumbarton Bridge (Highway 84 in East Palo Alto), and from Sunnyvale east through Coyote Creek north up the East Bay. The broad tidal flats of San Francisco Bay form a band around the entire edge of the IBA, and major blocks of marsh habitat include Bair Isl./Greco Isl. (vic. Redwood City) and Palo Alto Baylands (vic. Mountain View), which feature diked wetland, tidal marsh and tidal flats. The southeast edge of the Bay also features some of the most substantial upland habitats within this IBA, including a remnant vernal pool/grassland area south of Fremont (now nearly eliminated) and the Coyote Hills north of Newark (see Goals Project 1999 for a complete description of the area).

Birds: Most of the global population of the endemic Alameda Song Sparrow falls within this IBA. Surveys in the tidal marshes on Don Edwards S.F. Bay NWR lands have estimated 600 California Clapper Rails (at least 60% of the global population of this taxa, M. Kolar, *in litt.*). These are now limited to the handful of protected lands where Red Fox is being controlled. Snowy Plovers are locally common in winter and occassionaly breed in scattered sites, mainly near Redwood City and in the Alameda Co. section of this IBA, where they are joined by thousands of pairs of California Gull (11-14% of California's breeding population, Shuford and Ryan 2000) and Forster's Tern, with smaller numbers of Caspian Tern. Least Terns currently breed only at Hayward Shoreline (irregularly), but utilize salt pans throughout for post-breeding staging, and Black Skimmer has recently bred successfully at several sites. Carefully monitored by the San Francisco Bay Bird Observatory, a heronry near Alviso is one of the state's largest, and has recently included a handful of Little Blue Heron, Cattle Egret and White-faced Ibis (M. Rogers, via email). This IBA is a critical migration and wintering area for shorebirds, with an estimated half-million individuals (mainly Western Sandpipers) pouring through during spring migration, and large numbers in fall and winter. Other shorebirds are also well-represented, with spring Dunlin and Marbled Godwit numbers estimated to exceed 10% of their global populations (Page and Shuford 2000). Over 75,000 ducks have been counted wintering on the open water of the refuge, with Ruddy Duck and Northern Shoveler dominant (Accurso 1992). Other significant birds include Black Rail (winter only, *fide* Evens and Nur, in press) and even the occasional winter sighting of Yellow Rail, a species that has been nearly extirpated from the state (*fide* M. Rodgers). Northern Harrier, Short-eared Owl (mainly winter), Burrowing Owl and Loggerhead Shrike maintain small populations in grassy portions of the IBA, and have been essentially eliminated from inland areas by development.

Conservation issues: Conservationists are now racing to acquire the remaining open space within this IBA and elsewhere around San Francisco Bay, and millions of dollars are being sought to restore and enhance diked former wetlands (see Goals 1999 for complete discussion of recommendations). On already-protected lands, exotic species control remains a pressing conservation issue, with Spartina alterniflora and Pepperweed among the more serious invaders. Red Fox entered the system in the mid-1980s, and has been decimating the rail population of the IBA, as have feral cats (colonies fiercely defended in area by local residents) and non-native rats. Finally, urban encroachment and its associated threats (incl. urban runoff, off-leash dogs) continue to pose a constant (and likely permanent) threat to the managed portions of this IBA.

San Jacinto Valley
Riverside

Nearest town(s): Perris, Hemet, San Jacinto
Size: 1000-10,000 acres
Threat: High
Local Audubon Chapter: San Bernardino Valley
BCR: 32

IBA Criteria		Source/Notes
P	>1% Global population of Long-billed Curlew	244 birds on 1999 San Jacinto Lake CBC
L	19 sensitive species: White-faced Ibis, Northern Harrier, Ferruginous Hawk, Golden Eagle, Prairie Falcon, Mountain Plover, Long-billed Curlew, Burrowing Owl, Short-eared Owl, Long-eared Owl, Loggerhead Shrike, Cactus Wren, California Gnatcatcher, Yellow Warbler, Yellow-breasted Chat, Sage Sparrow, Grasshopper Sparrow, Tricolored Blackbird, Yellow-headed Blackbird	C. McGaugh, *pers. comm.*
S	>10,000 Shorebirds	D. Shuford *unpubl. data*
W	>5000 Waterfowl	25,217 waterfowl on 1999 San Jacinto Lake CBC

Description: Quite simply one of the most important bird areas in southern California, the San Jacinto Valley is dominated by the floodplain of the San Jacinto River, which runs northwest from the base of the San Jacinto Mountains. A portion of the river empties into Mystic Lake (a.k.a. "San Jacinto Lake"), just east of the community of Moreno Valley, while the rest is directed southwest from here toward the community of Perris and I-215, and eventually into Lake Elsinore. Low hills surround the valley on the north ("The Badlands"), west (Bernasconi Hills) and south ("Juniper Flats"), which are covered with Riversidean Coastal Sage Scrub and, where frequently burned, by grassland. A series of impoundments with freshwater marsh on the southwest side of Mystic Lake is maintained as the San Jacinto Wildlife Area, and smaller areas of marsh are found at the Hemet-San Jacinto WTP (a.k.a. "San Jacinto Sewage Ponds") along Sanderson Rd. to the southeast, and locally elsewhere in the valley (around stock ponds). Large areas of pastureland, including sparse alkali grassland, occur throughout.

Birds: The marshes of the San Jacinto Wildlife Area support one of the few remaining southern California breeding colonies of White-faced Ibis, rails and hundreds of pairs of Tricolored and Yellow-headed Blackbird. The pastureland, particularly the vast plowed fields southeast of Mystic Lake, are one of the few remaining areas left in southern California outside the Imperial Valley that support winter flocks of Mountain Plover (possibly extirpated, *fide* C. McGaugh), Long-billed Curlew, White-faced Ibis, and (historically) Sandhill Crane. Dozens of Ferruginous Hawks – one of the largest concentrations in the state – winter in this area, and virtually all of southern California's raptor community is represented here, perhaps concentrated by abundant rodent prey. A traditional roost of both Long-eared (olive groves) and Short-eared (weedy fields) owls exists along Davis Rd. within the San Jacinto Wildlife Area. Depending on water levels, thousands of shorebirds and waterfowl (esp. American Wigeon, Northern Shoveler and Green-winged Teal) utilize the wetlands of the wildlife area, Mystic Lake to the east and the water treatment plant (over 2000 dowitchers recorded at the wildlife area on single-day surveys in spring, Shuford *et al.* 2002). After wet winters, trees near Mystic Lake support rookeries of herons, egrets and Double-crested Cormorants. The scrub on the hillsides surrounding the valley supports high densities of resident Bell's Sage Sparrow, which are shared very locally by California Gnatcatcher and Cactus Wren. The whole region appears to be a critical migration corridor for certain species between the desert and the coast for a wide variety of species. A sizable springtime movement of Sage Thrasher – nearly unique in coastal southern California – occurs in late winter, followed by a push of Swainson's Hawks moving north.

Conservation issues: This area, like the Skinner Reservoir Area (see below), falls within the WRMSHCP planning area, and similar recommendations apply. The potential for habitat restoration in this area is enormous – the marshy shore of Mystic Lake was one of the last wintering areas for Yellow Rail and breeding Black Rail in southern California, and a Yellow Rail present here in the 1970s (Garrett and Dunn 1981) suggests that recolonization is not out of the question. Conservation groups, as well as the State of California, have made the San Jacinto Valley a priority area for acquisitions and easements, with recent activity focusing on much of the regularly-flooded lands in and around Mystic Lake. However, pressure to develop the surrounding uplands is intense; a new Indian casino is now (2001) being constructed less than a half-mile away from the shore of Mystic Lake.

San Joaquin Hills

Orange

Nearest town(s): Irvine, Corona del Mar, Laguna Beach, Laguna Hills, San Juan Capistrano
Size: 1000-10,000 acres
Threat: Medium
Local Audubon Chapter: Laguna Hills, South Coast
BCR: 32

IBA Criteria		Source/Notes
P	>1% Global population of California Gnatcatcher	USFWS 1998
L	14 sensitive species: Northern Harrier, Ferruginous Hawk, Burrowing Owl, Loggerhead Shrike, Least Bell's Vireo, Cactus Wren, Clark's Marsh Wren, California Gnatcatcher, California Swainson's Thrush, Yellow Warbler, Yellow-breasted Chat, Sage Sparrow, Grasshopper Sparrow, Tricolored Blackbird	Hamilton and Willick 1996; Gallagher 1997

Description: The flat coastal plain of the Los Angeles Basin is interrupted by three low, isolated ranges of hills: the Baldwin Hills, the Palos Verdes Peninsula, and the San Joaquin Hills of southern Orange County. Each has a distinctive avifauna, but that of the San Joaquin Hills is by far the most intact. In this range, the Coastal Subarea Reserve of the Nature Reserve of Orange County preserves 17,201 acres of grasslands, coastal sage scrub, low-elevation chaparral, and riparian and oak woodlands. From Upper Newport Bay, this reserve extends southeast approximately 16 miles to the confluence of Oso and Trabuco creeks, and includes Crystal Cove State Park, Laguna Coast Wilderness Park and Aliso/Wood Canyons Reg. Park. Although riparian habitat is mostly limited to narrow bands of willow and sycamore woodlands in seasonal drainages, just upstream from Upper Newport Bay, Bonita Creek and the silted-in Bonita Reservoir support extensive and important freshwater marsh and willow-riparian habitats.

Birds: The avifauna of the San Joaquin Hills is quite similar to that of the Puente-Chino Hills (see above), which is expected given a similar elevation and representation of habitats. The USFWS (1998) identified 2 Core Populations (50+ pr.) of California Gnatcatcher here, though the large San Joaquin Hills population was reduced in a 1993 fire. The wetland habitat Bonita Reservoir supports several locally-rare nesters, including Clark's Marsh Wren, Least Bell's Vireo and Swainson's Thrush (Gallagher 1997).

Conservation issues: As a result of extensive surrounding development, the San Joaquin Hills are essentially cut off from other natural open spaces, and so movement into and out of this range is impeded for resident species with low vagility, such as the Cactus Wren and California Gnatcatcher. This could have implications for re-colonization of the San Joaquin Hills if a population were to be extirpated as a result of fire, disease, etc. See Orange County Wilderness Parks (above) for additional issues.

San Joaquin River NWR Area

Stanislaus/San Joaquin

Nearest town(s): Manteca, Modesto
Size: 10,000 - 50,000 acres
Threat: Medium
Local Audubon Chapter: Stanislaus
BCR: 32

IBA Criteria		Source/Notes
P	Nearly entire global population of Aleutian Canada Goose	34,000 birds on 1999 Caswell-Westley CBC
P	>1% Global population of Long-billed Curlew	513 birds on 1997 Caswell-Westley CBC
P	>10% California population of Sandhill Crane	3228 birds on 1993 Caswell-Westley CBC
L	11 sensitive species: Tule Greater White-fronted Goose, Aleutian Canada Goose, Redhead, Northern Harrier, Swainson's Hawk, Sandhill Crane, Western Snowy Plover, Long-billed Curlew, Short-eared Owl, Long-eared Owl, Loggerhead Shrike, Yellow-breasted Chat	J. Gain, J. Hammond, via email
W	>5000 Waterfowl	110,525 waterfowl on 2001 Caswell-Westley CBC

Description: The San Joaquin River NWR covers 15,000 acres at the confluence of the San Joaquin, Stanislaus and Tuolumne rivers. While currently unstaffed and closed to the public, a small viewing area has recently open near Manteca. Together with 250-acre Caswell Memorial State Park, this IBA protects the most significant patch of lowland riparian woodland remaining in the San Joaquin Valley. Though other National Wildlife Refuges in the valley have only limited stringers of riparian thicket, this refuge features Christman Island, an 800-acre block of dense riparian jungle that has only recently (2001) been investigated by ornithologists (*fide* J. Gain), as well as an uncultivated floodplain dotted with enormous Valley Oaks. Christman Island has been selected to form the core of a 1300-acre riparian restoration project along the San Joaquin River (J. Hammond, PRBO, via email). Caswell, on the Stanislaus River just to the north, is relatively tiny by comparison, yet its Valley Oak riparian woodland represents "one of the most intact and ecologically diverse riparian systems in the state" (TNC 1998). Most of the refuge is maintained in agriculture (pastureland, corn, winter wheat), and is managed through the San Luis NWR Complex. Other important habitat areas include remnant wetlands and riparian habitat along the San Joaquin River, bounded by Keyes and Carpenter roads (including the settling ponds of the Modesto WTP and adjacent alfalfa fields that are flooded in winter).

Birds: San Joaquin NWR owes its existence to the Aleutian Canada Goose, whose Recovery Plan identified it as a key management area, supporting nearly the entire global population in winter (USFWS 2003b). This flock is joined by several hundred Sandhill Crane, a handful of the scarce "Tule" race of the

Greater White-fronted Goose, and by Cackling Canada Goose. The flooded fields in the area are notable for hosting large concentrations of wintering waterfowl, especially Northern Shoveler (c. 40,000), Ruddy Duck (20,000) and Gadwall (5000) (J. Gain, *unpubl. data*). About 30% of the world's Aleutian Canada Goose population that winters at the San Joaquin NWR roosts at night on the ponds at the Modesto WTP. Large numbers of shorebirds (mainly "peeps", Dunlin and dowitchers) utilize these habitats during spring and fall migration (incl. the nearby Ceres WTP), and small numbers of Pacific Golden-Plover are now regular. A handful of Snowy Plover bred recently at Modesto WTP, one of their few Central Valley nesting sites north of the Tulare Lake Basin (*fide* J. Gain). The nearby fields flooded with treated effluent are appealing to large numbers of White-faced Ibis and Long-billed Curlew in winter, along with Short-eared Owl. During the summer, Northern Harrier breed in abundance in the alfalfa. Riparian birds eliminated elsewhere in the San Joaquin Valley, including California Thrasher and Yellow-breasted Chat, continue to maintain small numbers, particularly at Caswell, which was the site of a recent summer record of Yellow-billed Cuckoo, offering hope that a population of this species may persist somewhere between the northern Sacramento Valley and the South Fork Kern River in the southern Sierra. Several woodland species that probably occurred throughout Central Valley woodlands breed here, including Western Wood-Pewee and Hutton's Vireo (TNC 1998). The remnant gallery forest along the San Joaquin River throughout this IBA has great restoration potential, and supports numerous pairs of breeding Swainson's Hawk. Other sensitive wildlife here includes the Riparian Woodrat and the Riparian Brush Rabbit, the latter occurring nowhere else on earth.

Conservation issues: The main management concerns of this IBA involve its small size relative to the vast amounts of ecologically sterile agricultural lands just outside its borders. The NWR staff is currently working with local landowners to increase the aggregate amount of wildlife habitat in the region through easements in order to alleviate some of the pressure on public lands. A less direct but still major threat involves the continued degradation of habitat connectivity between this IBA and the Sierra via the Stanislaus and Tuolumne rivers, major valley waterways that are probably critical to maintain the richness of the natural community here. Disturbingly, The Nature Conservancy (1998) reports that the Army Corps of Engineers has been acquiring river frontage easements along the Stanislaus River corridor, giving it "exclusive right to do whatever it needs to reduce the threat of flooding on its easements, including vegetation clearing, rip-rapping, and levee patching." It is hoped that the Modesto WTP can be encouraged to manage for wildlife as well as for water quality, as other plants have done elsewhere in California (e.g. Arcata Marsh in Humboldt Co.; Hemet-San Jacinto WTP in Riverside Co.). Because so much of the land in the area is private, all of the habitat outside the boundaries of the refuges and the state park should be considered to be somewhat threatened.

San Luis Rey River

San Diego

Nearest town(s): Fallbrook
Size: 1000 – 10,000 acres
Threat: High
Local Audubon Chapter: Buena Vista, Palomar
BCR: 32

IBA Criteria		Source/Notes
P	>1% Global population of Southwestern Willow Flycatcher	61 territories; Sogge *et al.* 2002
P	>1% Global population of Least Bell's Vireo	150 territories; B. Kus *unpubl. data.*
L	14 sensitive species: Least Bittern, White-faced Ibis, Golden Eagle, Southwestern Willow Flycatcher, Loggerhead Shrike, Least Bell's Vireo, Cactus Wren, Clark's Marsh Wren, California Gnatcatcher, Yellow Warbler, Yellow-breasted Chat, Summer Tanager, Sage Sparrow, Grasshopper Sparrow	San Diego Natural History Museum 2000

Description: The San Luis Rey River watershed supports some of the most extensive riparian habitat in southern California. Largely un-channelized and relatively undisturbed by the massive flood-control alterations suffered by other streams in the region, the San Luis Rey, like the Santa Margarita River just to the north, appears to be of major importance to riparian bird species in the region. The habitat quality generally improves upstream, and may be divided into a lower stretch (Bonsall east to I-15) and an upper stretch (Pala east to Lake Henshaw) that includes the communities of Pauma Valley and Rincon Springs. Major tributaries with significant riparian vegetation along the upper stretch include Pilgrim Creek. While the upper stretch is located largely within public lands (U.S. Forest Service), the lower stretch is owned by numerous small landowners, making large conservation efforts here more challenging.

Birds: The upper stretch of the San Luis Rey River, particularly the 4-mi. stretch below Lake Henshaw, is one of three main nesting areas for Southwestern Willow Flycatcher in California. This represents a significant proportion of the global population of this taxon. Least Bell's Vireo breeds in abundance, with nearly 200 pairs along the upper San Luis Rey River and Pilgrim Creek. Guajome Lake, located at the western end of the IBA, is a haven for breeding freshwater marsh birds, such as Snowy Egret, Least Bittern and Marsh Wren, as well as San Diego County's only nesting colony of White-faced Ibis, one of only a handful in southern California (San Diego History Museum of Natural History 2002). The lower stretch still supports a vibrant riparian bird community, and one of great local importance in this rapidly-developing area (Oceanside-Vista). Large numbers of Least Bell's Vireo breed here, along with a handful of Long-eared Owl (one of the few remaining coastal locations in southern California).

Conservation issues: Efforts to stem urban encroachment of the lower San Luis Rey River will continue to be important as the region builds out. The area is located in the heart of San Diego County's Indian casino country, and there are many proposals to site new gaming facilities and associated development such as hotel construction and road-widening/stream channelization (*fide* K. Weaver). The expansion and creation of new sand-mining operations have posed a serious threat to riparian birds for years. Associated disturbances (e.g. Brown-headed Cowbirds) are probably a major threat to breeding songbirds, at least on the lower San Luis Rey. Since cowbird parasitism appears to not be a major threat to the bird community along the upper San Luis Rey, the principal disturbance here is from recreation. As the key riparian areas happen to coincide with established campgrounds, large numbers of people may be found swimming or rafting (in inner tubes) on the river on summer weekends, and, locally, trampling the riparian vegetation. The impact of these activities should be assessed. Also, irregular water discharge from Lake Henshaw may be adversely affecting habitat values in both stretches and should be studied.

Applying herbicide to stands of Giant Reed (Arundo donax) in north San Diego County (photo courtesy Santa Margarita and San Luis Rey Watersheds Weed Management Area)

San Pablo Bay Wetlands
Marin/Sonoma/Napa/Solano

Nearest town(s): Vallejo, Sonoma, Novato, Petaluma
Size: >50,000 acres
Threat: Medium
Local Audubon Chapter: Marin, Madrone, Napa-Solano
BCR: 32

IBA Criteria		Source/Notes
P	Most of Global population of San Pablo Song Sparrow	H. Spautz, *unpubl. data*
P	Probably >1% Global population of Long-billed Curlew	R. Leong, *pers. comm.*
P	>1% Global population of California Black Rail	c. 4000 birds; Evens and Nur, In press
P	>1% Global population of California Clapper Rail	260-422 pr. in "northern reaches of San Francisco Bay; Evans and Collins 1992 (In: Burridge 1995)
P	>1% Global population of Saltmarsh Common Yellowthroat	H. Spautz, *unpubl. data*
L	13 sensitive species: Northern Harrier, Peregrine Falcon, Black Rail, California Clapper Rail, Western Snowy Plover, Long-billed Curlew, Burrowing Owl, Short-eared Owl, Loggerhead Shrike, San Pablo Song Sparrow, Saltmarsh Common Yellowthroat, Bryant's Savannah Sparrow, Tricolored Blackbird	Burridge 1995; R. Leong, *pers. comm.*
S	>10,000 Shorebirds	G. Page, via email
W	>5000 Waterfowl	24,004 waterfowl in "Marin-Sonoma" section on 17 January 2003; USFWS 2003b

Description: This IBA is located on the north side of San Pablo Bay, the northernmost extension of San Francisco Bay, and encompasses the low-lying areas from the town of San Rafael north and east, taking in the Petaluma River Marshes (north to Novato and Petaluma); Sonoma Creek; and the Napa River Marshes to Mare Isl. (adjacent to the City of Vallejo). Included are the well-known wetlands of Mare, Knight, Coon, Russ and Bull Isl.; and White, South, Dutchman's and Fagan sloughs. These marshes, bounded on the north by the foothills of the Northern Coast Range that define the Sonoma and Napa Valleys, are bisected into a coastal and inland section by Highway 37. The habitats here are a mosaic of wetlands dominated by diked former wetlands that are flooded during storm events and high tides (many of which are used for agriculture); and shallow, former salt evaporation ponds alternately filled and dried (some greatly exceeding the salinity of the ocean). Fingers of tidal saltmarsh weave throughout the landscape, widening along the edge of the bay and along the Petaluma River. Smaller areas of freshwater wetlands (also created and defined by dikes) are interspersed throughout, and a broad band of tidally-exposed mudflats at the edge of the bay extends across the length of the IBA. Much of the land on the south side of Highway 37 is federally managed as the San Pablo Bay NWR, and that on the north side is protected by the State of California as Petaluma Marsh Wildlife Area and Napa-Sonoma Marsh Wildlife Area. These reserves, along with several private duck hunting clubs, ensure that much of the area is managed as open space.

Birds: The San Pablo Bay Wetlands represent one of most important tidal estuaries in the state, and support essentially the entire range of the endemic San Pablo Song Sparrow, around half the global population of California Black Rail, the race confined to the western U.S. and adjacent Baja California, Mexico (Evens and Nur, in press). It is of major regional importance for other marsh species that require vast areas of open space, including breeding Short-eared Owl. Yellow-headed Blackbird has bred in the past (Burridge 1995) and may continue to do so locally. Exceptionally large numbers of migrant and wintering waterfowl occur here, particularly Canvasback (the original reason for the designation of the San Pablo Bay NWR). Roughly 65% of the state's wintering Canvasback occur on San Francisco Bay, and about 80% of the this population occurs within San Pablo Bay (Accurso 1992). Other waterfowl that occur in exceptional numbers include Northern Shoveler, Ruddy Duck, Bufflehead, and Greater Scaup. Thousands of shorebirds utilize the exposed mudflats for feeding and roost in the salt ponds during high tide, when they are joined by tens of thousands more from other areas of the Bay (G. Page, via email). The salt ponds also support breeding terns, Double-crested Cormorant and a handful of nesting Snowy Plover. Finally, the upland areas on the northern edge of this IBA are becoming increasingly important to Loggerhead Shrike and other grassland species as they are pushed toward the bay by urban development inland.

Conservation issues: The conservation priorities within this IBA are threefold, as identified by the Goals Project (1999). First, lands acquisition is urgently needed of both wetland and upland "buffer" habitat, particularly around rapidly-urbanizing areas of eastern Marin Co. and Vallejo. A proposal to create a "Marin Baylands National Wildlife Refuge" on the southwestern shore of San Pablo Bay is currently under consideration (B. Salzman, *pers. comm.*). Second, large-scale reclamation of former salt ponds to a more natural state would help realize the potential of this IBA for the original wetland bird communities. Finally, aggressive exotic species removal must be undertaken to secure the health of already-protected lands that are being overrun with weeds (e.g. Pepperweed) and mammalian invaders (e.g. Red Fox, feral cats). Unleashed dogs are a particular problem in the Huichia Creek Unit of the Napa-Sonoma Marsh W.A., the same area that supports nesting waterfowl, Snowy Plovers and wintering Burrowing Owls (RL).

San Pasqual Valley
San Diego

Nearest town(s): Escondido
Size: 1000-10,000 acres
Threat: High
Local Audubon Chapter: Palomar
BCR: 32

IBA Criteria		Source/Notes
P	>1% Global population of Least Bell's Vireo	150 territories; B. Kus, *unpubl. data*
P	>1% Global population of California Gnatcatcher	80-120 pr. at Lake Hodges alone; W. Pray, *in litt.*
P	Possibly >1% Global population of Southwestern Willow Flycatcher	2-4 pr., B. Kus, *unpubl. data.*
L	14 sensitive species: Least Bittern, Northern Harrier, Golden Eagle, Yellow-billed Cuckoo, Loggerhead Shrike, Least Bell's Vireo, Cactus Wren, Clark's Marsh Wren, California Gnatcatcher, Yellow Warbler, Yellow-breasted Chat, Sage Sparrow, Grasshopper Sparrow, Tricolored Blackbird	San Diego Natural History Museum 2000
W	>5000 Waterfowl	5000 – 8000 waterfowl on Escondido CBC during 1990s

Description: The San Pasqual Valley includes the lower Santa Ysabel Creek drainage east of the city of Escondido, including a portion of the upper San Dieguito River. This IBA also encompasses the Lake Hodges area just to the west, which extends along the south side of Escondido west of I-15. Lake Hodges is one of several large (>1000-acre) reservoirs in San Diego County, and is surrounded by 2350 acres of coastal sage scrub and grassland, 500 acres of chaparral, and smaller amounts of oak woodland, riparian woodland and freshwater marsh. Nearby Kit Carson Park (just northeast of the reservoir) supports a similar array of habitats, and seems to be more of a migrant hotspot, particularly during April and May. Aside from the high-quality riparian woodland in the area, it still features large tracts of Diegan Coastal Sage Scrub, grassland, and patches of oak woodland. The San Diego Wild Animal Park, essentially a large zoo without cages, protects hundreds of acres of lush coastal sage scrub and several ponds that have become attractive to nesting waterbirds.

Birds: The San Pasqual Valley is one of the most significant lowland riparian habitats in Southern California, supporting about 150 pairs of Least Bell's Vireo and 2-4 pairs of Southwestern Willow Flycatcher, along with strong numbers of other lowland riparian breeders. This valley is also one of three locales in the bioregion with recent records of summering Yellow-billed Cuckoo (Santa Clara River and

Prado Basin being the others), suggesting their reestablishment as a nester in the future. The open habitat in the valley is well-used by coastal sage scrub species, and, together with the grassland, appear to be important for wintering raptors, positioned between two other major San Diego raptor areas, Pamo Valley and Ramona Grasslands. Several locally-scarce species rely on the freshwater marsh at Lake Hodges for breeding, notably Least Bittern, Northern Harrier and Tricolored Blackbird, all of which have suffered serious losses of their breeding habitat in California. The coastal sage scrub specialists, including California Gnatcatcher, Cactus Wren and Bell's Sage Sparrow, all thrive here, with 3 distinct Core Populations of gnatcatchers southwest of Escondido (USFWS 1998). Other interesting breeders here include American Avocet and one of the southernmost breeding populations of Spotted Sandpiper in the state (*fide* K. Weaver). Of local interest, the ponds at the San Diego Wild Animal Park support rookeries of all the colonial waders, including one of the few rookeries of Great Egret in southern California.

Conservation issues: Like the San Luis Rey River IBA, the San Pasqual Valley area has seen proposals for resort hotels and associated development to support the region's growing popularity as an Indian Gaming area. While the open space surrounding the lake is reasonably secure from development, problems associated with unchecked active recreation must be addressed to ensure the persistence of its sensitive species. At Lake Hodges, W. Pray (*in litt.*) recommends increased visitor education and ranger activity to manage unauthorized OHV use (a very popular activity in San Diego Co.), which has degraded large areas of the coastal sage scrub through direct contact and by igniting fires. It would also encourage dog-owners to keep pets leashed, particularly during the nesting season near sensitive habitats such as freshwater marsh and coastal sage scrub.

Santa Ana River - Upper
San Bernardino

Nearest town(s): Yucaipa, Redlands
Size: 1000-10,000 acres
Sensitive species: 4 (California Spotted Owl, Southwestern Willow Flycatcher, Yellow Warbler, Sage Sparrow) (R. McKernan, via email)
Threat: Medium
Local Audubon Chapter: San Bernardino Valley
BCR: 32

IBA Criteria		Source/Notes
P	>1% Global population of California Spotted Owl	Up to 266 territories; LaHaye *et al.* 1994
P	>1% Global population of Southwestern Willow Flycatcher	1-3 pr., R. McKernan, *pers. comm.*

Description: Draining the southwestern portion of the San Bernardino Mountains, the Upper Santa Ana River and its major tributaries (incl. Mill Ck.) pass through a wide variety of habitats before ending in a broad, alluvial wash east of Redlands. At the headwaters, extensive mixed-conifer forests blanket the north-facing slopes, while the south-facing slopes support a mix of grassy Great Basin Sage Scrub and chaparral. The riverbed itself occasionally widens (e.g. near Seven Oaks and Barton Flats), where it then resembles a montane meadow, with lush grasses and willow thickets. Lower down, mixed woodland of oaks (especially Canyon Live Oak) and Big-cone Douglas-Fir dominates the north-facing slopes. Several interesting microhabitats are present, notably a series of small waterfalls along Mill Creek.

Birds: Black Swift is the most famous denizen of this drainage, and the largest colony south of the Sierras is found in waterfalls along Mill Creek and probably elsewhere in the watershed. This area lies in the heart of the largest southern California population of California Spotted Owls, which occur in the dense mixed evergreen woodland on north-facing slopes. Along with the Mount Pinos area, the San Bernardino Mountains support the richest southern California montane bird community, in contrast to the isolated ranges elsewhere (Garrett and Dunn 1981). One to three pairs of Southwestern Willow Flycatcher have recently been discovered breeding in alders along Mill Creek near the community of Forest Home (Stephenson and Calcarone 1999), and they may do so near Seven Oaks as well, where montane meadow taxa such as MacGillivray's Warbler and Lincoln's Sparrow (otherwise very rare breeders in southern California) maintain breeding territories in appropriate habitat (Garrett and Dunn 1981).

Conservation issues: Though this area is largely protected within San Bernardino National Forest, the most sensitive riparian and montane meadow habitat occurs in various private in-holdings and coincident with areas of high recreation use (e.g. campgrounds, OHV use). The rough, dirt road that follows the river east of Angelus Oaks (incl. to Seven Oaks) is probably keeping the habitat from more severe degradation. Brown-headed Cowbirds may represent a threat to the breeding songbirds, and though it is still scarce within the drainage, Arundo and other exotic riparian plants should be closely monitored.

Santa Ana River Valley

Riverside/San Bernardino

Nearest town(s): Riverside, Pedley, Rubidoux, Norco, Chino
Size: 1000-10,000 acres
Threat: High
Local Audubon Chapter: Pomona Valley
BCR: 32

IBA Criteria		Source/Notes
P	>1% Global population of Southwestern Willow Flycatcher	5-10 pr. in 2001; J. Pike, *unpubl. data*
P	>1% Global population of Least Bell's Vireo	336 pr. in Prado Basin alone in 2001; J. Pike, *unpubl. data*
P	>10% CA population of Yellow-billed Cuckoo	Up to 3 pr. in 2001; J. Pike, *unpubl. data*
L	18 sensitive species: White-faced Ibis, Ferruginous Hawk, Golden Eagle, Long-billed Curlew, Yellow-billed Cuckoo, Burrowing Owl, Long-eared Owl, Southwestern Willow Flycatcher, Loggerhead Shrike, Least Bell's Vireo, Cactus Wren, California Gnatcatcher, California Swainson's Thrush, Yellow Warbler, Yellow-breasted Chat, Sage Sparrow, Grasshopper Sparrow, Tricolored Blackbird	J. Pike, *unpubl. data*

Description: The bulk of the habitat along the middle portion of the Santa Ana River extends from Hwy. 60 just west of downtown Riverside southwest through the "equestrian communities" of Rubidoux, Pedley and Norco, and terminates in the vast riparian forest of the Prado Basin near the intersection of Hwy. 71 and Hwy. 91 near Corona. Though managed primarily for flood control, several parks and conservation areas with sizable chunks of riparian woodland dot the length of the river, with smaller areas of freshwater marsh, grassland and coastal sage scrub. Unfortunately, much of the riparian vegetation upstream of the Prado Basin has been overrun with Arundo, severely diminishing its utility for native birds. The main areas of habitat (east to west) include:

- Rancho Jurupa Co. Park/Rubidoux Nature Center (Riverside Co.)
- DeAnza Narrows Regional Park (Riverside Co.)
- Hidden Valley Wildlife Area (Riverside Co.)
- Lake Norconian (DoD)
- Prado Basin (Army Corps of Engineers)

The Rancho Jurupa/Rubidoux stretch consists of small patches grassland (formerly riparian bottomland woodland) and riparian thickets along the main stem of the Santa Ana River and former irrigation canals. Scattered remnants of degraded (repeatedly burned) coastal sage scrub are found in this section, particularly in the hills north of Limonite Ave., and south of the river near Norco. Downstream of Van Buren Ave., the undeveloped river plain widens considerably, and is even farmed in places (e.g. north of

Hidden Valley Wildlife Area), alternating with more extensive grassland. West of I-15 (south of Chino) into the Prado Basin, the habitat reaches its widest point, with extensive bottomland riparian woodland (mainly willow) bordered by pastureland (incl. several dairies) and grassland. Here, the habitat spreads north into San Bernardino County (to vic. Pine Ave.), where it receives some protection as Prado Regional Park. A large complex of water settling ponds associated with a treatment plant on the north side of the Prado Basin provide exceptional wetland and riparian bird habitat. Other significant wetland habitat (freswater marsh) may be found at Lake Norconian, within the Naval Surface Warfare Center. North of Pine Ave., dairies and scattered small wetlands (formerly much more extensive) still offer good waterbird and raptor habitat, but are slated for imminent residential development.

Birds: This IBA includes the Prado Basin, the largest intact patch of riparian habitat south of the Kern River Preserve. The birds of Prado have been closely monitored by biologists for over a decade, and from this research, we know that it supports one of the world's largest populations of Least Bell's Vireo, as well as southwestern California's only known breeding population of Yellow-billed Cuckoo, plus 5-10 pr. of breeding Southwestern Willow Flycatchers. Long-eared Owl was detected during the 1980s, but has not been surveyed for since. Small numbers of Burrowing Owls persist in the Chino Basin dairy lands on the north side of Prado Basin (and perhaps in culverts farther east), in what appears to be one of two remaining colonies in the Los Angeles metropolitan area. The freshwater marsh habitat is heavily used by waterfowl and waders year round, including some of the largest winter aggregations of White-faced Ibis in the state (Shuford *et al.* 1996). Hidden Valley Wildlife Area, its riparian habitats thoroughly invaded with Arundo, supports a few breeding Least Bell's Vireo, as well as a rich winter raptor community that includes multiple Ferruginous Hawks, Prairie Falcons and both Bald and Golden eagles among its regular visitors. Farther east (e.g. Rubidoux), the riparian habitat is more constricted and generally overrun with Arundo, yet still provides much-needed habitat for such nesting species as White-tailed Kite, Yellow-breasted Chat and Blue Grosbeak. The rugged hills bordering the river, where not developed (e.g. south of Hidden Valley Wildlife Area in the "Norco Hills") still support coastal sage scrub species like Cactus Wren, California Gnatcatcher (extirpated?) and Bell's Sage Sparrow, all of which have become highly localized.

Conservation issues: Urban sprawl, particularly on flatlands bordering the Prado Basin, remains the greatest threat to this IBA, followed closely by invasive species. The control of Arundo, which would be helped through more ecologically sensitive flood-control measures, is of paramount importance to this IBA. Small patches of open space, particularly ruderal grassland that don't support a particularly rich grassland bird community should be explored for coastal sage scrub restoration projects, such as at the Rubidoux Nature Center. Frequent fire remains a chronic threat to this urbanized yet vital IBA.

Santa Clara River Valley

Ventura/Los Angeles

Nearest town(s): Ventura, Santa Paula, Fillmore, Santa Clarita, Saugus, Canyon Country
Size: 10,000 - 50,000 acres
Threat: Critical
Local Audubon Chapter: Ventura, Conejo Valley, San Fernando Valley
BCR: 32

IBA Criteria		Source/Notes
P	>1% Global population of Southwestern Willow Flycatcher	13 territrories; Sogge *et al.* 2002; 6 pr. in 2002; J. Greaves, *pers. comm.*
P	>1% Global population of Least Bell's Vireo	100+ pr. 2001; J. Greaves, *pers. comm.*
L	11 sensitive species: Golden Eagle, Long-eared Owl, Southwestern Willow Flycatcher, Loggerhead Shrike, Least Bell's Vireo, Cactus Wren, California Swainson's Thrush, Yellow Warbler, Yellow-breasted Chat, Summer Tanager, Tricolored Blackbird	J. Greaves, *unpubl. data*

Description: The Santa Clara River is the longest free-flowing river in southern California, and is the only one that extends from the desert to the coast. As such, it is of critical biological importance, linking several major ecoregions (Coastal Plain, Coast Ranges, Transverse Ranges, Mojave Desert). The Santa Clara River and its tributaries are within one of the most rapidly-urbanizing watersheds in the state, with both Ventura and Los Angeles counties racing to develop tens of thousands of homes west and east of the I-5 corridor, which roughly bisects the river. Though much of the mountainous habitat high above the floodplain in the Los Angeles Co. stretch (and to a lesser extent in Ventura Co.) is well protected within the Los Padres and Angeles national forests, the most sensitive habitats along the river, its tributaries, and on adjacent terraces are in private hands. What was once a continuous expanse of bottomland riparian woodland (Fremont Cottonwood mixed with willows) is becoming increasingly fragmented, broken up by residential development and (in Ventura Co.) orchards. Other important habitats include dense riparian scrub of Mulefat, willows and Mexican Elderberry, as well as open fields and fallow pastures bordering the river. Major tributaries with well-developed riparian vegetation within this IBA include Piru Creek (below dam) and Sespe Creek (now nearly lost to development) in Ventura Co., and San Francisquito (lower portion destroyed by development in 2001) and Soledad canyons in Los Angeles Co.

Birds: The habitat along the Santa Clara River supports the largest community of riparian-obligate birds between the Santa Ynez River in Santa Barbara Co. and the Prado Basin in Riverside Co. Though large areas of habitat remain unexplored (on private lands), recent investigation has turned up a sizable population of Least Bell's Vireo along the Ventura Co. portion (esp. west of Santa Paula, *fide* J. Greaves), and scattered territories of Southwestern Willow Flycatcher (vic. Saticoy and along Soledad Canyon). Summer Tanager and other desert species breed along the Soledad Canyon stretch in Los Angeles Co.

While rarely observed, Long-eared Owl probably persists in wider sections of the floodplain one, of the few remaining populations of this once-common species along the southern California coastal plain. Even Yellow-billed Cuckoo has been reported in recent years from the ancient Fremont Cottonwoods near the Los Angeles/Ventura Co. border.

Conservation issues: Portions of the intact lowland riparian bird community of the Santa Clara River are teetering on the brink of disaster, particularly within Los Angeles Co. Even now, massive residential developments and associated river channelization have all but bisected the riparian habitat into a lower (Ventura Co.) and an upper (Los Angeles Co.) section, separated by an impenetrable gap of urbanization along I-5 (City of Santa Clarita). Other threats include sand and gravel mines that continue to expand (e.g. along Soledad Canyon), regular bulldozing of channels for "flood control" throughout the watershed, and the lining of tributaries with concrete as a requirement of development projects (e.g. Newhall Ck.). Exotic species (esp. Arundo) that thrive on altered water regimes and urbanization pose a serious risk to existing diversity, and threaten future restoration efforts, though several agencies have made some progress in their control.

Santa Clara River through Los Angeles County (Steve Hampton)

Santa Lucia Peaks
Monterey

Nearest town(s): None
Size: 1000-10,000 acres
Sensitive species: 5 (California Condor, Golden Eagle, California Spotted Owl, Purple Martin, Sage Sparrow) (Roberson and Tenney 1993)
Threat: Low
Local Audubon Chapter: Monterey Peninsula
BCR: 32

IBA Criteria		Source/Notes
P	Major release area for California Condor	C. Hohenberger, *in litt.*

Description: The Santa Lucia Peaks rise up to near 6000' in the Outer Coast Range about 40 miles southeast of Monterey. Like the Big Pine Mtn. Area to the south, they represent a cluster of highly-isolated patches of high-elevation Ponderosa Pine forest surrounded by chaparral. Major promontories include Junipero Serra and Cone peaks. Chews Ridge, a high area just southeast of Carmel with an introduced stand of Jeffrey Pine, has a similar avifauna.

Birds: The Santa Lucias were found to support some of the highest breeding bird species diversity in Monterey Co. (Roberson and Tenney 1993). Purple Martin still breeds (DR, *via email*), as do several species that become highly-localized south of the San Francisco Bay area and are more typical of the Sierra Nevada, including breeding Sharp-shinned Hawk, Flammulated Owl, Mountain Chickadee and Red-breasted Nuthatch. The coniferous forest of the peaks consists of a rare habitat type, Santa Lucia Fir Forest, dominated by the endemic Santa Lucia Fir. This IBA is one of two principal release sites in the state, for California Condor (managed by the Ventana Wilderness Society), which historically nested in the Santa Lucias.

Conservation issues: The Santa Lucia Peaks are fully protected by the Ventana Wilderness, and are considered very secure at this time. However, recent proposals from the U.S. Navy to increase the number of over-flights by aircraft on practice bombing raids are being investigated for their effects on wildlife, including condors.

Important Bird Areas of California

Santa Margarita Valley

San Luis Obispo

Nearest town(s): Atascadero, Santa Margarita
Size: 1000-10,000 acres
Threat: Critical
Local Audubon Chapter: North Cuesta
BCR: 32

IBA Criteria		Source/Notes
L	10 sensitive species: Golden Eagle, Prairie Falcon, California Spotted Owl, Loggerhead Shrike, Purple Martin, California Swainson's Thrush, Yellow Warbler, Yellow-breasted Chat, Grasshopper Sparrow, Tricolored Blackbird	S. Schubert, T. Edell, *pers. comm.*

Description: This IBA lies along Hwy. 101 north of the Cuesta Grade, a high ridge between San Luis Obispo and Atascadero. Encompassing the headwaters of the Salinas River, it features low, rolling hills cloaked with Blue and Valley oak savannah, extensive grassland, and numerous riparian draws with massive Western Sycamores.

Birds: The species of this IBA represent a diverse mix of lowland and foothill species, many of which become rare in southern and central California, including breeding Sharp-shinned Hawk, Wood Duck and Purple Martin. Cassin's, Warbling and Hutton's vireos coexist in riparian areas, which also support Yellow Warbler and Yellow-breasted Chat.

Conservation issues: This IBA is dominated by private lands in a rapidly-urbanizing region. As developers buy up sprawling ranches that are no longer economically successful, a typical scenario would involve a ranch subdivided into 20-acre lots with a dream house on the highest point, surrounded by sterile, newly-installed vineyards. Sprawling "planned communities" have already begun appearing in the area, resulting in massive habitat alteration, particularly along creeks. A concerted regional planning effort is needed to identify, protect, and link the most ecologically sensitive areas in and around this IBA.

Santa Maria River Valley

Santa Barbara/San Luis Obispo

Nearest town(s): Grover Beach, Oceano, Nipomo
Size: 1000-10,000 acres
Sensitive species: 7 (Northern Harrier, Western Snowy Plover, Long-billed Curlew, Least Tern, Loggerhead Shrike, California Swainson's Thrush, Yellow Warbler) (Lehman 1994; S. Schubert, T. Edell, *pers. comm.*)
Threat: High
Local Audubon Chapter: Morro Coast, La Purisima
BCR: 32

IBA Criteria		Source/Notes
P	>10% California population of coastal-breeding Western Snowy Plover	241 birds on 1993 Santa Maria- Guadalupe CBC; 246 birds in summer 1991, USFWS 2001

Description: This large complex of wetlands, dune and riparian habitats extends up to five miles inland from the coast to the base of Nipomo Mesa and is bounded by Oso Flaco Lake to the north and by the Pt. Sal headlands/Casmalia Hills (within Vandenberg Air Force Base) to the south. Ecologically, the area should extend north to the bluffs north of Pismo Beach, but the habitat in the north has been tremendously degraded within the Pismo Beach State Vehicular Recreation Area, and has a totally separate management regime. This IBA may be divided into three main habitats: riparian corridors along creeks (incl. the Santa Maria River, Oso Flaco Ck.); freshwater marshes and willow thickets around dune lakes, and the coastal estuary at the Santa Maria River mouth itself. This IBA has long been a focus of conservation groups and public agencies, and now receives protection as patchwork of reserves, dominated by the 600-acre Rancho Guadalupe Dunes Preserve (Santa Barbara Co.).

Birds: In addition to the thousands of shorebirds that utilize the wetlands at the river mouth and the waterfowl at the dune lakes during spring and fall migration, this area protects many sensitive taxa, including sizable nesting colonies of Least Tern (25 pr. in 2002, K. Keane, *unpubl. data*), and especially Snowy Plover. The riparian vegetation supports good numbers of breeding riparian passerines, including Warbling Vireo, Swainson's Thrush, Yellow and Wilson's warblers, and Yellow-breasted Chat. Though physiographically separate from the river mouth system, the coastal bluffs on either side of this IBA (rocks off Shell and Pismo Beach; Pt. Sal) are regionally important for nesting seabirds, including Rhinoceros Auklet and Pigeon Guillemot (Carter *et al.* 1992).

Conservation issues: The Rancho Guadalupe Dunes Preserve is managed for the county by the Center for Natural Lands Management, a conservation non-profit that employs a full-time on-site manager and relies on a network of volunteers for visitor education. Disturbance by human visitors, including trampling of nests and nest sites and discarded trash that attracts scavenging predators remain chronic problems for nesting Snowy Plovers and Least Terns (*fide* W. Wehtje). Off-leash dogs were a major threat, but are less of a concern now that dogs have been totally banned from the area. Cattle grazing in unprotected riparian areas within the IBA (including within the Santa Maria River estuary) may be impacting riparian and potential freshwater marsh breeders. Exotic plants such as European Beach Grass and various species of ice plant continue to depress natural diversity. The habitat just north of this IBA receives virtually no resource management, and much of it is taken up by an OHV park. The effect of these activities so close to this IBA deserves investigation.

Oso Flaco Lake with Guadalupe Dunes in background, Santa Maria River Valley IBA (Daniel S. Cooper)

Santa Ynez River - Upper
Santa Barbara

Nearest town(s): Santa Barbara
Size: >50,000 acres
Threat: Medium
Local Audubon Chapter: La Purisima
BCR: 32

IBA Criteria		Source/Notes
P	>1% Global population of Least Bell's Vireo	Ave. 25-30 pr.; J. Greaves, *via email*
L	10 sensitive species: Golden Eagle, Peregrine Falcon, Prairie Falcon, California Spotted Owl, Long-eared Owl, Southwestern Willow Flycatcher, Least Bell's Vireo, California Swainson's Thrush, Yellow Warbler, Yellow-breasted Chat, Sage Sparrow	Lehman 1994
W	>5000 Waterfowl	J. Greaves, *via email*

Description: The Upper Santa Ynez River Watershed lies within the Southern Coast Range directly north of Santa Barbara. The area is characterized by strips of riparian vegetation winding through dense chaparral and patches of oak woodland, with pinyon-juniper stands in the Mono Creek area. Ironically, some of the best-developed riparian habitat here occurs in association with Gibraltar Reservoir, where drawdown areas provide the fluctuation of water necessary to support dense stands of willows. Rugged hills extend up to 4500' both north and south of the river in this IBA, which is wholly included in Los Padres National Forest.

Birds: The willow riparian habitat of the upper Santa Ynez and Mono Creek supports the northernmost large population of Least Bell's Vireos in California, with 25-30 pairs regularly breeding, as well as a handful of Southwestern Willow Flycatchers. An estimated 11 pairs of California Spotted Owl are known from the watershed (*fide* J. Greaves). Other localized taxa occurring here that were historically more common in California include nesting Common Merganser (irregular; southernmost breeding area in state), Long-eared Owl and Bell's Sage Sparrow. More than 5000 ducks and grebes winter on the open water of Gibraltar Reservoir. Like other areas with extensive riparian habitat at middle elevations (e.g. Lopez Lake Area) this IBA supports a large diversity of breeding birds, including 4 species of vireo (Bell's, Cassin's, Hutton's and Warbling). Finally, long-term research conducted on Least Bell's Vireo on the site has been widely used to manage this and other sensitive riparian species throughout the western U.S.

Conservation issues: Cowbird control, "intermittently applied" by the USFS since 1989 (*fide* J. Greaves) is apparently necessary for the persistence of nesting songbirds within this IBA. Efforts by the USFS to eradicate exotic species (e.g. tamarisk, bullfrogs) from the drainage should also be encouraged.

Santa Ynez River Valley

Santa Barbara

Nearest town(s): Lompoc, Buellton
Size: 1000-10,000 acres
Threat: Critical
Local Audubon Chapter: La Purisima
BCR: 32

IBA Criteria		Source/Notes
P	>1% Global population of Southwestern Willow Flycatcher	7 territories during 1990s; M. Holmgren, *via email*
L	10 sensitive species: Northern Harrier, Ferruginous Hawk, Golden Eagle, Southwestern Willow Flycatcher, Loggerhead Shrike, Least Bell's Vireo, California Swainson's Thrush, Yellow Warbler, Yellow-breasted Chat, Tricolored Blackbird	Lehman 1994

Description: This IBA refers to the intact riparian habitat from Hwy. 101 (vic. Buellton) west through the broad agricultural lands west of Lompoc. The habitat of this IBA, bottomland riparian woodland along an unchannelized stream, is dominated by dense willows and scattered cottonwoods. This area supports one of the most significant and little-studied riparian systems in central California, and one of the two best examples of lowland riparian habitat in Santa Barbara County (the other being the upper Santa Ynez River to the east). The habitat east of Buellton (Santa Ynez Valley), while restorable, is patchy and intensively grazed/farmed to Lake Cachuma. The coastal zone, including the mouth of the Santa Ynez River, is treated as the Vandenberg Air Force Base IBA.

Birds: The lower Santa Ynez River supports a large, poorly-known population of Southwestern Willow Flycatchers, with the largest colony located about five miles west of Buellton. Southwestern Willow Flycatcher and Least Bell's Vireo have been observed in breeding habitat the length of the river (though not in recent years, *fide* M. Holmgren), and even Yellow-billed Cuckoo has been recorded recently in summer along Sweeny Rd. (July 2000, *fide* D. Compton), which follows the north side of the river east of Lompoc. Golden Eagle is a regular sight in summer, and probably breeds in the hills to the south (Lehman 1994). Purple Martin have maintained one of their southernmost colonies in massive Western Sycamores along a nearby tributary of the Santa Ynez, Nojoqui Creek, (within Nojoqui Falls County Park, five miles south of Buellton), and may eventually colonize this IBA. The oak savannah on either side of the river supports grassland birds, including wintering raptors (esp. Ferruginous Hawk). Tricolored Blackbirds breed in scattered farm ponds, and Yellow-billed Magpie is found in the eastern portion of this IBA near the southern edge of its global range.

Conservation issues: The lower Santa Ynez River flows entirely through private lands, with virtually no guidelines or mandates on how the river should be managed for conservation. The conversion of ranches from low-density cattle grazing to vineyards and/or housing developments continues unabated, and it is likely that the next decade or so will see a dramatic loss of open space in the lower Santa Ynez watershed. Conservation easements and acquisitions could forestall the transformation of this unique lowland riparian system.

Yellow-billed Magpie (Peter LaTourrette)

Seiad Valley

Siskiyou

Nearest town(s): Happy Camp, Seiad Valley
Size: 1000-10,000 acres
Threat: Low
Local Audubon Chapter: Mt. Shasta
BCR: 5

IBA Criteria		Source/Notes
L	10 sensitive species: Bald Eagle, Northern Goshawk, Golden Eagle, Peregrine Falcon, Northern Spotted Owl, Vaux's Swift, Willow Flycatcher, California Swainson's Thrush, Yellow Warbler, Yellow-breasted Chat	B. Helsaple, B. Claypole, *in litt.*

Description: Pronounced "Sy-add", this IBA refers to a 1700-acre section of the Klamath River canyon in extreme northern California that extends for about 10 miles along Hwy. 96 ("State of Jefferson Scenic Byway"). This broad, isolated valley lies about 30 linear miles west of I-5 and features mature riparian woodland dominated by willow, alder and Broadleaf Maple, with a dense, jungle-like understory. The land ownership here is a complex mixture of public lands (USFS – Klamath National Forest, incl. a small "Bald Eagle Management Area") and private parcels.

Birds: Within the overwhelmingly coniferous landscape of the Klamath Mountains, this habitat concentrates both breeding species and migrants. The Seiad Valley and surrounding highlands support a rich breeding avifauna with the characteristic montane species. Several of these nesters breed principally in the mountains above the valley floor, utilizing deep coniferous forests and extensive forb-dominated grasslands ("mountain prairies") and willow thickets (e.g. Sharp-shinned Hawk, Willow Flycatcher). This IBA is notable for being a relatively broad valley that seems to collect large numbers of migrant songbirds during spring and fall, especially riparian-breeding taxa. The Klamath Bird Observatory of Ashland, Oregon has conducted long-term bird research here for several years.

Conservation issues: Though no pressing Conservation issues have come up in the valley, the legacy of clear-cutting and summer grazing has seriously altered aspects of the bird community, most notably contributing to an abundance of Brown-headed Cowbirds, historically absent from the region (B. Claypole, *pers. comm.*).

Shasta Valley

Siskiyou

Nearest town(s): Yreka
Size: 10,000 - 50,000 acres
Threat: Medium
Local Audubon Chapter: Mt. Shasta
BCR: 5

IBA Criteria		Source/Notes
L	14 sensitive species: Redhead, Bald Eagle, Northern Harrier, Ferruginous Hawk, Golden Eagle, Prairie Falcon, Sandhill Crane, Burrowing Owl, Long-eared Owl, Loggerhead Shrike, Bank Swallow, Yellow-breasted Chat, Tricolored Blackbird, Yellow-headed Blackbird	R. Eckstrom, *in litt.*
W	>5000 Waterfowl	5753 waterfowl on 2002 Yreka CBC; B. Smith, *in litt*

Description: In the long shadow of Mt. Shasta, this large area of grassland (including remnant native grasses), juniper woodland, scattered wetlands and cropland is bisected by I-5 just south of the Oregon border. About 5,000 acres of habitat is managed as Shasta Valley Wildlife Area (DFG). The Shasta and Little Shasta rivers flow through the area and support riparian habitat, with that on the former being mostly confined to private ranchland. Several small reservoirs constructed for irrigation water storage within the wildlife area support small, marshes and riparian thickets where the water seeps out of their dams. Other important habitats in the region include Lake Shastina, at the southern end of the IBA, and the scrub habitat of the Kilgore Hills.

Birds: Shasta Valley supports a rich diversity of species within a relatively small area, including most of the representative Great Basin species, as well as several "Californian" taxa from the Cascades (e.g. Oak Titmouse). Bird records have been meticulously kept for many years by Ray Eckstrom. Bank Swallow has been found breeding near Lake Shastina, which hosts large numbers of grebes and diving ducks, and also supports small colonies of breeding "inland seabirds" such as Double-crested Cormorant and Ring-billed and California gulls (D. Shuford, *in litt.*). The grasslands in and around the Siskiyou County Airport north of Montague have held some of the region's few nesting pairs of Burrowing Owl (R. Eckstrom, *in litt.*). It is likely that increased exploration of the Shasta River and continued riparian habitat improvement will yield more avian surprises — both Willow Flycatcher and Yellow Warbler have summered irregularly and would likely respond to restoration.

Conservation issues: Though the area has been managed principally for livestock for the past 150 years, ranchers in the area have recently been very receptive to such conservation measures as constructing cattle fencing around riparian areas (B. Smith, *pers. comm.*.). Water availability remains the driving force for conservation within this IBA, and both the Shasta and the Little Shasta rivers are at the heart of the battle over salmon recovery in the Klamath Basin (both Chinook and Steelhead occur in the area). It remains to be seen what effect recent efforts to designate both fish as endangered species will have on local attitudes toward conservation here. Disturbance from hunting remains high at Lake Shastina. Ray Eckstrom writes: "it's not the last falcon that clears the lake, it's the hunter in a sneak boat who can reduce numbers in the thousands to hundreds in one morning and probably with little to show for his efforts." R. Eckstrom (*in litt.*) also mentions increases in breeding Brown-headed Cowbirds and European Starlings, the latter implicated in the apparent recent extirpation of Purple Martin from the valley.

Vermilion Flycatcher (Brian Small)

Shoshone-Tecopa Area
Inyo

Nearest town(s): Tecopa, Baker
Size: <1000 acres
Threat: Medium
Local Audubon Chapter: San Bernardino Valley
BCR: 33

IBA Criteria		Source/Notes
L	13 sensitive species: Least Bittern, Northern Harrier, Western Snowy Plover, Yellow-billed Cuckoo, Vermilion Flycatcher, Southwestern Willow Flycatcher, Loggerhead Shrike, Least/Arizona Bell's Vireo, Crissal Thrasher, Le Conte's Thrasher, Lucy's Warbler, Yellow-breasted Chat, Summer Tanager	T. and J. Heindel, *pers. comm.*

Description: This habitat gem is associated with the Amargosa River in the northeastern Mojave, less than 20 miles from the Nevada border. Located about halfway between Baker, on I-15, and the headquarters of Death Valley National Park, it is passed by hundreds of thousands of tourists each year, but remains nearly totally undeveloped for birding. One notable exception is China Ranch, which has been eager to spur ecotourism in the region. The vegetation consists of desert riparian thickets (dominated by willows and mesquite), with small areas of wetland and alkali marsh (esp. Grimshaw Lake, just north of Tecopa). Ownership is complex, mainly a combination of small ranches and BLM lands. Main areas for birds include Grimshaw Lake/Tecopa Hot Springs Co. Park area north of Tecopa, and China Ranch, a 218-acre ranch with lush riparian woodland. Several extensive riparian thickets (willows) associated with the Amargosa River are northeast of Shoshone, and mesquite thickets are found just northwest of Shoshone and at "Resting Springs" in Chicago Valley east of Tecopa.

Birds: This area boasts an exceptionally rich avifauna compared with the rest of the Mojave Desert, owing both the abundance of year-round water as well as to its low level of habitat disturbance. China Ranch, only recently opened to birders, has been found to support a tiny population of breeding Yellow-billed Cuckoo, one of only a handful left in California. Other specialties reaching the northern terminus of the ranges in the state at China Ranch include Vermilion and Brown-crested flycatchers and Crissal Thrasher. Small numbers of Bell's Vireo (either Arizona or Least) and Willow Flycatcher (see Sogge et al. 2002) have been found summering in riparian habitat within the IBA, though their racial affiliation is not known at this time. Grimshaw Lake and associated alkali wetlands support breeding Least Bittern, Northern Harrier and Snowy Plover (7 birds in 1978, *fide* Page and Stenzel 1981), otherwise highly localized in the north Mojave. Several endemic non-bird taxa are found here, including the Amargosa Vole (*Microtus californicus scirpensis*).

Conservation issues: Major conservation concerns in this area include the invasion of exotic plants (esp. tamarisk) into desert riparian systems and unauthorized use by OHVs. Fortunately, some of the best habitat in the IBA occurs within China Ranch, which, though private, is committed to managing its resources to attract birders. Still, aside from the areas mentioned, large stretches of the Amargosa River have exceptional potential for providing riparian bird habitat if restored.

Grimshaw Lake, part of Shoshone-Tecopa Area IBA (Jim Boone)

Sierra Meadows – Northern
Sierra/Nevada/Placer/Amador/Alpine/Mono

Nearest town(s): South Lake Tahoe, Truckee
Size: 10,000 - 50,000 acres
Sensitive species: 9 (Northern Goshawk, Golden Eagle, Sandhill Crane, California Spotted Owl, Great Gray Owl, Long-eared Owl, Vaux's Swift, Willow Flycatcher, Yellow Warbler) (T. Beedy, *pers. comm.*)
Threat: Medium
Local Audubon Chapter: Altacal, Plumas, Sacramento, Sierra Foothills
BCR: 15

IBA Criteria		Source/Notes
P	>1% Global population of California Spotted Owl	Grinnell and Miller 1944; Small 1994
P	>10% CA population of Willow Flycatcher	Grinnell and Miller 1944

Description: This IBA refers to several distinct meadow systems in the northern Sierra Nevada, both north and south of Lake Tahoe:

- "Yuba Pass Meadows", Sierra Co. (incl. Lavezola/Empire Ck. located north of Hwy. 49)
- Loney Meadow, Nevada Co. (north of Emigrant Gap/Hwy. 80)
- "Upper Truckee Meadows", Sierra/Nevada Co. (incl. Perazzo and Kyburz meadows and Sagehen Creek; north of Truckee/Hwy. 80)
- Martis Ck./Alpine Meadows, Nevada/Placer Co. (southwest of Truckee/Hwy. 80)
- Kirkwood Meadows, Amador/Alpine Co. (along Hwy. 88 south of Lake Tahoe)
- Leavitt Meadows, Mono Co. (along Hwy. 108 west of Hwy. 395)

The Yuba Pass Meadows, with their lack of roads and old growth forest, have emerged as major conservation priorities for the Sierra Nevada (T. Beedy, *pers. comm.*). All of these sites include USFS land dedicated to timber production and/or recreation, and several have a private component, such as an in-holding by developers (e.g. Kirkwood Meadows). Very little receives formal protection such as Wilderness Area status, and all but Loney Meadow are accessible by paved roads. The Yuba Pass Research Station (Sierra Nevada Field Campus of San Francisco State University) has been conducting research on the avifauna within this IBA for over a decade.

Birds: These meadows have two principal bird communities. First, there are the species that depend directly on the willow thickets for breeding and post-breeding dispersal. These include taxa such as Lincoln's Sparrow, Wilson's Warbler and Willow Flycatcher, with a large proportion of the world's breeding *brewsteri* race of the flycatcher occurring within this IBA. There are also species that seem to concentrate nesting and foraging at the interface between meadow and forest, such as several species of owls, woodpeckers (incl. Pileated) and flycatchers (e.g. Olive-sided). Nearly all of the characteristic Sierran taxa are found in and around these meadows, including Pine Grosbeak and Williamson's Sapsucker. Kyburz Meadow stands out as supporting 1-2 pairs of Sandhill Crane and irregular nesting by Black Tern (DS).

Conservation issues: The meadows located along major Sierran highways, including Kyburz, Sagehen Creek, Martis Creek, Kirkwood and Leavitt receive the heaviest use, with Martis Creek and Kirkwood emerging as popular outdoor recreation destinations year round (hiking/camping in summer, cross-country skiing in winter). Recent proposals for vacation homes at Kirkwood Meadows could have major consequences for the more sensitive components of the bird community there, and recreation pressures on the other sites are expected to increase with development in the Tahoe Basin and the foothills east of Sacramento (*fide* T. Beedy). Summer grazing by cattle and logging in and around these meadows (including the removal of dead and dying trees) continue to be major conservation concerns within this IBA.

Sierra Meadows – Southern

Tuolumne/Mariposa/Madera/Fresno/Tulare

Nearest town(s): Pinecrest, Oakhurst, Shaver Lake, Hume, Camp Nelson, Kernville
Size: 10,000 - 50,000 acres
Sensitive species: 9 (Northern Goshawk, Golden Eagle, Mt. Pinos Blue Grouse, California Spotted Owl, Great Gray Owl, Long-eared Owl, Vaux's Swift, Willow Flycatcher, Yellow Warbler) (B. Barnes, *via email*)
Threat: Medium
Local Audubon Chapter: Central Sierra, Yosemite Area, Fresno, Tulare County
BCR: 15

IBA Criteria		Source/Notes
P	Nearly entire global population of Mt. Pinos Blue Grouse	Grinnell and Miller 1944
P	>1% Global population of California Spotted Owl	Grinnell and Miller 1944
P	Nearly entire CA population of Great Gray Owl	Grinnell and Miller 1944

Description: From the area just north of Yosemite National Park and south to Tulare Co., the Sierra Nevada achieves both its highest peaks as well as its broadest widths. Some of the most critical bird habitat is found in its meadows, and most of these are centered at middle elevations (4500' – 7000'), and vary greatly in terms of habitat quality. The main factors that determine the appeal of meadows to Sierran birds include the health of their willow thickets, the intensity of grazing and the amount of water near the surface. During the late 1990s, the non-profit Institute for Bird Populations conducted an unprecedented survey of avian use of 208 meadows in the Central and Southern Sierra (combined here into simply the "Southern" meadows), in an attempt to document their importance to Sierran birds and to develop a ranking of meadows for inclusion in the California IBA program (Wilkerson and Siegel 2001). The study focused on birds that breed in meadows, those that establish territories preferentially near meadows and those that utilize meadows as post-breeding habitat (long-distance/upslope migrants and local dispersers). The highest-priority meadows are listed in Appendix III.

Compared with the northern Sierra, forest resources may be far better protected within this IBA, as tens of thousands of acres are contained in the massive, world-famous national parks of Yosemite and Sequoia/Kings Canyon. Unfortunately, not all of the most important meadows are particularly well protected within the parks, much less by the three national forests represented within this IBA that maintain a strong culture of timber production.

There are far too many individual meadows to mention here, but aggregations (clusters of three or more

Important Bird Areas of California

"highest priority" meadows) from north to south include (unless noted, all are on USFS land):

- East of Pinecrest, Tuolumne Co. (incl. Bluff)
- Southeast of Wawona in Madera Co. (incl. Topping Cow Camp)
- Dinkey Creek Rd. east of Shaver Lake, Fresno Co. (incl. Poison)
- Patterson area, vic. Wishon Reservoir, Fresno Co. (incl. Hall and Ross)
- Giant Forest area within Sequoia/Kings Canyon National Park, Tulare Co. (incl. Circle and Crescent)
- Quaking Aspen area near Camp Nelson, Tulare Co. (incl. Hossack, Deep and Quaking Aspen)
- "Redwood Meadows" west of Johnsondale, Tulare Co. (incl. Long, Holey, Double Bunk)

Of course, several other important Sierra meadows are not within aggregations, including Zumwalt, Fresno Co. (Kings Canyon National Park); Lower Rock Creek Crossing, Inyo Co. (vic. Cottonwood Lakes southwest of Lone Pine) and over a dozen other "highest priority" meadows (per Wilkerson and Siegel 2001) scattered across the western half of Yosemite National Park and adjacent lands, including Tiltill Valley, Ackerson, Hodgdon, Crane Flat, Big, McGurk and Wawona.

Birds: See Sierra Meadows – Northern IBA above. These meadows reach their highest species diversity in the Central Sierras (Yosemite to Sequoia National Park), and several Sierran species, including Great Gray Owl, Black-backed Woodpecker and Pine Grosbeak have not been recorded south of Sequoia National Park, even historically (B. Barnes, *pers. comm.*). In the far south, the Redwood Meadows area of Tulare Co. is apparently the southernmost regular site for such distinctive Sierran species as Blue Grouse, Pileated Woodpecker, Vaux's Swift, Hammond's Flycatcher and Winter Wren (with scattered potential sites farther south, e.g. Breckenridge Mtn., Kern Co.). The range of the "Mount Pinos" race of Blue Grouse *(Dendragapus fuliginosus howardii)* is apparently wholly contained within this IBA; its northerly contact zone with northerly taxa was placed at southeast Fresno Co. by Grinnell and Miller (1944), and it has not been confirmed south of the Greenhorn Mtns. in decades (Heindel 2001, BB).

Conservation issues: The diverse conservation issues facing each meadow depend largely on two factors – ownership and accessibility. Three main classes of ownership include USFS, wherein meadows are managed to support a mix of summer livestock grazing (cattle and sheep), logging, recreation and wildlife conservation in a broad sense; those managed by the National Park Service, which have seen extractive activities such as logging long banned, but often support heavy recreation use; and a handful of privately-held meadows (notably Ackerson Meadow/Camp Mather), generally operated as cattle pastures and woodlots for the owners. Threats to each depend on ownership, although summer grazing (USFS/private lands) may be the most damaging threat to the greatest number of meadow-dependent bird species by severely reducing or eliminating willow thickets needed for nesting and foraging. The weight of cattle also alters the delicate hydrology of these meadows, and encourages streams to incise into gullies, thus desiccating the meadow. Recreational uses are most severe outside the national parks, where threats include campgrounds and picnic areas located within (rather than adjacent to) meadows and degradation by vehicles (incl. OHV use, unofficial parking lots). Human disturbance, predictably, is most pronounced in meadows near well-traveled roads. Logging continues to have local impacts, especially where it has removed large nesting trees, including dead or diseased individuals. An ungrazed, un-trampled meadow big enough to support a meadow avifauna is a rare sight indeed in this IBA, but even somewhat "disturbed" meadows have emerged as being extremely important to Sierran bird conservation.

Holey Meadow, Tulare Co., part of the Sierra Meadows - Southern IBA (Alison Sheehey © NatureAli)

Sierra Valley

Plumas/Sierra

Nearest town(s): Sierraville, Loyalton
Size: >50,000 acres
Threat: High
Local Audubon Chapter: Plumas
BCR: 15

	IBA Criteria	Source/Notes
P	>10% CA breeding population of White-faced Ibis	Ivey *et al.* 2002
L	18 sensitive species: White-faced Ibis, Bald Eagle, Northern Harrier, Swainson's Hawk, Ferruginous Hawk, Northern Goshawk, Golden Eagle, Peregrine Falcon, Prairie Falcon, Sandhill Crane, Long-billed Curlew, Black Tern, Burrowing Owl, Short-eared Owl, Long-eared Owl, Loggerhead Shrike, Yellow Warbler, Yellow-headed Blackbird	D. Lukas, P. Hardy, *in litt.*
W	>5000 Waterfowl	P. Hardy, *in litt.*

Description: Sierra Valley, the largest intermountain valley in the Sierra Nevada, lies at 5000' elevation just 35 miles northwest of Reno, Nevada. Nearly the entire valley floor (c. 100,000 acres) is comprised of large, privately-owned ranches, and is covered with sagebrush scrub, broken by freshwater marshes, grasslands and riparian woodland. The western portion of Sierra Valley supports unique vernal pools, and the entire edge of the valley supports coniferous forest and chaparral, protecting the headwaters of the Middle Fork Feather River (a "Wild and Scenic River").

Birds: Like the Klamath Basin, Grasslands Ecological Area and the Salton Sea, superlatives define this IBA and its avifauna. But, unlike these areas, Sierra Valley is still in a relatively pristine state, not having been radically transformed by agriculture or human manipulation. Thanks to long-time monitoring by many professional and amateur ornithologists (including the Yuba Pass Research Station), the avifauna of Sierra Valley is exceptionally well-known. It contains what is probably the largest freshwater marsh in the Sierra Nevada, and supports several breeding species not found on managed wetlands (e.g. impoundments), including Black Tern, Wilson's Phalarope, Willet and 13 species of waterfowl (incl. Canvasback). The breeding colony of White-faced Ibis (c. 1000 pr., Ivey *et al.* 2002) is one of the largest in California. During the breeding season, the wetlands of Sierra Valley are heavily used by American White Pelican on feeding runs from Nevada's Pyramid Lake colonies (D. Lukas, via email). Up to 1000 Sandhill Cranes have been counted during spring migration. During early spring (mid-March to mid-April), Sierra Valley supports thousands of northbound waterfowl, notably Greater White-fronted Goose (up to 2000/day) and Cinnamon Teal (up to 1000/day) (P. Hardy, *in litt.*). Shorebird migration is less spectacular, but still significant for the Sierra, with over 200 Willet and 100 Common Snipe recorded during the same period. The concentration of wintering raptors may be unsurpassed in the

Sierra, rivaling the top locales elsewhere in the state. It has had the second-highest count of Rough-legged Hawk on national Christmas Bird Counts (recent high counts of 93 on single-day surveys in 2000, P. Hardy, via email). Burrowing Owl, now essentially eliminated from most of northern California, still maintains a small population here. Conditions for riparian birds are expected to improve with continued restoration activities – small numbers of Willow Flycatchers have been detected singing in the Carman Valley area, and may eventually nest.

Conservation issues: Currently, construction of second homes ("spillover" from the Lake Tahoe market) has been the greatest threat to open space and bird habitat in the Sierra Valley, with water running a close second. Although water is pumped for alfalfa and turf farms and diverted to irrigate pasture during the summer, the water table of this enclosed system is been replenished each year by snowfall. However, recent development pressures (including that related to the expansion of Reno) threaten to upset this balance. The result of this lowering of the water table has been the incursion of sagebrush into meadows and wetlands (often addressed by the ranchers by applying herbicide). Local overgrazing by livestock remains a constant conservation issue within the Sierra Valley, particularly given its lack of land explicitly managed for wildlife. Plumas Audubon has taken a proactive role in helping shape the Sierra Valley General Plan to minimize these effects and to encourage local ranchers to adopt grazing practices that also support wildlife.

Sierra Valley (Steve Hampton)

Skinner Reservoir Area

Riverside

Nearest town(s): Murrieta Hot Springs
Size: 1000-10,000 acres
Threat: High
Local Audubon Chapter: San Bernardino Valley
BCR: 32

IBA Criteria		Source/Notes
L	15 sensitive species: Northern Harrier, Ferruginous Hawk, Golden Eagle, Prairie Falcon, Burrowing Owl, Long-eared Owl, Loggerhead Shrike, Least Bell's Vireo, Cactus Wren, California Gnatcatcher, Yellow Warbler, Yellow-breasted Chat, Sage Sparrow, Grasshopper Sparrow, Tricolored Blackbird	C. McGaugh, *pers. comm.*

Description: Until recently (late-1980s), nearly all the land in this area of western Riverside County was privately-held, characterized by large ranches and dirt roads through the grassland. This facilitated an unprecedented building boom, with a half-million new residents arriving in the past two decades, housed in sprawling tract homes. Combined with widespread conversion of former pastureland to vineyards in the same time, this growth has left much of the open space fragmented and isolated. The Skinner Reservoir area ("Lake Skinner") consists of open water with a well-developed area of riparian woodland at its eastern end. The reservoir is surrounded by Riversidean Coastal Sage Scrub and grassland, including significant amounts of native grassland. This habitat extends southwest (across Borell Rd.) into the former Johnson Ranch area, recently purchased for conservation by the Trust for Public Land, which features pastureland (much of it regularly plowed) alternating with patches of grassland and coastal sage scrub. The third area is contiguous with Black Mountain to the north, which supports large tracts of lush chaparral and patches of oak woodland, including Engelmann Oak Woodland.

Birds: Along with the San Jacinto Valley just to the north and IBAs of north-central San Diego Co., the Skinner Reservoir Area is one of the key wintering raptor areas left in southern California. Prairie Falcon, Golden Eagle and Ferruginous Hawk are regular sights throughout the winter, and a handful of Burrowing Owls (declining sharply) still nest in ground-squirrel colonies. Small numbers of Bald Eagle are regular in winter. The riparian area of the reservoir supports breeding small numbers of Least Bell's Vireo among the expected riparian birds, along with a Great Blue Heron rookery. California Gnatcatcher, Bell's Sage Sparrow and Grasshopper Sparrow are all common in the scrub and grassland surrounding the reservoir. This IBA has become a major research site for the endangered Quino Checkerspot (*Ephydryas editha quino*), a once-abundant butterfly now on the verge of extinction.

Conservation issues: The Western Riverside Multiple Species and Habitat Conservation Plan (WRMSHCP), begun in the late 1990s, is attempting to link and expand the network of undeveloped lands throughout the area (many originally set aside to protect the federally endangered Stephen's Kangaroo-Rat). Much of the protected habitat within this IBA (including the 2500-acre Roy E. Shipley Reserve just north of the reservoir) was set aside by the Metropolitan Water District in the 1990s in exchange for the construction of the massive Diamond Valley Reservoir nearby. Many of the species most dependent on this habitat require vast areas of open space, so the establishment of protected buffers, free from roads, golf courses and new reservoirs will be critical. Careful monitoring of the WRMSHCP process is necessary to ensure that the open spaces designated by the planning process remain so.

Ferruginous Hawk (Brian Small)

South Fork Kern River Valley

Kern

Nearest town(s): Weldon, Lake Isabella
Size: 10,000 - 50,000 acres
Threat: Medium
Local Audubon Chapter: Kerncrest
BCR: 15/33/32

IBA Criteria		Source/Notes
P	Nearly entire global population of Kern Red-winged Blackbird	Grinnell and Miller 1944; T. Gallion, *in litt.*
P	>1% Global population of Southwestern Willow Flycatcher	20-30 pr./yr.; M. Whitfield, *pers. comm.*
P	>10% CA population of Yellow-billed Cuckoo	Ave. 40 birds/yr.; S. Laymon; *in litt.*
P	>10% CA population of Summer Tanager	Up to 40 pr.; S. Laymond, *in litt.*
L	16 sensitive species: Northern Harrier, Ferruginous Hawk, Golden Eagle, Prairie Falcon, Yellow-billed Cuckoo, Burrowing Owl, Long-eared Owl, Southwestern Willow Flycatcher, Loggerhead Shrike, Yellow Warbler, Yellow-breasted Chat, Summer Tanager, Grasshopper Sparrow, Kern Red-winged Blackbird, Tricolored Blackbird, Yellow-headed Blackbird	B. Barnes, S. Laymon; *pers. comm.*

Description: The Kern River is one of the major rivers of the Sierra Nevada, and its watershed, which extends from the highest point in the state south and west into the southern San Joaquin Valley, is totally isolated from other major drainages of the Sierra and the Central Valley. Its two main arms, the North Fork, which drains the High Sierra, and the South Fork, which originates on the Kern Plateau (the southern terminus of the Sierra), meet in a large reservoir called Lake Isabella, which straddles five major bioregions: the Great Basin, the Mojave Desert, the Sierra Nevada, the Central Valley and Coastal California. The South Fork Kern River Valley, about 15 miles in length, contains elements of all of these ecological zones, as well as one of the largest and best-preserved examples of lowland riparian woodland (Fremont Cottonwood-willow) in the state. Other major habitat communities include Joshua Tree woodland, wet meadow, freshwater marsh, Mojave Desert scrub, desert chaparral, and annual grassland. Though much of the 10,000-acre valley floor is privately-held by large cattle ranches, several thousand acres are protected as conservation lands from the eastern edge of Isabella Reservoir east past the community of Onyx, including South Fork Wildlife Area (1200 acres, USFS) at the eastern edge of Lake Isabella; the Kern River Preserve (1100 acres, National Audubon Society) just to the east; and Canebrake Ecological Reserve (1300 acres, DFG) beyond Onyx.

Birds: This IBA is best known for supporting one of a handful of large populations of Yellow-billed Cuckoo left in the western U.S. (ave. 40 birds/summer). It is the metropolis of the Kern Red-winged Blackbird, a poorly-known race confined to the lower Kern River watershed, and supports California's largest population of Summer Tanager, with an estimated 80 birds summering. Its breeding Willow

Flycatchers (20-30 pr. each year) is one of the largest population of the federally threatened "Southwestern" race in the world. Between 11 and 16 pairs of Brown-crested Flycatchers breed here, the state's largest aggregations away from the lower Colorado River. The riparian bird community is exceptionally rich, with 95 species documented as nesters, and over 130 species breeding in the valley as a whole. Mid-summer bird censuses have documented around 300 Yellow Warblers (most singing males) and over 1000 Song Sparrows covering only about 50% of the habitat (B. Barnes, *unpubl. data*). The wetlands in the IBA support large numbers of nesting Tricolored Blackbirds (up to 1500 pr., BB), which feed with other blackbirds in the agricultural fields and feedlots in the valley. Alkali meadows and wet grasslands here support an interesting interior-coastal blend of species, including White-tailed Kite, Northern Harrier, Common Snipe and Grasshopper Sparrow. Spring migration can be spectacular, with thousands of songbirds moving through the riparian forest in April and early May, and fall migration is highlighted by the arrival of 30,000 southbound Turkey Vultures that roost in the riparian forest during September and October (Rowe and Gallion 1996). Research at the Kern River Preserve has been ongoing since the 1980s when The Nature Conservancy was the owner, and has resulted in numerous publications on the Yellow-billed Cuckoo, the Southwestern Willow Flycatcher and Turkey Vulture migration. Most of the current work is coordinated by the Southern Sierra Research Station at the Kern River Preserve.

Conservation issues: Parasitism by Brown-headed Cowbirds was a major threat to the riparian songbird community, which rebounded dramatically following the initiation of cowbird trapping in the 1990s (with the notable exception of Southwestern Willow Flycatcher reproduction). Periodic inundation of the western three miles of riparian forest by Isabella Reservoir remains a threat (mainly in wet years), as does over-grazing by livestock on private lands adjacent to the reserves (mainly in dry years). A growing threat involves the lowering of the water table associated with a shifting away from grazing and toward irrigated row crops valley-wide, which could have a serious effect on the riparian habitat of the IBA (*fide* B. Barnes).

Southern Orange County

Orange

Nearest town(s): San Clemente
Size: 50,000+ acres
Threat: Critical
Local Audubon Chapter: Sea and Sage, South Coast
BCR: 32

IBA Criteria		Source/Notes
P	>1% Global population of Coastal Cactus Wren	Conservation Biology Institute 2001
P	>1% Global population of California Gnatcatcher	350+ pr., USFWS 1998
L	21 sensitive species: Least Bittern, Northern Harrier, Ferruginous Hawk, Golden Eagle, Western Snowy Plover, California Spotted Owl, Burrowing Owl, Long-eared Owl, Southwestern Willow Flycatcher, Loggerhead Shrike, Least Bell's Vireo, Purple Martin, Cactus Wren, California Gnatcatcher, Swainson's Thrush, Yellow Warbler, Yellow-breasted Chat, Sage Sparrow, Grasshopper Sparrow, Tricolored Blackbird, Yellow-headed Blackbird	Hamilton and Willick 1996; Gallagher 1997

Description: This area refers to more than 50,000 acres of a grassland/oak/riparian belt along the base of the foothills in southern Orange County (east of I-5), between the tract home development of Mission Viejo and Rancho Santa Margarita and the San Diego Co. (Camp Pendleton) border. Its most sensitive resources have been intensively studied and mapped through California's Natural Communities Conservation Plan (NCCP), and summarized by the Conservation Biology Institute (2001). This IBA may be divided the area into four distinct subregions: Arroyo Trabuco/Trabuco Canyon in the north, Canada Chiquita and San Juan Creek Watershed in the center, and the San Mateo Watershed in the south, along the San Diego Co. border. According to Stephenson and Calcarone (1999), San Mateo Creek is "probably the most pristine coastal stream south of the Santa Monica Mountains." This area includes most of the last remaining large, intact blocks of the coastal southwestern California ecosystem currently available for conservation acquisition. Much of the higher-elevation habitat, such as mixed evergreen woodland (Canyon Live Oak/Big-cone Douglas-Fir) is protected by the USFS (Cleveland National Forest), though significant blocks of lowland habitats such as coastal sage scrub and oak-sycamore riparian exist on the Starr Ranch Sanctuary (National Audubon Society) and Caspers Regional Park (Orange County). Long-term avian monitoring at Starr Ranch is overseen by the Starr Ranch Bird Observatory (P. DeSimone, *pers. comm.*).

Birds: Based on remaining habitat, this IBA is believed to support at least 50% of the remaining global population of San Diego Cactus Wren, the race endemic to Orange and San Diego Co. (and adjacent Baja) and 15-25% of the remaining U.S. population of California Gnatcatcher (Conservation Biology Institute 2001). The Coto de Caza-Canada Chiquita population was estimated at more than 350 pr. by

USFWS (1998), making it one of the two largest aggregations in the U.S. (along with Otay Ranch in southern San Diego Co.). True lowland taxa such as Burrowing Owl, Southwestern Willow Flycatcher and Grasshopper Sparrow still maintain highly localized breeding populations here. These, as well as a diverse wintering raptors community have been nearly extirpated from the coast of southern California. The IBA is of critical importance for the few remaining pairs of Golden Eagle and Long-eared Owl left in Orange Co., and may have recently lost its tiny remnant population of Purple Martin (Gallagher 1997). Some of the unique microhabitats used by birds here include alkali marshes along Chiquita Canyon that support hundreds of Tricolored Blackbirds (Conservation Biology Institute 2001). Large carnivores, including Mountain Lion and Bobcat, are still frequent sights in this area.

Conservation issues: These private lands represent virtually the last large, easily-developable area along the coastal plain between San Diego and Los Angeles, and the owners have recently disclosed plans for construction of approximately 14,000 homes (R. Hamilton, *pers. comm.*). The other major threat to these lands is the proposed southerly extension of the 261 Toll Road between Santa Margarita and San Clemente. The success of the NCCP in setting aside and defending the most important habitats is critical to the survival of this IBA. Locally, urban runoff from adjacent development has altered local hydrology and exacerbated exotic plant invasion at lower elevations throughout this area (P. DeSimone, *pers. comm.*). While additional conservation purchases along this foothill belt could add to the aggregate amount of protected area here, it is the lowland portions that are probably more critical to maintain the threatened biodiversity of the region.

Stone Lakes NWR Area

Sacramento

Nearest town(s): Sacramento, Elk Grove
Size: 10,000 - 50,000 acres
Sensitive species: 9 (Least Bittern, Northern Harrier, Swainson's Hawk, Ferruginous Hawk, Sandhill Crane, Long-billed Curlew, Burrowing Owl, Short-eared Owl, Loggerhead Shrike) (C. Conard, *via email*)
Threat: High
Local Audubon Chapter: Sacramento
BCR: 32

IBA Criteria		Source/Notes
S	Probably >10,000 Shorebirds	C. Conard, *via email*
W	>5000 Waterfowl	c. 16,000 waterfowl in winter; C. Conard, *via email*

Description: Originally part of the flood zone of the Sacramento and Cosumnes rivers prior to the creation of levees, this IBA also protects patches of remnant valley riparian woodland dominated by Valley Oak, as well as several vernal pools. Designated only in 1994, Stone Lakes NWR currently protects about 4000 acres (of a 20,000 project area) of grassland, cropland and freshwater wetland habitat straddling I-5 just south of Sacramento (T. Harvey, *in litt.*). The refuge area represents a mosaic of public (state and federal) and private land, about a third of which is under cultivation. The Sacramento Regional County Sanitation District Bufferlands ("Bufferlands") extend 2,650 acres of habitat north toward metropolitan Sacramento, and Delta Meadows River Park (State of California) extends the habitat south into the Sacramento Delta, essentially contiguous with the vast Cosumnes River Preserve. Delta Meadows features a remnant "Tidal Freshwater Swamp" along the Sacramento River, which, though small, provided a model for The Nature Conservancy's efforts to restore a portion of the Cosumnes River Preserve (J. Trochet, *pers. comm.*). Stone Lakes and the Cosumnes form a "V" around the southern border of the Sacramento-Elk Grove metropolitan area, and provide a critical buffer between the urban footprints of Sacramento and Stockton. Furthermore, Stone Lakes contributes strongly to the undeveloped land between the Sacramento Delta and the Sierra foothills via the Cosumnes River.

Birds: This IBA is known to support large numbers of waterfowl (at least 6000 per day in winter at Stone Lakes, with 10,000+ at Bufferlands) and both migratory and wintering shorebirds (2000+ each Dunlin and Black-bellied Plover winter at Bufferlands, *fide* C. Conard). The Bufferlands have seen peaks of Canvasback of the 15-20,000 individuals, and Ring-necked Duck exceeding 2000 birds (C. Conard, *via email*). During surveys in 1998, Stone Lakes was found to support the largest breeding colony of Double-crested Cormorants (180 pr.) in the Central Valley (Shuford *et al.* 1999). A handful of Swainson's Hawks and Burrowing Owls breed here, and heron rookeries hosts around 300 birds at Stone Lakes

Important Bird Areas of California

and 75 pairs at Bufferlands (Great Egret, Great Blue Heron). It is likely that continued investigation of the area and the restoration of the native habitats (especially riparian vegetation) will reveal additional sensitive species utilizing the site. Important non-bird species documented from the area include Valley Elderberry Longhorn Beetle and Giant Garter Snake, both endemic to the Central Valley.

Conservation issues: Aside from the Bufferlands and the patchwork 4000 acres of Stone Lakes NWR, much of the habitat in this area is under severe threat, and it is not known whether the qualities of this IBA can withstand these pressures (*fide* B. Treiterer, *pers. comm.*). The main conservation issue in the region involves the conversion of "bird-friendly" grassland, pastureland, and cropland to comparatively sterile vineyards, which have already claimed thousands of acres of wildlife habitat in the area around Stone Lakes (and elsewhere in California). Exotic species, including Pepperweed and Water Hyacinth, continue to threaten grassland and marshy areas of the refuge. Finally, pesticide use remains at high levels in the area, and may be impacting bird reproduction. Fortunately, an active staff at Stone Lakes is working with local landowners to acquire their unwanted parcels and to establish conservation easements on surrounding lands. For the past ten years, Bufferlands has supported a major riparian/wetlands restoration ("Upper Beach Lake"), and similar work at Stone Lakes continues, in both cases with the help of numerous volunteers from the community.

Suisun Marsh
Solano

Nearest town(s): Fairfield, Suisun City, Benicia
Size: >50,000 acres
Threat: High
Local Audubon Chapter: Napa-Solano
BCR: 32

	IBA Criteria	Source/Notes
P	Entire Global population of Suisun Song Sparrow	H. Spautz, *unpubl. data*
P	>1% Global population of Tule White-fronted Goose	Small 1994
P	>1% Global population of California Black Rail	Evens and Nur, in press
P	>1% Global population of California Clapper Rail	C. Jones and D. Feliz, *in litt.*
P	>1% Global population of Long-billed Curlew	R. Leong, *via email*
P	>1% Global population Saltmarsh Common Yellowthroat	Nur *et al.* 1997
P	Probably >10% California population of Yellow Rail	R. Leong, *via email*
L	16 sensitive species: Least Bittern, Tule White-fronted Goose, Northern Harrier, Ferruginous Hawk, Golden Eagle, Peregrine Falcon, Yellow Rail, Black Rail, Long-billed Curlew, Burrowing Owl, Short-eared Owl, Loggerhead Shrike, Saltmarsh Common Yellowthroat, Bryant's Savannah Sparrow, Suisun Song Sparrow, Tricolored Blackbird	C. Jones and D. Feliz, *in litt..*; R. Leong, *via email*
S	>10,000 Shorebirds	C. Jones and D. Feliz, *in litt.*
W	>5000 Waterfowl	54,480 at "Suisun Marsh" on 6 January 2003; USFWS 2003b

Description: Covering about 84,000 acres northeast of San Francisco Bay, Suisun Marsh is the largest contiguous estuarine marsh in the U.S. Along with the Concord Marshes on the south side of Suisun Bay, it ecologically links the Central Valley/Delta Area with the Pacific Coast. The area is dominated by a vast, central block of diked wetlands, which consist of former tidal marsh separated by levees and alternately drained and filled with water (both fresh and brackish), surrounded by tidal marsh and the open waters of Grizzly and Suisun Bay. Another large area of diked wetlands is found on the northwest side of the IBA, against Hwy. 680. Politically, the IBA is a patchwork of 14,300 acres of state-owned parcels (known collectively as the Grizzly Island Complex), plus several thousand acres of agricultural lands and private duck clubs. A significant private parcel of wetlands and grassland, Rush Ranch, has recently been acquired by the Solano Land Trust. Despite a history of disturbance, this remains a decidedly wild area, with abundant River Otter, an introduced herd of Tule Elk, several rare wetland plants and the Salt Marsh Harvest Mouse.

Birds: An endemic race of Song Sparrow, Suisun Song Sparrow, has essentially its entire global population (c. 20-50,000 individuals) within the IBA, and it is believed to be the only area in the world where the Saltmarsh Common Yellowthroat, another Bay-Area endemic, is common (Nur et al. 1997). Suisun Bay is one of the few areas of California that supports more than 100,000 waterfowl during the winter, with "dabbling ducks" (Green-winged Teal, Mallard, Northern Pintail, Northern Shoveler and American Wigeon) especially well represented. This is in contrast with the bay ducks (e.g. scaup) typical of San Francisco and San Pablo bays. Suisun is one of just three wintering areas for the rare "Tule" race of the Greater White-fronted Goose (Small 1994). With its mix of freshwater and tidal marsh, nearly every wetland bird species in the region occurs here, often in exceptional numbers. The number of California Black Rails here and in the adjacent Carquinez Straits rivals that of San Pablo Bay just to the west, which holds about half the global population of the taxon (Evens and Nur, in press). Unlike coastal wetlands, just a handful of California Clapper Rails have been noted in the IBA, associated with tidal sloughs. Short-eared Owl winters in large numbers and many still breed, the only regular nesting locale along the coast of California. The diked wetlands support breeding colonies of Tricolored Blackbird; American White Pelican have recently begun summering in large numbers and may conceivably begin to breed. The hundreds of Great Egret breeding at Suisun represent an estimated 35% of the San Francisco Bay Area population (Kelly et al. 1993). As the upland areas surrounding Suisun Marsh become increasingly developed, their conservation will be of greater importance in the region for raptors (Golden Eagle has nested recently in the Portrero Hills north of Grizzly Isl.) and open-country species like Loggerhead Shrike. Yellow Rail, an almost mythical marsh bird essentially extirpated in the state, was detected in February of 2002 (two birds), and may prove to be regular in winter (RL).

Conservation issues: From the Goals Project (1999), conservation efforts should focus on restoring and connecting tidal channels throughout the area, protecting vernal pools and other seasonal wetlands, enhancing natural transitions from tidal marsh to upland (e.g. grassland, woodland habitat in Portrero Hills), and maintaining open space for buffers around wetlands. This will rely on a combination of exotic species removal (the entire IBA is extensively invaded with Peppergrass and other exotics), dike reconfiguration, and land easements/acquisitions.

Surprise Valley

Modoc

Nearest town(s): Ft. Bidwell, Cedarville
Size: >50,000 acres
Threat: Low
Local Audubon Chapter: Eagle Lake
BCR: 9

IBA Criteria		Source/Notes
P	>1% Global population of Greater Sage-Grouse	S. Blankenship, *via email.*
P	Entire known CA breeding population of Yellow Rail	M. San Miguel, *via email.*
P	>10% CA breeding population of Greater Sandhill Crane	Ivey and Herzinger 2001
P	>10% CA population of interior-breeding Western Snowy Plover	494 birds Page *et al.* 1991
L	20 sensitive species: Redhead, Bald Eagle, Northern Harrier, Swainson's Hawk, Ferruginous Hawk, Golden Eagle, Peregrine Falcon, Prairie Falcon, Greater Sage-Grouse, Yellow Rail, Sandhill Crane, Western Snowy Plover, Long-billed Curlew, Short-eared Owl, Vaux's Swift, Loggerhead Shrike, Bank Swallow, Yellow Warbler, Tricolored Blackbird, Yellow-headed Blackbird	J. Sterling, D. Shuford, *pers. comm.*
S	>10,000 Shorebirds	c. 10,000 shorebirds in recent spring surveys, D. Shuford *unpubl. data*
W	Probably >5000 Waterfowl	J. Sterling, D. Shuford, *pers. comm.*

Description: This enormous valley parallels the California-Nevada border from Oregon to Lower Alkali Lake, 50 miles to the south. It encompasses three other major seasonal lakes, Upper Alkali Lake, Middle Alkali Lake, and, in the extreme northeastern corner of the state, Cowhead Dry Lake. These wetlands are filled after wet winters by water draining off the eastern slopes of the Warner Mountains. Agricultural fields (mainly alfalfa) and pastureland cover the valley floor west of the lakes, and most of the bird habitat of Surprise Valley is restricted to private lands.

Birds: A diverse raptor community (especially important for wintering Rough-legged Hawk, *fide* J. Sterling) and good numbers of Great Basin species that require wide, open spaces (incl. breeding Long-billed Curlew and Sandhill Crane) characterize Surprise Valley. The cranes, found to represent the second-largest breeding population in the state (14% of the total, *fide* Ivey and Herziger 2001), are of the "Greater" race that breeds in the western Great Basin. The vast sagebrush flats of this valley support several known leks of Greater Sage-Grouse (S. Blankenship, via email). The seasonal wetlands support a full compliment of wetland breeders scarce on managed wetlands (e.g. abundant Black Tern), including the only California population of (presumably) breeding Yellow Rail near Cowhead Lake north of Ft. Bidwell (MSM). The alkali lakes in the valley floor held the largest Snowy Plover population (hundreds of pairs) in California during a statewide survey in the 1980s (DS), and support thousands of shorebirds each day during spring and fall (D. Shuford *unpubl. data*). An unusual urban-breeding population of Vaux's

Swift occurs at Ft. Bidwell at the north end of the valley (JS). Though not particularly relevant to its IBA status, Surprise Valley occasionally supports eastern breeding species with western outposts in the riparian and meadow habitat at the northern end of the valley (e.g. Eastern Kingbird, Least Flycatcher, Bobolink).

Conservation issues: Given its remoteness and despite the private ownership, the wildlife resources of Surprise Valley are not threatened at this time. However, expansion of agriculture in the area could reduce the overall amount of water in the valley, which could affect its wetland habitats.

Yellow Rail (Brian Small)

Taft Hills

Kern

Nearest town(s): Taft, Maricopa
Size: >50,000 acres
Sensitive species: 8 (Ferruginous Hawk, Golden Eagle, Prairie Falcon, Burrowing Owl, Loggerhead Shrike, San Joaquin Le Conte's Thrasher, Sage Sparrow, Tricolored Blackbird) (S. Fitton, *via email*)
Threat: High
Local Audubon Chapter: Kern
BCR: 32

IBA Criteria		Source/Notes
P	Nearly entire global population of San Joaquin Le Conte's Thrasher	S. Fitton, *unpubl. data*

Description: This IBA refers to the low, rolling hills at the eastern edge of the Temblor Range in the southwestern San Joaquin Valley. It extends along the far western border of Kern Co. from Maricopa and Taft northwest to just north of McKittrick (vic. Lokern Rd.). Buena Vista Creek (usually dry) drains the eastern flank of the IBA just north of Taft. According to an assessment by The Nature Conservancy (1998), this site ranked highest of all "arid upland sites" in the San Joaquin Valley (essentially the last large example of this community left), owing to its strong populations of sensitive species, especially endemic plants. The dominant habitat is an alkali scrub of saltbushes (*Atriplex* spp.), dense and lush in some areas forming Interior Coast Range Scrub (see Holland 1986). This mixes with alkali grassland, much of which has been converted to exotic annual grasses. Public lands dominate here, with BLM holdings and Dept. of Energy oil fields accounting for most of the acreage. The Lokern Preserve, operated by the non-profit Center for Natural Lands Management, serves as a land bank for mitigation of impacts to endangered species habitat in the region.

Birds: This IBA draws attention to the last large population of San Joaquin Le Conte's Thrasher (*Toxostoma lecontei macmillanorum*). This taxon occurs within a distinct, intact natural community of birds that includes breeding Prairie Falcon, Greater Roadrunner, the canescens race of Sage Sparrow, plus wintering Sage Thrasher, Mountain Bluebird, and both Vesper and Brewer's sparrows.

Conservation issues: Much of the habitat of this IBA is located on active oil fields or on lands awaiting gas and oil exploration. While this has had considerable impact to the habitat, it has probably also contributed somewhat to its conservation by isolating it from human disturbance (e.g. OHV use). Unfortunately, fire (generally arson) remains the greatest threat to the alkali scrub here, as it can quickly convert vital alkali scrub to exotic grassland in seconds.

Tehachapi Oaks

Kern

Nearest town(s): Tehachapi/Bear Valley
Size: 10,000 - 50,000 acres
Sensitive species: 2 (Swainson's Hawk, Purple Martin) (B. Williams, via email)
Threat: Critical
Local Audubon Chapter: Kern
BCR: 15

IBA Criteria		Source/Notes
P	>10% CA population of Purple Martin	Williams 1998

Description: This IBA refers to the northwestern slope of the Tehachapi Mtns., southeast of Bakersfield, land that is wholly within the vast Tejon Ranch. Overlooking the southern end of the Central Valley, high ridges in this area support an extensive oak woodland ecosystem (one of the largest in the state) that includes many massive, ancient individuals. Warm summer winds sweep up from the valley floor, bringing with them abundant insect prey for the birds here, including large dragonflies that congregate in exceptionally high numbers on exposed ridges.

Birds: These oaks are the primary nesting habitat for what is by far the largest breeding aggregation of Purple Martins in California, and one of just a handful left in central and southern California. Brian Williams (*pers. comm.*) estimates close to 200 pairs breeding, nearly $1/4$ of the state population. These birds are apparently selecting massive Valley Oaks with commanding views for nest sites, as well as an absence (or rarity) of European Starlings, a major nest competitor that has been linked to declines throughout the West. This area appears to be of great importance to cavity-nesting birds, and was historically important for California Condor foraging. Swainson's Hawk has nested recently (SF), but its current status is not known.

Conservation issues: During the late 1990s, roads and houses began creeping up the slopes of the mountains in this IBA, bringing with them the associated urban birds, including starlings. It remains to be seen how the ecosystem responds to this combination of physical encroachment and introduction of competitors, but conservation of undeveloped ridges with remnant oaks is thought to be essential in maintaining martin populations.

Terminal Island Tern Colony

Los Angeles

Nearest town(s): Los Angeles (Wilmington)
Size: <1000 acres
Sensitive species: 4 (Royal Tern, Elegant Tern, Least Tern, Black Skimmer)
(K. Garrett, *pers. comm.*)
Threat: Critical
Local Audubon Chapter: Palos Verdes/South Bay
BCR: 32

IBA Criteria		Source/Notes
P	>1% Global population of California Least Tern	c. 300 pr. in 2002; K. Keane, *unpubl. data*
P	>10% CA breeding population of Elegant Tern	c. 5000 pr. in 2002; K. Garrett, *pers. comm.*
P	>10% CA breeding population of Royal Tern	20 pr. in 2002; K. Garrett, *pers. comm.*
P	Possibly >10% CA breeding population of Black Skimmer	<10 pr. in 2002; K. Garrett, *pers. comm.*

Not a natural island, but a 15-acre patch of fill-dirt within Los Angeles Harbor that, like Brooks Island and Alameda NAS in San Francisco Bay, has become attractive to nesting birds. With roughly 300 pairs in 2002, this site protects a significant proportion of the southern California's beleaguered population of California Least Tern. Roughly half the breeding Elegant Tern population in the U.S. nests here, as well as most of California's breeding Royal Terns. A few hundred Caspian Tern also breed, along with a handful of Black Skimmer. This site is apparently slated for major modification, which will wipe out the nesting terns. As mitigation, key areas of existing wetlands in the area (see Orange Coast Wetlands IBA) could be protected and portions managed for breeding terns prior to the loss of the Terminal Island site.

Tijuana River Reserve

San Diego

Nearest town(s): Imperial Beach, San Ysidro, Tijuana (Mexico)
Size: 1000-10,000 acres
Threat: Medium
Local Audubon Chapter: San Diego
BCR: 32

IBA Criteria		Source/Notes
P	>1% Global population of California Least Tern	233 nests in 2002; K. Keane, *unpubl. data*
P	>1% Global population of Light-footed Clapper Rail	98 birds in 1997; B. Collins, *in litt.*
P	>1% Global population of Least Bell's Vireo	c. 200 pr. in valley; B. Abbott, *pers. comm.*
L	16 sensitive species: Northern Harrier, Light-footed Clapper Rail, Western Snowy Plover, Long-billed Curlew, Least Tern, Short-eared Owl, Loggerhead Shrike, Least Bell's Vireo, Cactus Wren, Clark's Marsh Wren, California Gnatcatcher, California Swainson's Thrush, Yellow Warbler, Yellow-breasted Chat, Belding's Savannah Sparrow, Large-billed Savannah Sparrow	B. Collins, *in litt.*; San Diego Natural History Museum 2000

Description: The Tijuana River Reserve (one of three National Estuarine Research Areas in California) consists of about 2,500 acres of land at the extreme southwestern corner of California, adjacent to Mexico. It is dominated by two protected areas, Tijuana Slough NWR in the north, adjacent to the city of Imperial Beach, and Borderfield State Park to the south, along the Mexican border. The site consists of tidal saltmarsh associated with the mouth of the Tijuana River (which flows northwest from Baja California, Mexico), and also features natural coastal dunes, riparian thickets, and Diegan Coastal Sage Scrub.

Birds: The area supports a large population of Light-footed Clapper Rail (c. 100 individuals, second only to Upper Newport Bay) and breeding Northern Harrier (one of only a handful of nesting locales left on the coast of southern California). This IBA is a major nesting area for California Least Tern, and several other terns, including Gull-billed, forage here from nearby colonies (see South San Diego Bay IBA). Predictably, a small population of Snowy Plover is present as well, with 11 clutches produced in 1997 and up to 68 birds wintering (B. Collins, in litt). California Gnatcatcher occurs in patches of coastal sage scrub here, and the riparian thickets on the east side of the site support breeding Least Bell's Vireo. Like all large coastal riparian habitat areas in California, these thickets are important for large numbers of migrant (and wintering) songbirds such as Southwestern Willow Flycatcher, which may breed (San Diego Natural History Museum 2002).

Conservation issues: The foremost threats are posed by the encroaching urban edge and the associated exotic species invasions and by direct impacts from recreation. The eastern edge of the site is seeing increasing urbanization (esp. tract housing), which is eliminating the agricultural lands that once provided a buffer between the habitat and the urban sprawl of San Ysidro-Imperial beach and Tijuana. Recent cowbird trapping has been successful, at least for Bell's Vireo, which have rebounded from a low of 5 males in the early 1990s (B. Abbott, *pers. comm.*). The site is a major human movement corridor between Mexico and the U.S., and numerous illegal trails, along with the accompanying activities of Border Patrol agents, continue to degrade the habitat of the site.

Willow forest along Tijuana River (Dennis Parker)

Tomales Bay

Marin

Nearest town(s): Inverness, Point Reyes Station, Marshall
Size: 1000-10,000 acres
Threat: Low
Sensitive species: 9 (Least Bittern, Brant, Northern Harrier, Yellow Rail, Black Rail, Western Snowy Plover, Long-billed Curlew, California Swainson's Thrush, Bryant's Savannah Sparrow) (Shuford 1993)
Local Audubon Chapter: Marin, Madrone
BCR: 32

IBA Criteria		Source/Notes
P	>1% Global population of Pacific Black Brant	Kelly and Tappen 1998
P	>10% CA winter population of Yellow Rail	D. Shuford, *pers. comm.*
S	>10,000 Shorebirds	Shuford *et al.* 1989
W	>5000 Waterfowl	Kelly and Tappen 1998

Description: Tomales Bay is a narrow, 15-mile-long tidal estuary along the San Andreas Fault on the northeast side of Pt. Reyes. It is situated between Bodega Bay in the north and Bolinas Lagoon in the south, to the east of Drake's Estero – all critical estuaries of the Pt. Reyes region. Most of the tidal marsh and mudflat habitat forms at the south end, near the village of Inverness, with additional habitat at the mouth of Walker Ck. along the northeast shore. The south side of the bay grades into an extensive freshwater marsh/riparian corridor (incl. Olema Marsh), surrounded by humid coniferous forest. About 1000 acres of wetlands and adjacent uplands here is managed by the State of California (Tomales Bay State Park, Tomales Bay Ecological Reserve), which continues to add acreage with the help of the non-profit Trust for Public Land. The IBA has been intensively studied by both Audubon Canyon Ranch (through the Cypress Grove Research Station) and by PRBO.

Birds: Of all the Pt. Reyes wetlands, Tomales Bay consistently supports the highest numbers of wintering and migrant waterbirds, with up to 20,000 shorebirds spending the winter (Shuford *et al.* 1989). Winter surveys have documented thousands of Bufflehead and Brant, which represent 12% and 31%, *resp.*, of statewide wintering populations (Kelly and Tappen 1998). This site supports California's largest population of Black Rail on the immediate coast (though much larger numbers occur within San Francisco Bay), and in recent winters has even hosted Yellow Rail, a species nearly extirpated from California. Least Bittern maintains one of its only Bay Area colonies at Olema Marsh.

Conservation issues: Because this site is so well protected, no major threats such as development have been identified. However, Kelly and Tappen (1998) have pointed to potential disturbance of waterfowl by recreational and fishing boat (incl. kayaks) within the bay. Recently, high levels of mercury have been detected in the bay.

Topaz Lake Area

Mono

Nearest town(s): Topaz Lake, NV; Wellington, NV
Size: 10,000 - 50,000 acres
Threat: Medium
Local Audubon Chapter: None
BCR: 9

IBA Criteria		Source/Notes
L	11 sensitive species: Bald Eagle, Northern Harrier, Swainson's Hawk, Ferruginous Hawk, Golden Eagle, Prairie Falcon, Long-billed Curlew, Loggerhead Shrike, Bank Swallow, Yellow Warbler, Yellow-headed Blackbird	E. Strauss, *via email*

Description: One of a handful of IBAs shared with Nevada, this valley in the eastern Sierra Nevada at the northern tip of Mono Co. is formed by the west fork of the Walker River, which flows north into Nevada to feed Walker Lake in Nevada, one of the most important sites in the Great Basin for waterbirds. The California side of the valley begins at the town of Walker along Hwy. 395 and extends north to Topaz Lake, a medium-sized reservoir on the Nevada border. The southern side of the lake features a draw-down area where ducks, geese and shorebirds congregate during fall migration. The valley is extensively planted with alfalfa, but remnant stands of riparian woodland (highly restorable) persists along channels of the Walker River, all of which is located on private ranchlands.

Birds: The West Walker River is one of a handful of major rivers connecting the Sierra Nevada of California with the vast wetlands of Nevada. Though research is still in its infancy, it is likely that these corridors, including the Walker, Carson and Truckee rivers, are major avian movement corridors between the Great Basin and California. Topaz Lake is the only regular breeding site for Bald Eagle south of Lake Tahoe, supporting just one pair each year (with several more in winter, ES). Swainson's Hawk nests in the tall cottonwoods south of Topaz Lake, and Long-billed Curlew, another classic Great Basin breeder, nests in small numbers in the Antelope Valley, its only nesting site in Mono County. Finally, Bank Swallow maintains a small colony in a borrow pit (gravel mine) near the town of Topaz, and no doubt once bred commonly along the Walker River prior to its alteration. Occasional records of Yellow-billed Cuckoo from the Walker River (in Nevada) also suggest that this species may still be prospecting for breeding here. Today, large numbers of waterfowl visit Topaz Lake, particularly Common Loon migrating in early spring (*fide* T. Beedy).

Conservation issues: This IBA has been extensively altered. Originally, the Walker River would have flowed through the Antelope Valley, cutting channels, forming oxbows and supporting patches of natural wetlands. This historic landscape is nearly gone, with the river now largely relegated to a central channel (thankfully, unlined), surrounded by and tapped for alfalfa cultivation, and dammed to form Topaz Lake. While this scene is not particularly threatened, this is an area that could benefit greatly from riparian and wetland restoration.

Trinidad Rocks

Humboldt

Nearest town(s): Trinidad
Size: <1000 acres
Sensitive species: 3 (Fork-tailed Storm-Petrel, Cassin's Auklet, Tufted Puffin) (Carter *et al.* 1992)
Threat: Medium
Local Audubon Chapter: Redwood Region
BCR: 32

IBA Criteria		Source/Notes
P	>10% CA population of Fork-tailed Storm-Petrel	200 birds; Carter *et al.* 1992
P	>10% CA population of Tufted Puffin	82 birds; Carter *et al.* 1992

This IBA refers to several large offshore rocks between Elk Head and Little River State Beach, centered on the town of Trinidad. These include (north to south) White Rock, Green Rock, Flatiron Rock, the Trinidad Bay Rocks and Little River Rock (see Carter *et al.* 1992). These rocks support one of the most diverse seabird nesting colonies in California, including one of the few California colonies of Fork-tailed Storm-Petrel (200 birds on Little River Rock) and small numbers of Tufted Puffin (Green Rock, Puffin Rock), as well nearly 10,000 Leach's Storm-Petrel (2/3 of California's population) and over 30,000 Common Murre (Carter *et al.* 1992). Just ashore of these rocks, Little River State Beach has recently supported small numbers of breeding Snowy Plover (JS). Though the rocks are secure from human disturbance, Double-crested Cormorants, greatly increasing as breeders on the northwest coast, may pose a threat to nesting seabirds.

Tulare Lake Bed

Kings

Nearest town(s): Corcoran, Kettleman City
Size: >50,000 acres
Threat: High
Local Audubon Chapter: Kern or Tulare County
BCR: 32

	IBA Criteria	Source/Notes
P	>1% Global population of Mountain Plover	143 birds along S.R. 41 on 2 February 2002; S. Fitton, *via email*
P	>10% CA population of interior-breeding Snowy Plover	252 birds; Page *et al.* 1991
L	15 sensitive species: White-faced Ibis, Redhead, Northern Harrier, Swainson's Hawk, Ferruginous Hawk, Western Snowy Plover, Mountain Plover, Long-billed Curlew, Least Tern, Black Tern, Burrowing Owl, Short-eared Owl, Loggerhead Shrike, Tricolored Blackbird, Yellow-headed Blackbird	
S	>10,000 Shorebirds	Shuford *et al.* 1998
W	>5000 Waterfowl	5000 Ruddy Ducks on 17 January 2001; L. Cole, *unpubl. data*

Description: The ancient Tulare Lake Bed, once covering hundreds of thousands of acres in the middle of the San Joaquin Valley, has now been reduced to a vast, nearly lifeless agricultural landscape of cotton fields and cement-lined irrigation channels. Nature, however, has a way of reasserting herself, and this lake bed is no exception. Periodically flooded fields and basins recreate the vast natural wetland habitats that have been lost, and many of the birds can't tell the difference. Aside from large evaporation ponds, the largest, most consistently flooded regions are fields within the South Wilbur and Hacienda Flood Areas, located in the southeastern corner of Kings County, between I-5 and 6th Ave. (west of Alpaugh). South Wilbur, located on the southern shore of the original Tulare Lake Bed, area has been identified as "the largest remaining historic wetland in the San Joaquin Valley" (TNC 1998). Hacienda was historically upland habitat, but the owner, J.G. Boswell Co., uses it, along with South Wilbur, for water storage. These two areas, along with flooded agricultural fields in the area, support nearly 20,000 acres of wetlands during wet years (TNC 1998). During dry years, the vast floodwater basins are colonized by native alkali scrub and grassland, along with their associated sensitive species. There is no public land in or near this IBA, and private property rights are tightly controlled.

Birds: This area is a true magnet for birds year-round. During the spring, winter and fall, any flooded field in this area can attract thousands of waterfowl, gulls and shorebirds, and in winter, these same fields become raptor habitat. Fall migration use of this IBA by shorebirds (August-September) can be higher than any other site in the Central Valley, as wetland habitat is scarce at this time elsewhere (Shuford *et* *al.* 1998). Burrowing Owl is still common in the area, particularly along the remaining unlined irrigation channels, and Short-eared Owls cruise fallow fields on winter nights. Dozens of Mountain Plover have been found in flocks in winter, particularly along Utica Rd. During the nesting season, any reservoir or pond left un-cleared can develop fairly extensive freshwater marsh habitat, which have hosted Least Bittern, rails, Black Tern, Tricolored Blackbird and other marsh birds. Though these species breed throughout the IBA, they often shift locations based on water levels and habitat conditions. Even the bare dirt levees around agricultural evaporation ponds and constructed (as mitigation) wetlands here and to the north toward Corcoran have become key habitats for birds, utilized by a suite of "alkali playa" breeders that includes Snowy Plover and several tern species. In fact, the Tulare Lake Bed remains essentially the only site in the San Joaquin Valley supporting numbers of breeding Caspian and Forster's terns, once common nesters throughout the original wetlands of the valley (Shuford *et al.* 1999), and this area has emerged as the major Central Valley stronghold for Snowy Plovers, a handful of which breed (Shuford *et al.* 1998).

Conservation issues: Still, the fact that this IBA is currently managed solely for water storage and agricultural production and currently contains no protected lands, all of its wildlife resources should be considered at some level of risk. As with other large wetlands, communicable disease (e.g. avian botulism) has been a persistent problem, particularly during the breeding season. Agricultural runoff remains a major threat to breeding species, and this IBA contains many large settling ponds that fill with potentially lethal water. Unpredictable water management also poses an immediate threat, since nesting birds suffer if water is drained too quickly in spring. In upland areas, gazing pressure is intense, which limits its utility to grassland birds. Still, unmanaged (for conservation) flooded agricultural fields such as those within this IBA have emerged as key summer breeding sites for many wetland bird species otherwise excluded from nesting on refuges due to lack of summer water.

Vandenberg AFB

Santa Barbara

Nearest town(s): Lompoc
Size: >50,000 acres
Threat: Medium
Local Audubon Chapter: La Purisima
BCR: 32

	IBA Criteria	Source/Notes
P	>1% Global population of California Least Tern	65 nests in 2002; K. Keane, *unpubl. data*
P	>10% CA population of coastal-breeding Western Snowy Plover	242 birds in summer 1991; USFWS 2001
L	20 sensitive species: Least Bittern, Northern Harrier, Ferruginous Hawk, Peregrine Falcon, Prairie Falcon, Western Snowy Plover, Mountain Plover, Long-billed Curlew, Least Tern, Burrowing Owl, Short-eared Owl, Long-eared Owl, Southwestern Willow Flycatcher, Loggerhead Shrike, California Swainson's Thrush, Yellow Warbler, Yellow-breasted Chat, Sage Sparrow, Grasshopper Sparrow, Tricolored Blackbird	Lehman 1994; D. Compton, *pers. comm.*

Description: Vandenberg Air Force Base covers nearly 100,000 acres on the coast of northern Santa Barbara County, just north of Pt. Concepcion. Like Camp Pendleton in northern San Diego County, it is a DoD property that could easily qualify as a national park with its spectacular scenery and rich natural resources. Bisected by the Santa Ynez River (see above), it extends east to near Lompoc (Harris Grade Rd./ Miguelito Rd.) and supports a staggering diversity of habitats, from coastal Bishop Pine forest to tidal marsh to mature cottonwood-willow riparian woodland. It also protects several plant and animal taxa found nowhere else one earth, including an endemic California plant community, Burton Mesa Chaparral, found wholly within its borders. Barka Slough, along the San Antonio River, is one of the largest natural freshwater marshes in the bioregion, and another example of this marsh/riparian habitat is maintained at a series of "waterfowl management ponds" west of Lompoc. About 97% of the base is maintained "in essentially a wild state" (A. Naydol, Chief, Natural Resources Dept., VAFB, *in litt.*).

Birds: The list of the sensitive birds at this IBA reads like a who's-who list for rare and declining California species. The remote headlands around Pt. Arguello support the farthest-south site on the mainland for breeding seabirds (mainly Pelagic Cormorant and Pigeon Guillemot, but also a handful Rhinoceros Auklet, *fide* Carter et al. 1992). The broad, sandy beaches (esp. vic. Purisima Point and Santa Ynez River mouth) offer scarce nesting habitat for Least Tern (up to 100 pr. in recent years) and one of the state's largest population of breeding and wintering Snowy Plover. The tidal marsh and mudflats at the mouth of the Santa Ynez River can host hundreds of migrant and winter waterbirds, particularly when the river is allowed to reach the ocean, and supports a colony of saltmarsh-nesting Savannah Sparrows of an undetermined subspecies. Riparian and freshwater marsh birds such as Least Bittern

Important Bird Areas of California

and Yellow-breasted Chat breed in small numbers, and Southwestern Willow Flycatcher could eventually re-colonize the extensive habitat at Barka Slough. The scrub habitats, including the Burton Mesa Chaparral north of the Santa Ynez River, supports one of the largest colonies of the scarce Bell's Sage Sparrow in Central California, with up to 325 breeding pairs (A. Naydol, *unpubl. data*). Finally, open-country birds occur here in numbers unprecedented elsewhere on the Central Coast, with Ferruginous Hawk, Burrowing Owl and Mountain Plover (up to 27 birds in 1997, *Ibid*) occurring in winter and Grasshopper Sparrow breeding.

Conservation issues: Vandenberg has made admirable efforts to maintain suitable habitat for sensitive species on the base, including the removal of cattle from about a third of former grazing land (and from all wetlands and oak woodlands, A. Naydol, *in litt.*). Habitat known to support federally threatened and endangered species (e.g. Peregrine Falcon, Least Tern, Snowy Plover) is "totally protected", according to A. Naydol (*in litt.*). The biggest threat is now from exotic plant invasion, especially ice plant, Veldt grass, and European Beach Grass along the coast and tamarisk in riparian areas. Fires burning sensitive habitat (e.g. recently at Barka Slough) remain a constant threat. A local Audubon chapter, La Purisima, has recently cultivated a relationship with the base and is involved with surveying birds and small-scale habitat restoration at the waterfowl ponds. However, as a DoD installation whose primary mission is military preparedness (and not resource conservation), the resources on Vandenberg will probably remain somewhat threatened for the foreseeable future.

Important Bird Areas of California

Yolo Bypass Area

Yolo

Nearest town(s): Sacramento, Davis, Woodland
Size: 10,000 - 50,000 acres
Threat: Low
Local Audubon Chapter: Yolo
BCR: 32

IBA Criteria		Source/Notes
P	>1% Global population of Mountain Plover	200 birds on 2 February 2002; K. Hunting, *unpubl. data*
P	>1% Global population of Long-billed Curlew	1681 birds on 2001 Sacramento CBC
P	>1% Global population of Tricolored Blackbird	15,000 at single site in 1999; S. Hampton, *pers. comm.*
L	14 sensitive species: Least Bittern, White-faced Ibis, Aleutian Canada Goose, Redhead, Northern Harrier, Swainson's Hawk, Ferruginous Hawk, Mountain Plover, Long-billed Curlew, Short-eared Owl, Loggerhead Shrike, Yellow-breasted Chat, Tricolored Blackbird, Yellow-headed Blackbird	S. Hampton, S. England, *via email*
S	>10,000 Shorebirds	S. Hampton, *via email*
W	>5000 Waterfowl	238,230 waterfowl in January 2003; USFWS 2003b

Description: Though a largely artificial system of spreading basins and controlled water releases, the Yolo Bypass is nonetheless one of the key freshwater marsh ecosystems in California. Other wildlife habitats include riparian forest and grassland, much of which is currently being restored. This IBA is centered within the historical wetland sink of Putah Creek, which flows east into the Sacramento Valley from the Coast Range. The Bypass itself extends south around the west side of Sacramento for about 30 miles, rejoining the river in the Sacramento Delta. It is intersected by both I-5 and I-80, main arteries north and west out of Sacramento. About 3600 acres south of I-80 was acquired by the Wildlife Conservation Board (DFG) and is being managed and restored for habitat as the Vic Fazio Yolo Basin Wildlife Area (formerly "Yolo Bypass Wildlife Area"). Cache Creek Settling Basin, within the Bypass, extends the habitat north of I-80. Nearby and adjacent to the bypass, several private holdings and restoration sites contribute greatly to bird habitat within the IBA, notably Conaway Ranch (incl. Willow Slough), Trestle Ponds (City of Woodland) and Davis Wetlands (City of Davis).

Birds: The avifauna of the Yolo Bypass area is similar to that of the refuges north of Sacramento (see Sacramento Valley Wetlands IBA above). Winter duck counts within the Wildlife Area alone have approached 40,000 individuals, with Northern Pintail and Northern Shoveler particularly well represented. Mountain Plover has recently been discovered to winter here, with 200 birds found at Midway and Levee Rd. on statewide plover surveys on 2 February 2002. Up to 1000 Aleutian Canada

Geese have been recording staging in spring at the Yolo Basin Wildlife Area (S. England, *in litt.*). Tricolored Blackbirds are irregular nesters, although in 1999, 15,000 bred at Conaway Ranch (SH). Remarkable numbers of shorebirds use seasonal wetlands year round here, especially the ponds at Davis Wetlands and at the Yolo Basin Wildlife Area, which supports hundreds of Greater Yellowlegs each fall. An impressive 32 species of shorebirds have been recorded at the Davis Wetlands, including up to 2000 Wilson's Phalarope in migration, a handful of which remain to breed in 2001 (SH). Several thousand waterfowl occur here in late fall, including what may be one of the largest concentrations of wintering Cinnamon Teal in the U.S. (1000 birds, S. Hampton, *via email*). Trestle Ponds have hosted 10,000 shorebirds during spring migration when flooded. Species utilizing freshwater marsh habitat in summer include White-faced Ibis ("thousands" during the summer of 2001 *Ibid.*) and even Least Bittern at Conaway Ranch, which would represent one of a handful of Sacramento Valley populations for each. Northern Harriers nest in abundance in freshwater marshes, and even Short-eared Owl has been documented breeding in the Sacramento Bypass at the north end of the IBA (*Ibid*). Riparian habitat is rebounding within this IBA, and Yellow-breasted Chat is suspected of breeding in regenerating willow-cottonwood forest at Cache Creek Settling Basin. Another riparian species, Swainson's Hawk, maintains a large breeding concentration along Willow Slough, with an average of 20 pairs each year (S. England, *in litt.*). Grassland restoration could lead to more surprises – Grasshopper Sparrows have been recorded during the breeding season lately, though with no evidence of nesting (SH).

Conservation issues: The Central Valley Habitat Joint Venture Plan, developed by a consortium of private landowners, agency representatives and conservation scientists, called for the restoration of 20,000 acres of new wetland habitat within this IBA and over 10,000 acres were purchased in 2001 (S. England, *in litt.*). Since large amounts of open space have already been acquired here, exotic plant invasions associated with constructed wetlands and agriculture are among the top conservation concerns. Though most of the southern portion of the IBA is probably secure from the effects of development, urban sprawl from the north (e.g. housing tracts associated with Davis) threaten to constrict the habitat locally. During the 1990s, a proposal to create a "North Delta National Wildlife Refuge" to adjoin Vic Fazio Yolo Basin Wildlife Area at its southern end was being examined by the USFWS, and may reemerge as a viable plan in the future.

Bibliography

Abraham, C.L., K.L. Mills and W.J. Sydeman. 2000. Population size and reproductive performance of seabirds on Southeast Farallon Island, 2000. Unpublished Report, PRBO. Stinson Beach, CA.

Accurso, L. 1992. Distribution and abundance of wintering waterfowl on San Francisco Bay. M.A. Thesis, Humboldt State University, Arcata.

Allen, L. and K.L. Garrett. 1995. Atlas Handbook: Los Angeles County Breeding Bird Atlas. Los Angeles Audubon Society, West Hollywood, CA.

BirdLife International. 2000. Threatened Birds of the World. Lynx Edicions and BirdLife International, Barcelona and Cambridge, UK.

Boxall, B. 2001. Taking a Gander at Geese's Comeback. Los Angeles Times. B1. April 10, 2001.

Brown, S., C. Hickey, B. Harrington and R. Gill, eds. 2001. The U.S. Shorebird Conservation Plan, 2nd ed. Manomet Center for Conservation Sciences. Manomet, MA.

Burness, G.P., Lefevre, K. and C.T. Collins. 1999. Elegant Tern (Sterna elegans). In The Birds of North America, No. 404 (A. Poole and F. Gill, eds.). The Birds of North America, Inc. Philadelphia, PA.

Burridge, B., ed. 1995. Sonoma County Breeding Bird Atlas. Madrone Audubon Society. Inc., Santa Rosa, California.

California Department of Fish and Game. 2000. Annual report on the status of endangered, threatened and candidate species. Birds: Species accounts. Retrieved 2002, from the World Wide Web: http://www.dfg.ca.gov/hcpb/species/t_e_spp/ann_te_rpt.shtml

California Department of Fish and Game and Point Reyes Bird Observatory 2001. California Bird Species of Special Concern: Draft List and Solicitation of Input. Retrieved 2002, from the World Wide Web: http://www.prbo.org/BSSC/draftBSSClist.pdf

California Resources Agency 1994. California Bioregions. Retrieved 2002, from the World Wide Web: http://ceres.ca.gov/geo_area/bioregion_index.html

California State Water Resources Control Board. 1994. Final Environmental Impact Report for Review of Mono Basin water rights of the City of Los Angeles. Sacramento, CA. September 1994.

California Partners in Flight. 2001. Bird Conservation Plans. Point Reyes Bird Observatory, February 2001. Retrieved 2002, from the World Wide Web: http://prbo.org/CPIF/Consplan.html

Cardiff, S.W. and J.V. Remsen, Jr. 1981. Breeding avifaunas of the New York Mountains and Kingston Range: Islands of Conifers in the Mojave Desert of California. Western Birds 12:73-86.

Carter, H.R., G.J. McChesney, D.L. Jaques, C.S. Strong, M.W. Parker, J.E. Takekawa, D.L. Jory and D.L. Whitworth, Point Reyes Bird Observatory and Channel Islands National Park. 1992. Breeding populations of seabirds in California, 1989-1991. U.S. Dept. of the Interior, Minerals Management Service, Los Angeles, CA.

Center for Biological Diversity, Santa Clara Valley Audubon Society, Defenders of Wildlife, San Bernardino Valley Audubon Society, California State Park Rangers Association, and Tri-County Conservation League 2003. Petition to the state of California Fish and Game Commission and supporting information for listing the California population of the western Burrowing Owl (Athene cunicularia hypugaea) as an endangered or threatened species under the California Endangered Species Act. Submitted April 8, 2003.

Collins, C.T. and K.L. Garrett. 1996. The Black Skimmer in California: an overview. Western Birds 27:127-135.

Colwell, M. 1994. Shorebirds of Humboldt Bay, California: Abundance Estimates and Conservation Implications. Western Birds 25:137-145.

Conservation Biology Institute. 2001. On the global and regional ecological significance of southern Orange County: Conservation Priorities for a biodiversity hotspot. Prepared for Endangered Habitats League, Los Angeles, CA.

Cooper, D.S. 2000. Breeding landbirds of a highly threatened open space: The Puente-Chino Hills, California. Western Birds 31:213-234.

DeSante, D.F. and E. Ruhlen. 1995. A census of burrowing owls in California, 1991-1993. Institute for Bird Populations. Point Reyes Station, CA.

Edwards, A.L. 2000. Livermore Birds: Locations and Calendar. http://fog.ccsf.cc.ca.us/~jmorlan/livermore.htm.

England, A.S. and W.F. Laudenslayer, Jr. 1989. Distribution and seasonal movements of Bendire's Thrasher in California. Western Birds 20:97-124.

Evens, J.G. and N. Nur. California Black Rail in the San Francisco Bay region: Abundance indices and habitat affinities. Journal of Field Ornithology. In press.

Gaines, D. 1988. Birds of Yosemite and the East Slope. Artemisia Press. Lee Vining, CA.

Gallagher, S.R. 1997. Atlas of Breeding Birds, Orange County, California. Sea & Sage Press, Sea & Sage Audubon Society, Irvine, CA.

Garrett, K. and J. Dunn. 1981. Birds of Southern California: Status and Distribution. Los Angeles Audubon Society, Los Angeles, CA.

Garrison, B.A., J.M. Humphrey and S.A. Laymon. 1987. Bank Swallow distribution and nesting ecology on the Sacramento River, California. Western Birds 18:71-76.

Gilmer, D.S., K.A. Gonzalez, M.A. Wolder, and N.R. Graves. 1998. Nongame and upland gamebird surveys on Sacramento National Wildlife Refuges, 1986 and 1993. Western Birds 29:83-102.

Glover, S. 2001. Contra Costa Co., CA Breeding Bird Atlas. Retrieved 2002, from the World Wide Web: http://www.flyingemu.com/ccosta/

Goals Project. 1999. Baylands Ecosystem Habitat Goals. A report of habitat recommendations prepared by the San Francisco Bay Area Wetlands Ecosystem Goals Project. First Reprint. U.S. Environmental Protection Agency, San Francisco, California/S.F. Bay Regional Water Quality Control Board, Oakland, CA.

Gould, G.I., Jr. 1974. Breeding success of piscivorous birds at Eagle Lake, California. M.S. Thesis, Humboldt State University, Arcata.

Green, H. and D.A. Airola. 1997. Checklist of the birds of the Lake Almanor Area, Plumas County, California (unpublished).

Grenfell, W.E., Jr., and W.F. Laudenslayer, Jr., eds. 1983. The distribution off California birds. California Wildlife/Habitat Relationships Program. Publ. #4. Calif. Dept. Fish and Game, Sacramento, and USDA Forest Service, San Francisco, CA.

Grinnell, J. and A.H. Miller. 1944. The distribution of the birds of California. Pacific Coast Avifauna 27.

Halterman, M.D., S.A. Laymon, M.J. Whitfield. 1989. Status and distribution of the Elf Owl in California. Western Birds 20:71-80.

Hamilton, R.A. and D.R. Willick. 1996. The Birds of Orange County, California: Status and Distribution. Sea & Sage Press, Sea & Sage Audubon Society, Irvine, CA.

Hamilton, W.J. III. 2000. Tricolored Blackbird. 2000 breeding season census and survey. Observations and recommendations. Unpublished.

Harris, S.W. 1996. Northwestern California Birds. 2d ed. Humboldt State University Press, Arcata, California.

Heindel, M. 2000. Birds of eastern Kern County. Unpublished Report.

Hickman, J.C. 1993. The Jepson Manual: higher plants of California. University of California Press, Berkeley.

Holland, R.F., 1986. Preliminary descriptions of the terrestrial natural communities of California. State of California, The Resources Agency, Nongame Heritage Program, Dept. Fish & Game, Sacramento, Calif. 156 pp.

Holland, R.F. 2000. The Flying M Ranch: soils, plants and vernal pools in eastern Merced County. Fremontia 27:4 and 28:1.

Humple, D.L. and G.R. Geupel. 2002. Autumn populations of birds in riparian habitat of California's Central Valley. Western Birds 33:34-50.

Institute for Wildlife Studies. 2002. San Clemente Sage Sparrow. Retrieved 2002, from the World Wide Web: http://www.iws.org/sparrow.htm

Ivey, G.L., S.L. Earnst, E.P. Kelchlin, L. Neel, and D.S. Paul. 2002. White-faced Ibis Status Update and Management Guidelines: Great Basin Population. U.S. Fish and Wildlife Service, Portland, OR.

Ivey, G.L. and C.P. Herziger. 2001. Distribution of Greater Sandhill Crane pairs in California, 2000. Unpublished Report.

Jaques, D.L., C.S. Strong, and T.W. Keeney. 1996. Brown Pelican roosting patterns and responses to disturbance at Mugu Lagoon and other non-breeding sites in the Southern California Bight. National Biological Service, Technical Report No. 54, Tucson, AZ.

Kelly, J.P., H.M. Pratt, and P.L. Greene. 1993. The distribution, reproductive success, and habitat characteristics of heron and egret breeding colonies in the San Francisco Bay Area. Colonial Waterbirds 16:18-27.

Kelly, J.P. and S.L. Tappen. 1998. Distribution, abundance and implications for conservation of winter waterbirds on Tomales Bay, California. Western Birds. 29:103-120.

Kemper, J. 1999. Birding Northern California. Falcon Publishing, Inc. Helena, Montana.

Kushlan, J.A., M.J. Steinkamp, K.C. Parsons, J. Capp, M.A. Cruz, M. Coulter, I. Davidson, L. Dickson, N. Edelson, R. Eilliot, R.M. Erwin, S. Hatch, S. Kress, R. Milko, S. Miller, K. Mills, R. Paul, R. Phillips, J.E. Saliva, B. Sydeman, J. Trapp, J. Wheeler and K. Wohl. 2002. Waterbird Conservation for the Americas: The North American Waterbird Conservation Plan, Version 1. Waterbird Conservation for the Americas, Washington, DC, U.S.A., 78 pp.

Lamb, C. and A.B. Howell. 1913. Notes from Buena Vista Lake and Fort Tejon. The Condor 15:115-120.

LaHaye, W. S., R. J. Gutiérrez, and H. R. Akçakaya. 1994. Spotted owl metapopulation dynamics in southern California. Journal of Animal Ecology 63:775-785.

Laymon, S. and M. Halterman. 1987. Can the western subspecies of Yellow-billed Cuckoo be saved from extinction? Western Birds 18:19-25.

Lehman, P.E. 1994. The Birds of Santa Barbara County, California. University of California, Santa Barbara Vertebrate Museum, Santa Barbara, CA.

Linton, C.B. 1908. Notes from Buena Vista Lake, May 20 to June 16, 1907. The Condor 10:196-198.

Littlefield, C.D. 1995. Greater Sandhill Crane Nesting and Production in Northeastern California, 1988. Western Birds 26:34-38.

Long, M.C. 1993. Birds of Whittier Narrows Recreation Area, Los Angeles County, California. Whittier Narrows Nature Center Associates, South El Monte, CA.

LSA Associates 2001. Revised Resource Inventory Draft, Eastshore Park Project Site. September 2001.

Massey, B.W. and M.U. Evans. 1994. An eight-year census of birds of Vallecito Creek, Anza-Borrego Desert, California. Western Birds 25:169-177.

McChesney, G.J., H.R. Carter and M.W. Parker. 2000. Nesting of Ashy Storm-Petrels and Cassin's Auklets in Monterey County, California. Western Birds. 31:165-177.

McKernan, R.L. and G. Braden. 2001. Status, distribution, and habitat affinities of the Southwestern Willow Flycatcher along the Lower Colorado River. Year 4 – 1999. Unpublished report submitted to the U.S. Bureau of Reclamation, U.S. Fish and Wildlife Service, and the U.S. Bureau of Land Management.

Modoc NWR. 2003. Results of waterfowl, shorebird and raptor survey: March 11, 2003. Retrieved 2003 from the World Wide Web: http://modoc.fws.gov/current/html

Molina, K.C. 2000. Breeding populations of Gull-billed Terns (Sterna nilotica vanrossemi) in southern California, 2000. Contract No. 101810M393, final report to U.S. Fish and Wildlife Service, Carlsbad, CA.

The Nature Conservancy. 1995. Sacramento Valley and foothill bioregion biological scoping project. Unpublished report.

The Nature Conservancy. 1998. San Joaquin Valley and foothill ecoregional plan – Draft. Unpublished Report.

The North American Bird Conservation Initative – United States. 2002. Bird Conservation Regions. Retrieved 2002 from the World Wide Web: http://www.nabci-us.org/map.html

Nur, N, S. Zack, J. Evens and T. Gardali. 1997. Tidal marsh birds of the San Francisco Bay Region: status, distribution and conservation of five Category 2 taxa. Draft final report to U.S. Geological Survey – BRD. Point Reyes Bird Observatory.

Page, G.W. and T. Ruhlen. 2002. Summary of surveys for breeding Snowy Plovers and American Avocets at Owens Lake in 2002. October 1, 2002. Point Reyes Bird Observatory. Unpulished report.

Page, G.W. and W.D. Shuford. 2000. Southern Pacific Coast regional shorebird plan. Version 1.0. Retrieved 2002, from the World Wide Web: http://www.manomet.org/USSCP/files.htm.

Page, G.W. and L. Stenzel. 1981. The breeding status of the Snowy Plover in California. Western Birds 12:1-40.

Page, G.W. L.E. Stenzel and W.D. Shuford. 1991. Distribution and abundance of the Snowy Plover on its western breeding grounds. Journal of Field Ornithology. 62(2)245-255.

Page, G.W., L.E. Stenzel and J.E. Kjelmyr. 1999. Overview of shorebird abundance and distribution in wetlands of the Pacific coast of the contiguous United States. Condor 101:461-471.

Pashley, D.N., C.J. Beardmore, J.A. Fitzgerald, R.P. Ford, W.C. Hunter, M.S. Morrison, K.V. Rosenberg. 2000. Partners In Flight: Conservation of the Land Birds of the United States. American Bird Conservancy. The Plains, VA.

Ralph, C. John; L. George, Jr; M.G. Raphael, and J.F. Piatt, Technical Eds. 1995. Ecology and Conservation of the Marbled Murrelet. Gen. Tech. Rep. PSW-GTR-152. Albany CA: Pacific Southwest Research Station, Forest Service, U.S. Department of Agriculture; 420 p.

Remsen, J.V. 1978. Bird species of Special Concern in California: an annotated list of declining or vulnerable bird species. California Dept. of Fish and Game, Sacramento, CA.

The Resources Agency. 1992. Bird Species of Special Concern. California Department of Fish and Game, Wildlife Management Division, Nongame Bird and Mammal section. July, 1992.

Roberson, D. and C. Tenney. 1993. Atlas of the Breeding Birds of Monterey County, California. Monterey Peninsula Audubon Society, Carmel, CA.

Rosenberg, K.V., R.D. Ohmart, W.C. Hunter and B.W. Anderson. 1991. Birds of the Lower Colorado River Valley. The University of Arizona Press, Tucson, AZ.

Rowe, S.P. and T. Gallion. 1996. Fall migration of turkey vultures and other raptors through the southern Sierra Nevada, California. Western Birds 27:48-53.

San Diego Natural History Museum. 2002. San Diego County Breeding Bird Atlas: Species accounts. Retrieved 2002, from the World Wide Web: http://www.sdnhm.org/research/birdatlas/

Sedinger, J.S., D.H. Ward, R.M. Anthony, D.V. Derksen, C.J. Lensink and K.S. Bollinger. 1994. Management of Pacific brant: population structure and conservation issues. Transactions of the North American Wildlife and Natural Resources Conference 59:50-62.

Sequoia Audubon Society. 2001. San Mateo County Breeding Bird Atlas. May 2001.

Shaw, D.W.H. 1998. Change in population size and colony location of breeding waterbirds at Eagle Lake, California, between 1970 and 1997. M.S. Thesis. California State University, Chico.

Shuford, W.D. 1993. The Marin County Breeding Bird Atlas: A distributional and natural history of coastal California birds. Bushtit Books, Bolinas, California.

Shuford, W.D. 1998. Surveys of Black Terns and other inland-breeding seabirds in northeastern California. In 1997. Report 98-03, Bird and Mammal Conservation Program, Calif. DFG, Sac.

Important Bird Areas of California

Shuford, W.D., Hickey, C.M. R.J. Safran and G.W. Page. 1996. A review of the status of the White-faced Ibis in California. Western Birds. 27:169-196.

Shuford, W.D., J.M. Humphrey and N. Nur. 1999. Surveys of terns and cormorants in California's Central Valley in 1998. Final report of Point Reyes Bird Observatory.

Shuford, W.D., J.M. Humphrey and N. Nur. 2001. Breeding status of the Black Tern in California. Western Birds. 32:189-217.

Shuford, W. D., G.W. Page, J. G. Evens, and L. E. Stenzel. 1989. Seasonal abundance of waterbirds at Point Reyes: a coastal California perspective. Western Birds 20:137-265.

Shuford, W.D., G.W. Page and J.E. Kjelmyr. 1998. Patterns and dynamics of shorebird use of California's Central Valley. Condor 100:227-244.

Shuford, W.D., G.W. Page and L.E. Stenzel. 2002. Patterns of distribution and abundance of migratory shorebirds in the Intermountain West of the United States. Western Birds 33:134-174.

Shuford, W.D. and T.P. Ryan 2000. Nesting populations of California and Ring-billed Gulls in California: recent surveys and historical status. Western Birds 31:133-164.

Shuford, W.D., N. Warnock, K.C. Molina, B. Mulrooney and A.E. Black. 2000. Avifauna of the Salton Sea: Abundance, distribution and annual phenology. Contribution No. 931 of Point Reyes Bird Observatory. Final report for EPA Contract No. R826552-01-0 to the Salton Sea Authority, 78401 Hwy. 111. Su. T, La Quinta, CA.

Small, A. 1994. California Birds: Their Status and Distribution. Ibis Publishing Co., Vista, California.

Sogge, M.K., S.J. Sferra, T. McCarthey, S.O. Williams and B. Kus. 2002. Southwestern Willow Flycatcher breeding site and territory summary 2001. Prepared for: The Southwestern Willow Flycatcher Recovery Team, USFWS, Albequerque, NM. October 2002.

Stephenson, J.R. and G.M. Calcarone. 1999. Southern California mountains and foothills assessment: habitat and species Conservation issues. General Technical Report GTR-PSW-172. Albany, CA: Pacific Southwest Research Station, Forest Service, U.S. Dept. of Agriculture; 402 pp.

Thelander, C.G. and M. Crabtree. 1994. Life on the Edge: A Guide to California's Endangered Natural Resources. Heyday Books, Berkeley, CA.

Unitt, P. 1981. Birds of Hot Springs Mountain, San Diego County, California. Western Birds. 12:125-135.

Unitt, P. 1984. The Birds of San Diego County. San Diego Society of Natural History, San Diego, California.

Unitt, P. 2000a. Gray Vireos wintering in California Elephant Trees. Western Birds 31:258-262.

Unitt, P. 2000b. Focus on Royal and Elegant Terns. Wrenderings (newsletter of the San Diego County Bird Atlas). Summer 2000.

Unitt, P., K. Messer and M. Thery. 1996. Taxonomy of the Marsh Wren in southern California. Proc. San Diego Soc. Nat. Hist. 31:1-20.

U.S. Fish and Wildlife Service. 1998. U.S. Distribution of the California Gnatcatcher (map). Unpublished.

U.S. Fish and Wildlife Service. 2001. Western Snowy Plover (Charadrius alexandrinus nivosus) Pacific Coast Population Draft Recovery Plan. Portland, Oregon. xix + 630 pp.

U.S. Fish and Wildlife Service. 2003a. Update to the North American Waterfowl Management Plan (Draft). Retrieved 2002, from the World Wide Web: http://birdhabitat.fws.gov/NAWMP/2003nawmpdraft.htm

U.S. Fish and Wildlife Service. 2003b. Winter Waterfowl Survey, Pacific Flyway, January 6-10, 2003. Unpublished.

Ventana Wilderness Society. 2001. Notes from the Field. September 2001.

Walton, B.J. 1978. Nesting of Swainson's Hawk in San Luis Obispo County, California in 1977. Western Birds 9:82.

Warnock, N., S.M. Haig and L.W. Oring. 1998. Monitoring species richness and abundance of shorebirds in the western Great Basin. Condor 100:589-600.

Weaver, K.L. 1998. A new site of sympatry of the California and Black-tailed Gnatcatchers. Western Birds 29:476-479.

Wells, J.M. and B. Kus. 2001. Least Bell's Vireo surveys and nest monitoring at Anza Borrego Desert State Park in 2000. Final Report to California State Parks. Colorado Desert District. 200 Palm Canyon Dr., Borrego Springs, CA.

Wilkerson, R.L. and R.B. Siegel. 2001. Establishing a southern Sierra Meadows Important Bird Area: Results from meadow surveys at Stanislaus, Sierra and Sequoia National Forests, and Yosemite and Sequoia/Kings Canyon National Parks. Unpublished report. The Institute for Bird Populations. Point Reyes Station, CA.

Williams, B. 1998. Distribution, habitat associations, and conservation of Purple Martins breeding in California. M.S. Thesis. California State University, Sacramento.

Zembal, R., S.M. Hoffman and J.R. Bradley. 1997. Light-footed Clapper Rail management and population assessment. Final report to California Dept. of Fish and Game, Sacramento, CA. Contract FG4113-01.

Appendix I. Sites identified or nominated as IBAs prior to 2000

Adobe Valley (incl. Black Lake*)
Alameda NAS**
Argus Range – Southern**
Big Morongo Canyon**
Big Sur River Mouth/Pt. Sur Area (incl. Andrew Molera SP**)
Bodega Harbor (Bodega Bay**)
Brooks Island Regional Preserve**
Camp Pendleton**
Carrizo Plain**
Channel Islands – Northern**
Clear Lake Area (incl. McVicar Sanctuary*)
Colorado Desert Microphyll Woodland (incl. N. Algodones Dunes*)
Concord Marshes (incl. Concord NWS **)
Cosumnes River Preserve**
East Park Reservoir**
Elkhorn Slough**
Fall River Valley Area (submitted separately as "Ahjumawi Lava Springs State Park" and "McArthur-Burney Falls State Park", both RJ)
Goleta Coast**
Grasslands Ecological Area**
Klamath Basin (incl. Lower Klamath NWR**)
Lake Almanor Area * (submitted as Lake Almanor, Mountain Meadows Reservoir)
Lake Casitas** Area
Mendocino Coast (incl. Ten Mile River**)
Modoc NWR*
Mono Lake Basin**

Morro Bay**
Napa Lakes (RJ; submitted separately as Lake Berryessa and Lk. Hennessey)
North San Diego Lagoons (incl. San Elijo**)
Owens Lake**
Orange Coast Wetlands (incl. Seal Beach NWR**, Bolsa Chica**)
Point Mugu Area (incl. Mugu Lagoon**)
Richardson Bay**
Sacramento Valley Wetlands (incl. Sacramento NWR Complex**)
Salton Sea** (submitted as "Salton Sea NWR")
San Diego Bay**
San Diego NWR - Eastern (incl. Marron Valley*; "Spring Valley to Rancho Jamul"**)
San Luis Rey River (incl. Upper portion **, Lake Hodges**)
San Pablo Bay Wetlands (incl. Napa River Marshes*)
Santa Clara River Valley (incl. "Ventura Co. portion"**)
Santa Ynez River - Upper**
Seiad Valley* (submitted as "State of Jefferson Byway")
Sierra Valley**
South Fork Kern River Valley**
South San Francisco Bay Wetlands(Don Edwards NWR**)
Southern Orange County (incl. Starr Ranch** Area)
Stone Lakes NWR Area**
Suisun Marsh**
Tijuana River Reserve**
Vandenberg AFB**
Yolo Bypass Area**

* Nominated as an IBA prior to 1999
** Accepted as an IBA by American Bird Conservancy, prior to 1999
RJ Rejected by the ABC as an "Global, Continental, or National" IBA (but possibly to be considered a "State" IBA, R. Chipley, *via email*, 2002)

Sites nominated prior to 1999, considered by Audubon California as IBAs, but rejected because they do not currently meet criteria.

Butterbredt Spring
Napa River Ecological Reserve
Spenceville Wildlife Area

Appendix II. List of California's Audubon Chapters and the IBAs intersected by their membership boundaries

ALTACAL
Feather River – Lower
Sacramento River – Upper
Sacramento Valley Wetlands
Sierra Meadows – Northern

BUENA VISTA
North San Diego Lagoons
San Luis Rey River
Camp Pendleton

CENTRAL SIERRA
La Grange-Waterford Grasslands
Salt Spring Valley
Sierra Meadows – Southern

CONEJO VALLEY
Point Mugu Area
Santa Clara River Valley

EAGLE LAKE
Eagle Lake
Goose Lake, Modoc Co.
Honey Lake Valley
Klamath Basin/Clear Lake
Lake Almanor Area
Modoc NWR
Modoc Plateau
Surprise Valley

EASTERN SIERRA
Adobe Valley
Bridgeport Valley
Crowley Lake Area
Deep Springs Valley
Mono Highlands
Mono Lake
Owens Lake
Owens River

EL DORADO
Lower Los Angeles River
Orange Coast Wetlands

FRESNO
Lone Willow Slough
Mendota Wildlife Area
Merced Grasslands
Panoche Valley
Sierra Meadows – Southern

GOLDEN GATE
Alameda Naval Air Station
Brooks Island Regional Preserve
Eastshore Wetlands
North Richmond Wetlands

KERN
Buena Vista Lake Bed
Carrizo Plain
Goose Lake, Kern Co.
Kern NWR
San Emigdio Canyon
Taft Hills
Tehachapi Oaks
Tulare Lake Bed

KERNCREST
Argus Range – Southern
Kelso Creek
North Mojave Dry Lakes
South Fork Kern River Valley

KLAMATH BASIN
Klamath Basin

LA PURISIMA
Santa Maria River Valley
Santa Ynez River Valley
Santa Ynez River – Upper
Vandenberg Air Force Base

LAGUNA HILLS
San Joaquin Hills

LOS ANGELES
No IBAs within membership boundaries

MADRONE
Bodega Harbor
San Pablo Bay Wetlands
Tomales Bay

MARIN
Bolinas Lagoon
Corte Madera Marsh
Point Reyes – Outer
Richardson Bay
San Pablo Bay Wetlands
Tomales Bay

MENDOCINO COAST
Mendocino Coast

MONTEREY PENINSULA
Big Sur Area
Bolsa de San Felipe
Elkhorn Slough
Monterey Bay
Panoche Valley
Salinas River – Lower
Salinas River - Middle
San Antonio Valley
Santa Lucia Peaks

MORRO COAST
Lopez Lake Area
Morro Bay
Santa Maria River Valley

MT. DIABLO
Byron Area
Concord Marshes
North Richmond Wetlands
Sacramento-San Joaquin Delta

MT. SHASTA
Butte Valley
McCloud River – Upper
Shasta Valley
Seiad Valley

NAPA-SOLANO
Benicia State Recreation Area
Napa Lakes
San Pablo Bay Wetlands
Suisun Marsh
Jepson Grasslands
Sacramento-San Joaquin Delta

NORTH CUESTA
Carrizo Plain
Santa Margarita Valley

OHLONE
East Diablo Range
South San Francisco Bay

PALOMAR
Pamo Valley
San Diego Peaks
San Luis Rey River
San Pasqual Valley

PALOS VERDES/SOUTH BAY
Terminal Island Tern Colony

PASADENA
Los Angeles Flood Control Basins

PEREGRINE
None

PLUMAS
Lake Almanor Area
Sierra Meadows - North
Sierra Valley

POMONA VALLEY
Puente-Chino Hills
Santa Ana River Valley

REDBUD
East Park Reservoir
Clear Lake Area, Lake Co.

REDWOOD REGION
Cape Mendocino Grasslands
Del Norte Coast
Humboldt Bay
Humboldt Lagoons
Trinidad Rocks

SACRAMENTO
Cosumnes River Preserve
Sacramento-San Joaquin Delta
Sierra Meadows – Northern
Stone Lakes NWR Area

SAN BERNARDINO VALLEY
Aguanga Area
Baldwin Lake
Big Morongo Canyon
Cima Dome
East Mojave Peaks
East Mojave Springs
Imperial Valley
Lake Elsinore
Lake Mathews/Estelle Mtn.
Mojave River
Salton Sea
San Jacinto Valley
Shoshone-Tecopa Area
Skinner Reservoir Area
Santa Ana River – Upper

SAN DIEGO
Anza-Borrego Riparian
Elephant Tree Forest
Imperial Valley
Mission Bay
Salton Sea
San Diego NWR – Eastern
San Diego Bay
Tijuana River Reserve

SAN FERNANDO VALLEY
Los Angeles Flood Control Basins
Edwards Air Force Base
Lancaster
Santa Clara River Valley

SAN JOAQUIN
East Diablo Range
Sacramento-San Joaquin Delta

SANTA BARBARA
Channel Islands – Northern
Goleta Coast

SANTA CLARA VALLEY
East Diablo Range
Bolsa de San Felipe
South San Francisco Bay

SANTA MONICA BAY
Ballona Valley

SEA AND SAGE
Orange Coast Wetlands
Orange County Wilderness Parks
Southern Orange County

SEQUOIA
Ano Nuevo Area
South San Francisco Bay

SIERRA FOOTHILLS
Sierra Meadows - North

SOUTH COAST
San Joaquin Hills
Camp Pendleton /Santa Margarita River
Southern Orange County

STANISLAUS
Cooperstown/Red Hills Area
East Diablo Range
Merced Grasslands
Grasslands Ecological Area
San Joaquin River NWR Area

TULARE COUNTY
Central Valley
Creighton Ranch Area
Lake Success Area
Pixley NWR Area
Tulare Lake Bed

VENTURA
Channel Islands – Northern
Lake Casitas Area
Pt. Mugu Area
Santa Clara River Valley

WHITTIER
Puente-Chino Hills
Los Angeles Flood Control Basins

WINTU
Big Valley/Ash Creek
Fall River Valley

YOLO
Yolo Bypass Area

YOSEMITE AREA
Sierra Meadows - Southern

YUMA (Arizona)
Colorado Desert Microphyll Woodland
Lower Colorado River Valley

Sites outside the ranges of current chapter membership boundaries

Carson River – Upper
Farallon Islands
San Clemente Island
Cuyama Valley
Topaz Lake

Appendix III. List of "High Priority" Southern Sierra Meadows (from Wilkerson and Siegel 2001)

Sequoia National Forest
Quaking Aspen
Double Bunk
Hossack
Long I
Beck Rodeo Flat
Huckleberry
Crane
Deep
Upper Parker
Troy
East Rowell
Dunlap
Taylor

Sequoia/Kings Canyon National Parks
Alta
Grouse
Zumwalt
Upper Bubbs Creek
Metroyhoy
Sugarloaf
Upper Cabin
Lone Pine
Redwood
Dorst
Cahoon
Willow

Long
Circle
Mather
Crescent
Lower Rock Creek Crossing
Hockett

Sierra National Forest
Fresno Dome
Markwood
Hall
Jackass
Unnamed Meadow C
Poison
Long Dusy
Meadow 197
Poison Grade
Ross
Garlic
Lower Graveyard
Topping Cow Camp

Yosemite National Park
Big
Hodgdon
Wawona
Sunrise
Tiltill Valley
Crane Flat

Empire
Aspen Valley
Gin Flat East
McGurk
Cottonwood
Westfall
Harden Lake
Upper Paradise
Mt. Gibson
Tall Grass
Joie's
Poopenaut

Stanislaus National Forest
Ackerson
Bell
Eagle
Lower Relief Valley
Ackerson South
Randalls
Bluff
Hay
Willow I
Gretel's
Upper Gardner
Tryon
Greely Hill